Unlocking the Chinese Gate

SUNY series in Chinese Philosophy and Culture
—————
Roger T. Ames, editor

Unlocking the Chinese Gate

Manifestations of the Space "In-Between" in Early China

GALIA DOR

Cover Credit: Courtesy of Galia Dor

Published by State University of New York Press, Albany

For information, contact State University of New York Press, Albany, NY
www.sunypress.edu

Library of Congress Cataloging-in-Publication Data

Name: Dor, Galia, [date] author.
Title: Unlocking the Chinese gate : manifestations of the space "in-between" in
    early China / Galia Dor.
Description: Albany : State University of New York Press, [2024] | Series:
    SUNY series in Chinese philosophy and culture | Includes bibliographical
    references and index.
Identifiers: LCCN 2023039271 | ISBN 9781438497532 (hardcover : alk. paper) |
    ISBN 9781438497549 (ebook) | ISBN 9781438497525 (pbk. : alk. paper)
Subjects: LCSH: Philosophy, Chinese. | Boundaries (Philosophy) | Gates. |
    Liminality.
Classification: LCC B126 .D67 2024 | DDC 181/.11—dc23/eng/20240130
LC record available at https://lccn.loc.gov/2023039271

10 9 8 7 6 5 4 3 2 1

For Namiko

There is a theory which states that if ever anyone discovers exactly what the Universe is for and why it is here, it will instantly disappear and be replaced by something even more bizarre and inexplicable. There is another theory mentioned, which states that this has already happened.

—Douglas Adams, *The Restaurant at the End of the Universe*

Contents

Illustrations

Figures

ix

Tables

Notes on Chinese Language and Translation

1. All translations from Classical Chinese are by the author, unless otherwise stated.

2. Throughout this study, the *Pinyin* 拼音 transliteration system is used (with the exception of "word by word" citing that might contain the old Wade-Giles system).

3. There is an ongoing debate about the translatability of core Chinese philosophical concepts, to the extent of pronouncing them untranslatable.[1] My approach in this book is case-specific; some terms are left untranslatable, such as *dao* 道 (before which I omit the determiner "the" as in Classical Chinese it is not necessarily a noun but could be a verb or a process).[2] As for *tian* 天, I prefer to render it "heavens" instead of "Heaven" (and sometimes "heaven-like" when I find it fits the meaning of the text better).[3]

A (Semipersonal) Preface

Every day I go to my study and sit at my desk and put the computer on.

At that moment, I have to open the door.

It's a big, heavy door. You have to go into the Other Room. Metaphorically, of course.

And you have to come back to this side of the room. So it's literally physical strength to open and shut the door.

So if I lose that strength, I cannot write a novel any more. And you have to shut the door.

—Haruki Murakami[4]

This is a book about the efficacy of in-betweenness in Chinese thought and material culture, and, in a curious way, it is by itself a product of an *interval*: written during the COVID-19 outbreak in which the human world stood still—and an opening offered itself as a singular and rare opportunity. As the above epigraph by Haruki Murakami suggests, sometimes it's the opposite case, that is, when the gate is in fact closed and it is up to us (if we wish for self-realization) to open it again and again, each time, in the same way that we open our eyes every morning and start another day—an action that requires continuous effort, determination, and inner strength. Whether open, closed, or any state in between, however, an opportunity is just that: a situational dilemma that necessitates choice, that is, *decision-making* (and theory)—a subject that was found highly associated with the various manifestations of gates in early China.

Indeed, if ways (*dao*) go straight or curve, bend and twist, split into two, go up and down, through mountains or valleys, have difficult-to-pass obstacles or easy-to-cross sections, then it is the Chinese gate (contextually interlinked with *dao*) that occupies a point of efficacious potentiality on them. But in the most general way, the very act of opening or closing a gate seems to be significant in many cultures (see introduction); indeed, it was Gaston Bachelard who said that if "one were to give account of all the doors one has closed and opened, of all the doors one would like to re-open, one would have to tell the story of one's entire life" (1964, 224). This specific act, which I name "decision-gating," impresses directly upon our lives and the paths that were consequently taken—which, so inevitably and (at times) tragically, leaves out all those other potential pathways—the paths and lives that *could* have been. Indeed, the image that has repeatedly surfaced in the study is that of a tree-branching pattern, the forking or bifurcation of roots and branches *benmo* 本末, within which two-leaved gates occupy nexuses and junctions. This visual image entices me to the story "The Garden of Forking Paths" by Jorge Luis Borges:

> The Garden of Forking Paths is a picture, incomplete, yet not false, of the universe such as Ts'ui Pen conceived it to be.
>
> Differing from Newton and Schopenhauer, your ancestor did not think of time as absolute and uniform. He believed in an infinite series of times, in a dizzily growing, ever spreading network of diverging, converging and parallel times.
>
> This web of time—the strands of which approach one another, bifurcate, intersect or ignore each other through the centuries—embraces every possibility.
>
> We do not exist in most of them. In some you exist and not I, while in others I do, and you do not, and in yet others both of us exist.
>
> In this one, in which chance has favored me, you have come to my gate.[5]

The association stems from multiple ideas and themes in the story . . .first, the Chinese ancestorship of the protagonist (Ts'ui Pen); secondly, the emphasis Borges puts on the intellectual difference with Western thought; and thirdly, the "labyrinth of time," which is made of parallel realities or futures in time and space; this always takes me to Zhuangzi's butterfly dream—a dream that is no less real than life.[6] The Chinese gate *men* 門 has taken me along such winding road—experiencing its "forking paths" but in equal amount—the convergence of ideas through Chinese correlative thinking and modern science. Indeed, my academic endeavor had started with the life sciences with emphasis on ethology and evolution—being driven by some "big questions" about the laws of nature and the secrets of life; then, when my academic path took a turn into East Asian studies, an intriguing convergence back into the life sciences has taken place—this time through the lens of ancient Chinese texts.

Though it was my fascination with Chinese and Japanese philosophy, aesthetics, and medical thought that brought the above change, it came about when I was already feeling uncomfortable with certain attitudes to animals (in research) and conceptual approaches to nonhuman species—to the extent of sensing remnants of Cartesian philosophy still lingering on.[7] It was as if something was holding the whole field back and preventing a true account and realization of nonhuman species (perhaps with the exception of apes and dolphins), but certainly not toward species such birds, invertebrates, social insects, and more.

But fortunately, the field is experiencing a quantum leap as study after study either from ethology, genetics, or cognitive sciences reveals traits and capacities that (not long ago) were considered uniquely human (e.g., thinking and planning, the making of sophisticated tools, problem-solving, and cognitive abilities). In these nonhuman *cultures*, individuals feel fear but also joy, have a sense of play and mischief and even humor. But it seems some people feel unhappy and even threatened by this newly discovered continuity between animals and humans. The primatologist Frans de Waal (2001) calls such people anthropodenialist, connecting it to the ancient Greek fear of anthropomorphism (i.e., the sin of comparing animals to "human form").

The significance of this huge shift in the way we grasp ourselves as one more species among others (a human–nature continuity that is expressed in early Chinese texts), goes beyond the life sciences: it bears heavily on various theories that have tended to conceptualize characteristics of "the human" as universal (which, I argue, partly stems from its separation from the nonhuman). A good example is the field of linguistics—in which new data and innovative theories challenge the

Chomskian paradigm of an innate, grammatically universal language shared by all human cultures (thank you brother Prof. Daniel Dor for continuously enlightening me on the subject). Looking at it from the prism of the Chinese gate's mechanism, it always comes down to whether something is included (allowed in through openness) or excluded (left outside of the gate).

In effect, the same phenomenon occurs *within* the human circle—when theories that claim to be universal hide a resistance to or exclusion of the "other," and here (as in the above example of linguistics), I refer explicitly to the centuries-long dominance of Western ideas, dogmas, and beliefs over non-Western schools of thought. But things are changing in this department, as well—as Roger Ames says, it is due to the existence of "a competing meaning that recognizes the potential contributions of non-Western cultures. This second sense that we might tease out of *quanqiuhua* 全球化 or 'inclusive globalizing' might alternatively refer to the mutual accessibility of cultural sensibilities" (quoted in D. Zhao 2007, 38).

On the other hand, contemporary Western thought includes one area which exhibits intriguing resonance with early Chinese ideas, namely, modern science (e.g., biology, physics, etc.); one idea that is absent in both, to begin with, is the very belief in a personal God and its related, contextual conjectures (e.g., teleology). Indeed, in Chinese thought, as Tu Wei-ming aptly says, "the conception of a Creator as the ultimate source of morality or spirituality is not even a rejected possibility" (1985, 19).

It is thus from its liminal local that the gate takes us in between the boundaries of knowledge—within Chinese thought and beyond it. In fact, the gate as the subject of this study has transformed to a sort of *koan* that, by untangling its conventional boundaries, has repeatedly offered new perspectives—from the space of in-betweenness (to which the Chinese eye is uniquely sensitive)—out to actualized forms in any dimension on the Chinese psychocosmic continuum.

Indeed, in the context of forms (*xing* 形), I have always been attracted to the *visual*, that is, to nature's recursive patterns (e.g., fractals) or man-made artistic designs. As a student of biology, I would spend hours at the electronic microscope observing micropatterns and deciphering their visual resemblance to the macroworld. Then, while living in Japan and Taiwan, the artistic, architectural, and graphic creations of these cultures have been a constant source of intrigue and fascination.

And in this world—of Chinese architecture and spatiality—gates cannot be missed . . . they slowly but surely become an inseparable part of one's living experience; but they also pop up in Chinese vernacular . . . for instance, while having a conversation on the determination needed to succeed in university exams, I was once told a folkloristic tale named "The Carp Jumping Over the Dragon Gate" (鯉魚跳龙門) in which a determined carp goes through a strenuous journey in order to arrive at the Dragon Gate, at which point he gathers his last remaining strength and attempts to jump over it . . . since it is the only way to cross the threshold between the ordinary and mythical—and transform into a dragon (see figure P.1).[8]

Figure P.1. Carp leaping over the Dragon Gate. After Wang Shucun 王樹村. 1985. Ancient Chinese Woodblock. New Year Prints. Beijing: Foreign Languages Press. Public domain.

The gate as a singular locus for transformation is evident in the very opening *kai* 開 of Chinese intellectual history, namely, the *Yijing*. It is here that the tens of thousands of living things are created with the emergence of the first (dividing) line of *form* and order—out of chaotic formlessness. In this warp-and-weft interconnecting universe of Chinese thought, ways and gates metaphorically coalesce, becoming a paradigm and an efficacious apparatus for human behavior and choice-making. The Chinese gate, which sometimes creates *dao* out of its own multiplication (figure P.2), will certainly take me further to ways and fields unknown as it has done so far—gate after gate after gate.

Figure P.2. Memorial archways form a way (*dao*). Wikicommons.

These gates along one's "long and winding road" (as the Beatles sang) include singular encounters that prove (immediately or upon reflection) to be significant landmarks on one's path. I have been fortunate to live for lengthy periods in truly exceptional East Asian cultures and natural landscapes, and through travel, studies, and practice of local arts encounter, befriend, and learn from many gifted individuals to whom I will be forever grateful; among those I would like to extend my deep thanks to my Japanese *sensei* and Taiwanese *laoshi* (above all to *laoshi*

Wang Yen-nien in Taipei), and to a very unique individual who placed a copy of the *Daode jing* in my hands and changed the course of my life (Deviam Preaux: どうもありがとうございました).

I am indebted to Galia Patt-Shamir, who, literally, "opened the gate of the Chinese gate" to me . . . and was my supervisor in both my M.A. and Ph.D. I thank my teachers at the East Asian and Philosophy departments in Tel Aviv University, especially to Yoav Ariel for his ever-stimulating discussions, to Zhang Ping—for his traditional methods of teaching Classical Chinese and his enthusiastic readiness to share his knowledge with me, and to Shlomo Biderman—whose lectures on early Buddhism I will never forget. I am honored to have met, discussed ideas with, or absorbed knowledge from inspirational scholars of East Asian thought worldwide, such as, to name but a few, Michael Puett, Alan Fox, Michael Stanely-Baker, Yuri Pines, Gil Raz, Fabrizio Pregadio, and many others. Among these, I am especially grateful to Roger Ames—not only an inspiring scholar and the editor of the SUNY series in Chinese Philosophy and Culture, but also, on the personal level, as a teacher who is always readily there for guidance along the path. I wish to express my thanks and appreciation to the anonymous readers of the manuscript: your critical remarks have been invaluable and improved this book to no end! I would like to express my gratitude to the wonderful team at SUNY Press: first and foremost, to James Peltz, editor in chief, for his wise and personal guidance throughout the publishing process, as well as to Jenn Bennett-Genthner, Ryan Morris, Aimee Harrison, the language editor Brian Kuhl and the rest of the team: you have made the publication of this work an enjoyable task by being always so knowledgeable, accommodating, and cooperative. I am grateful to my students for listening (*wen* 聞) and asking questions (*wen* 問)—two of the most important themes revealed in association with the Chinese gate. I thank you close family and friends, and, last but certainly not least, thank you daughter of mine—my most significant teacher.

Introduction

Life and death, beginning and end, are indeed the great laws of the universe. Yet the similarities and differences of things are not uniform. Some are this and some are that. Tens of thousands of varieties are in constant change and transformation, strange and without any definite pattern. Whether things are this way or that, whether they are regular or irregular in their essential and subsidiary aspects, cannot be reduced to uniformity.[9]

—Ge Hong, *Baopuzi* 抱樸子 (*The book of the master who embraced simplicity*)

In his *Shiji* 史記 (*Records of the Grand Historian*) Sima Qian documents that under the State of Qi at the close of the fourth century BC, thousands of scholars from all corners of the land traveled to the capital city of Linzi to join the "Gate of Qi"—the common name of the intellectual magnet of the era, namely, the Jixia Academy 稷下學宮. Imagine the intellectual brainstorming that took place within the "boundaries of a gate"—a singular amalgamate of spatiality, architecture, research, and philosophy.[10] The academy's location near the western gate of the city notwithstanding, the reasons for referring to it as a "gate," I argue, lie deep in the roots of Chinese thought and its manifestations in material culture.

This book invites the reader to take a deep dive into the "boundaries of the Chinese gate"—as an innovative prism through which to observe ancient Chinese thought and culture; it analyzes gates from the perspective of their states (between open and closed), as well as their respective idealities, philosophical inclinations, or political agendas. This means that the reader will encounter such gates as water sluice gates that might have contextually developed to be the pivot between chaos and order, gates in a continuous open and closed state that constitute the center of creation—both in the natural (evolution of living things) and the human spheres (textual creation), gates that open out to an undifferentiated cognitive state, gates of the private Chinese home that correlate with the mouth and body-mind, architectural gates that were erected with the aim of achieving sociopolitical order (and thus are closed by default), half-closed gates that are depicted on Han period tombs symbolizing the fantasy to break gender distinctions in the after-world, or gates that need to be destroyed because they still constitute a trace of duality . . .

This versatile array of gate-related interpretations necessitated a multidisciplinary approach to begin with—in order to enable an investigation of various dimensions and fields in parallel. In Chinese context, however (as shall be discussed ahead), an interdisciplinary approach exposes a deeper interrelation that exists a priori, namely, correlative thinking. Notwithstanding, due to its wide scope, it needed a counter line that will give it boundary—and the one chosen was historic: the beginning of China's intellectual timeline. The study therefore constitutes an exploration of concrete (in tangible form) and abstract (textual, metaphorical, cognitive) gates in early China, that is, between the semi-legendary Xia dynasty (2070–1600 BC) and the Jin dynasty (晉朝 265–420).[11] It aims at understanding the ways in which gates conferred coherence and significance in the workings of the ancient Chinese and their semantic universe. The "behavioral mechanism" of Chinese gates in the above dimensions has revealed it to constitute a "bio-philosophical membrane" that exists in close association with some of the most fundamental ideas of Chinese intellectual framework, namely, *dao*, emptiness, change, chaos and order, as well as questions debating boundaries, methods of self-cultivation, epistemological queries, and more. This introduction thus includes some necessary background on these principles—with some comparative reflections to Western thought. It consists of some preliminary "infrastructures" as part of "paving the way" toward the proposed thesis, as follows: laying down some of the rudimentary characteristics of gates, drawing an outline of Western-Chinese cultural gaps and metaphorical interpretation, and discussing Chinese *xiang* thinking and correlative thinking as the contextual framework of the study and a key to its exegesis. I will then present a succinct summary of the conceptualized thesis of the Chinese gate presented in this book; this will be followed by a list of the primary textual sources analyzed. Finally, I will explain the rationale behind the arrangement of the book and a succinct summary of its chapters. But first and foremost, the first tier: What makes gates an important subject of inquiry?

What Is Significant about Gates?

Swiss architect Mario Botta famously said, "the first gesture of architecture is to draw a perimeter; in other words, to separate the microclimate from the macro space outside. This in itself is a sacred act. Architecture itself conveys this idea of limiting space. It's a limit between the finite and the infinite" (Mortice 2008). Indeed, it is in the appearance of this demarcating line between any two spheres that the intensity and significance of architectural and metaphorical boundaries lie. And in recent years, as Michele Lamont and Virag Molnar say, "the concept of boundaries has been at the center of influential research agendas in anthropology, history, political science, social psychology, and sociology" (2002, 167).[12] In this context, the significance of gates stem from their inherent function as an apparatus that either allows for continuity or breaks it; it is probable that well before man-made doors and gates started to be built, natural "gate-like" formations had appeared on man's way and planted the seed of entrances, openings, or barriers in his mind. Think of openings in rock precipices, caves mouths, or narrow passages between mountains—as cultures worldwide testify, such naturally occurring openings even acquired legendary reputation as entrances to "worlds beyond."[13]

An important part of the conceptualization of the Chinese gate as presented here, is indeed the contextualized part of openings, creeks, and narrow passages in the early Chinese imagination. They have caught the attention of the early Chinese in a particular way—as part of their meticulous observation and documentation of earth's phenomena, with special attention to "flowing substances" such as water, wind, and *qi*. Figure I.1 is one of the finest examples of this captivation with "natural openings to otherworldly lands": the Gate of Heavens *tianmen* in Zhangjiajie geological park (Hunan Province)—a place that continues to attract the (Chinese) multitudes who ascend the stairs to get a glimpse of the foggy mist of the "heavens" through this natural "gate."

Figure I.1. Natural "Gate of Heaven." *Source:* Author provided.

In chapter 1 I delve further into the significance of such openings, with special attention to *qi*, water, and wind as formless substances that pass through them. To continue with rudiments of gates in general, it is important to consider their uniqueness in comparison with other architectural components that connect the inside and outside (*wai/nei* 外/内), such as windows, for instance. Note that as opposed to windows, gates constitute a structure that completely *envelopes* the person passing through—thereby constituting a metaphor for a process or change *one goes through*. A gate's basic structure is made out of a structured frame of two vertical posts and one or more horizontal girders on top, with either an empty space within or single- or double-leaved doors inside. The passage through gates positions one on paths and ways (in the Chinese context, to *dao*) along which a "before" and "after" are connected—both in the temporal dimension (i.e., remembered past and unknown future), and naturally, the spatial one, that is, the invisible space that lies ahead or beyond. It thus inevitably centers gates in a heavily invested mental and emotional environment that ranges from curiosity as to what lies ahead to fears and doubts; in addition to all these characteristics, gates present *possibilities* to the treader on the path, that is, a choice must be made (i.e., enter through if open, force-open if closed, forsake it altogether, and more)—taking us to the intriguing subject of decision theory.

Indeed, the *liminal locale* of gates has served extensively as an ubiquitous element of architecture, but also as a metaphor in multiple literary works, expressions, and idioms—not only in China but cultures worldwide.[14] However, as will be argued ahead, as components of *boundaries*, gates not only signify, detect, and shed light on deep elements within a particular culture, but can, in effect, venture outwardly right into the gaps in between cultures and ways of thought.[15] In his book *On the Way to Language*, Heidegger discusses the ancient Greek deity Hermes, who crosses *thresholds of meanings* to create a real "transformation of thinking" (1971, 42). Intriguingly, the very etymological root of "hermeneutics" is Hermes—who presides over *liminal* spheres and border-crossing. It is only through authentic intertextuality and openness, Heidegger stressed, that one can in fact enter a dialogue across huge linguistic, cultural and historical gaps.[16]

This treatise on Chinese gates is thus to no lesser extent about *cultural meaning*—as the ways in which "a particular system of symbols . . . confers order, coherence, and significance upon a people, their surroundings, and the workings of their universe" (Basso and Selby 1976, 3). As the gate inhabits the space in between dimensions and spheres—or cultures, for that matter, it is necessary to allow some space to a comparison between characteristics of Chinese and Western thought; however, it is by no means an attempt to cover or discuss this wide and complex subject in depth, but to direct the torchlight to a few paradigms that bear impact on hermeneutics and philosophical perspectives—especially when some gaps constitute, as Roger Ames dubs it, a "fundamental character of cultural difference" (Olberding and Ivanhoe 2011, 117; the final discussion of the book includes further implications from a comparative Chinese-Western point of view).

Cultural Gaps in Interpretation

Edward Slingerland remarks that it is becoming more and more clear to sinologists that instead of "translating" Chinese arguments into rational Western propositions (modeled by formal logic), "the key to grasping arguments and concepts in early China is to focus on and unpack the specific metaphors and images that are deployed in the texts" (2011, 3). Indeed! But then why not take it one step further? What about metaphors that are still taken by many scholars (in general) and Sinologists to be conceptual, that is, universal? The specific, cultural, physical (bodily), and cognitive contexts of metaphors constitute the key to unlocking their meanings—instead of (consciously or not) interpreting them on the basis of dogmas, conventional concepts, or deep-rooted presumptions of the interpreter's cultural background. Benjamin Schwartz, for instance, aptly describes the cultural gap between Western and Chinese thought in the context of Confucian thought: "The very effort to translate this vision [of the *Analects*] into modern Western discourse may inevitably involve the kind of distortion that would result from filling empty spaces of a sparse Chinese landscape painting with the details of a Dutch painter" (1985, 62).

But does that indicate incommensurability? If indeed individuals are able to relate to and embrace ideas born out of a completely different background to their own, it necessarily means that the cognitive potential is there . . . but in some cases (e.g., cultural and academic circles) it might be locked behind a closed gate. A good instance might be the Mencian metaphor of "sprouts" (*duan* 端) that, according to Slingerland (*Mind and Body in Early China*, 2019), suggests that Mencian thought contained "internal essences and natural teleologies," meaning that sprouts, and plants in general, grow for a certain purpose or end goal. Jim Behuniak responded in the following way: "that is false. I have thought about evolution. I am thinking about plant life right now without essence and teleology. Why could Mencius not have had similar thoughts? Is his mind so different than mine?" and then adding that "I find it altogether plausible that Mencius was able to break free from the baseline cognitive tendencies that we share" (2019, 311).

I agree. Individuals can indeed relate to concepts and categories different to their own background, but, as mentioned in the semipersonal preface, when it comes to wider circles of nations, cultures, and disciplines, sometimes we see an almost automatic transference of those inherent presumptions and conceptual roots. Such gaps between Western and Chinese thought seem to be especially wide in the context of epistemological enquiries and subject-object relations—two topics that relate to the body-mind question that extensively resurfaced in association with gates.[17] Indeed, the many and varied sources analyzed illustrate the Chinese body to be an organic and holistic whole in the sense of interconnectivity (nothing in it operates separately or independently, including the mind or the soul), but—just as any in any biological, living system, there must also be distinctions, confined spaces, and barriers—which means a qualitative gradation in degrees of perviousness. The fact that the early Chinese talked of mind and soul does not mean, in my eyes, that they constitute a different entity that resides in mind and soul or is ontologically made of a different substance.

A good example of such conceptual gap is the metaphor of "body sensation" that has been called "universal conceptual metaphor" by Lakoff and Johnson, two influential scholars who define it in the following way: "each of us is a container . . . bounded off from the rest of the world by the surface of our skins, and we experience the rest of the world as outside us" (1980, 29).[18] To me, the problematic point in this "closed body" schema is (again) its claim to universality—isn't it highly culture-specific? I argue that in the context of Chinese thought, the above scheme loses ground in light of multiple textual descriptions that differ greatly from a "container bounded off from the rest of the world." Jane Geaney similarly argues that according to numerous Chinese texts the body is "far from being a closed system that only occasionally ingests and expels things . . . bodies in early Chinese texts are like a constant interface, any firm sense of interiority is an achievement not a given" (2012, 18). This conclusion is enforced by my own findings: an emphasis on the protection and guarding of "internal space" in several correlating circles, for example, the state, the city/village (against foreign invasion and intruders), one's privacy at home, and finally, body-mind. Indeed, it has been one of the most interesting aspects of the study to repeatedly encounter that the *cause* for this deep need to protect the inside is feelings of anxiety and fear from "what is out there" in early Chinese civilization.

The way cultures conceptualize body and mind bears heavily on other subjects, such as the question of free will versus determinism—yet another Western dichotomic pair of either-or that is alien to early Chinese conceptualization of the individual and his or her will. Indeed, the individual, as a variety of opinions and philosophies from early China indicate, is not a separate agent and thus the *will* cannot be completely devoid or "free" of (unconditioned by) multiple factors in this complex matrix we call life; it is constantly affected by internal factors such as the body itself (from which is *not* separated) or by external circumstances (see, for instance, a discussion of Mencian will *zhi* 志, in chapter 5).[19]

In order for a "clean" approach to the ideas of a different culture, I believe we can learn from Chinese *yinyang* complementarity: it can only work when each side lets go of its own principles and transforms to become the other. Tetragram number 57 ("Guarding") from the *Taixuan jing* 太玄經 (*The Canon of Supreme Mystery*) remarkably illustrates this point:

> (when) *yin* guards the door and *yang* guards the gate,
> (subsequently) things cannot mutually correspond.

陰守戶, 陽守門, 物莫相干

Cleverly manipulating the inherent Chinese conceptualization of *yinyang* as continuously and mutually intermingling, the author demonstrates what happens when they don't . . . this line can take up different interpretations depending on context (in chapter 2, the context is the *yinyang* of natural creation), but when it comes to an attempt at a dialogue, clearly it cannot take place when each side zealously protects its own concepts or beliefs.

All the above themes that shed light on gaps between Chinese and Western thought stem from different approaches to objects and things, that is, "a being bound in form" versus "that which is in between" or absent. In other words, it all goes down to one of the most important root ideas of Chinese thought—emptiness. Pre-modern Western thought had a complex relationship with emptiness (and in certain areas it still does), and was even abhorred because it opposes being, presence, and substance. Parmenides said that "void is non-existent" and Aristotle joked in *Physics* VI 8 216a 26–27 that "even if we consider it in its own merit, the so-called vacuum will be found to be really vacuous," and coined the phrase "nature abhors a vacuum" with regard to early Christians who forbade the usage of zero (if God is omnipresent, there cannot be a zero). It was modern scientific investigation that embraced emptiness: from early mathematicians to present-day biologists and physicists (particularly quantum physicists) who recognize it as the essence of the universe—from outer space to the atom level.[20]

The subject of emptiness brings us back to the various ways we construct our own mind . . . whether full of distinctions between "this or that" or empty of absolute values, ideas, and beliefs. A mind that is stuck in a *form* is known as an "either-or" thinking of radical dichotomy (a separation of traits that do not actually exist or apply in the world). Indeed, in his work *Structure, Sign and Play in the Discourse of the Human Sciences* (translated 1978), Jacques Derrida maintained that Western thought has been founded upon the "logic" of binary oppositions, such as mind/body, rational/emotional, freedom/determinism, nature/culture, and scared/profane, stressing that part of the problem is the elevation of one term over the other or the awarding of a privileged position to one side, which is "the way ideologies are created."[21]

Traits of "binary thinking" are interlocked with the Western conceptualization of "being" (Greek, ousia οὐσία) versus Chinese "becoming," as Liu and Berger point out: "while the history of Western philosophy began primary with concerns involving the constituents and fundamental nature of being and existence, the notion of nothingness or emptiness plays a central role in Asian philosophical traditions from the start" (2014, 6). This unreconciled line between opposites is also conspicuous in Western (and monotheistic) attitudes to the "sacred and the profane"; Cassirer refers to this pair of opposites, emphasizing that "only in this separation does it achieve an individual religious form. All movements into and out of this ring are governed by very definite sacral regulations" (1955, 104).[22]

As briefly mentioned in the semipersonal preface, an additional characteristic of early Chinese scientific-like scrutiny and understanding of the world is, as Joseph Needham states, "the lack of orders of a superior authority external to themselves"—as opposed to Abrahamic beliefs. Indeed, Needham stresses that it has been Western science and modern "philosophy of the organism" that have come to "a new understanding of cosmic, biological and social evolution" (1956, 582), thereby getting closer to the Chinese worldview. See the discussion for further elaboration.

Chinese Correlative thinking, *xiang* Thinking, and Concentric Circles

It is due to Chinese correlative thinking, *xiang* thinking, and the Chinese gate's characteristics of a "form that contains *potential* formlessness" on the edge of conceptual boundaries, that three themes have repeatedly and stubbornly surfaced, namely, image *xiang* 象, form *xing* 形, and pattern *li* 理. "*Xiang* thinking" rests upon a deep layer in our cognitive perceptions, namely, concreteness and visuality—qualities that are different from conceptual and rational thinking (particularly in its avoidance of strict provisions of conceptual boundaries); it means a tendency toward relativity, or, as Man-to Tang calls it, the "Abstract West" and the "Concrete East" from a linguistic point of view (2018).[23] Interrelated to *xiang* thinking is Chinese correlative thinking—a term which in modern terms might be called "associative thinking"; this type of thinking does not analyze things and phenomena separately but constitutes a widthwise cut through (from the object studied outwardly).

This is expressed in the fields of cognitive studies and education—and the conceptual boundaries between disciplines; for instance, what lies behind the necessity to coin the (relatively new) term of "interdisciplinarity" in Western scholarship? The answer lies in the (default state of) strict separation between them. . . . Indeed, William H. Newell claims that interdisciplinarity "is the latest response to the dominant Western intellectual tradition of rationality and reductionism (i.e., specialization) that is ultimately grounded in dichotomous (i.e., either-or) thinking" (2010, 360). This study had in fact purposely begun as interdisciplinary research, but with time the gate has shed its conventional boundaries and emerged as a "semiotic apparatus" that cuts through disciplines and resonates *ganying* 感應 through the various dimensions (or concentric circles).

Chinese *ganying* means the principle "by which things belonging to the same class or category *lei* 類 influence each other" (Pregadio 2010, 1:56). For instance, if we have previously discussed gaps in conceptualizing the body, Chinese correlative thinking sees correspondence between the universe and the body in relation to boundaries and gates. Vivienne Lo demonstrates this through the following passage from medicinal texts of the Western Han period: "Ostensibly the *neiguan* in the Western Han period relates to the perception of the body as a microcosm of the imperial body politic. In early imperial times the most important *guan* 'passes' were the *wuguan* 'Wu Pass' and the *hanguguan* 'Hangu Pass' through the mountain barrier as you travelled from the Yellow River plain through modern day Shanxi into Shaanxi, which was then the land 'west of the pass'" (2000, 22). Such passes indeed marked boundaries of land beyond which lay lands unknown, dangerous regions or just unfamiliar territories, but similar boundaries exist in the body itself (in fact, the very term for the afterlife as the world beyond is *daxian* 大限, literally, "the great boundary"). Chunyu Yi, a physician of the early Western Han period, stated, as another instance, that when an illness has progressed to the *neiguan* "inner pass," it means that it "has entered a deeper space where it is more difficult to treat" (V. Lo 2000, 15).

Such correlations did not stop there: paralleling the unobstructed flow of *qi* in the body through gate-equipped meridians (strategic points), the *Art of War* (*Sunzi*) says that "whether (through) mountains or forest, dangerous and blocked swamps and marshes, all these make the roads (*dao*) difficult for travel —a ruined terrain" (山林、險阻、沮澤, 凡難行之道者, 為圮地). Such efficacious operations through homologous dimensions, or correlative cosmology, constitutes, as A. C. Graham states, the "primordial and quintessential expression of the 'Chinese mind'" (Fung 2010, 296), and Roger Ames sees it as an idea "that parallels the defining force of metaphysical realism in shaping the categories and grammar of the Western philosophical narrative" (2011, 119). John E. Wills emphasizes that within this quintessential way of Chinese thinking, order and boundaries resonate through all concentric circles: "At every level from the skin as the boundary of the human body to visions of the cosmos, Chinese thinkers insisted on the importance of boundaries and at the same time of proper relations across them, so that order within and openness to the outside remained compatible" (2007, 192). One of the most remarkable texts that exemplifies Chinese correlative thinking and concentric circles is the well-known passage from the "Great Learning" *Daxue* 大學:

> In ancient times, those who wished to ascertain the fulfillment of the "inherent potency" of the whole world, first had to govern their own states in an orderly way; wishing to govern their states in an orderly manner, they first had to do the same with their own households; wishing to govern their own households, they first had to cultivate their bodies; wishing to cultivate their bodies, they first had to rectify their hearts; wishing to rectify their hearts, they first had to have sincerity in their thoughts; wishing to have sincerity in their thoughts, they first had to extend their knowledge; extending knowledge lies in studying the "underlying principle."

> 古之欲明明德于天下者, 先治其国; 欲治其国者, 先齐其家; 欲齐其家者, 先修其身; 欲修其身者, 先正其心; 欲正其心者, 先诚其意; 欲诚其意者, 先致其知, 致知在格物.

These (correlating) concentric circles start from the macrocosm and go deeper and deeper to the innermost sphere of the mind, only to start again in the opposite direction.[24] As said in the beginning, what resonates among them is the need to put order and harmony *he* 和 into each, because each is the consequent result of the former and a prerequisite for the latter.[25]

Playing on the same theme and principle, the study found strong correlations between concrete life and the afterlife expressed through gates and doors depicted on the inner walls of ancient tombs; the tomb of Marquis Zeng-hou Yi (early Warring States), for instance, exhibits small doors constructed in the walls of the casket to connect different burial chambers (see figure I.2). Mu-Chou Poo says that "although the doors were perhaps only symbolic and without any practical function, the meaning seems clear: the souls of the deceased were expected to move around in the tomb through the doors, much as they did in a house when alive" (Olberding and Ivanhoe 2011, 16).

Figure I.2. Tomb of Marquis Yi of Zeng, Hubei Province, China. Hubei Provincial Museum. Creative commons.

I suggest also that this *resonating* worldview and concepts of continuity are interlinked with "how it all began," that is, the various creation myths that refer to the origin of the world and man. In China, as opposed to Judeo-Christian traditions, the first creation or the beginning of all phenomena was not marked by a miraculous appearance of forms (by a transcendental entity) which proceeds linearly, but by a process of endless transformations that take place in between heavens and earth. Even after separation, the heavens and earth continuously correspond and intermingle as the *yinyang* model of complementary opposites.[26]

Importantly, it is this space in between heavens and earth that man "inhabits" as part of the trinity of "heavens-man-earth" (*tian dì rén* 天地人). Observing the gate within this Chinese context elucidates its *benmo* 本末: the hidden roots that feed its bifurcated branches. This image of roots and branches can serve us in setting a visual and conceptualized background to the Chinese interconnectivity of form, text, and potentiality.

The Warp and Weft of the Chinese Gate: A Succinct Abstract

The study conceptualizes Chinese gates (whether abstract or concrete) as efficacious apparatuses at the center of a tight warp-and-weft contextualized matrix, which functions as a "bio-philosophical membrane" for the realization (fulfillment of potentiality) of natural and human lives; the potentiality of the gate stems from its ability to embrace all states between open and closed—which determines tendencies and idealities between the formed (ordered) and the formless (chaotic), openness and closedness, inclusion and exclusion, continuity and discontinuity, and others—in any dimension whatsoever. According to this contextualized model and in Chinese terms, I propose that the Chinese gate inhabits the threshold or pivotal space in between *dao* 道 and *de* 德—efficaciously manifesting inner potential into the concrete and actual.

The efficacy of the Chinese gate stems from its singular setting right at the highly potential center between convergence to the threshold and emergence of boundaries, and their "states of potentiality" or "degrees of perviousness" between outside/inside *wai/nei* 外/內 determine the relationship between various pairs of complementary opposites, such as chaos/disorder (*hundun* 渾沌 and *luan* 亂) and order *zhi* 秩. In this context, order means a state of distinct forms around which the system is organized and ordered, while chaos means a state of formlessness. This model correlatively functions through all concentric circles, for example, spatial and temporal (past-future) realms, the natural world and the cosmos, down to the political/national circle, yet further inside to the social circle, the family, and the individual (possessing the innermost circle of the body-mind).

The relation of the above characteristics to self-actualization resembles the biological phenomenon of *homeostasis*—as key to the survival of every organism and each and every living cell. Homeostasis means that a cell will survive only if its specific orderliness is created as rapidly as it degrades into disorder—and for that to happen, a careful close-open monitoring of gates and channels between the inside and the outside need to take place. In the Chinese human world, this close-open, chaotic-ordered adjustment corresponds to the manifestation of different *idealities*, for instance, cosmo-philosophical, political, cognitive, or medical. These idealities rarely stay abstract . . . they are concertedly fulfilled through practical strategies, techniques, and skills *shu* 術 that can pertain to the individual, society, or the world at large.

Among the various methods encountered in association with the gate, two skills distinctly stand out, namely, *shi* 勢 and *shi* 時— the first relates to a unique feeling of the shaping force and propensity of materials and the immediate environment, while the second refers to "right timing." The meaning of actualizing an ideality is the manifestation of potentiality in the concrete world that, in Chinese philosophical vernacular, is intrinsically linked with some of early China's centermost ideas, namely, *dao* 道, its manifestations into actuality *de* 德, and the process of self-cultivation *xiu-yang* 修養.[27] The Chinese gate is involved in the theme of decision-making (or decision-gating) as it is inseparable from ways and path (*dao*) and thus presents before the man walking (living) multiple choices and possibilities; intriguingly, the different concepts or strategies of "decision-gating" elucidate the very diversity of Chinese philosophical schools, for example, Daoist-inclined *wuwei* or the learned and calculative ritualistic (*li*) behavior of the Confucian school.

Some Chinese characters resurfaced repeatedly in association with Chinese gates, conveying their conceptual infrastructure, if you like, or the semantic field that is associated with them; the following is a nonexhaustive list: characters of emptiness, namely, *wu* 無, *xu* 虛, and *kong* 空 (void; used also in Buddhist context), as well as the important character *jian* 間—denoting the empty gap within a gate in both the temporal and spatial dimensions. Other characters of contextual importance are related to cracks, gaps, rifts, clefts, or openings, such as *xi* 隙, *xi* 巇 (also meaning dangerous passage between mountains), *qiao* 竅 (hole, orifice, etc.), *xue* 穴, and of course, *bu* 卜, the cracks on the oracle bones. In this context, *tong* 通 is also significant as the "breakthrough for unification"—that is, "going through empty passageways and uniting everything."

Some senses and actions are emphasized in association with gates (containing the gate radical), such as to listen and hear (*wen* 聞), or ask questions (*wen* 問). As for the former, it is said in the *shuo wén jie zi* dictionary that it means "something from the inside that could be heard from outside and the outside from inside," thus is directly related to the inside/outside of the gate and to skills and techniques around it; for instance, "to hear the sound" ("聞, 知声也") carries an added meaning of "sniffing an odor"—a way of describing an attempt to gain information at the gate. The list continues with *Bai* 捭—"forcing a gate open" that appears in various sources, such as the *Guiguzi* and the *Yijing*, and is related to the concept of seizing opportunities; *he* 闔 and *kai* 開 or *pi* 闢—as the acts of closing and opening a gate; *kai* has been especially significant as synonymous to the first act of creation.

Guan 關—traditionally rendered as the verb "to close" but which, as I argue throughout, refers to a "strategic pass" (the character inside the "gate" radical is *guan* 絭, which fascinatingly means "to run threads though a web in weaving"). The original meaning of *guan* is thus to connect the two doors of a gate and lock them, or, on the other side, "to connect two sides before and after the gate". Either way, it manifests an image of a "warp and weft" net or fabric, which has been suggested as the Chinese gate's framework (with pivot, hinge, center, and axis as the gate's synonyms). In addition, characters pertaining to two types of *forms* appeared closely with gates, namely, skin-like membranous shape, such as *nang* 囊, and storage rooms filled with *qi* or water that function as a gate's hinge, such as *dou* 斗 or *fu* 腑—in medical texts.

The metaphor of "warp and weft" is in fact a well-known Chinese image; it is said in *Huainanzi*, 7.1, "heaven as father, Earth as mother, *yin* and *yang* as warp, the four seasons as weft" (Major et al. 2010, 242), demonstrating a remarkable image of the universe as a woven fabric—all interconnected. In the very midst of this "double-emptiness" at the gate, a trigger-like efficacy has the potential to possess and encapsulate all situational possibilities—between the widely open and the tightly closed.

List of Primary Sources

Although the architectural gate constitutes a significant part of this book, the study did not venture into the technical aspects of the craft since it is, first and foremost, a philosophical study but also because my premise conceptualizes Chinese architecture as a concrete manifestation of philosophy and ideology, as is hinted in multiple textual sources; Cai Yong, for instance, a scholar of the Eastern Han, said that "the eight doors represent the eight trigrams (of the *Yijing* [Book of Changes])" (Tseng 2011, 67)—this constitutes an analogy between architecture and text (the *Yijing*) and between door and transition/change: an example of architectural symbolism that is metonymic *and* metaphorical.[28]

The attempt to study gates in ancient Chinese architecture is challenged by the fact that, beyond excavated gates in archeological sites, there is a paucity in primary textual sources; as for secondary sources (whether Chinese or Western), these tend to concentrate on later periods or on technicalities. Among those, I have studied the following: the *Qingnanjing* 青囊經 (*Green Satchel Classic*)—the earliest manual of *fengshui* composed in the ninth century AD by Yang Yunsong; the Zhou dynasty *Jiangren* (匠人), which was composed "for the purpose of inspecting, evaluating, and maintaining the quality of handicraft production" (Feng 2012, 26); the *Lu Ban jing* 魯班經 (*The Mirror of Woodwork Craftsmen*) composed by Lu Ban; and the *Yingzao Fashi* 營造法式, composed by Li Jie 李誡 in the Song dynasty.

Textual Gate *men* 門

Chinese intellectual history has produced a vast "cognitive library" that has branched and evolved out of its pre-Qin textual roots. The first stage of the study was thus devoted to searching the character *men* 門, and some of its significant compounds in as wide as possible a range of texts—to enable a selection of the most interesting and significant gate-related passages. The following list is the result: the *Yijing* 易經, commentaries of Wang Bi (226–249 AD) and Kong Yingda (574–648 AD), the *Shi Jing* 詩經 (*Book of Poetry*), the *Shang Shu* 尚書 or *Shu Jing* 書經 (*Book of Documents*), the *Li Jing* 禮記 (*Book of Rites*), the *Chun Qiu* 春秋 (*Spring and Autumn Annals*), the *Zhou li* 周禮 (*The Rites of Zhou*) and *Yili* 儀禮 (*Etiquette of Rites*), the *Taixuan jing* 太玄經 (*The Great Mystery*), the *Daode jing* 道德經, *Zhuangzi* 莊子, *Lunyu* 論語, the *Mengzi* 孟子,

the *Mozi* 墨翟, *Yuan Dao* 原道 (the first chapter of the *Huainanzi* 淮南子), *Guiguzi* 鬼谷子, *Hanfeizi* 韓非子, the *Sunzi bing fa* 孫子兵法 (*Master Sun's Military Methods*). Also included are the hagiographies of Laozi (老子), as follows: the *Liexian zhuan* 列仙傳 (*Immortals' Biography*) by Liu Xiang 劉向 dated 100 BC, the *Shenxian zhuan* 神仙傳 (*Biographies of Spirit Immortals*) by Ge Hong 葛洪 dated 320 AD, and the *Laozi ming* 老子銘 (*Inscription for Laozi*) by Bian Shao 邊韶 dated 165 AD. I have also analyzed passages from the *Lunheng* 論衡 (first century AD) composed by Wang Chong, and the *Heshang gong* 河上公. Outside the historical framework notwithstanding, I have decided to include the thirteenth-century Chan Buddhist text *Mumonkan* 無門關 (*The Gateless Barrier*) for its significance in any study of the gate metaphor. This list is not exhaustive—additional sources are used and quoted, such as Liu Hsie's *The Literary Mind and the Carvings of Dragons*, and it goes without saying that, even within the historical framework, not to mention beyond it, a long list of primary sources that are "heavily gated" await interpretation as well as specific themes that have been found to be associated with gates but exceeded the space and scope of this volume.[29]

The Rationale Underlying the Arrangement of the Book and a Succinct Description of Its Chapters

The arrangement of the book reflects my wish to present the exegesis of the gate through Chinese correlative thinking instead of locking it in strict domains of knowledge, that is, arranging the chapters according to "architecture," "philosophy," or "religion." Such conventional categorization would fail to "bring out to the light" its shared *roots* and efficaciousness in all dimensions. Thus, out of several ways or options according to which the various gates could be presented, I chose the gate's degrees of perviousness or "states of potentiality," such as double-leaved gates in continuous interchange of open *and* closed, gates in a state of open *or* closed, and closed gates by default (barriers). Importantly, this arrangement also stems from the finding that a certain gate-method (e.g., close the gates) might serve two entirely different viewpoints or ideological outcomes.

Chapter 1 ("Chinese Gates in Fourfold Context: Observation, 'Existential Thought,' Spatiality, Etymology") presents my argument that the idea of the gate, its metaphorical significance, and its concrete construction in early China might have stemmed from the very life conditions on the early Chinese on their land, for instance, rivers and topographical patterns, combined with their unique skill of observation—with emphasis on *qi*, water, and wind. I suggest that the attention given to water (particularly in the form of rivers, as said), wind, and *qi*, and the fascination these substances held for the early Chinese, stems from their common unique characteristic, namely, possessing the highest efficacy for the sustainment of life, but simultaneously having *no form*. I thus present the gate idea through the contexts of existential thought in early China, which looks at the very conditions of life on the Chinese land with emphasis on rivers and floods, and the unique way in which the early Chinese observed the natural world; a short discussion of the systemized formulation of *fangshui*, and a suggested framework for the idea of *dao*; this is followed by a discussion of spatial ideas in early China and their implementation in architecture, and finally, an enquiry into the etymological meanings of *men*.

Chapter 2 ("Gates of Creation: Correlates between Man, Text, and Cosmos") introduces "prototype gates" that are located in between complementary opposites and which relate to creation in parallel dimensions, namely, cosmic, mental, and textual. Significantly, the "opening gate" to the successive analysis of gates in this book is from the *Yijing*—as I find both gates (the text and the gates mentioned in it) to constitute roots of ancient Chinese thought.

Chapter 3 ("Gates to Inner Formlessness") discusses the gate as metaphorizing the need to go backward to the formless and the chaotic (as was found in Daoist philosophies and the *Taixuan jing*). Although intuitively we would assume that an aspiration to the formless state would necessitate open gates . . . in many cases (particularly with Daoist sources) it is actually the opposite: the advice is to close the openings of the body.

Chapter 4 ("Should I Open or Close My Gate? An Individual's Home, Mouth, and Mind") looks at the opening/closing of the gate as an act placed in the hands of the individual and is presented through the correlative circles of the front gate, the mouth, and the mind. I have included the front gate of Confucius in this chapter as well.

Chapter 5 ("Gates to Sociomoral Order and Distinctions") looks at the gate as metaphorizing the need for order and appropriateness as was found in the classics and humanistic philosophies.

Chapter 6 ("The Gate as Authority: The Construction of Order and Control") discusses the gate in its closed state, that is, a barrier which is controlled by external forces; it includes gateways on inland roads (paralleling real-to-imagined journeys), gates of cities, and gates in "legalist" thought.

Chapter 7 ("Destroy the Mind Barrier! An Opportunity for Personal Transformation") studies the phenomenon of destruction of the gate barrier as a manifestation of the wish to eliminate all traces *ji* of dichotomy (*Zhuangzi*), or an internal barrier that needs breaking through (*wumenguan* and the hagiographies of Laozi).

The "Discussion and Further Reflections" expounds further on the practical applicability of the suggested "gate philosophy" for current human lives by exploring its potentiality in cognitive psychology, decision-making, personal growth, and more. It also discusses parallels between ancient Chinese thought and modern scientific finds on the natural world and the universe.

Chapter 1

Chinese Gates in Fourfold Context

Observation, "Existential Thought," Spatiality, Etymology

The opening and the closing are the phases of order and chaos.

The doors (being opened or closed) have pervasive effects on "all under heaven."

—Wang Bi[1]

According to Sima Qian, it was in 109 AD that emperor Wudi commenced the restoration of a dike that had ruptured on the Yellow River and ceremoniously composed the following poem:

> The river raged from its boundaries . . .
> It has left its constant course . . .
> Dragons and water monsters leap forth,
> Free to wander afar. (Viollet 2007, 243)

Indeed, I propose in this chapter that the construction of dikes, dams, or floodgates against the chaotic facet of the river that "rages from its boundaries," "wreaks havoc and chaos," and "releases monsters into the human realm," carried a deep, almost visceral, meaning for the ancient Chinese—a meaning that starts with technical apparatuses but contextually goes beyond them to become the axis or pivot between chaos and order. However, these technical solutions constituted the end result of a process of multiple steps, that is, documented observation of a repeated, natural phenomenon and its investigation and subsequent applied thought. As will be stressed throughout, I argue that early Sinic society was characterized by a unique skill of observing and documenting natural phenomena, to the extent that it impresses me as distinctive among cultures. The chapter will thus begin with Chinese observation of their land (with emphasis on rivers, and other "flowing substances," e.g., *qi* and winds), to be followed by a look at Chinese "Existential Thought," as I call it, as a characteristic that might have played a significant part in the metaphorical development of the Chinese gate; I will then proceed to one of the most important contexts to architecture in general and gates in particular, namely, Chinese spatiality; the chapter will then end with some elaboration on the etymology of *the character men* 門. Let us look first at textual sources that indicate early examinations (observation) of ontological phenomena. In the Ten Wings of the *Yijing* 易經, it is said:

> When in ancient times Lord Baoxi ruled the world . . . he looked upward and observed the images in heaven and looked downward and observed the models that the earth provided. He observed the patterns on birds and beasts and what was suitable for the land . . . he thereupon made the eight trigrams in order to become thoroughly conversant with the numinous and bright and to classify the myriad things. (Lynn 1994, 54)

As mentioned in the introduction, the key point here is the systemized study of the universe and the natural world and its phenomena; the formulation of the hexagram system was the result of this search for repeated shapes *xiang* 象 and forms *xing* 形, attempting at *penetrating dao* or the source underlying all phenomena—through the deciphering of its concrete traces *ji* 跡. The *Yijing* can be thought of as a semiotic system which takes change as its conceptual basis and enables decision-making in resonance with the cosmos (see chapter 2).

It seems that during the Shang this conscious search for signs and patterns stemmed out of reverence to the land itself. As Li Feng remarks, "to the Shang, the landscape was not merely the location of the natural features, it was inhabited by the spirits, and the successful operation of the Shang state and the good fortune of the royal court would need to be ensued by enlisting their cooperation" (2013, 100).[2]

Shang oracle bones' divination indeed attests to this reverence; in parallel to natural traces, man-made marks created on the oracle bones were also taken as clues that might point man in the vast and confusing map of endless possible choices and paths. The oracle bones divination-queries tell us of the various subjects that occupied the mind of the ancient Shang, namely, victory or failure in wars, calendric, climatic and agricultural issues, auspicious times and sites, and more. They also catalogued topographical landforms and physical features of animals and the human body (Henderson 1994, 218); chapter 3 of the *Guanzi* attests to this remarkable observation skill:

> The sages learnt social order from bees, textiles and nets from spiders, ceremonies from rats, and war from fighting ants. Thus, the sages were taught by the myriad things, their turn taught the worthies, who taught the people. But only the sages could understand the things (in the first place); they could unify themselves with natural principles, because they had no prejudices and preconceived opinions. (Needham 1956, 447)

This is an intriguing passage. The wisdom of the sages was in this awareness (and respect) to the natural world around, and an understanding that this world offers hidden knowledge worth studying for human beings: from the ants, they learned "social order" (which can be thought as parallel to study of "emergent behavior" in modern biological studies, e.g., of social insects); from the spiders, they learned of textile (a natural warp and weft fabric which can be utilized in the human world); from the rats, ceremonies (indeed, animals demonstrate "ritualistic" behavior); and from fighting ants, war strategy. Out of the many and varied patterns, behaviors, and forms observed and detected by the ancient Chinese on earth, some stand out as significant in the context of gates, namely, (a) natural openings and creeks, terrestrial contours of the earth, gorges, passages, and natural barriers, and (b) the flow and behavior of water and rivers, wind, and *qi*.

A famous story from the Jin dynasty demonstrates this captivation with openings, namely, the Peach Blossom Forest story written by Tao Yuanming (376–427 CE):

> In the time of Emperor Taizhong of the Jin dynasty, a man from Wuling, a fisherman by occupation, happened to travel along the edge of a creek, and completely forgot the distance of his route. He suddenly found himself in a peach blossom forest; still edged in-between the creek, he kept forward for a few hundred paces; inside there were no other trees, only

the delicious fragrance of the grass; the fallen blossoms had all kinds of colors, which the fisherman could not distinguish. He went back and forth wishing to find the end of the forest. He saw a small and narrow opening in the mountain, which seemed to have light shining through; so he abandoned his boat and went through the opening; at first it was extremely narrow for a person (to be able to cross), but then, as he resumed his walking for another ten paces, it suddenly (just like that) opened up to a wide clearance of a vast and flat ground, with neatly arranged residences. There were fertile fields and beautiful ponds, mulberry trees, bamboo groves, and raised paths for easy passage.

晉太元中, 武陵人, 捕魚為業, 緣溪行, 忘路之遠近; 忽逢桃花林, 夾岸數百步, 中無雜樹, 芳草鮮美, 落英繽紛, 漁人甚異之. 復前行, 欲窮其林. 山有小口, 髣彿若有光, 便捨船, 從口入 初極狹, 纔通人; 復行數十步, 豁然開朗 土地平曠, 屋舍儼然. 有良田、美池、桑、竹之屬, 阡陌交通, 雞犬相聞.

This "Shangri-la" story that narrates a sudden passage into another world while on a journey through mysterious openings (basic form of a gate) in mountains or narrow creeks sounds like a Chinese version of Alice in Wonderland . . . and indeed it continues to occupy and inspire the minds and imagination of the Chinese people through poems, stories, and paintings (it even inspires works of modern architecture, as I. M. Pei himself attested while planning the Miho Museum in Japan).

As a fine example to the continuous influence and intertextual interplay of the above story—this time involving a gate—is a poem that was written three hundred to four hundred years later by Liu Yuxi (772–842) named "On the Sweet Pear House at Shouan":

In front of the gate, there is the road to Louyang.
Inside the gate, there is the path to Peach Blossom Spring,
Between the dusty ground and the misty rosy clouds,
There are only a dozen paces. (X. Yang 2003, 53)

Xiaoshan Yang believes that the poet leads us to the significance of the thin border between the road to Louyang and the path to the spring—notwithstanding its thinness, it possesses efficacy in direction: it can lead to segregation or proximity "of the two diametrically opposed worlds divided by the front gate" (2003, 53). But what are these *opposing* (yet intermingling at the gate) *worlds*? Let us get closer.

The first line points at the road to Louyang, which is an actual path and an actual place—a down-to-earth description of concrete life. But the second line says that *inside* the gate is the road to Peach Blossom Spring . . . what is this place? It is the Spring of Liu Yuxi . . . an otherworldly land! It hints that at the threshold of the gate and (in parallel)—in the mind of the poet—two worlds coalesce: the concrete, mundane life and an autoptic world that lies somewhere beyond.

The next lines give us further clues: the very thin line that exists between the dusty ground (concrete life on earth) and the misty clouds (heavenly land) . . . perhaps hides a deep personal contemplation, that is, his own life and his death—and the thin line that separates them. Importantly, it also involves decision-making . . . in the earlier story, it was the fisherman's decision to explore the creek and enter the opening, and in the poem, the protagonist can decide whether to close his front gate (closing himself in) or open it so that he can venture out or allow others in. Such natural openings constitute heavily invested foci: they can either lead us into a wonderful experience and opportunity (one that requires courage) or risk the traveler's life.

Studying the topography of the earth—its openings, creeks, rivers, and natural boundaries—was also a major factor in the development of walls and check-point gateways, including the most famous landmark of China, the Great Wall. Yuri Pines investigates part of the Great Wall in the area of the Chu (the southerly state of the Warring States period, which had its main territory around the valleys of the Han River and then spread further to the Yangtze River), emphasizing the utilization of the natural boundary: "These crescent-like ranges and hills served as a natural boundary of the Nanyang Basin, which was the major gate to Chu's heartland to the east of the Han River. That in the Warring States period a Long Wall was built along parts of this 300 km long defensive perimeter is undeniable" (2018, 759). However, the observation of patterns of the earth was also part of the Chinese preoccupation with clues to auspiciousness: Where and how should one reside in life and in the afterlife? For that aim, they looked for patterns *li* 理, a character which is, in fact, related, as Brook Ziporyn remarks, to the verb "divide or make a border according to the contours of the land or for carving of jade according to its own patterns" (2014, 27). Chan Wing-Tsit adds that the word *li* means "to put in order (*zhi*) or to distinguish" (1964, 123).[3] The adherents of the Form school of *fengshui* (associated with Jiangxi Province), for instance, "made use of schematic topographical maps that showed how the currents and concentrations of the energetic *qi* or pneuma that pulsed through the ridges and *watercourses* of the earth could be traced in order to identify auspicious locations" (Henderson 1994, 218). See the idealized pattern in figure 1.1, which follows the counters of the earth.[4]

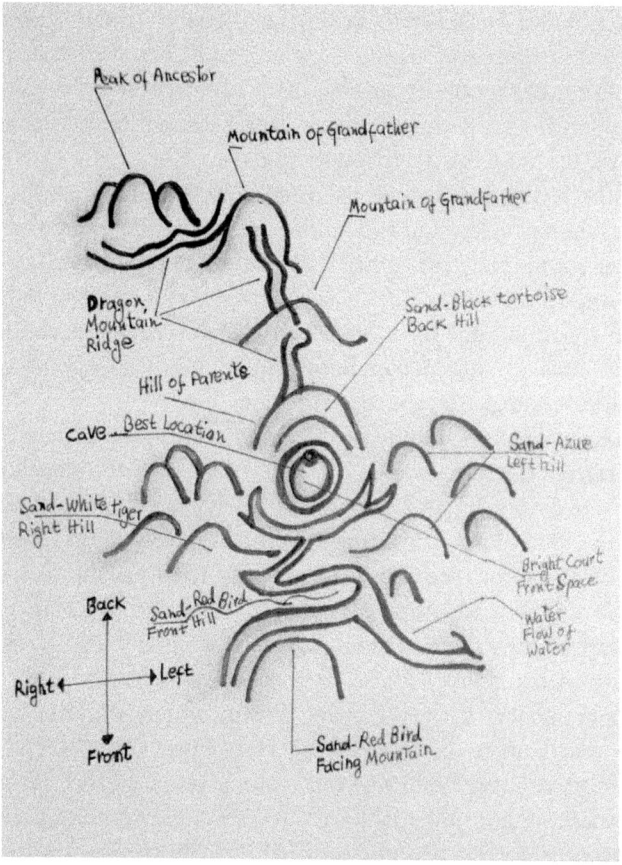

Figure 1.1. The "Form school" of *fengshui* follows the contours of the earth. After Michael Y. Mak and S. Thomas Ng. 2005. "The art and Science of Feng Shui—A Study on Architects' Perception." *Building and Environment* 40, no. 3: 427–34. Illustration by the author.

Observing the contours of the earth and its patterns means following the outlines and boundaries of *forms*, but also the formless or empty passages in between them. Through spaces of in-betweenness flow formless substances, namely, *qi*, water, and wind. In Warring States thought, *qi* was most often defined as an animating life force that provides both sustenance and energy to living things. P. J. Ivanhoe describes *qi* as "a kind of vital energy found in both atmosphere and the human body and existing in various densities and levels of clarity or turbidity that is responsible for, among other things, the intensity of one's emotions" (2002a, 87).

The prevalence of *qi* in almost every genre of texts in Chinese thought attests to its conceptual ontological ubiquitousness—from the cosmic to the body and the innermost sphere of the mind. The doctrine of *fengshui* developed out of the aspiration to find the most favorable locations for the inhabitance of the living and the dead (burial sites), but also out of the attempt to survive in an agrarian society with low agricultural productivity (Sun et al. 2014)—but, ultimately, they searched for "the proper space arrangement for channeling the positive flow of *qi* (the life energy)" (Li Xiaodong 2002, 89). If there exists a positive *qi*, there is also a negative one that can damage homes and lives. The balance was not only between right and wrong *qi* but between a state of surplus *qi* (overflowing) and a deficiency in *qi*.

The recently excavated *Xing zi ming chu* 性自命出 (fourth century BC) indicate that *qi* was believed to impact a man's character as it mentions *qi* alongside *xing*, human nature: "the vital energies (*qi* 氣) of pleasure, anger, grief, and sadness are *xing*. Their appearing on the outside is because things stimulate them" (Liu Zhao 2003, strips 1–3).[5] Yet another formless substance that seems to be of great interest for the ancient Chinese was wind; so significant, in fact, that it forms half of the term *fengshui*, alongside water.

A clue for the significance of wind might be found in the etymology of *feng*, which reveals a conjunction of two pictographs: *fan* 凡, which means "whole," "everyday," "origin," and its inner character *chong* 虫 which is some sort of an insect or snake. The *Shuowen Jiezi* dictionary (120 AD), makes reference to the Chinese idea of "when the wind blows, insects are born," an important observation that situates winds as a prerequisite for life itself. Like water, though these substances are formless, they are highly efficacious for life! Elisabeth Rochat de la Vallée makes three important points (which are significant to the exegesis of gates): the first, the way winds blow through openings and caverns in the mountains; the second, believing the etymological roots of *feng* are related to *shen* (spirit) and *feng* 鳳; and the third, the evolution of living creatures:

> What appears nowadays as a metaphor was then most probably believed to be a reality: the wind brings life from Heavens on Earth; it penetrates the earth through its opening, at the image of the caverns in the mountains (*feng xue* 風穴) which are also where the phoenixes dwell at sunset. Blowing in the spring, it triggers the process of transformation leading to germination, growing of the vegetation, and maturing of grains. (2012, 3)

This unites two significant ideas: the passage of flowing substances through empty spaces and passages (winds blowing through openings and caverns in the mountains) and the efficacy of the formless (emptiness) in creating and sustaining life. The wind might be a uniting metaphor or theme for the gate's main significance: passage, flow, unification, transformation. In the chapter called "Leveling-out Opinions" *qiwulun* 齊物論 of the Inner Chapters by Zhuangzi, the following (remarkable) passage pays special attention to winds:

> Ziqi said: when the great mass (of nature) emits *qi*, it is called wind; alone, it doesn't grow (so you don't hear it), but when it goes through the myriad orifices you can hear its vigorous sound; when alone, don't you hear the soaring sound of the wind? The mountain forests are scary and beautiful (at the same time), myriad orifices and cavities twist through and around the big trees, some resemble the nose, some resemble the mouth, some resemble the ear, some resemble jugs, some resembles loops, some resemble a mortar, some resemble swamps; exciting, stinging, shouting, inhaling, calling, roaring, biting; at first it sounds like singing, but it is followed by loud breathing sounds. Winds over water creates small harmony, floating winds create great harmony, and when (these) severe winds cross by, then the numerous orifices become empty; when alone, don't you see this profusion?

子綦曰: 夫大塊噫氣, 其名為風. 是唯无作, 作則萬竅怒呺. 而獨
不聞之翏翏乎? 山林之畏佳, 大木百圍之竅穴, 似鼻, 似口, 似耳,
似枅, 似圈, 似臼, 似洼者, 似污者; 激者, 謞者, 叱者, 吸者, 叫者,
譹者, 宎者, 咬者, 前者唱于而隨者唱喁. 風則小和, 飄風則大和,
厲風濟則眾竅為虛. 而獨不見之調調、之刁刁乎?

The passage contains a description of the various types of winds and the
various types of orifices and crevices—as two symbiotic phenomena of
emptiness and flow that exist alongside concrete and (relatively) steady and
constant mountains and forests—nature as "self-so" consists of both aspects.
This detailed account is highly imaginative . . . the winds are animated to
resemble a living creature, and thus it is also visual in our mind—though
it relates to something we cannot *actually* see! But we can feel it. This is
the reason, I believe, for the characters "hear" *wen* 聞, and "see" *jian* 見,
in lines 2 and 5, respectively: these senses are not used in the usual sense,
but through the skill of seeing without seeing, listening without listening
(isn't it the reason for the emphasis given in both questions as to "being
alone"—that is, a lone man in nature versus man in the company of people?).

Indeed, the winds in this story are central not only as "the invisible
that is highly efficacious" but also in relation to sounds (and, in direct
association, to music); the sound is enabled and manifested due to the
cavities and empty passages, and will always be related in this context
to the operation of the human senses and their respective desires (what
is external/internal), and to the idea that sounds (in general) and music
(specifically as a human endeavor) depend on the mind of listener! The
subject of music in Chinese thought and culture is naturally extensive
and beyond this volume, but some gate passages will take us right into
this context—due to its contextual connection with emptiness and
openings (including the "opening of the human mind and senses"), but
in no lesser degree due to its locale between complementary opposites
(see chapter 2 in the context of the *Yijing*). Indeed, music was believed
in the pre-Qin era to stem from the cosmic forces of heavens and earth
and, as "the proper appearance and prominence of certain forces and
phases—especially *yin-yang* and the Five Phases—at appropriate times of
the day, month and season. Thus, music and the cosmic were both idealized—and therefore linked—as harmonious processes" (Brindley 2012, 4)

Conceptualizing winds in such a way resonates with water—one
of the most conspicuous metaphors in Chinese thought, which begs the
question: What is the common dominator of winds, water, and *qi*? To

begin with, all three substances are not bound by a fixed form, and then, as a direct consequence of their formlessness—they are (or should be!) in constant *flow*, and finally, from the ancient Chinese point of view, it is worthwhile to observe and study their "behavior" for the following reasons: (a) the three substances could then be controlled or manipulated; (b) they could serve as a paradigm for other "substances" or dimensions, and (c) they teach us about the efficacy of formlessness (i.e., how is it that something without form *underlies* formed life?). Such characteristics of water and watercourses made it a central metaphor in Chinese thought, as Sarah Allan states: "its multiplicity of forms and extraordinary capacity for generating imagery, provided always the primary model for conceptualizing general cosmic principles, which applied to the behavior of people, as well as to the forces of nature" (1997, 4).

Water's inherent tendency to follow the "path of least resistance," never detesting or favoring anything—as in the way it "deals" with obstacles—embodies the state of "being one with *shi* 勢" at any given instance. Passages from the *Daode jing*, chapters 66 and 78, respectively, best express this principle: "The ability of rivers and seas to be the king of the hundred valleys, stems from being excellent at 'going down'" (江海所以能為百谷王者，以其善下之), and, "in the whole world there is nothing more supple or weaker than water, yet when it comes to dealing with the strong and unyielding, there is nothing as able (as water) in overcoming it" (天下莫柔弱於水，而攻堅強者莫之能勝，其無以易之). The use of water here is, of course, not only descriptive but metaphoric, relating to man's behavior and rulers' advised conduct, but it also highly relates to everyday lives.

Archaeological excavations and textual evidence indicate that as early as 8000 BC the Chinese utilized spring water and dug shallow wells; furthermore, as Yu, Zwahlen, and Yang note, more than 305 poems relate to spring water as an expression of its significance; these poems shed light on "daily lives, hopes, complaints and beliefs of ordinary people in the early Zhou Dynasty" (2011, 1104) but can be thought of as the very foundation of intellectual thought in China. Yet more evidence of the crucial significance of water in ancient Chinese thought can be found in the very text of the *Zou Yi*: it is suggested that when the divinatory symbols that constitute the hexagrams are put together, (it) makes for a very meaningful water cycle scheme; as Yu, Zwahlen, and Yang claim, this water cycle is even more detailed than some modern-time hydrogeological models (2011, 1114). Figure 1.2 demonstrates this:

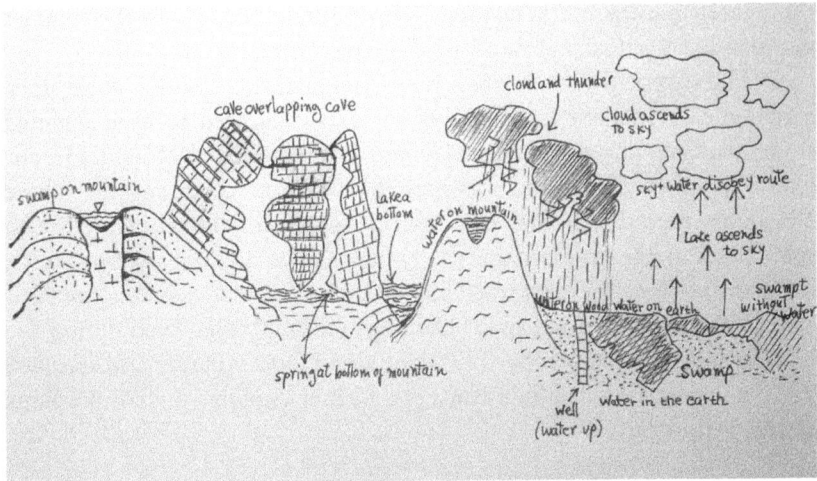

Figure 1.2. An ancient Chinese hydrogeological scheme based on the Zhouyi. After Yu Zhou, François Zwahlen, and Yanxin Wang. 2011. "The Ancient Chinese Notes on Hydrogeology." *Hydrogeology Journal* 19: 1103–14. Illustration by the author.

Now, the significance of water in Chinese thought and culture deepens further when it comes to the rivers that crisscross its land; as suggested at the beginning of this chapter, I argue that rivers (and subsequent phenomena) constitute one of the main agencies molding the idea and technological device of gates in Chinese thought and material culture; that means that it has begun very early indeed—with the first attempts to control rising water levels and floods (such as dams), or as an inseparable part of man-made canals (such as dikes and sluice gates). Concretely and then metaphorically, the gate has come to represent the transitionary locus between chaos and order.[6] In what follows I will attempt at demonstrating this idea through textual and archeological evidence, beginning with characteristics of rivers and canals and their respective technologies.

It is hard to exaggerate the significance of rivers in the growth of Chinese civilization (intellectually, technologically, and economically), with two rivers that in particular that stand out in their sheer impact on Chinese lives (and culture), namely, the Yangzi (長江) and the Yellow River (黃河). The second is considered to be the "cradle of Chinese civilization," and has received a twofold name that changes according to season: it is the "Mother River" and "China's Pride" (Cheng and Yuan 2009) during the winter months but is referred to as "China's Sorrow" in the summer months due to monsoon rains, floods, and changes in its course.

The extent to which rivers have occupied the Chinese mind since early times is evident in a number of texts dedicated to their detailed study; the *Shui jing* 水經 (*Water Classic*), for instance, described 137 different rivers of China and was presumably compiled during the Three Kingdoms period by Sang Qin (桑钦)—a geography scholar (though some place it the third or fourth century as the original text was lost); notwithstanding, the text that followed, *shui jing zhu* 水经注 (*Commentary on the Water Classic*) by Li Daoyuan (郦道元) who lived during the Northern Wei dynasty (386–535), contained forty volumes and specified 1,200 rivers in detail. Linda Rui Feng further explores textual accounts of the Yellow River:

> There was already a long tradition of accounts on the source of the Yellow River. The *Shanhai jing* (Mountain and Water Classic) from the first-century BCE, in its various sections, describes the river as issuing from Mount Kunlun; the "Yugong" (Tribute of Yu) in Shangshu (Book of Documents) identifies Mount Jishi as the river's source; other texts that discuss the river's origins include *Huainanzi* (Master of Huainan) by Liu An (179–122 BCE), and lexicons such as *Erya* and *Shuowen jiezi*. (quoted in G. Olberding 2022, 125)

The fact that Chinese folklore and mythical legends revolve around rivers is thus no surprise; one such instance is the *Ruoshui* 弱水 (*Weak River*) that sees its beginnings during the Warring States period and contains a collection of stories and poems referring to mythological rivers flowing near Mount Kunlun. These rivers, it is narrated, had such weak streams that they could not be traveled, thus protecting the sacredness of Kunlun against unworthy elements; intriguingly, the famous Ming dynasty novel *Journey to the West* (西遊記) refers to these rivers as a barrier on the way of its protagonist—"the monkey that comprehends emptiness"—Sun Wukong 孙悟空.

An additional facet of the need to arrest dire situations or utilize the qualities of water for life's various needs has also been the construction of numerous canals throughout Chinese history; Zhang and Zhou indeed emphasize that "in order to meet the needs of political, economic, military and socio-cultural exchanges, a great number of man-made canals or waterways had been excavated either by the use of convenient rivers and lakes or by overcoming the difficulties in topographical drops and insufficient water resources, finally forming a national water transport network connecting the major water systems, which is called the great canals of China" (quoted in Hua and Feng 2020, 214).

It is said in *Huainanzi* 18:20 that "supervisor Lu was sent to transport their provisions; he also used soldiers to dig canals and thus open the route for supplies. They fought with the people of Yue and killed Yi Xusong, the ruler of Xi'ou" (Major et al. 2010). In this short passage the canal is associated with three contexts: opening a way, transport of goods for people's survival, and military advantage. Indeed, the construction of canals involved advanced engineering by itself but promoted the development of innovative technical solutions for water management, namely, the invention of the first navigation lock (in the world) which, as Zhang and Zhou describe, "successively experienced three developments, namely, that of single-gate navigation locks, multi-gate navigation locks, and navigation locks with pond" (quoted in Hua and Feng 2020, 213).

These sophisticated locks consisted of a gate, a water storage room, and drains—which are all synchronized through the opening and closing of the gate—to adjust water level. Needham brings the following passage from the *Song shi* 宋史 (*History of the Song*), composed in the fourteenth century: "The distance between the two locks was rather more than 50 paces, and the whole space was covered with a great roof like a shed. The gates were 'hanging gates'; when they were *closed* the water accumulated like a tide until the required level was reached, and then when the time came it was *allowed* to flow out" (1971. 351).

Hua and Feng (2020) relate that the earliest single-gate navigation (found to date) belongs to the Lingqu canal (now in Guilin, Guangxi Province)—and could date back to the third century BC; such locks, which were locally known as *doumen* 斗門 (giving the canal the nickname of the "sluice gate canal"), were used specifically "to reduce the gradient and velocity of the canal, and increase its navigation depth" (250). The difference between sluice and weir gates is that the first has horizontal doors (opens and closes along its width—to the right and left sides) whereas the later has vertical doors (opens as it goes up and closes down). The character *dou* 斗 (which has its root meaning in the dipper constellation) refers to a water ladle that is used to scoop liquids up but in the compound *doumen* points to the storage room for water which forms part of the gate mechanism; the character *dou* 鬥 is a variant (interestingly resembling the character *men*) acquired the meaning of "fight" or "struggle" but also "to put together" or "coming together"—an interesting mixture of seemingly contrasting ideas, unless we think of it as "the coming together of two parties into a fight or a struggle" or other plausible explanations; notwithstanding, it is vacuous space that determines between exclusion or inclusion, openness and closedness.

A mechanical component of the sluice gate sits well with this premise, namely, the gate-entwining stone—a device for opening and closing the gate; in the center of this stone, as Zhang and Zhou detail, "there is an axle made of wood or iron, which belongs to fixed pully kind. When the rope of opening-closing the gate passes through the pulley axle, the sluice gate could open or close under the pull by man or animal power" (Hua and Feng 2020, 254). This "stone of in-between-ness" upon which the opening and closing of the water gate depends, functions efficaciously just as the axial hinge of a gate, and evokes in association the Zhuangzian metaphors of the potter's wheel *tianjun* 天鈞 and the whetstone *tianni* 天倪.

Last but not least is an interesting anecdote from the eleventh century in which Cheng Xun (a Buddhist monk) records the canals and multigate navigation locks he was passing through on his way to holy Buddhist sites in China; he attested how, by the next day (18th), "the second gate opened at 7 p.m. to 9 p.m. and the ships sailed out of the chamber" (Hua and Feng 2020, 258). This simple testimony binds together the act of opening and closing with a daily schedule—an important fact when it comes to gates: as shall be discussed ahead, city gates opened and closed according to a specific, authoritative schedule—though differing in hours (i.e., tides influenced the timing of canal gates as opposed to city gates).

The above-described water gates and dams developed out of the need to cope with river floods and manage canals' water levels and velocity; when it comes to floods of the Yellow River, for instance, the ancient Chinese constructed dams, weirs, and dikes that withheld its lower reaches in order to prevent floods; such dikes were administrated by Duke Huan (齊桓公), to give but one example, ruler of the state of Qi (685–643 BC) who aspired to bring about order in the very turbulent times of the Spring and Autumn period. But how frequent were such river floods? Liu Zhenhua (2014, 751) extracted data from textual sources and counted the number of "serious flood disasters" in each dynasty (e.g., Han dynasty 76; Wei-Jin dynasty 56; Northern and Southern dynasties 77; Sui and Tang dynasties 120; Five Dynasties 11; Song dynasty 193; Yuan dynasty 92).

These numbers indicate that floods constituted a frequent occurrence in early China—each (potentially) disastrous to Chinese lives—which, in turn, found its way into flood myths. Anne Birrell studied the fascinating myth of the flood in ancient Chinese culture and says that "the theme of flood control and myths of a great deluge constitute a fundamental and recurring topic in classical Chinese writings. This mythic theme forms an instructive point of contrast and comparison with mythologies worldwide at the literal and symbolic levels" (1999, 214). Indeed, floods were considered a disorderly phenomenon, and posed, as Mark E. Lewis says, a "universal social disorder" (2006, 49)—beyond their physical threat.[7] In the *Mengzi* (see chapter 5) mythological Great Yu will be encountered as the one who had conquered the floods and drew clear borders between ordered civilization and chaotic wilderness. In the context of the gate, floods signify the breakdown of boundaries and the various philosophical approaches that developed in relation to water's manipulation.

The technical solutions (as those already mentioned) were instrumental in restoring order and as a device that balances the two extreme facets of water (vital for life but simultaneously disastrous); the delicate balance between having just the right and beneficial level of flow (per location, time, and situation) and devastating (flood) situations translated, as said, into practical means with which to cope.

This remarkable use of chamber gates in order to control water levels had begun as an existential necessity—but metaphorized into an efficacious entity that either "allows flow" by opening the gates or "puts a barrier" by closing the gates.[8] This represents the inseparateness of abstract thought and concrete and practical ways of living in early Chinese culture. Indeed, Li Feng aptly characterizes Chinese philosophy as "a method to solve problems in the world, rather than the inquiry into the relationship between man and gods as was frequently the case in Greek philosophy" (2013, 209).[9]

This fusion between theoretical knowledge and practice and applicability in Chinese early culture is pronounced in numerous sources; in *Yuan Dao* 1.2, for instance, we encounter the two "August Lords" whose *de* was accorded with the heavens and earth, who harmonized *yin* and *yang* and thus were able to flow like water and fly like the wind. These "August Lords" are in fact the mythical deities Fuxi (holding a carpenter's square to measure the earth), and Nüwa (holding a compass to lay out the round heavens) (see figure 1.3). The compass and a carpenter's

Figure 1.3. Fuxi and Nüwa depicted on Eastern Han dynasty sarcophagi, Sichuan Province, China. Photo: Courtesy of Dr. Hajni Pejsue Elias.

square were used for *fengshui* calculations and architectural construction; as Roger T. Ames and D. C. Lau remark, the Two Lords are connected to "Tai Huang and Gu Huang," which are, "associated with both spatiality and temporality—they stand at the center and work the handle of the *dao*" (1998, 41).

Indeed, the Chinese compass, which in the Han dynasty was named the "south-governor" (*sinan* 司南), was used in geomancy and fortune-telling (Merrill 1983, 1) rather than navigation. In addition, the mythological pair is associated with the creation of man, the saving of the world and humanity (i.e., by mending the torn sky), the creation of the *Yijing*, the establishment of the institute of marriage (i.e., the blend between female and male), and importantly, the earliest flood myth in Chinese textual history. Given the unique and complex amalgamation of dimensions surrounding Nüwa and Fuxi—embodying myth, philosophy, and technology (tools made by man) together—the pair certainly deserves further study.[10]

As it relates to the *practical* means by which man manifests potentiality ontologically, it might just be a fascinating instance of the complementary *fusion* of two types of knowledge, namely, the square, "which is symbolic of the crafted, worked, planned, humanly altered environment that is the man-made world," and "the compass" or "outside of the circle" which, as Willard J. Peterson defines it, is "the mysterious, not wholly fathomable realm of Heaven, heaven-and-earth, and the ten thousand things . . . (which) men are involved in and affected by" (1979, 307).

In the context of the metaphorical meaning of water technology in early Chinese psychology and thought, as described above, an additional aspect takes us beyond myths and folkloristic narratives to the actual formulation of a philosophical framework: this happened when at a certain stage water hydrology stopped being the sole "intellectual property" of engineers or emperors—and began to occupy the mind of philosophers! Needham relates how Daoists and Confucians disagreed on the means of flood control employed; he says, "it took the form of a conflict between two systems of morality, one in [favor] of confining and repressing Nature, the other in [favor] of letting Nature take her course, or even assisting her to return to it if necessary" (Needham 1971, 249). I follow Needham in this intriguing observation and suggest further that we might find in rivers and man-made canals not only roots for the articulation of the abstract idea of gate but even the foundation of the very idea of *dao* 道.

Indeed, multiple sources indicate how water's unique characteristics evoke the efficacy of *dao*; in *Yuan Dao* 12 we read a praise to water, which, by resembling *dao*, serves as a metaphor for human behavior:

> (They) do not meet them with force but rather with a mental attitude based on the model of the persistent weakness of water. This is a quality of mind to be cultivated and is related to the notions of suppleness, pliancy, non-striving, and Non-assertiveness. It is through this normative model of water that we can, as the Laozi says, understand the benefits of acting without asserting the human will over and against the patterns of nature (*tianli* 天理). (Major et al. 2010, 45)

As for *dao*, Ge Zhaoguang says that when the ancient Chinese wanted to express the authoritative and self-evident nature of their knowledge and thought, they would have to give the reasons for their positions, because "this so-called 'Way' and 'Reason' or 'Principle' (*dao* 道 and *li* 理) were no less than that original and ultimate foundation" (2014, 23). As a "way," *dao* indeed constitutes a path or journey, as is said in chapter 64 of the *Daode jing*: "(even) a hike of a thousand *li*, commenced from the (space) under one foot."[11]

Still in the context of *dao*, let me illustrate a visual map: a river might just start its life as a thin stream that, following "the path of least resistance," penetrates into holes in the ground, flows along ruts in the soil, and falls into cracks and folds in the terrain and, while it runs down a mountain slope, continuously being fed by snow, ice, or rainwater, it fills up and, cojoining with other streams, grows wider, larger and deeper . . . to become a river—with its *own* inner momentum and strength. It thus consists of two developing stages: (a) a pre-existing topography (ruts in the terrain) along which water flows (due to water's characteristic of flowing along "the path of least resistance"), and (b) a river of volume, force, and intensity which still "listens" to the topography but is able to create its own path. This model sees *dao* as the sum of both the initial "terrain" that sets its primary course and the river that is formed out of it—a river with inner force and energy (*qi*). Just as its first stage consists of following contours of the earth to become a river, so do living creatures, man included, follow *dao*. Then it is up to man (in parallel to the second stage of the independent river) to create his own *dao* (in the words of Confucius, "man broadens *dao*"). But there is more here: the river offers multiple possibilities either for a lonely boat, a people, or entire civilizations—between two main strategies: one is "giving in" to the currents (*kai*, "opening to them") and flowing along their course; the second, traveling upstream (against it) and blocking the water course.

This is in fact a highly dynamic system that constantly monitors its (open-close) strategies and behavior—and this is exactly the function of a gate apparatus. Furthermore, these two "river sailing" strategies—with the stream or against it—might have developed into ancient China's main philosophical concepts and methods of self-cultivation, for example, Daoist-inclined flow along "the path of least resistance." Interestingly, it says in *Daode jing* 32, that, "*dao* to the whole world is like a river gorge to streams and seas" (譬道之在天下，猶川谷之與江海). This idea will be further discussed throughout the book and in the final discussion.

Chinese Spatiality

The second context that enables us a better conceptualization of gates is spatiality, and, specifically, architectural characteristics that bound and define the space around man. The following is but a succinct outline of the main spatial and architectural ideas and concepts that developed in ancient China (further elaborations on the city, mausoleums, tombs, etc. will be interwoven with their respective gate types in other chapters). In the most general way, spatial concepts constitute a highly culture-bound expression; as Li Xiaodong and Yeo Kang Shua say, "there may be as many forms of space as there are cultures" (2002, 50). As mentioned before, textual sources indicate a high level of semiotic, that is, tangible manifestation of abstract ideas, philosophical tendencies, and cosmological homologies.

An instance of such "link of meanings" between spatiality, temporality, and architecture is the Chinese word for cosmos *yu-zhou* 宇宙, in which *yu* means *shang-xia-si-fang* 上下四方, that is, above, below, and four directions, and *zhou* means *wang-gu-lai-jin* 往古来今, that is, going past and coming present. Hwang Ming-chorng says that the term originally "represented the eaves of the roof and the primary beam supporting the ridge of a roof" (1996, 11–12.). This a *warp-and-weft* image of the universe as crisscrossing location, spatiality (space), and temporality tell us something deeper about Chinese homologies between cosmology and architecture; in "Aspiration" (*zhi* 志)2/49 of the *Hanshu* 漢書 (*Book of Han*), composed by the Eastern Han court official Ban Gu (32–92 AD), there is a reference to this important expression in the context of the seasons and the dynamics of universe, saying, "(due to) the warp and weft of the universe, the four seasons rise and arrive at completion" (經緯天地, 作成四時). Nelson I. Wu indeed says that "the reality of the universe is understood as the combination of 'a six-sided world' (top, bottom and four sides) plus 'past, present and future.' As this cube of a universe spins down the central axis of time, Chinese history unreels, the four seasons revolving with the Chinese cyclical calendar" (1963, 13). As this very matrix or systemized form that captures the universe, a particular trilogy has developed in Chinese cosmology—that of heavens, earth, and man *tianren heyi* 天人合一. Emphasizing the importance of the concept, Ge Zhaoguang adds that the real meaning behind it is "the entire rationality of Heaven (the cosmos) and the Human realm is basically built upon the same foundation and this foundation is, in reality, the supporting background of all ancient Chinese knowledge and thought (2014, 27).

At a certain stage in the architectural history of China, this view manifested itself in the arrangement of capital cities—transforming to become an exact model of heavens and earth; Xianyang, for instance, the capital city of the Qin, dated 350–206 BC, transformed from the "capital of the state" to the "capital of an empire," and, as Wu, Xu, and Wang state, "along with the transformation, a new and important tradition of 'modeling Heaven and Earth' in capital city planning was founded" (2016, 1634). The essence of this "modeling" was the application of constellatory knowledge into the very concrete construction of the city, and both texts and archeology attest to the practice: archeologists Wu, Xu, and Wang have studied the location of relics in the site of Xianyang and found their form to correspond exactly to names of constellations described in the *Tianguanshu* ("Official Treatise of Astrology") of Sima Qian's *Shiji*, namely, "the Apex of Heaven, the Royal Chamber, the Milky Way and the Heavenly Corridor" (2016, 1634).

As a result of cosmological conceptions, the *bagua* 八卦 system was generated: a scheme which means "eight directions" and symbolizes the belief that orientation has an impact over the lives of the people because *qi* flows through these directional channels; *yin* and *yang* are also linked with the space and time and this influences the arrangement of the house. The *Yijing* allows us a glimpse into this metaphoric and physical arrangement of time and space—and man in between, but we have further sources that make such analogies between human tools (of construction) and the cosmos: Tang scholar Li Hua (715–766), for instance, said that "between the carpenter's weight strings and marking lines [is something] close to government order and enlightenment (繩墨之 間鄰於政教)" (*Yingzao fashi* 營造法式, trans. Daming Chen 1993), and Jiren Feng remarks that "the craftsmen's regulating process could be seen as embodying government order and virtue" (2012, 1).[12]

Correlations continue with *intangible* philosophical ideas, the most significant of which is emptiness; Yinong Xu remarks that in Chinese architecture, "the essentiality of the void was appreciated very early in China" (1996, 196). To realize how emptiness can indeed be manifested in man-made concrete environments, let us review the main characteristics of Chinese spatiality and architecture: first, instead of a single building, the Chinese construct a complex, a compound—built along a central axis. Second, there is a strong emphasis on the center from which concentric circles spread out. Third, whole structures are built out of units of empty space called *jian* 間 (see figure 1.4).

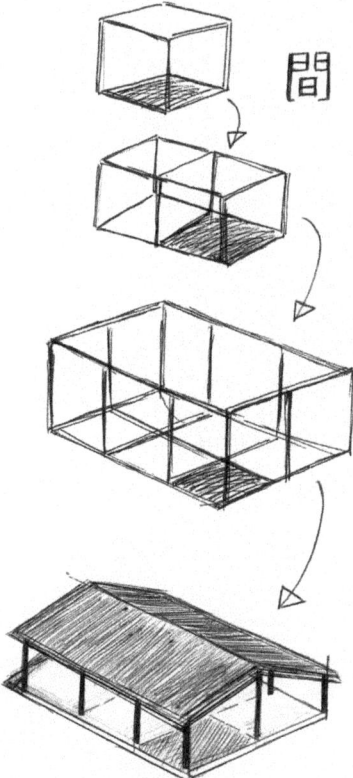

Figure 1.4. *Jian* as "empty or negative space unit" in Chinese architecture. After Ronald G. Knapp and Lo Kai-yin, eds. 2005. *House Home Family: Living and Being Chinese*. Honolulu: University of Hawaii Press. Illustration by the author.

I hold that *jian* constitutes one of the most significant roots of Chinese thought (and consequently, in its material culture and architecture). The character, which consists of a gate with sun/light (formerly, moon), penetrating through, is probably connected with the urban Chinese custom to close the gates of cities at sunset and have them reopen early next morning (as said before, it might be that canal lock gates, that scheduled their opening and closing according to the tide, served as a preliminary model for city gates); thus, light penetrated city gates throughout the day, constantly changing in color and intensity—as the signifier of "movement in space" (within the posts of the gate) and of temporality. *Jian* can be conceptualized as an "expecting void" waiting to be fulfilled; as Richard B. Pilgrim says, "this negative space/time . . . is a pregnant nothingness that is 'never unsubstantial or uncreative'" (1986, 258).

Fourth, *Jian* constitutes a parallelepiped space (from Greek: "an object having parallel plane") limited by pillars or walls. *Jian*, as the basic measurement unit, is repeatedly multiplied, which means that, as Li Xiaodong says, "every individual unit, from smallest room to city, is planned to achieve the maximum balance between what is 'within' and what is 'without'" (2002, 98).[13]

These characteristics attest to an emphasis given in Chinese spatiality on a play between emptiness and boundaries—divisions that create enclosures and generate an interplay of *wai/nei* 外/內 (outside/inside) and a tension between an open flow (*qi*, people, or merchandize) and blocked paths (barriers). The first principle that was mentioned—that of a complex compound aligned along a main axis—constitutes a skeleton that is highly distinctive in almost any Chinese compound, that is, from the private home to temples or cities. This south-to-north axis forms a social, political, or religious gradient along several structures (including gates) that are positioned at symbolic waypoints. In his book on early Chinese cities, Hong Xu mentions the scholar Yang Kuan who differentiates between "city avenues" and "streets," referring to the former as the *dao* that were "leading from the city gate through the outer city" (2021, 42), and the latter as *jie*—a road inside the city of Chang'an of Western Han.

The gradient dictates that as one walks further inside the complex, one reaches more private, sacred, or restricted areas. M. E. Lewis describes how the principle is pronounced in different structures, so that "in a household these would be the private chambers of the men and women of the house, in an imperial palace they would be the emperor's living quarters" (2005, 116). Hong Xu brings archeological evidence to the early existence of courtyard-shaped houses from the important Fengchu site located in Qishan County (Shaanxi Province) saying that "the building consists of the main base in the north, two sides based in the east, and a gate based in the south. The centre forms a rectangular courtyard" (2021, 138), and it is the largest single building known from the Western Zhou dynasty. The main axis is thus remarkably processional, that is, it allows (through *way*-walking) the unfolding of the various visual vistas and spaces to the eye of the "man on the path."

From this aspect, the main axis inevitably recalls, as Paul Wheatley aptly remarks, "the Chinese scroll paintings" (1971, 461) and is manifested also in Chinese traditional gardens in the sense that they constitute a consciously designed choreography. In this processional axis, the courtyard of an early Chinese home constituted a key role in spatial symbolism of the courtyard-house: it contained three spaces: the courtyard (*ting* 庭), the hall (*tang* 堂), and the inner room (*shi* 室 or *ao* 澳); the hall was built on an elevated platform and had to be reached by stairs; the inner rooms were further deep inside and signified a more private and intimate part of the house (into which only family members and intimate friends/relatives could enter). This "courtyard paradigm" manifests a typically Chinese dialectical play between the empty and the tangible—designed through the relationship between walls that confine and deny passage and openings that connect and grant movement. We will encounter the significance of this processional symbolism (succession of discoveries being unfolded along the way) in the context of self-cultivation according to the various philosophical schools.

Indeed, the examination of the relationship between the inside and the outside in the private Chinese home and the processional direction in between these spatial entities constitutes one of the most important points of this study—particularly because it sheds light on the Chinese conceptualization of the inside! As said before, the study has found a strong emphasis on the protection and strengthening of the inside—in all dimensions, that is, city, home, body, mind, and so on. Can we deduce thus that the two sides are asymmetrical? Or that one side has dominance or even control over the other? In his book on Chinese spatial strategies of Imperial Beijing, Zhu indeed argues that "a relative domination of inside above outside is established. A right of control and of access, from inside to outside, can be assigned to, and also supported by, the threshold and the wall" (2004, 49); the term "threshold" naturally refers to gates and doors or openings that connect inside and outside. This emphasis or dominance of the inside corresponds well with the attitudes discovered (in this study) in the context of the body—a particular attention to the inside and its protection. The miniature model in figure 1.5 exemplifies a rectangular compound from the Tang dynasty (618–907), which has two courtyards, pavilions, buildings, and gates that are located on an axial line with symmetrical west-east side halls.

Figure 1.5. Tricolored model of Tang dynasty rectangular house, excavated at Zhongbu Village, Xi'an, China. Shaanxi History Museum. Public domain.

The third principle is that of a center *zhong* 中, from which concentric circles spread outwardly, evoking the ideological-philosophical idea mentioned before in the context of Chinese correlative thinking. The following illustration, based on a reading from the *Zhou Li* 周禮 (*Rites of Zhou*) constitutes a fine instance in the context of concepts of (Chinese) self-identity and concepts of civilization and culture; referring to the illustration, John B. Henderson explains that, "the degree of barbarism increases with the square of the distance from the center" (in Harley and Woodward 1987, 207). This further attests to the correlation between architecture and cultural cultivation—of a whole civilization!

A fine and rare example of the principle of the center rendered into geometrical space is found in the *Book of Documents*, in the chapter "Announcement of the Duke of Zhou" *Shao Gao* 召誥:

Let the King come and continue the sovereignty of the High Emperorship, let himself become the embodiment of obedience as the center of the land. I, Dan, say, "this Great Settlement is constructed so that from now on it corresponds with the August Heaven, carefully scarifying to the upper (heavens) and the lower (Earth), and from now on embodies the very center of governance.[14]

王來紹上帝, 自服于土中. 且曰: "其作大邑, 其自時配皇天, 毖祀 于上下, 其自時中乂."

The passage illustrates that behind the construction of a city lies the idea that a King's residence (*zhai* 宅) constitutes the embodiment of a civilization's center, from which he governs in a way that corresponds with a cosmological order. Yinong Xu points out that that this concept of centralism, "is clearly characteristic of Han ideology" (1996, 54). Yet another instance of such correlations is found in the *Shundian* 舜 典 (*Canon of Shu*):

On the first day of the month, Shun went to (the temple of) Ancestor Wen, inquiring the Four Yue Powers on how to open the four gates, making bright his visual perceptions (of the four directions), attaining the utmost listening (to the four directions).

月正元日, 舜格于文祖, 詢于四嶽, 闢四門, 明四目, 達四聰.

Here, the gate is the point in which communication with the four quarters of the land is made possible; the emphasis here is on *how* to "open the gates," *how* to open the eyes to really *see*, and *how* to open the ears to really *listen*. Indeed, one of the oldest Chinese character dictionaries, the *Shuowen jiezi* 說文解字 ("Explaining words and analyzing characters"), which was compiled by the Later Han–period scholar Xu Shen 許慎, defines the character *men* 門 as "door" but also as the locale "where news are joined/followed and heard" (Zhang 1992, 267).

This association between listening and hearing and the gate has been conspicuous in multiple sources. Additionally, it indicates how the city or temple and their gates projected outwards to the corners of the universe as they were indeed thought to mirror the universe; Paul

Wheatley says that "the city gates, where power generated at the *axis mundi*, flowed out from confines of the ceremonial complex towards the cardinal points of the compass" (1971, 468). Chinese architecture was not only the means by which to create a harmonious universe as a reflection of the cosmos, but was also used as a political tool in the hands of the ruling authorities; one structure that remarkably manifests this aspiration toward cosmic harmony in early China is the "Bright Hall" *mingtang* 明堂 (see figure 1.6), which in order to be efficacious, as noted by J. B. Henderson, "all its microcosmic parts must correspond to the macroscopic parts" (1994, 213).[15]

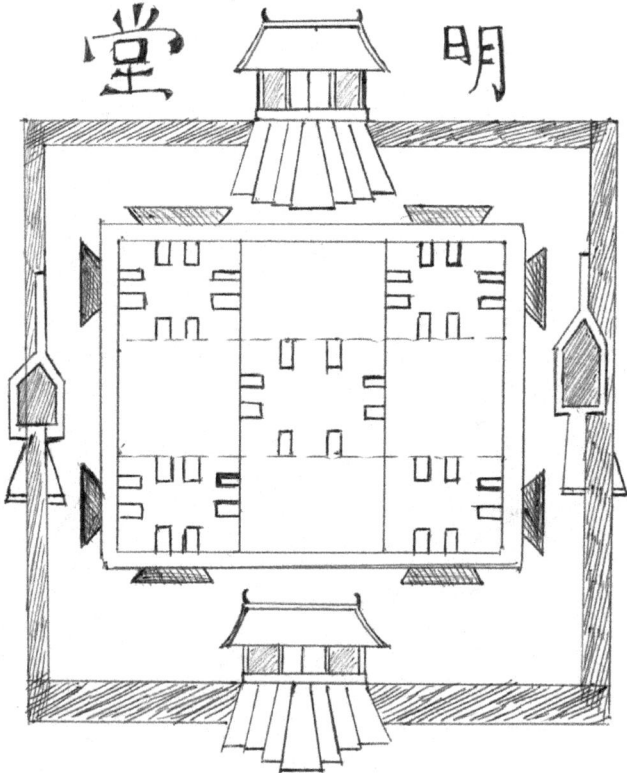

Figure 1.6. Illustration of *mingtang* 明堂. After Zhu Tianjun 朱天俊 (1993). "*Siku quanshu zongmu* 四庫全書總目," Beijing/Shanghai: *Zhongguo da baike quanshu chubanshe.* Illustration by the author.

Such parallels between ideology and architecture are also found in the Chinese "architecture of the afterlife"—tombs and mausoleums. Jessica Rawson describes the tomb, artifacts, and art found in the tomb of the Liu family (who founded the Han dynasty) and says something that I find significant: "the great tombs and the miniature landscapes had similar purposes; namely to realize the universe and to make that potential manifest for the benefit of the Liu family associates" (1999, 54). The connection m/e afterlife is indicative of *a* conceptual worldview of resonance and continuity between the past and the future—life and afterlife. An interesting shift occurred from the tomb as the end destination to a transcendent paradise in the minds of the ancient Chinese; the tomb was, as Guolong Lai says, "the 'happy home,' or the underground 'permanent home' of the deceased" (2005, 4).[16]

Figure 1.7 shows three clay bricks from three different tombs (Han dynasty), each decorated with various themes, such as boars and tigers (the right), trees, tomb doorways, and horses(top), and on the left side there are a few identified.

Figure 1.7. Bricks from three different Han dynasty tombs. Victoria and Albert Hall Museum. Public domain.

Great efforts were made in the way of decorations, depictions, and murals to the extent that some tombs aimed at achieving a sophisticated atmosphere that aspires or evokes philosophical ideas or ideologies. The arrangement and murals of tomb caves, for instance, hint at an aspiration of its designers for the creation of a dark and mysterious atmosphere inside. This attempt to evoke a "mystic vision" (*xuanlan*) in the cave refers, as E. Y. Wang says, "to the dark mental or interior space" which means that one needs to "cultivate the soul" as a prelude to cleansing "the mirror of mysteries." He adds that "shapeless as this dark mystery is, it is accessed in Laozi by way of a gateway: "Mystery of mysteries, the gate of all wonders" (2005, 31). This is in effect the meaning of the character *xuan* 玄, which will be discussed in the context of certain philosophical texts, such as the *Taixuan* or the *Daode jing*.

As shall be seen and individually analyzed, there is great variety in type, size, function, and design of gates within the above-described spatial and architectural design. They range from inner doors of the private home to one's front gate to city gates; watchtowers; open archways such as *paifang* 牌坊 or *Pailou*; checkpoints erected on the roads; watchtower gates named *guan* 觀 or *wanglou* 望樓, from which guards looked out for threats; and the important Twin Towers or *que* gate 闕 that appear by different names in early texts, such as *xiangwei* 象魏, *jique* 冀闕, and *diehuang* 経皇 (Chien 2018), and is associated in early dictionaries as a *guan* gate and as a gap (that is, emptiness). *Que* gates were highly important in three contexts, namely, as landmarks of city walls, as signifying social status, and as loci on imagined journeys of the soul to the afterlife along *shendao* 神道 or "spirit roads" (each context and its *que* gate will be discussed separately). Yang Kuan points out that in the Han dynasty's city of Chang'an, the gates of the inner city are described as *chengmen* 城門, while the gates of the outer walled city are described as *dumen* 都門 (H. Xu 2021, 36).

Massive gates (sometimes with whole offering halls) were also erected in front of tombs and mausoleums—especially when it comes to tombs of emperors. In the case of high-ranking officials, nobles, and royal families, we also find funerary art depicted on the gates of their tombs (Howard 2003, 139), alongside exact models in miniature (*mingqi* 明器) of their homes, watchtowers, and other architectural structures. This is indicative of the strength of the belief in the afterlife as an identical existence to life—which requires the creation of exact replicas of the material culture that surrounded the deceased in their lives.[17]

One of the factors that influenced the construction of watchtowers and barriers in the most general way was warfare . . . in times of war, there is an urgent need to strengthen the walls of the city, which only emphasizes their weakest link, that is, where their continuous line is broken in the form of gates. This must have been a defining factor in the development of the architecture of defense, but also in the formulation of intellectual notions of chaos and order and strategies and skills of warfare (in which gates fulfill a key role). Frank A. Kierman even suggests that, as opposed to Western expansiveness, China's concern for social order at home "instead of expansion abroad, came from her landlocked situation in North China remote from other centers of civilization and from sea routes communicating with them" (1974, 3). Li Feng emphasizes that during the Warring States period, "warfare was the most important aspect of social life, the principle of the state and the compass that directed government policies . . . in the late Warring States the entire state was organized for the very purpose of war" (2013, 197).

Furthermore, the conflict of *wen* 文 and *wu* 武, that is, between civil and military realms might have become a fundamental principle in early China; Christopher C. Rand (2017, 15) even coins this conflict "an axiom in developing the philosophy of war in ancient China," with intriguing complementarity of its derivatives, for example, virtue and punishment. As will be discussed in the context of Mozi's doctrine, for instance, the utilization of gates in defense and attack, and military strategies in general, revolve around ethical issues, which pre-Han texts do discuss, but which as Chris Fraser writes, "do not treat the issue of 'just' war per se, using a Western concept of justice or what is just. Instead, they evaluate, for instance, whether or not warfare is righteous (*yi* 義), benevolent (*ren* 仁), permissible (*ke* 可), or consistent with the Way (*dao* 道)" (2016, 7).

Etymology of *men* 門 and Associated Concepts

As said in the notes to Classical Chinese, *men* can mean a fixed object but also a verb or a process (meaning "to gate," "gating," or "passing through a gate").[18] A fine example is *yinyang*—taken as "things" in English but constituting in effect a dynamic and ever-changing process. In this study, thus, *men* is discovered and accordingly conceptualized as a polysemous metaphor and a sign of diverse semiotic significances. The character is made out of two symmetrical doors or posts that face each other, with an empty space or gap in between them—significant to its exegesis. How old is the character? Importantly, it is found on the *jiagu* 甲骨 "oracle bones," both on ox scapulae and tortoise plastrons, dated to 1200 BC. Early representations always have two posts with different accompanying components, a horizontal beam or two-leaved doors. The two-leaved doors in between gates raise the number of possible states within it (open, closed, half-open, etc.).

The compound image in figure 1.8 demonstrates the evolution of the character *men* as quite an exact pictograph of real double-leaved gates—but simple wooden ones. The character above is found on Shang oracle bones, while the one below is the character *men* itself. Note also the visual resemblance between the Shang character and the gate extracted from the famous scroll *Qingming shanghe tu* 清明上河圖 by Zhang Zeduan 張擇端 (twelfth century AD).

The etymology of *men* points to a gate or a door but also "an opening" and (on the other hand) a closed gate (a barrier). The chapter *shigong* 釋宮 in the *Erya* dictionary includes a list of components of gates and doors, such as "door panel" (*fei* 扉), small entrance to the women's quarter (*gui* 閨), and threshold (*yu* 閾). Furthermore, it defines various components of architecture in relation to the rituals; for instance, in the definition of "the front gate of a palace," *zheng men wei zhi ying men* 正門 謂之應門, *ying* 應 is defined as "audience or court," attesting that the court and/or audiences were assembled at the front gate.

Figures 1.8a and 1.8b. Similarity between Shang dynasty gate character and gate depicted in a Song painting. Museum of Tianjin. Author photos.

The character also means "friends" and "group," which points to the suffix *men* 們 having its roots in the specific sense of a "clan" (Iljic 2001, 74), as well as meanings of "turning point" (change) and an association with texts (discovered to be highly significant), "locus of instruction" (as indeed was revealed in the *Analects*).[19] Table 1.1 has a summary.

Table 1.1. Table showing layered meanings of *men* 門.

Dimensions	Etymology
Ontological/Architectural	Anything between an opening and a barrier
The Social	Family, Clan, Sect, Friends
The Individual	Locus of instruction, School, Doctrine, Teacher, Turning point, Self-cultivation.

Source: Author provided.

Chapter 2

Gates of Creation

Correlates between Man, Text, and Cosmos

At the meeting [in the Gate] at the second month, the myriad creatures come to life.

At the meeting [in the Gate] in the eighth month, the herbs and trees begin to die.

—*Huainanzi* 3.17[1]

This chapter contains gate passages that have been found to embody prototype characteristics of Chinese cosmology and thought, that is, emptiness, complementary opposites such as *yinyang*, center (threshold), and the cultivation and evolvement of all things and phenomena. These particular 'apparatuses of creation' constitute double-leaved gates that either exhibit a mechanism of continuous opening and closing or serve as the space 'in-between' in which an intermingling of complementary opposites take place. But an added significance has surfaced around these particular gates: a resonance with the text they constitute part of, specifically, and with the *written word* in general, that is, *texts* as a unique human creation that correlate with natural and cosmological creation. The main textual sources found to exhibit these characteristics are the *Yijing*, the *Huainanzi*, the *Taixuan jing*, and certain chapters from the *Daode jing*.

Let us actually begin this discovery with the context of the gate as a portal through which all the myriad things and phenomena are created and evolve to full fruition. A beautiful instance of such description is found in *Huainanzi* 1.13:

> All living things (without fail) go through one orifice; the root of the numerous phenomena always emerges from one gateway.

> 萬物之總, 皆閱一孔, 百事之根, 皆出一門.

The two parts of the line parallel each other, the first relating to "all living things" that "go through holes *kong* 孔," and the second, to the root of all phenomena that emerges from one gateway *men* 門; this is a cyclic process of life and death, of creation and destruction. The hole is an empty, vacant channel all things pass through to completion (*tong*); the second refers to the root of all phenomena, which, if I am correct, refers to the word "root" and not the phenomena themselves, meaning that "the root of all phenomena" constitutes the "return back to emptiness" through the gateway.

The idea and concept of the gate as a spatiotemporal apparatus for biological evolution (i.e., the creation and evolvement of all living things) is conspicuous in the *Yijing* but it carries an added significance of textual creation and decision-making in the face of constant change. That the *Yijing* constitutes the ultimate source of such cosmo-textual gates is not a great surprise for readers of Chinese philosophy . . . as Roger Ames aptly defines it, isn't the very axis of the *Yijing* "the coordination of the relationship between the changing world and the human experience" (2015, 2)? I indeed contend that the gates described in the *Yijing* manifest the idea of change in both the natural and the human spheres; however, the prediction of change as postulated in the *Yijing* can hardly be called divination or prophecy, as the consultee obtains no deterministic solutions nor specific advice as to his or her situation. Furthermore, as a nineteenth-century Chinese commentary states, "the Changes is the mirror of men's heart-minds" (易者人心之鏡也), meaning that "there are as many versions of the *Yijing* as there are readers of the document and commentators upon it" (Smith 2009, 2).

Any meaningful insights that one might extract from its contextual way-pointers mirrors his or her mind and predicts nothing that is absolute or certain; this is because, as Xiaosui Xiao says, fate, by its own definition, "is never determined in itself" (2006, 3).[2] As is indeed clear from multiple Chinese sources presented in this book, that the line that stretches from the present to the (unknown) future is not linear nor deterministic but a complex, ever-changing matrix. As shall be seen, textual sources point to several external factors and internal skills that might help man in the ever-present, existential dilemmas of *choice* and decision-making, namely, timing, circumstances, location, inner state of mind, and *shi* 势.

But in what way does the *Yijing* grasp this ever-changing matrix? The hexagrams were originally grasped as actual representations of cosmic patterns, but with time they went through an intellectual shift (at times as a response to crises of self-doubt) until the fall of the Han dynasty (220 AD); Hon Tze-Ki (2019a) claims that in the next seven hundred years, the Chinese turned their attention to "ordering the human world and looked for its deep structure" instead of attempting a full discerning of the cosmic pattern and its application to human affairs. Intriguingly, it is Wang Bi who conspicuously plays a part in this shift, emphasizing the hexagrams to be way-pointers to human creativity, prowess, and efficacious activism (Hon 2019), in addition to stressing the deep meaning of images *xiang* for human intellectual endeavor, saying that "nothing can equal image in giving the fullness of concept" (Geiger 2013, 615).

One of the most important references to the concept of *xiang* and *xing* in the *Yijing* appears in the *Xi Ci* I ("Great Treatise"):

> That which is above form is called *dao*, that which is below form is called a thing.

> 形而上者謂之道, 形而下者謂之器.

What is above form? The formless—a state in which forms are not separate one from the other—that is *dao*: obscure and hidden. What is below form? The separation into distinct things or objects: once things are contained within clearly defined boundaries (which could refer to the mind, the body, living things, or man-made tangible manifestations), they constitute the *de* of *dao*: the tangible realization of the ten thousand things. In connection to the suggested model presented in chapter 1, I believe that this very idea underlies the formulation of the *Yijing*: by deciphering patterns and signs in the visible world (the world of forms), the ancient Chinese wished to penetrate into the formless and the empty—*dao*. I thus argue that the conceptualization of and attitudes toward form *xing* 形 constitute a core question in early Chinese thought and material culture—to the degree that it can elucidate differences between schools of thought—precisely because it pulls us directly into the space that is "in between" the forms. A significant passage describes the efficacy of a double-leaved gate in this very context of creation as the process in which "things and phenomena become and take on form"; it is extracted from the *Xi Ci* I ("Great Treatise"):

> Thus, closing the swinging doors (of the gate) is called *kun* and opening the swinging doors (of the gate) is called *qian*. Each (repetition of) closing and opening is called *transformation* and this inexhaustible (process of) alteration is called "perfect breakthrough (for unification)."[3]

是故, 闔戶謂之坤; 闢戶謂之乾; 一闔一闢謂之變; 往來不窮謂之通.

The passage relates to a continuous opening and closing mechanism of the inner doors *hun* 戶, of a two-leaved gate; but what is the nature of the process described here and in which dimension does it take place? I find that it points to the cosmogenic process of creation in all dimensions, that is, the cosmic, biological, as well as the human sphere. The act of closing is associated with earth, or extreme *yin*, and the act of opening is associated with heavens, extreme *yang*. The first (closing) is interlinked with marking a boundary (a division, separation, containment) which can relate to any dimension, that is, the mind (thoughts coming out of the mind, external influences coming in) or bodily *qi* or the natural world; as it is associated with *yin*, it is soft and yielding, directed at the inside and towards the invisible, the dark.

The opening act *pi* 闢 is associated with the release of *yang* type *qi*, which is intense and determined; it parallels an "eye-opening" experience, an unveiling or seeing something *beyond*—through a *crack* in a wall. It is interesting to note the hexagram named *guan*, which further attests to the significance of *seeing* (and observing) in Chinese thought (in fact, it has been revealed to constantly occupy the same conceptual field as the gate). A further parallelism is manifested in concrete architecture—the flanking watchtower *guan* 觀 from which patrolling guards looked far into the distance. However, according to the *Erya* dictionary, this multistoried tower not only allowed for looking afar outwardly, but carried the significance of an *inward* observation. Joseph Needham speculates that the original meaning was "to observe the flights of birds, perhaps with a view to making predications from omens obtained from them" (Ronan 1978, 95), and adds that its meaning had changed between 430 and 250 BC to a watchtower.

Still, it seems that the original meaning (especially for Daoists) remained: an observation of the natural world.[4] In reference to "seeing" in a divinatory sense, Chung-ying Cheng asks, "What is *guan* (as comprehensive observation?) It is to observe all things in nature and the world in an extensive and comprehensive way, so things are seen as a whole. All things emerge from this whole and manifest the whole. At the same time, one observes the rich things" (2011, 346). The endless repetitive process of opening and closing is a very *delicate* interplay, influenced by numerous factors that can potentially alternate its consequential evolving life; this refers to the tiniest detail or event that can alter the situation and lead to far-reaching consequences (resonating with the phenomenon known as the "butterfly effect"). As noted, the intermingling of closing (as looking backwards or inwardly) and opening (looking forwards or outwardly) creates a highly efficacious potential for seeing (i.e., evoking *insights*). This unique skill of penetrating into spatiotemporal past and future simultaneously constitutes the cutting through to the very unfolding of *dao*—right at the threshold of the gate; as it is said in *Liezi* 8, "staying at front by keeping to the rear" (Graham 1990a, 158). Further, as a gate's hinge repeatedly turns on its axis, the potency of the space in-between increases—similarly to the combined electric charging power of plus and minus.

In the dimension of the mind, through the intermingling of *yin* and *yang* at the threshold, neither side takes precedence . . . it is an *abandonment* of any "side" or a letting go of any absolute values, which actually means a return to emptiness—the prerequisite condition for change that is taking place at the gate. A somewhat similar paragraph in the "Providing the Sequence of the Hexagrams," Part 1.6, reads as follows:

> The Master said: "Aren't *qian* and *kun* the gate of Yi?" *Qian* corresponds to *yang* phenomena, *kun* corresponds to *yin* phenomena; *yinyang* join together through their corresponding "inherent potential" (*de*), hard and soft are manifested in form, and form constitutes the compilation of Heavens and Earth.

> 子曰: 乾坤其易之門邪? 乾, 陽物也; 坤, 陰物也; 陰陽合德, 而剛柔有體, 以體天地之撰.

Here we have a description of the way *qian* and *kun* intermingle at the gate, but with an added meaning as to the *Yijing* itself. Lynn brings forth Wang Bi's comment on the passage:

> *Qian* and *kun*, do they not constitute the two-leaved gate into the *Changes*? *Qian* is purely a *yang* thing and *kun* is purely a *yin* thing. The hard and the soft exists as hexagrams only after *yang* and *yin* have combined their virtues, for it is in this way that the numbers of Heaven and Earth become embodied in them and so perfectly realize their numinous bright virtues. (1994, 86)

The emphasis on the intermingling of complementary opposites continues, but here the correspondence is not only between *yin* and *yang* but with the very lines *yao* 爻 that constitute the hexagrams: *yin*—a broken line (the break is discontinuity, that is, change, an open gate) in its ultimate performance is *kun*, and *yang* (a continuous line, a border) in its ultimate performance is *qian*, and the rest of the hexagrams are pointers to change. Significantly, the *yao* are also referred to as the "six empty places" of a hexagram which "stipulate the patterns, directions, and principle of change" (Guo-Ming Chen 2008, 8); an "empty place" is a space devoid of "this or that" as only through emptiness can transformation be carried through (*tong* 通). There is more to say about the significance of the *yao* and their *form* and I will do that in the final discussion.

Yet an additional reference to the same process is found in the *Xi Ci II* ("Great Treatise II"):

> Qian and Kun, do they not constitute the generative force of change!"

乾坤其易之縕邪

Wang Bi comments: "Generative force refers to the deep, mysterious well-spring." This reference to the well as an endless source of water that is "mysterious" is significant (see chapter 1) and is found in other sources as well (such as the *Daode jing*); a well-spring is a metaphor for something that is inexhaustible, which comes out from the deep and into to light (in the same way that a text is created inside the heart-mind and goes outward to the light)—to become part of all life. Chung-ying Cheng refers to the inherent qualities of *qian* and *kun*, saying that "we may call *qian* the positive creativity whereas we may call *kun* the receptive creativity, for it is in *kun* that we find provisions of nutritive elements and support for substantiating impulse of the *qian* that provides initiative motive power for creation. The togetherness and mutuality are explained in the notion of the 'great ultimate'" (*taiji*) (2011, 350). Indeed, the "great ultimate" *taiji* 太極 fulfills a key role in the cosmogenic processes from which all things and phenomena fulfill their inner potential. In chapter 42 of the *Daode jing*, for instance, the cosmogenic process describes how "the way (*dao*) begets one; one begets two; two begets three; three begets the 'the thousand things'" (Lau 1964).[5] Can we thus infer that emptiness *wuji* 無極 at the very center of the gate parallels *dao*, whereas the "two" parallels *taiji*? Chung-ying Cheng suggests that, "we have to think of the *dao* as both empty and not empty, and this make the *dao* inconceivable and unspeakable in concepts" (2011, 361). This resonates with the interpretation I have just given to the *yao* as "empty places."

But is it a state of *this* and *that* or *yin* and *yang* fused together? In other words, is there still a trace of dichotomy from the previously distinguished sides? This distinction might just be the very conceptual difference between *wuji* and *taiji*; Isabelle Robinet says that "the *wuji* is a limitless void, whereas the *taiji* is a limit in the sense that it is the beginning and the end of the world, a turning point. The *wuji* is the mechanism of both movement and quiescence; it is situated before the differentiation between movement and quiescence, metaphorically located in the space-time between the *kun* 坤, or pure *yin*, and *fu* 復, the return of the *yang*" (quoted in Pregadio 2010, 1058).[6] Taking into consideration that the etymological meaning of *ji* 極 is "a limit," I believe *taiji* should be taken as the *first divide*—the first line that constitutes the very precondition for any perceptible thing in life as it gives it form without which it cannot survive; it is also reminiscent of the first separation between heavens and earth! *Wuji*, on the other hand, parallels the mechanism of the gate's doors that simultaneously combines *yin* and *yang* in a state of limitless void.

The emptiness in *taiji* is relative—that is, meontological—and should be regarded, as David Chai says, "as the meontological milieu in which the potentiality of *Dao* 道 (the progenitor of all things) is realized" (2012, 5). This very fine attunement and balance between an advance or a withdrawal, between a *yin*-type act and a *yang*-type act, between chaos and order, between covering and unveiling, is the mechanism through which *dao* is manifested into form—right at the threshold.

This meontology approach is reflected in my exegesis of chapter 11 of the *Daode jing*, which significantly relates to concepts of the formed and the formless, emptiness and tangibility:

Thirty spokes are shared by one wheel;
Acting out of (the potency of) both its "tangible form" and
  "empty space,"
The vehicle has utility.
Knead clay in order to make a vessel;
Acting out of both its "tangible form" and "empty space,"
  this vessel has utility.
Chisel out doors and windows for a room;
Acting out of both its "tangible form" and "empty space,"
The room has utility.
This happens because of the advantage of the "formed";
(but) it is "empty space" which enables its utility.[7]

三十輻, 共一轂, 當其無, 有車之用. 埏埴以為器, 當其無, 有器之
用. 鑿戶牖以為室, 當其無, 有室之用. 故有之以為利, 無之以為用.

This translation reflects a certain relationship between the formless and
the formed—as *equally* important in the context of *efficacy*. I argue that
the author/s of the *Daode jing* observed that it is the natural tendency of
man to see usefulness in the "there is" (what they see with their eyes),
missing that a thing's efficacy lies in the combination of both the tangible and intangible (*yinyang*). Indeed, as we cannot acknowledge "what
there is *not* there" or "what is *not* happening," we tend to attribute the
usefulness of a tea bowl to its concrete clay walls and bottom; we would
fail to realize that if the concrete and tangible bowl "lacks empty space"
inside (i.e., it is full), it would not be possible for the bowl to hold tea
or, to "accept new tea."

As an analogy to the human mind, if one is "full" (of himself, of
opinions, of convictions, etc.), nothing new can enter—hence, literally,
there is *no room* for change and transformation (see discussion in final
chapter). But importantly, the passage *does not* negate ontology, that
is, tangible forms: without walls and bottom a tea cup cannot function
either in the same way that *dao* expresses its potentiality through actual
forms—as its *de*: it is indeed the meontological efficacy of *dao*. The very
manifestation of *dao* into *de is* the performance of transformation that is
able to "go through to completion" (*tong* 通)—the iterative and repetitious
process of the intermingling of complementary opposites constitutes the
way *dao* is becoming tangible in the concrete world, as Wang Bi says,
"the reciprocal process of *yin* and *yang*, that which allows the *Dao* to

continue" (Lynn 1994, 53). But what is the nature of this change *yi*? Is it a gradual change, a step-by-step process of slow accumulation, a sudden, "quantum leap" transformation?[8]

In the above passage from the *Ci Xi* I ("Great Treatise" I), change is represented by the character *bian* 變, the etymological meaning of which relates to reins of a horse. *Bian* is made out of 夂, a hand 又 holding a stick *bu* ⼘, which might mean "to strike or otherwise act upon something," that is, "to control chaos"[9] but *bu* ⼘ is also a divinatory crack on an oracle bone, suggesting an additional meaning of *bian* as "hand holding (something) to make a crack," that is, "hand attempting to predict change or bring about order out of chaos."

As for horse reins, these are used to control wild horses . . . which can be likened to a dike controlling an overflowing river—the function of both is to control *chaotic behavior*. However, the reins and horsemanship metaphor involves the accumulation of knowledge and a continuous learning process and skill, so that familiarity with the horse is acquired (I would also emphasize "learning through a feedback mechanism"), the result of which is a *change* in the horse's behavior—from chaotic to ordered.[10] It hints at a steady and gradual change which reaches culmination and is then replaced by its opposite force, and vice versa. This is yet again a process known to modern science as the "tipping point." Guo-Ming Chen describes this nature of gradual change through the structure of the hexagram:

> The first or the bottom line indicates the foundation of change; the second line is the sprouting period which indicates the formation of a change of things; the third line is the embodiment indicating the concretizing stage of change; the fourth line is like the leaves of a tree, indicating the strong growth of change; the fifth line is the blooming period, indicating the flourishing of change; and the sixth or top line is the fruit, indicating the fullness of change which implies a stage of transformation to another cycle. (2008, 8)

As in the natural world, change goes through cycles of blooming, flourishing, and finally, fruit bearing; it reaches a certain limit or "tipping point" and returns. Guo-Ming Chen describes this cycle of interchanging slow and fact changes: "The sudden change refers to the acceleration or violence of movement when the gradual change reaches its saturation level. Thus, the sudden change is considered as the result of the gradual change in which the old system is replaced by a new one in a quick pace" (2008, 13). As discussed in chapter 1, the ancient Chinese detected the phenomenon of cyclic change and discerned patterns of the living world. In the *Zhuangzi*, for instance, we find ten references to the term *wuhua* 物化 "transformation of all things," and the *Huainanzi* contains ten occurrences of *bianhua*, which, as Major et al. indeed claim, refer to biological transformation, or as occurring "naturally in the nonhuman world," thus rendering *hua* as "metamorphosis" or "to turn into" (2010, 924). A passage in chapter 7 titled "utmost enjoyment," *zhile* 至樂 in Zhuangzi's Outer Chapters, stands out in its description of transformation and natural evolution at a *liminal singularity* ("at the border between water and soil") at which species evolve:

> Species contain (certain) germs *ji* 幾; when in water, they become *kui* 蟲 (successful in sustaining life). When they *are* at the border between water and soil, they "wear the cloths of" (evolve into) frogs and oysters. When they are on the bank, they become *ling-xi*; when on fertile soil the *ling-xi* become *wu-zu*.

> 種有幾, 得水則為蟲, 得水土之際則為蛙蠙之衣, 生於陵屯則為陵 舄, 陵舄得鬱棲則為烏足 . . .

The description then continues with more and more species evolving, until eventually human beings arrive, and ends with, "each of the ten thousand things *comes out* of these germs, and *goes in* from these germs" 萬物皆出於機, 皆入於機. Remarking on the *Yuan Dao*, with emphasis on the different attitudes of China and the West, Major et al. point out that for the authors of the *Huainanzi*, "everything in Heaven and on Earth is both natural and supernatural, secular and sacred, the natures and patterns that constitute them attain a normative prominence often unfamiliar to us in the West. That is, these patterns, sequences, propensities, and natures are themselves divine" (2010, 49).[11]

However, on the edge of these predictable and gradual changes there exists another—a sudden, chaotic, and unpredictable phenomena. Interpreter Kong Yingda (574–648) distinguishes between *bian* (in the following quote, rendered "alternation"), and *hua* (rendered "transformation"), as follows: "'Alternation' refers to afterwards changing from a former state, it has gradually changed. This is called 'alteration.' 'Transformation' refers to existence in one moment and absence of existence in the next, it has suddenly changed. This is called 'transformation'" (Nielsen 2013, 115). This important passage hints that two types of change were observed, a *bian*, which is a gradual, predictable change, and *hua* which constitutes a complete transformation. Joseph Needham mentions Cheng Yi, who implies that *bian* constitutes an "inward change with full or partial conservation of the external Gestalt or form, and *hua* as *fundamental* change in which the outward appearance is also altered" (1956, 74). Needham also remarks that in modern Chinese usage, *hua* tends to mean sudden and profound transmutation or alteration (as in a rapid chemical reaction).[12] Natural disaster (e.g., river floods or earthquakes) stood for such sudden and unpredictable change which carries far-reaching consequences.

As discussed in chapter 1, the careful observance and study of the various types of change and transformation constituted the elementary basis for the development of innovative means by which to survive and keep (or restore) order; as Chung-ying Cheng says, the *Yijing* is full of "creative potential to encounter difficulties and develop new possibilities" (2011, 351). To return to the two forces combined at the gate, the "closing" force defines external contours—which is the first and preliminary act in the evolvement of any biological creature (as it gives it substance and form that separates it from its environment), while the opening force can be grasped as giving living things their first breath and life essence and enables them to prevail and grow to maturity—and fulfill their inborne potential.

It is an interplay between the ultimate (invisible) reality, and its manifestation in the visibly concrete. F. M. Doeringer even compares the gate's threshold in the *Yijing* to the concepts of Nagarjuna's "Absolute and Relative Truths": "The gateway of change, therefore, is a passage between the ultimate and non-ultimate aspects of reality, connecting them so as to fuse constancy and change in an enigmatic whole" (1982, 315).[13] In an attempt at visualizing this cyclic movement of complementary opposites inside this gate, I have drawn the back-and-forth, open-and-close movements of a double-leaved gate (figure 2.1), and a certain shape has started to appear. I then encountered the following *taijitu* suggested by Marcel Granet in 1934, and found that both images are identical:

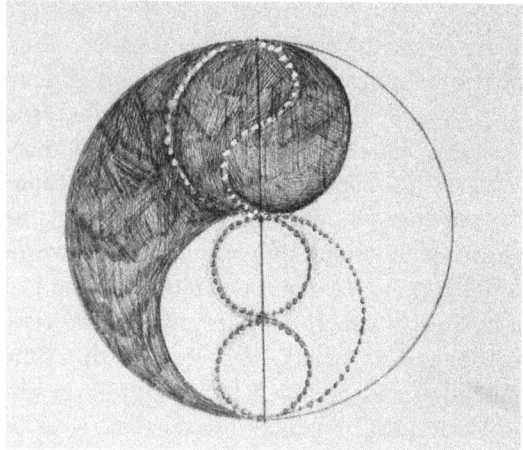

Figure 2.1. Inner cycles inside the *taijitu* symbol. After Marcel Granet. 1934. *La Pensée chinoise*. Paris: La Renaissance du Livre. Illustration by the author.

It is now the time to take a look at a passage that demonstrates the correlation between the text itself (the *Yijing* as human creation) and cosmogenic phenomena, change and the gate in the midst of it all; it appears in *Xi Ci* I ("Great Treatise" I)

> The Master said: "The *Yi* is ultimate! The *Yi* is the mean by which the sages reached the highest virtue and broadened the scope of their deeds. Wisdom made them honored, ritual propriety made them humble. In Honor, they followed the patterns of Heaven; in modesty, they followed the patterns of Earth. As the Heavens and Earth established their positions, the *Yi* performs from within them; thus, as the nature (of all things) comes to exist—it is the very gate of *dao* and integrity."

> 子曰: 易其至矣乎! 夫易, 聖人所以崇德而廣業也. 知崇禮卑, 崇效天卑法地. 天地設位, 而易行乎其中矣, 成性存存, 道義之門.

What a praise to the *Yijing*! According to the author, the ancients consulted with it as a means by which to "exalt their virtue," and acquired wisdom; this wisdom is the result of combining the patterns of the heavens and of earth by standing right in between them—in the liminal singularity in which change takes place.

The text emphasizes that such transformations are not a given, but depend on the appropriate actions carried out by man—actions that are accorded with cosmic forces, timing, and circumstances. Importantly, according to the *Jinlu zhai qitan yi* 金錄齋啟壇儀 (*Liturgies for Inaugurating the Altar of the Golden Register Retreat*), "the gate of the heavens" is the nose and the Door of Earth is the mouth; "through the nose comes in and goes out *qi* of the heavens, and the mouth absorbs *qi* of Earth through food" (Miura Kunio, quoted in Pregadio 2010, 978). When the gate of heavens (as the nose) is closed, no breathing and hence, potentiality for life, is possible. Perhaps this nose gate—as the channel through which air comes in and out in an iterative motion—constituted the very first image from which the *Yijing's* gate of creation has been borne out.

As for the purpose of the *Yijing*, I believe it did not only refer to the "big decisions of life" but to the mundane and minute steps we carry out each and every moment. As will be discussed in the final chapter, such mindful awareness demands a constant heart-mind attunement to everything that exists and occurs around us. It constitutes a way to "cut through" the spatiotemporal web of phenomena, actions, connections, and forces that constantly change (and in which nothing is predetermined or programmed towards some end target). Chung-ying Cheng indeed points to this open experience of *guan*, which "does not lead to dogmatic beliefs" (2011, 347). Indeed, when "dogmatic beliefs" or "absolute values" in our mind fill up original, primordial empty space, they allow for no change to take place.

Change constitutes numerous situational possibilities that are further multiplied by the inner world of man and its own multiple states . . . as in a room full of mirrors, we always face infinite possibilities that flow and constantly start anew within the dynamic matrix of the world. The passages discussed so far demonstrate that the process of the evolvement of all living entities starts with the appearance of the *first contour outline* that awards every living thing a form; this form separates it from the environment but at the same time awards it *life*: as it creates a unique and singular *communication* between external environment and internal characteristics—a behavior, a way, strategies of survival and self-actualization (in the discussion, I will correlate this first contour line to the first brush stroke in the creation of a Chinese painting).

In the context of emptiness and tangibility, the formed and the formless, I have already offered a somewhat different exegesis of chapter 11 of the *Daode jing*; although the *Daode jing* is definitely one of the most known and analyzed Classics in Chinese intellectual history (and more and more so in the West), I contend that this text *in particular* demands of us a "beginner's mind" (*shoshin* 初心)—one that is not overshadowed by preconceived knowledge and interpretations . . . so that the text always stays freshly enigmatic and on the edge of the unfathomable . . . as indeed it was 2,500 years ago.

I would now like to return to the text, and in fact, to its very beginning: the first chapter—a chapter that I conceive to be the gate to the text's deepest hermeneutical roots. Furthermore, the chapter as "root" has also begun to acquire in my mind a sort of vertical shape— from the ground to the depths of the earth or perhaps like a man-made architectural construct, with deep foundations below (in the dark) and tiers upon tiers above (in the light): whatever the visual metaphor that comes to mind, the chapter constitutes a path and the reader treads along it from the first *dao* to the final "crescendo"—the gate at its end.

In the most general way, doesn't the first chapter of any book constitute its "opening gate"? Doesn't it invite the reader in? When it comes to the first chapter of the *Daode jing*, David Loy indeed suggests that it is "a key to the whole work" (1985, 369), and Hansen takes it "as setting the background against which we should read the other fragments" (1992, 214).[14] Needless to say, the *Daode Jing* or the *Laozi* 老子 is one of the most influential texts in the intellectual history of China, inspiring countless Chinese and Western studies, heavy debates, and controversies on manuscript variants, authorship, dating, and most importantly, inter-pretation.[15] The gate is one in a long list of metaphors, analogies, and riddles used in the text, all manifesting, in the words of A. C. Graham, not an illustration of abstract thoughts, but "thinking itself" (1989, 218).

As an architectural construct, then, the chapter is made of four tiers, each supporting the next—as a ladder along which the reader climbs up to reach its intended realization. The following translation expresses this underlying conceptualization:

1. 道可道, 非常道, 名可名, 非常名.

Ways (that) one can speak about, (cannot be) the ubiquitous *dao*.
Names (that) are given, (cannot) encapsulate the ubiquitous *dao*.[16]

2. 無名天地之始, 有名萬物之母.

Thus, "nameless" is the beginning of heavens and earth;
The "named" is the mother of the living things.

3. 故常無欲, 以觀其妙, 常有欲, 以觀其徼.

Therefore, through (a state of) constant lack of inner-intentions,
one can see the mysterious;
Constantly having inner-intentions, one can see its boundaries.

4. 此兩者, 同出而異名, 同謂之玄, 玄之又玄, 衆妙之門.

These two (sides) of the same (source), issue forth with
separate names;
Being (from) one source, (I) call it a mystery; Mysterious and
(more deeply) mysterious, the gate to all (the many) wonders.

The exegetical challenge the first two lines have been posing for thousands of years lies in understanding the various meanings of the characters *dao*, *chang*, and *ming* and their relationships.[17] The traditional view sees the second *dao* as a verb meaning "to speak, to talk," thus rendering the inability of words to describe *dao* as words, and names are man-made construes (*formed* definitions) and are inevitably bound entities into narrow confines. This is, of course, the much discussed and immediate paradox with which we are faced while holding a five-thousand-character-long book—devoted to *dao*.[18]

I believe the clue to this question lies in the character *chang* 常, which is traditionally rendered "constant," "enduring," "permanent," and "eternal" (*chang* appears thirty times in the *Daode jing* with meanings ranging from "always" to "permanent" or "continuous").[19] If that is the meaning of *chang*, does it hint at an eternal *dao* that exists beyond the visible world—a world characterized by impermanence, decay, and death? Alan Fox renders such interpretations as "ontological readings"—those interpretations that take *dao* to be "a monolithic, fundamentally real, static, abstract and uniquely ineffable eternal *dao*" (2017, 30). Kurtis Hagen and Steve Coutinho remark that *chang* might refer to some *quality* of *dao* that is indeed *eternal* in itself, saying that "the constant *dao* is that which gives rise to change and yet is itself not the change just because it is the change" (2018, 362).[20]

We might have a clue in the Mawangdui silk manuscripts: there, instead of the character *chang*, a different character appears before *dao*, namely, *heng* 恆.[21] What can *heng* tell us and how is it related to *chang*? Qingjie Wang remarks that the two terms are connected "directly or indirectly, to movement on water, where a boat moves on an earthly river or the moon moves across the celestial 'river'" (2000, 150). Interestingly, *chang* denotes something that is constant, while *heng* refers to movement—isn't that contrary? I suggest that in effect it is the combination and intermingling of both: the ability of the boat to *stay steady* and balanced even when all around it there are "fast eddies and tranquil pools, shallow and deep water, movement forward and backward, up and down, slow and rapid, and so on" (Q. Wang 2000, 150).[22] Man and water become a *yinyang* entity—complementary motion of order (steadiness) and chaos (unpredictable behavior of water).

The shared characteristics of *chang* and *heng* is thus an immediate responsiveness to circumstances, the becoming one with the surroundings, which is the embodiment of change itself (the *Yijing*). It is the ability to "be one with change" and adapt to it through the use a unique "this and that together" or "either one" mechanism: boat and water becoming one, each forsaking its own *fixed identity* (much like *yinyang*). This is reinforced by Jing Liu who interprets *chong* 沖 (in the *Laozi*) as originally meaning "the surging-up and the swing of water, and later comes to also have the senses of 'mingle together' and 'harmony' or 'harmonize'" (2017, 89).[23] Therefore, *chang* means the quality of continuous adaptation and transformative flow which can only be manifested through emptiness. According to this exegesis, *chang dao* is formless, invisible, highly responsive, adaptive, and in continuous evolvement and change and endowed with immense efficacy.

This is the fusion of the ultimate and limited, unconditioned *wudai* 無待 and conditioned *youdai*, 有待, which constitutes the two aspects of *dao*. This is how, as David Chai says, "*dao* imbues things with its essence while ensuring harmony pervades the universe." (2010, 94).[24] With this in mind, how can we understand *chang ming*? Here it is easier to understand the interpretation of *chang* as permanent, since a word or a name and language in general fixate things; as the act of naming had a significant and central role in the period, it might be a direct criticism of the "school of naming," which means, as Cao Feng says, "that 'the Way' and 'names' are the two most critical factors of real politics, and only those who grasp the Way, can grasp the Way 'that cannot be spoken' and names 'that cannot be named'" (2013, 87). This does not belittle naming by itself! It just claims that because words are a human construct, they can only grasp the *formed* (concrete) part of *dao*—its manifested *de*. In effect, the breaks in between words constitute the formless or emptiness, that is, silence or interval (*jian* 間). This also corresponds to chapter 56, which says, "(those or he) who know/s, do/

does not speak; (those or he) who do/doesn't know, speak" (知者不言, 言者不知), and which says further that "therefore the sage keeps his mouth shut and his sense-gates closed" (塞其兌, 閉其門).

Furthermore, the *ming* might be a reference to the *Daode jing* itself as if saying that "talking about *this* text (written about *dao*) is *possible*, but this will not get you far in knowing the real mystery of *dao*."[25] Also, as all things are in constant flux, man's moral judgment and its constructed values should also be transforming. It might be that we have here a direct reference and criticism on things people say about *dao* as a doctrine: that people mistakenly and deludingly take doctrines to be eternal . . . a way that would always apply—notwithstanding changing times, situations, and circumstances. My translation attempts at reflecting these ideas—note that *dao* is rendered in plural at the beginning and singular *dao* at the end, to emphasize that the minute *dao* is talked about, it is no longer *dao* . . . but merely human constructed ways.

The next two lines continue to relate to names, the first referring to an entity "without name" or without concrete form, the second "with name." Here, the "nameless" is the beginning of heavens and earth, which is the nonhuman world of no forms and no name-giving; the named, on the other hand, is the limited, conditioned human world—the *mother* of all those (man-made) defined phenomena.

The mother constitutes a significant metaphor in the *Daode jing* as the nurturer who brings to fruition. Chapter 52, for instance, reads "the world had a beginning; and this beginning could be the mother of the world" (Lau 1964). What is the meaning of this feminine power? Is it the ability to act out of unconditional love and carry no selfish interests? Indeed, having no self-interest can be thought of as having no desires of her own, that is, an act of ultimate giving (of which breastfeeding is perhaps the best example).

From this aspect, it is understandable why the mother is mentioned as part of the world of the named (the formed and tangible)—because although she might lack desires, she cannot function without the physical senses of listening, breastfeeding, holding the child, and so on. In fact, a mother is the epitome of both states (thus perhaps coming closest to *dao* in the human world).[26] As a natural continuation of the previous tier, the third part indeed relates to the senses. I take the character *yu* 欲, traditionally rendered as desire, as referring to the inner intentions (conscious and rational thought) which leads to deliberate actions; these intentions are the opposite of meditative-like thought that manifests into effortless, spontaneous, and undeliberate action. When one acts out of "inner intentions," he or she is able to see the formed and bounded, while in their absence, one is able to witness the mysterious (formless).

An important clue as to the (literally) thin line that separates the formed and the formless comes in with the meaning of the characters *miao* 妙 and *jiao* 徼. *Miao* relates to a secret or the mysterious and contains the radical for "few" or "little," but it also carries the significance of "the marvel of the undifferentiated state," which is "neither small nor big" (無小無大).[27] Furthermore, *miao* also refers to "biological seeds," as Roberts says: "Laozi imagery, however, belongs more to the realm of biology than to physics. The 'seed germs' (*miao*) are fertile germ cells" (2001, 28).

This is yet again a reference to the natural world in which seeds or germ constitute *potentiality*—the yet unactualized, formless state that (given the right cultivation) is fulfilled (into form). *Jiao*, on the other side, relates to boundaries and borders; thus, between *jiao* and *miao* lies a thin line of continuous exchange—at the liminal space which is the gate—a biological membrane. At this singular threshold the "simultaneous existence in between states" translates into transformation; it occurs at the very edge of the formed—as David Loy says, "the fact that reality has two aspects and yet is one, is here declared to be a 'great mystery'" (1985, 378).

The final tier continues the reference to the two states as coming out of one source, namely, the space in between being and nonbeing, formed and formless; it is the skill and ability to simultaneously see and realize the *dao* and its *de*, the empty and tangible. As Chung-Ying Cheng says, "all things will return to the state of *wu* because *wu* is the source from which all things are generated" (2011, 363). Thus, these two diverge because *dao* is within the formless, while its manifestations (from the very first divide between the heavens and earth) do receive names, as they belong to the world of forms.

The process that takes place in this singular space is transformation *bianhua* (變化), which in the *Laozi* means going back to the undifferentiated source, to emptiness.[28] The gate at the very end signifies this unique state of potentiality in the concrete universe, and we can perhaps get closer to its significance by looking into the character *xuan*. Wang Bi said that "*xuan* (mystery) means silent, mysterious, and unspeakable," adding that "we cannot settle only on one *xuan*, or we would lose [its sense]; therefore [the *Daode jing*] says 'mystery and again mystery'" (Robinet 1977, 109). Cheng Xuanying gives yet another interpretation, saying that "the second *xuan* aims at not being attached to the first one, i.e., at not being attached to non-attachment," and adds that "the illness of pretending that any one statement—be it you or *wu*, or negating as well as asserting both—is true, disappears" (quoted in Pregadio 2010, 274). Isn't it that the moment an idea formulates into concrete words, it immediately loses its "truth" as it becomes confined and formed? It has left the "absolute reality" to reside in "relative truth," to evoke Nagarjuna's terms. This coincides with Hansen's view (above) that the first two lines indicate the futility of any textual guidance.

From a gate perspective, I would like to offer an additional exegesis of the two *xuans* as a process of getting deeper and deeper into the undifferentiated, to the singular source in which *dao* manifests itself in both the visible and the invisible worlds. As it is said in chapter 34, "constantly without desire, this can be named small; when all living things return to it, (and) it doesn't behave as (their) master, this can be named great" (常無欲, 可名於小; 萬物歸焉, 而不為主, 可名為大). The first *xuan* points at the realization of the mystery of transformation, which means *seeing* the gate of creation itself, while the second *xuan* stands for *enlightenment*. As *xuan* hints deeper into darkness, I wonder whether there is a play on dark and light in the text, that is, darkness that is followed by light as *enlightenment* (an etymological connection which appears in many languages and cultures).[29] Chang Chung-yuan refers to Daoist "enlightenment" as one which "no thought will disturb. One becomes aware of the heavenly radiance within. It is light in darkness" (1963, 76).

The wonder awarded at the gate consists of the simultaneous seeing of the formed and the formless—the very threshold in which creation (manifestation of *de* from *dao*) takes place: because being able to witness the very instance in which creation is taking place—is indeed a wonder. This unique ability of *seeing* allows one a glimpse of the wonderful or mysterious (related to the character *guan* 觀)—acquired through the process of emptying oneself (*wuwei*) of the constraints of language, opinions, and attachments, among other things. Importantly, this ability of *seeing* also requires the letting go of the attachment to the very idea of "letting go" or "emptiness"—even if such ideas are worthy or beautiful. In their article on "seeing," Miranda Brown and Uffe Bergeton find in the Spring and Autumn Annals *chun qiu* 春秋, a reference to the ability of the sage, and speculate that, "the ability to perceive the hidden or formless—here, represented by secret plots—was not something everyone was thought to be capable of. Instead, as Guan Zhong's reactions reveal, it was unique to sages" (2008, 651–52).

This "light in darkness" is a unique state of clarity achieved by suddenly *seeing* the gate and then standing at its threshold, center *zhong* 中, experiencing the creation or beginning of life. The visual image that comes to my mind is a gate within a gate within a gate—deeper and deeper down to the very "wonders of creation"—both of the physical world and the depth of the mind. Each gate forms yet another developing stage along the path (*dao*) leading into *ao*.[30] A beautiful description of this "within and within" appears in chapter 5 of the *Neiye* 內業 part of the *Guanzi*:

> The heart/mind 心 is such that it hides heart/mind. Within the heart/mind there is another heart/mind. As for the heart/mind of the heart/mind, thought and intention precedes speech. Only when there is articulated sound, does (thought) takes shape. Only when it takes shape, is there speech. Only when there is speech, is there internal control. Only when there is internal control, is there order. When one does not order things, there is bound to be chaos. (Needham 1971, 48)

Rudolf G. Wagner observes that this state of mind is "being one with the ultimate," and in fact—as referring to the gate itself; he says that "the Laozi itself thus establishes an important interpretive principle, namely, the legitimacy of identifying various makeshift appellations for the Ultimate, in this case *men* 門" (2000, 214). This fascinating description of almost a "fractal" entity of a mind, contained and contained within itself—an endless matrix of "concentric circles" embodies the very state from which creativity is embodied and enabled. As Roger T. Ames and David Hall say, "the swinging gateway . . . is where and when *Dao* spontaneously 'opens out' to provide creativity a space through which to make its 'entrance,' qualifying the processive nature of Dao with the immediacy and specificity of the creative act (2003, 59).

Chinese correlative thinking detected this creative act (in nature and in man's mind) as taking place on the very edge between chaos and order—again, at this very line between the undifferentiated (no form *as yet*) and the differentiated (having forms).[31] I argue that the idea of "roots and branches" sets the best background against which to understand the message encoded in this chapter; moreover, this image, of a *development* from roots to branches, as a constant process of change and transformation, seems to me to convey an inherent characteristic of Chinese thought in general, but it also denotes the very (visual) image that characterizes biological processes in nature, scientifically called "branching pattern." In this representative image, the gate constitutes the very center (*zhong*) at which transformation occurs.

A remarkable passage from the *Taixuan jing* (*Canon of Supreme Mystery*) presents the idea and principle of the efficacy of complementary opposites through a rare conceptual scheme, in order to "make a point."[32] I refer to tetragram number 57 named "Guarding": "*Yin* guards the door; *yang* guards the gate. No things make contact. *Yin* guards what is relatively inside; *yang* takes care of what is comparatively outside. Thus, *yin* may be said to keep watch over earth, while *yang* watches Heaven. Since yin and yang are each at their separate stations, apparently defending their own territories, there can be no mutual contact. With the marvelous capacity for interaction lost to the myriad things, nothing can germinate or grow" (Nylan 1994, 339). The passage starts by telling us that *yin* and *yang* *do not* intermingle, and, furthermore, that each "side" guards his own territory so that no cooperation or contact takes place. This is an extremely counterintuitive statement to make in the context of Chinese thought, but it is only used as an intriguing rhetoric as it is followed by this sentence: "with the marvelous capacity for interaction lost, nothing can germinate or grow." The author in fact wishes to emphasize that as long as people hold on to their opinions, conventions, tendencies, concrete territories, among other things—no breakthrough, contact or, in fact, harmonious life is possible.

Therefore, the gate symbolizes *possible options* open for man—between the closed state in which both sides (nations/parties/people) guard their own values/property/etc (which only lead to hostility and even death), and the open state, in which a connection and intermingling can take place. The "Diagram of the Mystery" *Xuan tu* 玄圖 reinforces this philosophy, "two by two they go, [like] leaves of the gate. Such is the meeting between friends. One day and one night make a single day. One *yin* and one *yang* give birth to the myriad things" (Nylan 1994, 372).

Chapter 16 in the *Daode jing* gives us hints at the subject of returning to the roots and awards us with an additional clarification of *chang* (Chapter 1):

The "the thousand things" are numerous (and diverse),
each returning to their source.
"Returning to the source" is called stillness,
Which is their (natural way of) completion.
Their (natural way of) completion,
is (called) ubiquity (being in constant evolvement).
Knowing this ubiquity is called clarity.

致虛極, 守靜篤.
萬物並作, 吾以觀復.
夫物芸芸, 各復歸其根.
歸根曰靜是謂復命.
復命曰常, 知常曰明

This passage relates to the "the thousand things" that rise from emptiness and return to emptiness as the natural circle of life and death. The main point here is the singular *root* in which the formed things and the formless converge. Again, it's an analogy to natural "roots and branches" as the process of evolutionary development. I suggest that this passage corresponds with the "gate to all the various wonders" in the first chapter: it is the root from which all things are borne and return to. Wenyin Xie says in relation to "return" that

> the opposite of a thing is also the origin of the thing. Weak is the opposite and origin of strong; poor is the opposite and origin of rich; and so on. In other words, when one becomes the strongest, he begins to return to weak, and becomes weaker and weaker. Weak is the opposite of strong, yet it is the origin of strong. The identification of opposite with origin in Laozi's observations of the sensible world implies that opposition is also reversal. In this treatment, "reversal" (*fan*) combines two meanings: opposite and origin. When it is used as a noun, it is the opposite of a thing; when used as a verb, it refers to a movement of returning. (2000, 471)

As was emphasized, these processes occur on different levels simultaneously and correlatedly—from the mind of man to the natural world, and heavens and earth. In the sphere of man, this evolvement is the concept of self-cultivation—an idea that, notwithstanding its place in all schools of Chinese thought, widely differs in the actual *how* (applicable means) and aspirational result. While the Confucians emphasized a process of learning and accumulating knowledge (a *forward direction* to the more complex state), Daoists advised the opposite direction . . . a return backwards to the simpler state, the origin, the roots, the formless.

This return to the spontaneous mind is named "uncivilized spontaneity" by Allinson, who stresses that according to the Daoist view, "people have lost contact with the ontological depths in which it rests," so there should be a "recovery of the uncivilized spontaneity, the soupiness, the unformed ready fecundity of the ontological depths of existence (1989, 63). Burik refers to chapter 5 of the *Daode jing*, saying that "the *Daode jing* chapter 5 talks about 'space between' Heaven and Earth as man's abode. The 'space between' character is closely related to the gateway character and can therefore be seen as that shifting place that is itself nothing but from which all diversity issues" (2010, 503). Just like a mother—the natural world exhibits such "effortless yet efficacious behavior" as water or sunlight, for instance, that sustains plants but possesses no conscious will to help the plant. The *Zhuangzi* delivers remarkable instances of biological creation; in the Outer Chapters, *zhi bei you* 知北遊 ("Knowledge Wandering North") number 5, for instance, we find a dialogue between Lao Dan and Confucius, in which a sequence of *organic* developments are described; for instance, illumination was born out of obscurity, these with form were born out of the formless, the spirit out of *dao*, the body from the essence of sperm; then comes a remarkable "taxonomy" of different species (some born from the womb, some born from eggs, each with its own number of openings).

As for these species, Zhuangzi says, "their comings leave no trace, their goings leave no scarp; (they have) no gate, no abode, (they roam) in the magnificence of the whole universe." (其來無跡, 其往無崖, 無門無房, 四達之皇皇也). Varied and distinct, notwithstanding, all these "species" share a common characteristic—they do not "leave any trace behind." This characteristic is not only the result of the natural cycle, which always goes back to emptiness—as opposed to human beings who act upon the world consciously and/or exploits it with direct intent; animals seem to be completely immersed in it. It certainly reminds one of chapter 27 in the *Daode jing*, which says, "an excellent traveler leaves no wheel tracks behind him." Indeed, a good traveler is in complete harmony with the topology, plantation, valleys, streams, and mountains; he or she travels without exerting his own presence on it by, for instance, cutting his way through aggressively.[33]

I would like now to focus on yet another theme that revolves around these "gates of creation" in the *Yijing* and the *Daode jing*—the textual perspective that is taking place at the gate *in parallel*. As Livia Kohn says in regard to the hagiography of Laozi (which will be discussed in chapter 7), "the text is part of the mystic effort to bridge the eternal gap between realization and knowledge, between practice and teaching" (1991, 26). Through the context of *dao* and *de*, what is a text? As human beings themselves are one of the things and phenomena of the world, that is, one of the manifestations of *dao*, their own creation of text (or tools, technology, etc.) can be thought of as their *de*; in other words, textual creation constitutes a *"de of de"* or double *de*—a *manifestation within manifestation*—as the two *xuan* in the first chapter.

Another point to consider is the Chinese characters themselves as they constitute a *visual* construct that conveys abstract (that is, formless) meaning, and thus they embody a mediatory entity by themselves; we can therefore grasp the very act of reading as "seeing this and that" together. As the reader opens the "gate" of the book (in the case of the *Daode jing* it might be the first chapter or the first *xuan*), he or she instantly realizes its essence, and gets *enlightened* by it: and this enlightenment is the meaning of the second *xuan*. This motif of successive actions will then continue on for generations of readers—as a potential transformer that offers an opportunity for change. Only when the gate opens and/or allows a disappearance into realization (enlightenment) its potentiality fulfilled and manifested; the text is never a given (correlatedly to *interality* in general! e.g., the Chinese grasp of the inner body)—meaning that only those readers whose mind is entuned through emptiness would be transformed and enlightened. When text and mind comingle at the gate, we have fertile soil from which the reader can grow and fulfill his or her potentiality.

In their linguistic study of the first chapter, Yoav Ariel and Gil Raz analyzed the *qi* 其 (in lines 5 and 6), and concluded that it might very well point to the "gate of all the various wonders," leading to the idea that "the ambiguity of the two *qi* is intended, and that the reader is to realize that the contextual referent, Dao, and the grammatical referent, 'gateway,' are in fact one and the same" (2010, 394, 399). "One and the same" applies to three dimensions: *dao*, gate, text. Only at this singular "in-betweenness" at the gate does a state *open up* for the simultaneous amalgamation of both the formed and the formless. I suggest that in both the *Yijing* and the *Daode jing* the gate passages do not only refer to creation of life in the cosmic and natural (biological) dimensions, but reflect on themselves. Humans can indeed be creators given they are entuned to the myriad things, as indeed Puett says in reference to chapter 13 in the *Zhuangzi*: "the sage is defined as a creator, the creator of the worlds in which the myriad things grow and develop" (quoted in A. Olberding 2011, 238).

Indeed, aren't books the very intellectual *openers* of the mind? Aren't they a door through which people transform—in any civilization? Indeed yes, but I sense an added significance of textuality in Chinese culture and thought—a "pillar of strength" holding its "intellectual architecture," if you like. The remarkable book *The Literary Mind and the Carving of Dragons*, written by Liu Hsie (465–522) during the Northern and Southern dynasties, constitutes the first comprehensive work of literary criticism in China; though beyond the scope of this volume, one line in it is too significant to exclude: "from these things we know that Tao is handed down in writing through sages, and that sages make Tao manifest in their writings" (Shih 1959, 12). And if we wish to even step further back—to the invention of writing itself for the Chinese, *Huainanzi* 8.5 uses dramatic words to describe its emergence: "In ancient times, when Cang Jue invented writing, Heaven rained corn, and demons wept all night" (Major et al. 2010). In chapter 7, the issue of textuality will be further discussed in the context of Laozi's hagiography. Finally, the term for civilization or culture in Chinese is *wenhua* 文化 that is literally "a transformation of writing."

Chapter 3

Gates to Inner Formlessness

Great image has no form, *dao* hides in no name.

大象無形; 道隱無名

—*Daode jing*, Chapter 41

This chapter includes passages from the *Taixuan jing*, the *Daode jing*, the *Huainanzi*, and the *Zhuangzi* . . . grouped together around gates that have been found to play a role in an aspiration for the formless state in the dimension of the body-mind: a philosophical inclination toward the unknown and ineffable as the desired state for man's cognitive state (involving methods of purging and emptying out). Importantly, due to Chinese correlative thinking which produces parallel worlds between body-mind and the cosmos, man-made architecture and the heavens, as well as a *tian/ren* (heavens-man) dialogue, the "exegetical destination" of these passages can relate to either one or the other but in some cases might very well be a simultaneous reference to both spheres. An inseparable part of such aspiration for the formless and ineffable constitutes methods of self-cultivation, which constitutes the "pulling down the abstract to concrete and practical means"—a trait which I find to be highly characteristic of Chinese culture and thought (see introduction). The gates in these particular passages are described as a portal through which one goes *backwards*—from complexity to simplicity, from the clearly divided to the chaotically muddled.

As explained in the introduction, the book's chapters are arranged along a closed-to-open gradation, and, when it comes to "gates into formlessness," we might intuitively expect them to be the most open on this range, that is, closely associated with inseparability; however, in many cases (particularly with Daoist sources) and specifically when it comes to the gates of the body (openings)—the repeated advice is actually to have them in a closed state.

As paradoxical as it may sound (i.e., *blocking* the gate in order to *open up?*), the underlying conceptual reason is a constant need to protect the interiority of the body-mind from external factors that might corrupt it. Let's see, for instance, Tetragram number 33, ("Closeness") in the *Taixuan jing*:

> Appraisal 1: He seeks a glimpse of the Great Unknown; but there is no gap in the gate.

> Fathoming 1: Peering into it, there is no gap means: it is shut up tight on every side.

The gate in Appraisal 1 is supposed to allow one a glimpse of the world beyond, the unknown, invisible and undifferentiated; a gate which is probably, as Michael Nylan says, "the border between potential and actual existence, between life and death, between the tangible and the ineffable. Behind our everyday world lies the inchoate source we call the Tao" (1994, 157). However, intriguingly, there is no gap in the gate . . . does it mean that the gate is closed? I hold that it actually hints (as in other tetragrams) that the efficacy inherent in the gate is dependent upon openness and that a glimpse of the unknown is possible, by "death or by a flash of sudden illumination" (Nylan 1994, 158).

This "sudden illumination" is associated with the architectural structure named Hall of Light *mingtang* 明堂, a common motif in the *Taixuan jing*; Tetragram number 16 ("Contact"), for instance, mentions it as "the sacred site where the king makes ritual contact with the gods" (Nylan 1994, 90).[1] In both the spatial and temporal spheres, the Hall of Light fuses together the meaning of "seeing beyond" or "seeing the light" (as enlightenment). *Huainanzi* 16.82 awards us with a significant (literally) insight into the meaning of "illumination" and light in the mental dimension, mentioning the doorway as one step before utter and complete illumination:

> If you get light through a crack (*xi* 隙) or gap [in the wall],
> it can illuminate a corner; if you get light from a window, it

can illuminate the north wall; if you get light from a doorway (受光於戶) it can illuminate everything in the room, omitting nothing. How much more [would be illuminated] if the light received were from the whole universe! There would be nothing in the world it did not illuminate. Looking at things in this way, if what you get [light from] is small, what you see is shallow (Major et al. 2010, 591; Chinese characters added).

This progression from a crack through which light comes in, to light received from the whole universe relates, I propose, to its perception by human beings. The source of light itself is the same (the sun or any conceived transcendental entity that projects light). The difference lies in the how it manages to illuminate one's mind, meaning that the descriptions of the openings (gradually getting bigger and bigger) correspond with the openness of one's mind—in other words, one's ability to really *see* beyond form, to the absolute, or *dao* itself. The end of the passage indeed supports this interpretation, saying that "if one's channel of vision is narrow or blocked, one can only manage to scratch the surface of reality."

A similar progression that utilizes an architectural component (as the previous passage in which we had window, room, door) is in Appraisal 5 of the *Taixuan jing*: "heaven's gate is opened wide, extending the steps of its hall, this may give rise to error." The Fathoming that follows remarks that "virtue cannot fill the sacred hall." What can the act of "extending the steps right into the formal audience hall" (before the gates) mean? The act of extending the steps makes it easier to approach the gate . . . as a metaphor for an easier process of self-cultivation (which is long and arduous); the reference here is to the self-cultivation of the ruler himself which leads to transformation of his people—as a bridge between heavens and earth (through the gate); by transforming his people to the level of sages he allows them to enter the Inner Sanctum *ao* 奧. However, it seems that in this particular case, the ruler lacks the required qualities so "he cannot hope to measure up in terms of virtue. Rulers like this, even though they may have 'ascended to the hall,' have not entered the Inner Sanctum *ao* 奧" (Nylan 2014, 292). This is a remarkable correlation between mind and architecture, in which the Inner Sanctum *ao*—a deep, dark, hidden and important part of the house—serves as a metaphor for a mysterious abode in the cosmos and in our mind:

Steps → audience hall → gates → *ao* 奥

The Inner Sanctum is a layered term with parallel meanings in philosophy, theology, architecture, and other fields. Benjamin A. Elman, for instance, refers to the Inner Sanctum in Imperial China, saying that

> by taking care of both imperial sacrifices and imperial family matters, the Ministry of Rites had the further distinction of being the only ministry that was a member of the inner court of the emperor and at the same time a full-fledged member of the outer court bureaucracy. It thus had access to the Inner Sanctum of imperial prerogative and could affect its policies through the education bureaucracy down to all county levels outside Beijing. (1989, 385)

Ao portrays an important singular locus in Chinese Buddhist caves of worship, as well as constituting a significant idea in Japanese aesthetics and thought.[2]

But what does the sage possess that grants him entrance to the Inner Sanctum, as opposed to the general populace? Clues might be found in further understanding the mysterious *xuan*. In the *Daode jing*, the quality that connects one with the ineffable and intangible is closely associated with the female; chapter 6 reads:

The gate of the mysterious female,
Is called the root of heavens and earth.

玄牝之門，是謂天地根

Robinet refers to the *xuan* in this chapter as the powerful meeting point of opposites at the gate, saying, "this gate is dual, just as the Center is in Taoism, and therefore suggests the dynamic bipolarity of the world" (quoted in Pregadio 2010, 2:1138). *Xuanpin* 玄牝 literally means the mysterious female or mysterious valley, which carry parallel meanings, for example, deep, dark, hidden, *yin*, yielding, and so on. The female possesses characteristics which allow it to be the creative power for realization. Indeed, Chung-ying Cheng says that as the female is "soft and yet capable of conquering the hard, it is similar to water" (1991, 178). In the Wang Bi commentary to the chapter, we find the following: "'door' is that on which the dark female is based. Basically what it is based on has the same substance as the *Taiji* 太極, the great Ultimate of the *Zhouyi* which 'creates the two formations' (Yin and Yang). This is why (this door) is spoken of (by Laozi) as 'the root of Heaven and Earth!'" (Wagner 2000, 139). Thus, the dark female is a symbol of "reversion" and "going back" *through the gate*, which evokes one of the most important concepts of Daoist thought, namely, *wuwei*—as a way of no action or effortless action ("path of least resistance"). Richard Lynn refers to nothingness in Wang Bi as a key concept in the Laozi, saying, "The perfect absence of conscious design, deliberate effort, prejudice, or pre-direction. . . . The Dao always 'acts out of nothing' (*wuyiwei* 無以為) and thus never functions deliberately or with conscious design; that is, it never 'acts out of something' (*youyiwei* 無以為). As the true sage embodies nothingness and is one with the Dao, he never makes a false or wrong move" (1999, 17). A strong affiliation of *wuwei*'ing is *ziran* 自然, literally the "self-so-ness" of natural dynamics and spontaneity of nature. Karyn L. Lai articulates that "while *ziran* pertains to the spontaneous articulation of the self-in-environment, *wuwei* refers to the conditions that engender *ziran*" (2007, 88). I find emptiness to constitute the underlying root of both terms, in the sense that both "act out of emptiness" *wuyiwei* 無以為; its *spontaneousness* constitutes acting in accordance to time, location, conditions, and circumstances and through the natural dynamics scientifically called entropy. Yet another instance that carries an association between "gates of heavens" and the female is found in chapter 10 of the *Daode jing*:

> When the soul is embraced in unity, can one be away from it?
> When focusing *qi* to the utmost softness, can one be like an infant?
> When polishing the mysterious mirror, can one be blemished?
> When loving the people and governing the state, Can one remain without knowledge?
> When the gate of heavens opens and closes, can one act as a female?
> When the brightest light reaches all corners of the earth, can one remain without knowledge?
> Giving life (and) nurturing all creatures, giving life (but) without claiming ownership.
> Acting (for them) (yet) not expecting (their) reliance.
> And (neither) exercises no authority (over them).
> This is called *de* (inner-potential) of the mysterious.

載營魄抱, 能無離乎? [3]
專氣致柔, 能嬰兒乎?
滌除玄覽, 能無疵乎?
愛民治國, 能無知乎?
天門開闔, 能為雌乎?
明白四達, 能無知乎?
生之、畜之, 生而不有,
為而不恃, 長而不宰, 是謂玄德.

In a similar way to chapter 1, this chapter can also be conceptualized as an architectural structure in which every line consists of a situation or act followed by an exclamational response or rhetorical question. The mirror symbolizes something that "reflects everything but does hold to it as its own" as a metaphor intertwined with the creation and the nurturing of life—in the same way that a mother provides for her children unconditionally. I argue that the line "when the gate of heavens opens and closes, can one act as a female?" refers to the qualities of the mirror because it allows for no attachment or preference to any of the sides (e.g., "close" or "open," *yin* or *yang*, etc.). Can our mind be polished *back* to such rudimentary undifferentiation? The *Daode jing* parallels such a state to the baby: symbolizing softness, spontaneousness, and a mind that is (as yet) unconstrained by education and morality. This metaphor constitutes yet another instance of "going back" to a mind of no distinctions, the formless state.[4]

An important source for gates to the undifferentiated is the *Huainanzi*, one of the most comprehensive texts in Chinese intellectual history.[5] The arrangement of the text is significant in the context of the gate as it revolves around the metaphor of roots (first six chapters) and branches (last six ones), with nine chapters constituting "the embodiment of *dao* into the tangible world." This metaphor resonates with the overall usage of correlative thinking and emphasis on *actualization* in the text (*de*)—both of which constitute the conceptual framework for the gate's exegesis. Robin Wang refers to the metaphor in the *Huainanzi* and says that "*yinyang* is like a root (*ben*) of the branches of Chinese thinking: as soon as you stimulate the root, the hundred branches all respond" (2012, 6).

As the *Huainanzi* contains 108 gate passages (deserving perhaps a separate volume), I have chosen to concentrate on its first chapter, the

Yuan Dao 原道 "Original Way"; this decision is not merely technical (the *Huainanzi* is an extensive text), but, similarly to the first chapter of the *Daode jing*, I believe the *Yuan Dao* serves as a significant opening to the whole work. As Major et al. say, it provides "the cosmological basis for the entire *Huainanzi* collection" (2010, 48).[6] *Yuan Dao* 4 reads thus:

> They transverse the frost and snow but left no tracks. Illuminated by the light of the sun, they cast no shadows. (trans. Major et al.)

> 經霜雪而無跡, 照日光而無景.

> Traversing mountains and rivers, they strode over Mount Kunlun. Pushing through the Chang He [gate] they surged through the gateway of Heaven. (trans. Major et al.)[7]

> 經紀山川, 蹈騰昆侖, 排閶闔, 淪天門.

They leave no trail or sign behind (trace *ji*), they rise up and reach *Changhe* gate 閶闔, and if they manage to pass through it, they will arrive at the gate of the heavens. The meaning of "leaving no trace" is that though you have form, you manage to act formlessly, just like a dragon on the wings of the wind; in fact, it evokes the following passage in the *Shiji* in which Sima Qian narrates how Confucius admits that, though he knows how birds fly, how fish swim, how beasts walk the earth, and so on . . . he has no idea how dragons ride the winds (至於龍, 吾不能知其乘風雲而上天), but then the text continues, "today I saw Laozi—he is just like a dragon!" (*wu jin ri jian laozi, qi you long xie* 吾今日見老子, 其猶龍邪).

Riding the winds means leaving no trace behind! This connects well with my argument presented in chapter 1 that sees the attention given in early China to winds, water, and *qi* stemming from an awe of the life-sustaining efficacy of these three formless substances. As will be seen in other chapters, concrete *Changhe* gates were excavated in archeological sites, mainly serving as the main (southern) gate of palaces, as in, for instance, the Northern Wei palace compound (figure 3.1) in which "the throne conducted affairs, tribute audience from other countries gathered, and where other major events were held" (Goodman 2010, 254).[8]

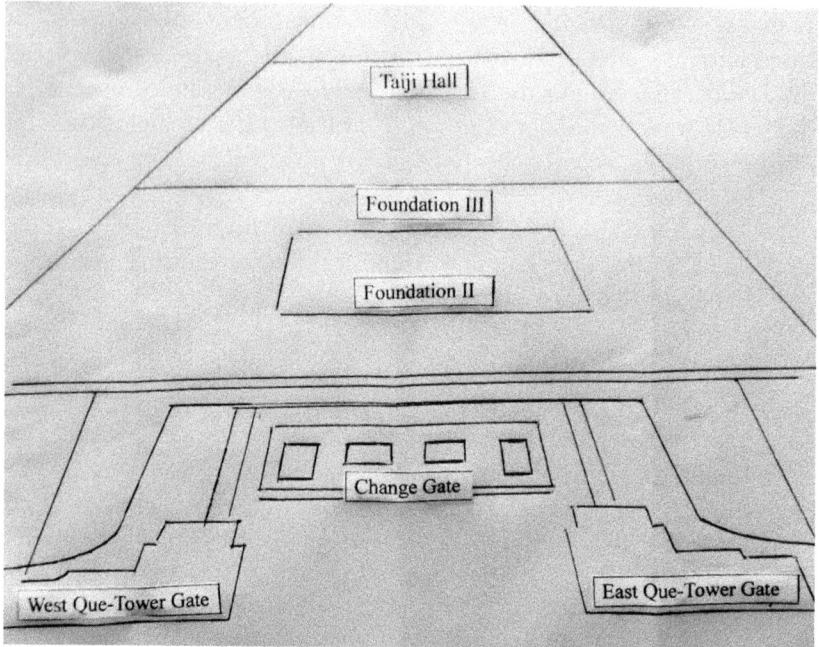

Figure 3.1. *Changhe* gate, *que* gates, and *Taiji* Hall in the layout of Northern Wei palace. After Qian Guoxiang and Guo Xiaotao. 2011. "Architectural Foundation III of the Northern Wei Palace found at Han-Wei Luoyang City, Henan." *Chinese Archaeology* 11: 106–110. Illustration by the author.

Note the typical progression from the outside inward, with two *que* gates on the sides and *Changhe* gate as the first hurdle before the internal journey begins . . . ending at the curious *Taiji* Hall at the rear . . . resonating with or even replacing *ao* in the same role (of emptiness)—as encountered in previous instances.

Further, a close look at the character *chang* 閶 reveals one of its inner components is *chang* 昌, the original meaning of which was "light" and "bright" as it depicts the sun and the eye—evoking, I suggest, the sense of "seeing the light" (as discussed before), but carries in addition a significant resemblance to *jian* 間! In both cases, the emphasis is on light penetrating through a crack or a gate, thus creating a singular "in-betweenness" in which temporality and spatiality and the intermingling of opposites takes place. The second character *he* 闔 used to refer to a door or a leaf of a door; thus, combining the two meanings together, *changhe* can be rendered "the door of in-betweenness/emptiness" or "door of seeing the light." Does the *Changhe* gate constitute a challenge—perhaps a trial of courage before the final stage (gate of the heavens)? As discussed before (in reference to the *Taixuan jing*), it appears that the gate of heavens opens only to those who go through intense self-cultivation.

In order to understand (again) what this process *is* (or, in other words, what is it that makes someone a sage?), we need to look for descriptions of skills or extraordinary abilities that make sages unique human beings. The text indeed *compares* the present and the past through a certain ability—the riding of carriages by the figures Feng Yi and Da Bing. Hans van Ess remarks that "it seems clear here that the text deliberately uses the strong particle *shi qu* in order to show that the great man has to draw a conclusion from the fact that living in an end time he is not able to compete with the sages living in highest antiquity: All he can do is to at least try to get close to them" (2005/6, 260). This is indeed a reoccurring theme in Chinese textual thought and philosophy, and in the *Huainanzi* in particular: using symbolic figures of a past era ("looking backwards *historically*") as an exemplar and a rhetoric tool which enhances the argument. With some additional illuminating hints at historical reference and skills, the passage further reads:

> If we compare it with the charioteering of recent times, although there are light-weight carts and good horses, strong whips and sharp prods, they cannot compete with or overtake them. (trans. Major et al.)

末世之御, 雖有輕車良馬, 勁策利鍛, 不能與之爭先.

I suggest the author uses the ability to ride carriages as a metaphor of "correct governing," as opposed to current means of control. Do the authors direct their criticism only to the rulers or are the ordinary people (who are unable to follow *dao*) included in it? Is it that in the present time man is unable to change and transform while on the path? Also, the ability to ride carriages points yet again to the winds and the ability to be entuned with their flow and momentum.

Indeed, the metaphor of riding or skills of horsemanship was discussed in chapter 1 (the "Great Treatise" of the *Yijing*), in which it was suggested that good horsemanship does not constitute the mere knowledge of using the reins (controlling the horses), but first of all "listening" to the needs of the horses. This listening can be thought of as *wuwei riding* . . . in other words, becoming one with the instinctive, animalistic dynamics of the horse. Indeed, the passage continues with a description of the "Great Man" who has no worries, taking the heavens as his canopy and earth as his carriage; he decides when it is time for his horses to walk or to run—because, again, he listens attentively to locality, time, circumstances, and the *shi* of the Horses; the lightening is his whip and thunder as his wheels. Then,

> above he rambles in the free and roaming vastness. Below he goes out of the gates of boundlessness. Having scanned all round and left nothing out, remaining whole he returns to guard what is within. He manages the four corners of the earth, yet always returns to the pivot. (trans. Major et al.)

上游於霄霓之野, 下出於無垠之門, 劉覽偏照, 複守以全. 經營四隅, 還反於樞.

The free and vast is associated with gates of boundlessness, and a play on the complementary opposites of above and below; by first traveling to both ends, he manages to guard what is within (the soul), and, though he goes to the four corners of the world, he remains in the *pivot* (or hinge *shu* 樞). This is yet again an example of correlative thinking—the body *is* the cosmos so that, though he roams to the four corners of the world, it is as if he never left the core of his body.[9]

Importantly, these rare qualities of the man on the journey of self-cultivation are mirrored through the capabilities of spirits *shen*. It evokes a key question (for any culture) that revolves around the conceptualized distance between man and the transcendental entities he has faith in and awe for. In the context of Chinese psych and belief system, specifically, could humans reach the level of spirits? In *Xici* I. 9 of the *Yijing*, it says that "knowing *dao* of transformations, is knowing the doings of the spirits" (知變化之道者, 其知神之所為乎); thus, it seems that the "knowing of doings the spirits" is the highest form of knowledge.[10] A further clue as to spirits and gates is found in *Yuan Dao* 10:

> Hence, one who understands Dao
> Returns to his limpidity and stillness,
> And one who knows all there is to know about things

Always ends up with nonactivity.
If one nourishes his nature with tranquility
And lodges his spirit in emptiness,
Then he has entered the Gateway of Heaven. (trans. Major
    et al.)

是故達於道者, 反于清靜; 究于物者, 終於無為。以恬養性, 以漠
處神, 則入於天門.

In this passage, although the gate of heavens is not preceded by the
Changhe gate, we have further confirmation to its precondition: acting
through "nonaction" *wuwei* 無為 while the spirit *shen* 神 lodges in emptiness *xu* 虛. I argue that the meaning of *shen* in this passage is the vital
power or agency that not only preserves life but is efficacious in fulfilling
life's potential to the fullest. *Huainanzi* 8:8 hints at this "spirit-illumi-
nation" that is stored in formlessness (神明藏於無形), enabling fruitful
self-cultivation through the practice of *wuwei*. This brings the person to
realize his innermost core, which, according to Major et al., "entails the
systematic elimination of the emotions, distractions, desires, preferences,
thoughts, deliberations, and attachments to the sense-objects that usually
flood the conscious mind. Through this, one may break-through to the
level of 'spiritlike illumination' (*shenming*) and realize what lies deep
within the innermost core of one's being, the one Way" (2010, 66). In
the same chapter, the four openings (gates) of the body, namely, eyes,
ears, mouth, and heart are mentioned (the mouth as a special case is
discussed in chapter 4) along with advice to close them. The reason?
In order to let the spirit go back to its "formless roots"—undisturbed by
external signals of colors, sounds, tastes, and so on (similar philosophy
is expressed in the *Laozi* and the *Zhuangzi*).

I suggest taking the act of closing as the means by which one
connects with the root, the ineffable or the unknown—rather than a
wish to be closed to the external world *as an end result*. It is not a case
of abrupt blockage of the senses but an ability to remain *undisturbed* by
them, that is, developing a mental skill of remaining stable in the core
(center) in the midst of all the stimuli and information coming from
the outside—Reminding us of the concept of *heng dao* discussed in the
context of the first chapter of the *Daode jing*. Miranda Brown and Uffe
Bergeton stress that "the *Huainanzi* went so far as to question the value
of sensory knowledge and conventional ways of apprehending the world
altogether. Most strikingly, it stressed the importance of shutting down

the senses to protect the spirit, the means by which one perceived the Way" (2008, 657). This interplay between open and close can serve the sage in controlling his inner gates in order to keep and preserve the vital essence. Harold Roth assumes that this "blocking of gateways" in the *Huainanzi* refers to the "periods of meditation (in which) sensory stimuli are reduced to a minimum, thus preventing the egress of the vital essence" (1991, 641). Indeed, one of the most beautiful passages in the *Huainanzi*, that demonstrates the importance of such "gatekeeping of the senses" appears in chapter 9.1:

> Now,
> if his eyes looked recklessly, there would be profligacy;
> if his ear listened recklessly, there would be delusion;
> if his mouth spoke recklessly, there would be disorder.
> One cannot fail to guard carefully these three gateways.
> If you wish to regulate them, that is in fact to distance your-
> self from them;
> if you wish to embellish them, that is in fact to injure them.
> (trans. Major et al.)

In saying "one cannot fail to guard carefully these three gateways," the authors might refer to the act of opening these sense-gates *without discernment*—which could lead to recklessness, delusion, and disorder. (In the *Mencius* we will meet with a similar technique but in different context.) As opposed to cases in which the disorder exists outside and the gate is there to prevent it from penetrating in, here the emphasis is on *ways of sensing things* (how we utilize our senses), and not on *what* we sense (i.e., the *content*).

This is important because, as opposed to the humanistic philosophies, there does not seem to be a *selection of external content* (coming in), but advice for *awareness* to the state of these gates. This puts the responsibility on the cultivation of the mind instead of on the mere *avoidance* of *certain* external stimuli or influences. Preference as to certain values is not the way of the sage, because *dao*, as Mark Berkson says, "has no absolute boundaries or divisions (so) the sage does not work with absolute distinctions" (quoted in A. Olberding and Ivanhoe 2011, 200).

If we search for other passages that shed light on ancient Chinese attitudes toward psychological states or the relations between the inner mind and the external world, then *Yuan Dao* 16 constitutes one of the most remarkable; the author sets a scene which contains all the various things that bring people pleasure, joy, and happiness—namely, music, soft cushions, beautiful girls, alcohol, and more—but then describes how, when these things are taken away, one not only feels sad, but in effect, as if he were in mourning . . . as if all that is dear to him is taken away from him. Then the author explains why this happens: because man does not rely on his inner, intrinsic qualities but uses (instead) external things for his own well-being.[11]

In this way, man damages his own internal vitality and potential, day after day. The author emphasizes the ability of man to reach a state of tranquility that is not dependent on the external, so the mind can reside in constant happiness. The authors of the *Huainanzi* thus suggest that people can cultivate themselves to such a degree that their inside stays calm and their responsiveness *qing* 情 is preserved. ("Externally they transform together with things but internally they do not lose their true responsiveness [*qing*]" [trans. Major et al.]). True joy cannot be acquired from the outside (external pleasures are anyway temporary) but is achieved through internal cultivated. Hans van Ess, analyzing the chapter linguistically, remarks that "the whole section on 'formlessness,' which is dealing with the senses, culminates in the words 'highest virtue' and 'joy.' The author concludes that conventional means to satisfy one's senses certainly are only inferior forms of joy. To grasp the Dao is joy, and to arrive at the state when one does not have desires anymore is highest joy" (2005/6, 265). Chapter 16 then continues with a fascinating psychological observation: "Why is it that man is happy when he has all these lovely things, and depressed when they are taken away from him?" The answer that follows is:

(This is indeed what happens when) it is not through the intrinsic, that happiness radiates outside; but when the extrinsic creates inner happiness.

不以內樂外, 而以外樂內.

As said, this (so-called) "inner happiness" is the result of being undisturbed by external influences and is unconditioned; isn't this 2,160-year-old text still remarkably relevant to twenty-first-century readers?

Chapter 9 of the *Huainanzi* contains further advice for self-control through the blocking of the openings:

thus, not letting inner desires emerge is called "barring the door"; not letting external depravity enter is called "blocking the gate": if what is inside is locked in and what is outside is blocked out, what matter would not be properly regulated? If what is outside is blocked out and what is inside is locked in, what matter would not be successful?

故中欲不出謂之扃, 外邪不入謂之閉. 中扃外閉, 何事之不節? 外閉中扃, 何事之不成? (Queen and Puett 2014, 168).

It is noteworthy that the character used here is not *men* but *jiong* 扃—which refers to an external bar that shuts the door—and *bi* 閉, which means "to close" or "obstruct." This is a more extreme case than shutting a gate—as a gate is decoded to open as well, whereas here the door is blocked on both sides.

How then can we understand Laozi's advice "to block the basis from which inner intentions for action arise" and to "shut the basis on which inner intentions for action are pursued"? It tells us that these external objects (that attract the mind-body or create a craving for them) are not to be blamed . . . things will always be out there . . . and whether beneficial, tempting, or destructive, their presence or occurrence it is not in our hands or control by default; however, the ability to cope with any stimuli that happen to be out there is entirely up to us—through the development of inner skills. Chapter 12 of the *Daode jing* gives us a further clue: "the five colors make man's eyes blind; the five notes make his ears deaf; the five tastes injure his palate" (trans. D. C. Lau). Colors, musical notes, and tastes do not ruin man's senses by themselves, it is the *psychological* involvement with them that determines their impact (from the outside) on the inside.[12] Burik indeed thinks that "what is meant here is an awareness of the possible consequences of attaching to various external values and things. It is a way to 'keep your mirror bright'—to use an often employed Daoist expression—unblemished by non-essential factors . . . it can then be understood as gathering and keeping the focus, not being distracted by artificial distinctions" (2010, 503). This closing of the openings further hints at an additional type of fear: that the openings are *too* wide or too open so that the spirit or bodily essence might escape out, or that the body-mind would be over-stimulated; Brown and Bergeton emphasize that these two phenomena are linked, and that too much stimulation could cause the spirit to leave the body and find no opening through which to return (because when the spirit leaves the body, it loses its *form* and openings) (2008, 657).

At times, instances demonstrate a unique skill of closing a gate without actually closing it in the physical sense; *Daode jing* 27, for instance, says,

> A. skillful shutting (of a gate) uses no "blocking bars,"
> Yet, the gate cannot be opened.

善閉無關楗而不可開.

This means that the undeveloped or untrained mind requires blocking bars that physically prevent the gate from opening, whereas the skillful mind manages to close the gates without the use of any such external or physical accessories.

Yuan Dao 15 describes the sage in the following way: "Standing head and shoulders above others, reaching the nine celestial fields above and the nine divisions of territory below; although he is round, he does not accord with the compass, and though (he is) square, he does not accord with the carpenter's square" (Lau and Ames 1998). This is followed by a curious reference to a gate: "pocketing the cosmos, it is the bar that shuts the *Dao* behind the gate" (Lau and Ames 1998) or "it envelopes Heaven and Earth like a sack, it closes the gates to the *dao*" (Major et al. 2010). Both translations of the line *huai nang tian ye, wei dao guan men* 懷襄天地, 為道關門 set *dao* behind closed gates/bars, which I find curious: can *dao* be locked or be denied access to anything? I argue that the character *guan* 關 in the above line might just be the key to (literally) unlocking the gate; though in modern usage, the character *guan* means "to close," in ancient times it referred to a "gate of a strategic pass." The line then changes in meaning and becomes, I argue, more "contextually Chinese"; here is my translation:

> Harboring the whole cosmos like a sack,
> it is (like the) *dao* of a strategic gate.

As will be discussed in chapter 6, a gate erected on a strategic pass was vital to the safeguarding of the state because it constitutes the "weakest link" for enemies to attack. I hold that the hinge of both gates carries parallel significance as even the tiniest alteration in its operation can potentially lead to far-reaching consequences (a small hinge can move a huge gate). It is thus a gate that possesses great potency and efficacy—in the same way as *dao*.

We continuously tread the thin line of in-betweenness when it comes to gates, which (as said in the introduction) throws me to modern science and the critical function of biological membranes to life; in this double-fold context, I find some Chinese characters stand out in significance: one such character is definitely *nang* 囊. Appearing in the Zhuangzian story of *hundun*, *nang* stands for some type of envelope, such as a sack for granary and rice, or a pocket; one of its earliest appearances is in Hexagram 2 of the *Yijing* (line 4): 括囊, 無咎無譽. *Kuo nang* 括囊 means a "tied up, large sack" with a "bottom," which carries the meaning of "one who knows his mind but does not speak of it." In the Commentary on the Hexagram, it says, "'tied up the bag,' so there will be no blame, no praise"; Lynn says that "'tied up' means 'bind up' that is, 'keep confined.' Thus, a worthy person should 'stay hidden,' it is only by exercising caution that he can get by" (1994, 148).[13]

Nang thus refers to an expanded thin film or sheet that inhabits the very edge of formation (*just* formed), acquiring a shape but still shapeless, which ascends to any height and pockets the whole universe.[14] I interpreted *nang* as a layer that envelopes any living creature or the *contour lines* (between inside and outside) of any form. It can also be thought of as an egg shell or the first line that protects the chaotic fluid inside— and the order that emerges out of this fluid in the form of an embryo.

Isabelle Robinet elaborates on the etymological meaning of *nang*:

> It is also akin to the expression "something confused and yet complete" (*huncheng* 混成) found in the *Daode jing* 25, which denotes the state prior to the formation of the world where nothing is perceptible, but which nevertheless contains a cosmic seed. Similarly, the state of *hundun* is likened to an egg; in this usage, the term alludes to a complete world round and closed in itself, which is a receptacle like a cavern (*dong* 洞) or a gourd (*hu* 壺 or *hulu* 壺盧). (quoted in Pregadio 2010, 524)[15]

It is a biological phenomenon that, in order for any living cell, organ or organism to live and prevail, the thin borderline that envelopes it (from subcellular structures and membranes to the outer skin of the body) needs to be *carefully* monitored and adjusted according to multiple internal-external variables; defined as a "fluid mosaic" structure, membranes define the borders of the cell and are critical in its interaction with the environment and with other cells (e.g., cells need to identify themselves, share information and more), and *nang* might very well be such an enveloping structure (see discussion of *hundun* ahead). The awareness to and communication with external conditions determine the behavior of all living things, humans included, and in this specific context, Chinese sources refer to a unique set of mental and physical skills that involves a "listening to the situation and to the propensity of things"—namely, *shi* 勢. *Huainanzi* 9:27 is highly significant in this context:

> Therefore, through the acquirement of the advantage of *shi* 勢 (inherent propensity), the smallest grasp can sustain the largest thing; guarding what is very limited and concentrated, is in fact what enables controlling the very wide. Thus, an encircling beam of 10 *wei* (in length) holds a house of 1000 *chun* (in weight); a linchpin of only 5 *cun* (inch), controls the opening and closing of a gate; does it matter whether the material is large or small? (no), what is vital is exact position. (trans. Major et al.)

> 是故得勢之利者, 所持甚小, 其存甚大; 所守甚約, 所制甚廣. 是故十圍之木, 持千鈞之屋; 五寸之鍵, 制開闔之門. 豈其材之巨小足哉? 所居要也.

The concept of *shi* 勢 constitutes the sensing of position, situations, or materials and utilizes it to efficaciously "make most of a situation." An intriguing reference is made here to *jian* 键, which is the thin linchpin that is inserted into the gate's hinge *shu* 樞 . . . it emphasizes that this tiny and seemingly insignificant component can in effect determine the mechanism of the opening and closing of a heavy gate. From this angle, *shi* constitutes the *inherent possibility* of all situations per specific locations and times, which in turn means actualizing potentiality to the fullest. The knowledge acquired is the ability to "be one" with the surroundings, perfectly attuned to the flux of things. This again brings us back to *wuwei* but from a different aspect, that is, by staying in the center and hardly making a move; from this perfect stillness the sage is still able to exert its impact on the world.

Other "gate-methods" have been encountered in the overall context of this chapter, some constituting the actual operational action required as a prerequisite of seeing, experiencing, or being one with the unknown and formless state. One source that points to this state is the *Zhuangzi* 莊子. The *Zhuangzi* is a textual amalgam of baffling, tantalizing and at times very humorous poems, stories, fables, allegories, metaphors, and fantastic imaginary. As Hansen says, "he wrote philosophical phantasy; this style is at once irresistibly attractive and yet maddeningly frustrating" (1992, 265).[16]

Outer chapters 3, named *zai you* 在宥 ("In the midst of letting go"), contains nine *dao* 道 and is rich in characters that are compounded with the gate radical, such as "questioning" *wen* 問, "listening" *wen* 聞, and "closing" of the gates *bi* 閉. The narrative describes how the Yellow Emperor (Huangdi 黄帝) came twice to see the Master of Vast Accomplishment on Mount Kongtong 空同山 and asks him for directions as to the "essence of the ultimate *dao*" *zhi dao zhi jing* 至道之精 in order that he would be able to apply it for the prosperity of his empire. The first time, the master refuses to satisfy him with an answer, which leads the emperor to renounce his seat and go for a three-month retreat; when he comes the second time, the master tells him to direct attention to his inner body, so that he may live long (乃可以長生).

The last line in the passage is curious as it uses *chang* in reference to the self ("I")—a self that will become constant and enduring, completely unmoved by whether people agree or disagree. Guoping Zhao remarks that *wo* and *ji* often represent first person pronouns used in a reflexive or emphatic sense, not in the sense of a substantive entity, which is implied in the Western term "self" (2012, 147). Thus, it is not a reference to one's self—as a personal identity—but a *self* that is not bound by attachments, conventions, and distinctions. The passage emphasizes the *need to protect the body-mind* as key to enlightenment because when the mind is kept still and quiet the "essence" can be contained and cultivated.

This requires the closure of all apertures because, as the master warns, a flood (surplus) of knowledge from the outside is malevolent. As said, this deep need to protect the inside might stem from a feeling that the "internal is not a given" (!) . . . in other words, it hints that the inner body is actually far from being closed—if at all, it is *perhaps too open!* As Pregadio says, "only in a perfectly sealed vessel is it possible to reproduce the state prior to the 'ten thousand things,' causing matter to reveal its original, authentic state" (2005, 154). The following passage points to the opposite direction: from the senses outward. It says, "eyes do not see, ears do not hear, the heart-mind doesn't know" (目無所見, 耳無所聞, 心無所知), which means that as the very essence of the senses is to be drawn to external stimuli (eyes to sights, ears to sounds, etc.), anyone wishing to be united with *dao* (widest cosmic circle) needs to monitor these openings.

The desired outcome of this awareness and practical monitoring, if I understand it correctly, would be "the safeguarding of the spirit" (女神將守形), which would in turn lead to the next level, namely, "the great Illumination," *dai ming* 大明. An interesting point in the passage is the fact that the emperor is answered only the second time—because one cannot aspire to be one with *dao* or even begin to realize it before taking the first step of *choice-making*, inner contemplation, and self-awareness (three months' retreat); the second step consists of "what I let in and what I leave outside"!—which constitutes *the very definition* of the gate philosophy presented in this book (and the very rudimentary definition of a membrane). When one is able to enter this level of calmness (*jing* 靜) and stability (*ding* 定), the body will survive forever, "as you perpetually dwell at the source of the *dao*" 常住道源 (Eskildsen 2015, 19).

In a similar way to the first chapter of the *Daode jing*, there is an interesting play on light and dark here. First, the "great illumination" as a state of clarity (*ming*), which is linked to an enlightened state of mind (*yang*), and then—entering darkness (*yin*); as in the *Yijing*, the gate is built into the singular locus of the threshold between *yin* and *yang*. Being one with this endless and formless sphere is also mentioned in relation to the second gate, which reads, "entering the 'gate of the inexhaustible,' (is the means by which one) wonders in unbounded space" (入無窮之門, 以遊無極之野). Is this passage a preliminary reference to meditative techniques used by practitioners of "religious" Daoism who wished for immortality? Indeed, the same passage continues with a description of the master who managed to live 1,200 years due to these techniques—so it is a possibility.

In his book on meditative techniques of Daoism, Eskildsen writes that "the teachings conveyed in the anecdote anticipate what Common Era Daoist religious texts would have to say about the physiological necessity and benefits of serenity" (2015, 19). Indeed, this unity that is "light of the sun and the moon" together is the clarity *ming* found in the center, which constitutes emptiness—as the gate to *dao*. Robinet refers to the Daoist view of human nature, saying that those who consider human nature to be good, bad, or a mixture of both have simply lost sight of its authentic aspect. They are unaware of the "truthful and empty" nature of the human being, its immobile and quiet essence, which the texts refer to as "cavern" (*dong* 洞) or "gate of all wonders" (*zhongmiao zhi men* 眾妙之門). The deluded have no knowledge of the fundamental cosmic nature which itself forms the basis of human nature. This nature is found in the "middle." (quoted in Pregadio 2010, 1104)

This state of clarity in the middle requires a mind that is "skillfully and immediately responsive" to all that that comes its way—a path in which no conscious evaluation or judgment is involved; in other words, a mirror-like mind. The mind stays calm notwithstanding external affairs or whether conventions defined these affairs "good" or "bad." It relates again to the character *heng* in the first chapter of the *Daode jing*—the boat that manages to stay steady even if the outside (stormy waters) is extremely chaotic. Humans live in a world of constant change and unpredictable transformations, and their minds are being bombarded by multiple factors every second, "digesting" the vast ocean of information and stimuli and constantly (as Zhuangzi calls it) conducting an "investigation of things." Through this spontaneous investigation the sage makes minute choices at every step on the path, particularly as to either blocking or allowing data from the outside to penetrate. Isn't it *always* relevant when it comes to the emotional pendulum that is the human mind?

A peculiar and highly significant narrative in the *Zhuangzi* relates to many of the themes discussed within the gate's warp and weft, namely, the question of form, emptiness, body openings in the thin "sack" (*nang*) that give the body its very initial form, and chaos/order. Moreover, it evokes an intriguing debate revolving around "what it is that constitutes a human being." I am referring to the story of Mr. Hundun, which, as Wu Kuang-ming says, "is pregnant with multifarious implications of cosmological and contemporary significance still to explore, to be 'read' out with attentive care" (2007, 263). The narrative is quite simple: Mr. Hundun, the Emperor of the Middle, had seven openings drilled into him by his friends Shu and Hu; these friends had good intentions as they wanted to make him more human (after their own "form"!) and thus gave him the senses of seeing, hearing, eating, and breathing (once sense per day) and on the seventh day, he dies.

The narrative then depicts an initial cosmological stage of the world consisting of central oneness that is void of any shape: "Hundun as an axis mundi around which the world is organized" (Girardot 1983, 89). In that sense, the story tells us of the destruction of the cosmic structure, due, supposedly, to human action. Girardot saw the story as a mythical representation of the cosmic principle of an origin that self-generates (such as the cosmic egg or the primal gourd) or indeed, the giant flood (as in the *Mencius*). Does the story constitute a direct criticism of Confucian ideas that "destroyed" Mr. Hundun? Did they kill him by "drilling moralist holes" in him (K.-M. Wu 2007, 266)? Yet another exegesis takes Mr. Hundun to represent an ideal paradise-like state, which, alas, was destroyed because people just cannot let things be . . . instead of *wuwei living* that allows all things to develop according to their inherent nature, human beings enforce their will on things and interfere; even though their intentions might be positive (they want to help), their actions still lead to destruction. Importantly, the names of his friends are *hu* 忽 (furious) and *shu* 儵 (fast), which summons yet another exegetical point: Does the author suggest that a human action that stems from anger or is carried out too quickly leads only to destruction?

Mr. Hundun's friends wanted to change him into (what they grasped) as a "better version" of himself—closer to their own human image and "physiology." However, what drives them from within and constitutes their mistake is pure vanity . . . as they presume the "human form" to be the best possible model. Mr. Hundun, who "fell" for their kindness, accepted their offer and was consequently destroyed. Frank W. Stevenson emphasizes the difference between the *de* of *shu* and *hu* and that of Hundun himself, saying that "Hun Dun is so 'open' (one vast formless 'hole') that he *allowed* his friends to drill holes in him."[17] Is the *de* of Hundun total openness? The clue might be found in his title, the Emperor of the Middle, residing in "in-betweenness" and thus encompassing infinity! Because the *de* of his friends is limited (locked in their form and identities), they wish to give a "face" to Hundun, that is, to limit and enclose him.

I believe that Hundun constitutes the embodiment of both form and formlessness—to the extent that they are indistinguishable (just as dream and wakefulness in the butterfly story); Zhuangzian philosophy grasps life and death as equal (as in the story of Zhuangzi's wife), and as Michael Puett says it is a generally Zhuangzian vision in which "the sage takes life and death as equal and sees himself as part of the larger transformations of the cosmos" (quoted in A. Olberding and Ivanhoe 2011, 228). Therefore, the (conventionally) *sad* meaning of death might not be what the author had intended. Looking at it from this point of view, the story becomes a purely biological description of life (starting from emptiness to develop form and collapsing back to formlessness). Importantly, in the first preliminary state, Mr. Hundun was *nang*—a huge, undefined "sack" or gourd which was sealed by a thin membranous layer. This state cannot be defined as complete chaos, but in fact as something that had already begun to take on shape and distinction: *hundun* is thus not chaos nor order but the center itself—the "Zhuangzian man" in between heavens and earth . . . (*hu* and *shu* are also north and south seas, respectively); Wu Kuang-ming says that the story "positions these cosmic aspects in spatial perspective, to auspiciously connote that by harmonizing the Yin and the Yang, the four seasons, and the dark and the bright, in the central Land of the Emperor Hundun, myriad things are allowed to nestle and give birth and thrive quite naturally" (2007, 264). Mr. Hundun constitutes the meeting ground for the two sides, serving as a pivot and axis, in fact—a gate that stands at the very mingling of "two" that came out of the "one"! This is indeed the cosmogenic process of *taiji* 太极 that is borne out of one unity and transforms into "three-in-one," a state created, as Pregadio says, "when the original Oneness of the cosmos first divides into *yin* and *yang* and then rejoins these forces in a new harmony; in this way a set of three is created that recovers a renewed original Oneness" (2010, 854).

If my exegesis makes sense, the Zhuangzian advice to close the body openings obtains a different significance: by having no openings (that is, before his friends drilled into him), the body remains in its primordial state. If that is the case, then Zhuangzi demonstrates a remarkable "biological" intuition that goes through *reduction ad absurdum*, that is, if openings (as a functional membrane) are a prerequisite to life and its inevitable return to death, thus, having a form yet no openings means never dying . . . As stated in one of the *Taiqing* texts, "leaving an opening as big as the nose of an ant on the crucible would result in the failure of the whole alchemical undertaking" (Pregadio 2005, 154). This interpretation strengthens my (previously mentioned) impression that certain schools of thought (mostly pronounced in early Daoist and medicinal texts) had carried a deep anxiety and fear of "that which is external to the body-mind" and its destructive influence on the inside, and consequently developed certain means and methods to protect this vulnerable and wholesome life that is inside—with the aim of reaching immortality. This would suggest that the *Zhuangzi* already contains seeds of immortality, but what remains under dispute, is whether or not these ideas were already accompanied by breathing exercises and meditative techniques (i.e., that are more typical to the so-called "religious Daoism").[18] Notwithstanding the indifference with which Zhuangzi treats life and death, the story constitutes a gate by itself—opening man's mind through rich analogues and metaphors that stand on the threshold between the "civilized" and the "chaotic."[19] An additional intermediary state in the *Zhuangzi* (beyond *nang*) is sleep and dream; Wu Kuang-ming points out that "Neither death nor wakefulness, sleep is a regular Hundun interruption of activity that replenishes life" (2007, 269).

A good path to follow into Zhuangzian attitudes toward life and death is *dao* itself—as underlying all facets and forms of existence; in the following passage we find clues to its characteristics according to Zhuangzi:

> Tungkuo Shun-Tzu said to Chuang Tzu, "Where is this so-called Tao?" Chuang Tzu answered, "Everywhere." The other said, "You must specify an instance of it." Chuang Tzu said, "It is here in these ants." Tungkuo replied, "That must be its lowest manifestation, surely." Chuang Tzu said, "No, it is in these weeds." The other said, "What about a lower example?" Chuang Tzu said, "It is in this earthenware tile." "Surely brick and tile must be its lowest place?" "No, it is here in this dung also." To this Tungkuo gave no reply. (Needham 1956, 47)

Zhuangzi sees *dao* as ubiquitously existing everywhere, even in places people would find "low," very much like water. The next extract appears in the Miscellaneous Chapters, in a passage named "The whole world," *tian xia* 天下:

> He, who is not away from (his) origin, is called "man of the heavens";
> He, who is not away from (his) essence, is called "man of spirit";
> He, who is not away from (his) genuineness, is called the "man of full realization."

不離於宗, 謂之天人.
不離於精, 謂之神人.
不離於真, 謂之至人.

This is a description of the different types of sagehood, perhaps in ascending order of "sagely achievements": "man of the heavens" is one who is not separated from his origin; "man of spirit" is one who is not separated from his essence *jing* 精; the "man of full realization" is one who is not separated from his *zhen* 真—genuineness, true nature, authenticity. The first level refers to the man who "keeps to the source"; the character used here is *zhong* 宗, which means "model"; in the context of this sentence, the heavenly-like is self-so (*ziran* 自然), the way of nature—as the model for one's behavior. Chen Guying remarks, in relation to this very line, that "the sage" judges the true beauty of heaven and earth and discerns the principles that underlies all things" (2016, 217)—bringing us back to the very origins of the *Yijing* . . . principles detected from heavens and earth by observance and discernment.

Then, when he "keeps to the essence" he adheres to the innermost "seed," which is the very pure vitality that exists inside man. This "seed" needs to be protected from external influences that might damage it. A. C. Graham rendered *qing* as "essential" and regarded it an inseparable part of a thing's definition; thus, a thing exists to its full potential when it realizes its "essentials by itself" (1989, 7).[20] The third stage is the "fully realized" man who keeps to his *zhen*—true nature, authentic self. The three stages start with the heavens as the most external, proceed with essence as the innermost, and achieve culmination at their very center—*zhen*! It is in effect the combination of a specific kind of knowledge (from the heavens) and the efficacious utilization of one's inner essence that leads one to be whole at any given instance. Roger Ames refers to this subject in his book on the *Zhuangzi*: "Instead of focusing on the sage-ruler and the manifestation of his personal of his personal enlightenment in the appropriate government of the state, the *Zhuangzi* concerns itself more with the realization of the particular person, assuming perhaps that enlightened government is simply a natural extension of the enlightened person . . . the Authentic Person" (1998, 3). Indeed, this is the meaning of *authentic*—realizing oneself through timely knowledge and a manifestation of the particular and singular spatiotemporal conditions through a spontaneous and authentic mind. In this context, the next line is of great interest:

By the means of the heavenly-like (becomes) his origin; by the means of *de* (becomes), his root; by the means of *dao* (becomes) his gate; from which (he knowingly enters) into transformation; this is who is called a sage (*shengren*).

以天為宗, 以德為本, 以道為門, 兆於變化, 謂之聖人.

Burton Watson translated this passage as follows: "only the sage has the ability . . . to make the *dao* his gate, revealing himself through change and transformation" (2003, 287). The use of *de* here, "by the means of *de* (becomes) his root" 以德為本, is significant; as I have argued before, I find *de* 德 to embody the efficaciousness and potency of *dao* as it is manifested into the ten thousand things and phenomena; I argue that at least in Daoist thought it is devoid of any moral "wrapping" that might appear in humanistic schools. S. A. Barnwell says that "the Laozi authors used *de* as the term to refer to, what Roth called, 'the nurturing aspect' of the *dao*" (2013, 47).

Can the etymology of *de* shed light on its meaning and significance? Moss Roberts says that "the graph for *de* consists of three elements: walking legs on the left and on the right 'mind' under 'straight, go straight.' Closely related to another *de* (meaning attain, obtain), *de*-virtue means the inner power to reach result or affect a situation . . . translators tend to prefer 'virtue' . . . 'power' is the second choice; 'potency' has also been used" (2001, 19). Indeed, I find that "potency" and "the inner power to reach result or affect a situation" best captures the meaning of this complex character and term; each and every living thing is endowed with *de*—which awards them with unique qualities and skills for adaptation. The sage (described above) is similarly endowed with unique skills through which his self-realization achieves "being one with the world"—perhaps as the highest form of adaptability. Moeller and D'Ambrosio refer to the expression *zhi de zhe* 至德者 as "one who has attained perfect *de*" and say that "these men are protected from harm! No disease can hurt them nor 'the spears of soldiers and the claws of animals'" (2017, 173).[21]

But what is it that prevents harmful things from hurting the *zhenren* 真人? This expression ("authentic person" *zhenren*) occurs nineteen times in the *Zhuangzi* and it pertains to a person in possession of unique knowledge—which, as Alan Fox says, is concrete and practical knowledge, "rather than abstract, scholarly or dispositional (*bian*) knowledge" (quoted in Kohn 2015, 60). It seems that they possess a barrier that stands against hostile elements, as in the expression *de zhi hou* 德之厚 "thickness of *de*"—a shield that protect the *zhenren* from all external affects. The Outer Chapters in the *Zhuangzi* contain an important clue as to the meaning of *de* and its prowess:

> In the times of ultimate *de*, (the people) were proper (in behavior), though (they) did not know *yi* 義; they loved each other, but did not know *ren* 仁; they were true, but they not know loyalty *zhong* 忠; they were equal, but did not know "trust" *xin* 信; they just moved about, and enabled each other, but did not think it to be a (special) blessing.

> 至德之世 . . . 端正而不知以為義, 相愛而不知以為仁, 實而不知 以為忠, 當而 不知以為信, 蠢動而相使不以為賜.

Here, Zhuangzi takes us back to the "age of *perfect de*" in which people behaved in a correct, loving, honest and responsible way . . . but, importantly, they were not aware or conscious of their behavior and conduct—it was as "second nature" to them. They lived their life lacking ego or self-interest and their conduct was never forceful, nor did they obey or follow any doctrine or authority. They are described as being free from the bounds of language, having techniques or skills *shu* 術 that involve "living the moment," "feeling the shaping force and propensity of materials and the immediate environment *shi*"—so that their *de* was perfect.

These skills, pronounced throughout the *Zhuangzi*, carry a double-fold significance in the context of gates, namely, the means by which the human body-mind senses and listens to the surroundings, and the gate itself as having its own *shi*—a highly-tuned hinge that opens or closes according to a situation. Qi Zhu explores *shi* in the *Zhuangzi*, saying that the sage's self-so body, "engenders an innate efficacy that differentiates him from the others as a true artist" (2008, 192). This *self-so shi* is the very embodiment of *ziren*, spontaneity and *wuwei* which senses for every moment and each step the best-of-all-options choice (never a "best" as an absolute value!), which includes all possible states of the gate—from the open to the closed.

This skill is born out of a process of distillment or fasting of the mind—named *xinzhai* 心齋 in the *Zhuangzi*. A. C. Graham remarks that for a sage there is only one "right action" among the multiple choices, and that is because he perceives it "with perfect clarity, as though in a mirror" (1983, 24). The sage senses his immediate surroundings as the result of the utilization of the "in-between line" between chaos and order; the sage is able to see right into the very unfolding of a certain situation—from which he has the ability to see the future from within the present! I believe that is precisely what the *Yijing* refers to (and the first chapter of the *Daode jing*): an ability to see the very onset of creation, of *foreseeing* the way all phenomena develop—and the wisdom of choosing the appropriate action.

This *wuwei* living-performance is brought to light in the *Zhuangzi* through a fantastic line of artisans, whose "art" is not the product (as an end target), but the actual spontaneous skillful action that is always "effortless" or goes along the least resistant path (as cook Ding). David Chai compares the "Gate of heavens" to the wheel hub from the *Daode jing*: "The Heavenly Gate was for Zhuangzi what the wheel hub was for Laozi: a place where all things come together in tranquil harmony. Though things enter and leave the world through it, the gate itself remains unchanged; though the spokes are what give a wheel its motion, the hub is unperturbed" (2012, 101). This is a direct reference to meontology that was discussed in the *Laozi*, but with a significant philosophical difference: whereas in the *Zhuangzi* the tangible frame of the gate disappears, in the *Laozi* we have the tangible and emptiness working together. In the *Zhuangzi*, as David Shulman and Guy G. Stroumsa say, "the axis of the Dao is located where no position can find its opposite. All are metaphors of flux, inclusivity, and mediation" (1999, 33–34). Metaphors such as the potter's wheel *tianjun* 天鈞 and the whetstone *tianni* 天倪 transcend opposites by their very meaning: they both constitute a device that mingles, combines, and polishes by the means of water! Roger Ames relates to the illuminating skills of the Zhuangzian sage, saying that these devices "enable one to interchange and accumulate the available alternatives within the context of the problem and to harmonize them as contingent approaches to resolution within a specific situation" (1998, 12).

Chapter 4

Should I Open or Close My Gate?

An Individual's Home, Mouth, and Mind

The mind lies within a realm of crystal,
While my clothes are soaked by spring rain.
I pace slowly through the series of gates,
In a deep courtyard plans for seclusion are realized.
Every door I come to opens and closes again,
The struck bell means that meal time is now.

—Du Fu, 8th century[1]

This chapter contains individual strategies of behavior and decision-making, with particular emphasis on three dimensions or types of gates functioning correlatedly and similarly, namely, one's mouth, one's front gate, and one's mind. The hinge in these gates is conceptualized to be in the hands of the individual—who decides (per time, circumstances, and location) whether to open the gate or close it, or perhaps—leave it half-closed. The sources and subjects analyzed include the (architectural) front gate (e.g., the front gate of Confucius), the *Guiguzi*, and the Classics—for example, the *Shijing* and certain "gate-hexagrams" from the *Yijing* which relate to behavioral strategies. Let us begin with the front gate of a Chinese home: What characterizes its form, parts and usage?

The Front Gate of One's Private Home

In the most general sense, one's private and personal inhabitance, that is, *home*, constitutes a manifestation of the correspondence between human beings' most private space (a space psychology) and the external environment. Chinese homes, as mentioned in chapter 1, translate this deeply psychological connection through a central south-north axis and a series of walls and openings that are designated for a proposed gradated pattern of movement—from the outermost (public) to the innermost (private). In such a setup, the front gate and/or front door—as the first opening that connects the inside and the outside—is of crucial importance.

In the Chinese private home, we encounter the *nie* 闃—an important device that functions in the closing of the front door—it is a small wooden block that prevents the door panel from closing and keeps it at a ninety-degree angle. The etymology of *nie* (appearing already on oracle bones), combines a nose and an ancient sundial apparatus and represents the center and the threshold (L. Zhang 2002, 82), or as Qi Zhu notes, the *nie* provided "a reference to divide the homogenous space into its east and west orientations" (2008, 143). An additional component of architecture that is typical to the Chinese home and related to the front gate is the highly familiar and recognizable doorsill *menkan* 門檻—a wooden plank that stretches horizontally at the bottom part of the door (figure 4.1). This probably developed as a practical device to help protect the house from incoming water, such as monsoon rain or floods, or in order to contain *qi* inside. With time, it transformed into a symbolic threshold that evokes awareness to the threshold in between entering or leaving.

Guests entering the house would not tread on it (out of respect to the owner) and, furthermore, the height of the doorsill itself signified the status of the owner of the house—the higher the status, the higher the doorsill. Knapp writes on this important threshold, saying that

> the threshold, typically raised 3–5 inches to help control rainwater, must be stepped over upon passing through this doorway. This brings the act of entry into the conscious thoughts of the person entering. It impresses upon the visitor an awareness of the privilege of their entry into the property. On occasions where a non-family member is asked to visit the home, this threshold reminds the person of the significance of having received the invitation to enter. (1999, 30)

Figure 4.1. The doorsill *menkan* of a private Chinese home. Photo by the author.

It is thus not surprising that folkloristic superstitions referring to the doorsill have developed in China; they detailed the bad consequences of treading on the threshold, such as that "one will float between the two worlds of *yin* and *yang*, unable to become a deity or gain rebirth" (Huber and Zhao 2011, 31). This is a remarkable indication of the threshold as the embodiment of *yin* and *yang* and its deeply engraved symbolism in the Chinese psyche—turned into a superstition. Slingerland offers two possible explanations for the phenomenon, saying that "most prosaically, one does not stand in the middle of the doorway as a courtesy to others, to avoid impeding their movement, and one does not tread upon thresholds to avoid dirtying them, which would in turn dirty the flowing robes of others" (2006, 99).[2] Such early strategies of personal behavior at the gate are encountered in the hexagrams of the *Yijing* that allow us a glimpse into the various attitudes and forms of actions recommended around it, for instance, response, advance, unify, be humble, approach, watch, turn back, retreat, increase, decrease, take action, or keep still, among others. In the most general way, it seems that from an individual's behavior to warfare strategies, the choice ranges between acting and refraining to act, between proceeding and withdrawing. Hexagram 52 *gen* 艮, for instance, is commented upon by Wang Bi, as follows:

gen (restraint) means "stop." When it is a time to stop, one should stop; when it is a time to act, one should act. If in one's activity and repose he is not out of step with the times, his *dao* (path) should be bright and glorious. The *dao* of restraint cannot always be used; it is something that one must employ only when it is not possible to take any action. If used when it suits its moment, this *dao* turns out to be bright and glorious . . . let Restraint operate where Restraint should take place, that is, let the restraining be done in its proper place. (Lynn 1994, 467)

What is it if not an algorithm for decision-making when one is faced with multiple possibilities and situations on the path? How is one to act? In the Commentary on the Appended by Wang Bi, the following poem is presented:

In the Dao of the noble man
There's a time for going forth
And a time for staying still.
A time to remain silent
And a time to speak out.
But for two people to share mind and heart,
Such sharpness severs metal,
And the words of those sharing mind and heart,
Such fragrance is like orchids. (Lynn 1994, 217)

The poem refers to timing *shi* and its crucial role in deterring action (including when to speak and when to be silent), alongside circumstantial and situational considerations. Even fellowship (sharing heart and mind) will not be fruitful or beneficial if acted out in the wrong moment and in the wrong way.

The gate of the private home carries multiple meanings because, first and foremost, it stands at the threshold between an individual's private space and the public sphere outside. As Xiaoshan Yang stresses in his book on Chinese gardens, "the drive towards fixing boundaries frequently manifested itself in the poetic imaging of the front gate" (2003, 50). In the poem "stopping at the banquet in old Zhano in Jizhou" by Wang Wei, it says "although your house borders on the realm of people, shutting the gate it turns into a hermitage" (X. Yang 2003, 52). The front gate thus constitutes an inseparable part of the Chinese home, and by extension, the family—the most basic social unit in Chinese culture. R. G. Knapp indeed states that "wherever it stands, the house is the single most profound symbol of the Chinese family. It is a symbol as powerful as the Great Wall is for the country" (1999, 37). Even the Great Wall of China began as a symbolic line between the civilized "Middle Kingdom" and barbaric tribes on its outskirts. As John Hay says, it was originally constructed "as a lengthy hill of low pounded earth until the 16th century" (1994, 11).

As said in chapter 1, the *fengshui* manuals emphasize that the process of selecting a site and the act of construction on it are almost synonymous; in the *Shih-ming*, a dictionary complied by Liu, it is stated that "the Chinese word *tse*, or dwelling is related to its homonym *tse*, or (site) selection" (Lewis 2006, 6). And the entrance to the house, the gate, receives outstanding attention—to the extent that it is conceptualized to function similarly to one's face openings. Li Hongmei stresses that the gate of the house is called "the air exhaling and gathering portal . . . it is the air inlet of welcoming fortune and gathering luck. The environment and orientation of the gate are vital for the home's fortune" (2014, 107). The in-out flow of *qi* constitutes a key factor when it comes to the front gate, and thus the gate's location within the site "is considered most important among the house elements" (Lee 1986, 250).

The *fengshui* details a particular order according to which construction is to be carried out, with the main gate as most important—even more than the house itself since, as opposed to the gate, the manuals state, "the house itself does not denote auspiciousness and inauspiciousness" (Lee 1986, 253). In addition, specific definitions are given to the various types of gates; the *Pa-chai ming-ching* states as follows: "*ta-men* is the doorway which is connected to the outside of the house. It is the most important one (among the doors). It must be open to the most auspicious direction of the main house building" (Lee 1986, 251). The manuals refer specifically to the size of the gate door leaves and how they compare and relate so that the inhabitants of the house will enjoy auspiciousness. Evoking the interplay between emptiness and form in Chinese architecture (*jian*, walls and gates), the Beijing courtyard dwelling, for instance, demonstrates its key role in its arrangement and settings: "the entrance is located at the southeast corner of the house, the direction from which, according to *feng-shui*, the vital *Qi* comes" (P. Xu 1998, 273). Additional information on front gates comes from archeological finds; the Yangshao and Banpuo archaeological sites expose two types of dwellings from early Chinese dwellings that, as Li Min says, "reveal that the disposition of the entry door plays a critical role in organizing space within the chamber" (2008, 193).

It is in the *Shijing* that we find other indications that gates were the first to be constructed as an act bringing auspiciousness; the poem *mian* 緜, for instance, which relates to the construction of the first Zhou temple, states the following:

> They set up the gate of the enceinte;
> And the gate of the enceinte stood high.
> They set up the court gate;
> And the court gate stood grand.
> They reared the great altar [to the Spirits of the land],
> From which all great movements should proceed. (Waley 1937)

It is noteworthy that instead of describing what would appear to be a more crucial component of temples, for instance, sacrificial halls or inner quarters, the author emphasizes the walls and gates. The poem pronounces how the gate constitutes a sort of "first step" so that if "it stands high" all other components will follow suit. An invaluable source of knowledge on such early gates is the "Lessons from the States," in *Beifang* 邶風 (*Odes of Beifang*), in which the following poem, dated to the Western Zhou, refers to a home gate:

> Beneath my door made of cross pieces of wood,
> I can rest at my leisure;
> By the wimpling stream from my fountain,
> I joy amid my hunger. (Waley 1937)

The characters used for this simple wooden gate in the first line are *heng men* 衡門; *heng* literally means "something heavy" and relates to the one of the earliest known forms of doors to exist in China. It is a very plain blockage made of pieces of wood crossed and connected together in a warp and weft texture to form a sort of gate; this is interesting as it contextually connects the gate to warp and weft matrix—which denotes it with two axes, namely, a back-to-front ax (before and after the gate), but also in-between the posts of the gate (between its sides). A different interpretation holds that *heng* was a piece of wood placed in horizontal position to stop anyone from entering an existing gate. Indeed, Ping Xu emphasizes that as far as guests were concerned, gates with such screen walls constituted the threshold before which guests stopped and ask for permission to enter (1998, 280). This stresses the significance of the Chinese home as sense of identity and self and the need to protect it.

The simple gate in the above poem thus consequently symbolizes the *boundary* between the inside and the outside, or an "improvised means of blockage." However, interestingly, the poem conveys a content state of mind in the face of *adverse* conditions—poverty and hunger. This humble door, assembled loosely, can hardly provide protection for his home—only a symbolic threshold of sense, self, and privacy. An interesting intermingling of two opposites takes place at this gate: rest at leisure versus bare simplicity and joy versus hunger. We have no reason to believe that the poet's home is any fancier than the door, but he still chooses the very threshold to emphasize his positive mood in spite of adversity.[3]

Recently, scholarly attention in the field of psychology has started investigating the home as indicative of the openness-closeness of the culture it is part of, noticing the analogue between openness of the front door and openness of the mind. This is because the home reflects the dialectic interplay between individuality and society: it is the threshold at which assimilation of an individual in a society is enabled but also his or her (need of) separation from it. Notice how cultures differ in this aspect alone (i.e., "my home is always open" versus cultures that are less enthusiastic to have unannounced guests).[4] This analogue is highly pronounced in Chinese textuality, with special emphasis on poems.

The personal decision as to the closing or opening of the front gate relates to one's mental sphere, as Xiaoshan Yang emphasizes: "shutting the gate had always been an emblematic gesture of enclosing oneself within a mental space of reclusion" (2003, 52) and "when the front gate was configured as an absolute boundary, entering the gate became a symbolic act of going out into a world of seclusion" (2003, 54).[5] The psychological boundaries that separate an individual from "others" constitute an inseparable part of his or her personality, but it is also highly influenced by cultural characteristics. In this context, I could not resist including the following poem by the poet (and painter) Gong Xian

(龔賢), who lived in the seventeenth century, as it beautifully illustrates the psychological significance of one's front gate:

> Content in the mountains as no guest is coming (to visit);
> my poor gate follows the opening and closing of this self of
> mine.

> 可容山巾無客來, 柴門随我自關開.

The poem manifests the correlation between the boundary of the poet's home and his heart-mind (self): it marks an in-betweenness of feelings (between desiring a human contact and wishing to withdraw into seclusion). The following Zhou dynasty text was posted on a gate to a private house:

> In the house we also see assignments and symbolism of the gate. The inner chamber, the outer hall, the courtyard, the gate and the alley and the main street, the wilds. . . . In the eleventh month, virtue dwells in the inner chamber thirty days, fifteen days before, . . . When virtue is in the inner chamber then Punishment is in the wilds. When virtue is in the outer chamber then Punishment is in the main street. When Yin and Yang share in potency then punishment and virtue meet at the gate. (Lewis 2005, 117)

The fact that the passage pronounces symbolism to the gate (beyond its mere functionality) is intriguing, but beyond that, it creates an image of concentric circles that start from the inner chamber and end at the wilds, like the following scheme:

> Inner Chamber → Outer Hall → Courtyard → Gate → Alley → Main Street

Through these circles, *virtue* and *punishment* get closer and closer to each other until they meet at the gate; in chapter 5 we will encounter a process almost exactly as described in the *Analects*, which parallels the process of self-cultivation as analogous to a sequence of architectural units!

Western Zhou archeological sites reveal that there was a small courtyard between the main hall and the front gatehouse which was shaped like a U and was called *chen* 陈, as part of a sequence of ritualistic halls and gates through which guests passed, as James Legge explains: "the palace, mansion, or public office was an aggregate of courts, with buildings in them, so that the visitor passed from one to another through a gateway, till he reached the inner court which conducted to the hall" (1885, 69). The threshold between punishment and virtue is very thin . . . but highly potent—because the smallest alterations in its state oscillates the scene either toward *chaos* or *order* (the "wilds" hints at chaos, the inner chamber, at order) and (as said in the introduction) *wen* versus *wu* (civil versus military life). A similar "quantum boundary" was mentioned in chapter 1 (between this life and the world beyond lies but a thin line).

In the *Yijing* we find reference to this continuous personal tension between one's inward tendency (self-isolation and privacy) and the reaching-out as part of the need of an individual to assimilate in society. I would even suggest that in the Chinese context, it constitutes a key variable in philosophical schools (especially between humanistic and Daoist thought). In the *Yijing*, Hexagram 13 named *tong ren* 同人 ("Fellowship") there is an important reflection on the connection between individuals:

> The first nine: "fellowship of men" gathering at the gate.
> No fault.

初九: 同人于門, 无咎.

Tong ren 同人 has various meanings: "fellowship," "union of man," "colleagues," and "sameness among men," among others. Here the gate stands for the center, threshold, or line of *union*—it represents a connector among man—not a divider. I sense an underlying tone that actually stresses the relations between people of *different* backgrounds, that is, *not* of the same family or clan or such-like degree of closeness. The character *yú* 于 carries a meaning of "something that is issued forth from the gate," pointing perhaps to the gate itself as possessing the ability to radiate outward a shared feeling or cause . . . a sort of *extension* of the family union.

But what is it that can be extended outward that would unite people of different orientations and backgrounds? Does the hexagram encourage people to free themselves of extreme particularism and cultivate their heart/mind toward wider and wider circles? The remark by Wang Bi on this hexagram says something along these lines: "one's heart and mind here should not be bound by particularism. Instead, one thoroughly identifies with the great community. So, when one goes out of his gate, he treats all with fellowship" (Lynn 1994, 217). Wang Bi offers man an extension of his immediate boundaries (the narrow circle of one's identity), the significance of which is that one can literally go out from his *own* gate to the symbolic *other* so that genuine fellowship can be achieved.

Any reader of Chinese philosophy would probably recognize the familiarity of this philosophical approach; both Confucius and Mencius pondered over it but it was Mozi 墨子 who developed the concept of *jian ai* 兼愛 or "universal love" that conceptualizes love as something that should be distributed and received equally—regardless of physical or national closeness or blood relation.[6] Interestingly, in specific reference to the "close and distant" in the context of one's state and far-reaching fields of the "other," Kong Yingda comments that "in entering into congenial fellowship with people, one must do so far and wide and leave no one out and, in so applying one's heart and mind, one must be free of partiality" (Lynn 1994, 221). Still in regard to this hexagram, Wang Bi takes it one step further—a warning against ultrapatriotism: "The more extreme one loves his own state, the more this will bring about calamity for others, and this happens because people do not pursue Fellowship on grand enough scale" (1994, 221). I find this a fascinating (and so relevant) insight . . . a warning that extreme nationalism and patriotism could bring about a social and political catastrophe. In Hexagram 17, named *sui* 隨 ("Following") it says,

> The first Nine: when an official is changing (his location or pursuit) and, leaving his home (and the familiar) in the correct way means creating relationship (with others). He will thus be accomplished.

> 初九: 官有渝, 貞出門交有功.

And in the *xiang zhuan* 象傳 ("Treatise on the Symbolism of the Hexagrams"), there is an added explanation:

> Upon change, an official needs to follow the correct way; he will not fail if he goes (beyond his own) gate to meet others.

> 官有渝, 從正吉也; 出門交有功, 不失也.

This hexagram is connected to number 13 in the context of correctness and timing; the pursuit itself, whether it is an official position, a teacher's change of school, or perhaps a change in one's line of work, should still be conducted in the right way (which emphasizes creating friendships). I believe the point being made here is not necessarily the actual befriending recommended, but the will to let go of one's "previous gates," that is, former attachment to one's identity, and looking out beyond the gate's demarcation line with an open heart and mind.

If this is done in a careful and accurate attuning to the objectives pursued and its circumstances, accomplishment will come one's way; otherwise, all can be lost in one second. Wang Bi refers to it, saying,

> to deal with a time of following and yet fail to get things to go smoothly on a grand scale means that one is acting contrary to the moment, and if one gets others to follow and yet does not deal with them in terms of the fitting practice of rectitude, this will result in a *dao* that leads to disaster. (Lynn 1994, 242)

Again and again we encounter this emphasis on efficacy of the minute, small, or thin as carrying the inner potential for a significant impact—in the same way that a tiny hinge can open and close a huge gate. In reference to the first *yang* of Hexagram 17, Wang Bi says, "When this one leaves his own gate, he stays free of any contrary behavior, so what violation could ever occur?" (Lynn 1994, 243). Here, the "inside" refers to one's home, village, city, or indeed nation, all of which belong contextually to conventions, proper and familiar ways to behave, and so on. However, once one leaves these familiar grounds and goes out of its boundaries, it is a different matter altogether; though it is up to the person (as decision-making) to take with him these familiar behavior patterns, he needs to take into account future encounters with foreigners, different attitudes and customs. As Roger Ames indeed phrases it, "the coordination of the relationship between the changing world and the human experience is the main axis of the *Yijing*" (2015, 2).

Guo-Ming Chen stresses that it is the ultimate fruit of the ability to abide and act upon the three core principles, namely, timing (*shi*), spatiality (*wei*) and the onset of change (*ji*): "The secret of appropriately regulating change is in the ability of holding the *zhong* (centrality) . . . *I Ching* points out three possible abilities embedded in *shi* (temporal contingencies), *wei* (spatial contingencies), and *ji* (the first imperceptible beginning of movement) to achieve the goal of holding the *zhong*" (2008, 15). The principle of *shi* 時 constitutes a key factor in the ability to decide upon an action and the means by which to "hold on to the center," and will be further encountered in other sources. In the *Zhong yong* 中庸, for instance, the *shi* is used as the means by which the noble man achieves oneness with the center.[7]

In the *Taixuan jing*, Tetragram 46, named *kou* ("Enlargement") is interesting. It says, "Enlarging his gates and doors, he protects himself from robbers and rogues." In the tetragram named "Fathoming" (no. 4) it says, "Enlarging the gates and doors, he extends what he plans and builds." As the size of gates was strictly regulated by law, the fact that the owner managed to enlarge his gates means he had high socioeconomic status, but perhaps we can look at it from a different angle altogether: a "wider entrance" that allows for more openness, or, as Michael Nylan suggests, an increased contact with the outside world. He adds that "such contact can continue in safety so long as the basic structural elements of the house are strong. By analogy, so long as the good person is strongly committed to the Way, he is able to realize future plans without endangering himself" (1994, 292). This interpretation resonates with the line "he extends what he plans and builds," as a way of saying that the front gate constitutes the very embodiment of one's inner creativity.

Due to the significance of the front gate of one's home, it has been the custom to hang signs and posts on the front gate for protection of the home (still very common in present-time Chinese villages). A most common post constitutes the *menshen* 門神, "Gate Spirits" (figure 4.2),

Figure 4.2. Gate spirits posted on the door of a private Chinese home. Photo by the author.

which serve as guardians of the house; others include a "range of calligraphic and pictographic prints used to ensure protection for the family and its home (Knapp and Lo 2005, 228).

These gate entities, as A. Plath states, constitute "a representation epitomizing the traditional Chinese home as quaint and earthy, yet also a closed entity of walls within walls that never revealed more than a glimpse of what lay within" (quoted in Knapp 1999, 325). This further attests to the need for *degrees of privacy inside* the house—not merely between the outside and inside, but the various distinctions that proceed deeper and deeper through inner doorways, partitions, screens, and so on (in the same way that the "Forbidden City" is arranged). The layers are circular and concentric and the overall complexity hints at the complexity of the Chinese inner spheres, that is, the mind-heart of the individual and the family. In the *Qu li* of the *Records of Rites*, we find how this gradation corresponds to ritual conduct within the family and appropriate courteous behavior:

> As for the conduct of one's son, he cannot reside in the "Inner Sanctum" (*ao*), nor can he sit in the middle of the mat, nor can he walk in the middle of the road, nor can he stand in the middle of the gate.

為人子者, 居不主奧, 坐不中席, 行不中道, 立不中門.

This is a wonderful instance of right conduct interwoven with architecture—with three significant markers of space included and referred to, namely, *ao*, *dao*, and *men*. Here we have a reference to spatial appropriateness between members of the family, especially between father and son. It would be an expression of disrespect to occupy the space destined for the elders (or high official, dukes, emperors, etc.). It seems that the son did not achieve the level required to enter this deep space or to walk along the middle of the path.

This indicates the significance of the center—the place that is neither inside nor outside but the fusion of both into a singular locus of transformation or, in this case, of social and virtuous standing. Knapp says that "as the threshold of house, the point through which the 'communication with the outside' takes place and as a point of rituals, the gates of private homes played a significant role in the daily life of the family as well an important representation of their cultural beliefs and spiritual faith" (1999, 337). Furthermore, as rituals to the *menshen* became customary, the gate itself naturally evolved and transformed into a religious singularity by itself, becoming "the chief of the five household things sacrificed to" (1999, 337).

An important type of front gate is that of private gardens. Interestingly, as Xiaoshan Yang says, the shutting of these gates was "a conventional gesture of withdrawing from the world" (2003, 4)—again signifying parallelism between the gate and the mind. The furthest that one could withdraw from the world, in architectural symbolism, seems to be the "Inner Sanctum" *ao* 奧 as the innermost and private-most room in the home. It seems that only a few individuals could enter this singular locale, and in analogy—*ao signifies* one's innermost sphere of heart-mind (chapter 62 of the *Daode jing* even hints that *ao* resembles *dao*). In addition to personal growth as a prerequisite for entering *ao*, rituals had to be performed in just the correct way as otherwise they lose potency—as the Classics demonstrate (see chapter 5); also, references that pertain to the *wu* gate 烏門 or the *wutoumen* 烏頭門 (figure 4.3), for instance, hint that they could not be built for "those ranking below the sixth and seventh levels" (Feng 2012, 56)—but only for high-ranking officials.

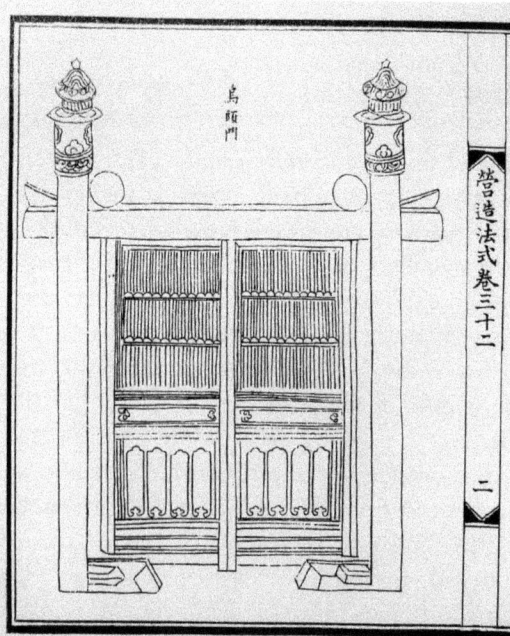

Figure 4.3. Timber frame *paifang* from the *Yingzao Fashi*. Public domain.

In the *Li jing*, in the "Summary of the Rules of Propriety," part 1:27, the following passage details the appropriate behavior of guests and hosts:

> When a guest comes in, at every gate the host should yield to the guest; (but) if the guest enters as far as the inner gate (of the reception room), the host will ask (the guest) to enter first (in order) to arrange the mats; then, after having done it, he will go back out to welcome the guest; the guest will then refuse strongly (to enter first), but the host will show his respect and they will enter; the host will enter through the western side (left) of the gate, while the guest will enter from the eastern side (right) of the gate.

> 凡與客入者, 每門讓於客. 客至於寢門, 則主人請入為席, 然後出迎客. 客固辭, 主人肅客而入. 主人入門而右, 客入門而左.

This *li* 禮 as ritualistic behavior requires that each individual fulfills a role in society, so that the whole scene is *choreographed* to the last detail, from the right location, timing, and behavior, combined and intertwined with the surrounding architecture, arranged according to numerology and cosmology.

The inner gates constitute points of entry and exit from each and every sphere and therefore symbolize levels of closeness between the host and guest. These structures potentially invite "explosive" situations if one of the parts of the synchronized and choreographed "dance" is conducted in the wrong manner or in the wrong time. Indeed, if the guest is received less respectfully (than his status dictates), a grave insult might ensue; furthermore, even if the spatial specification is correct, but the timing is wrong . . . the whole ceremony can be ruined and harmony damaged.

The Master's Front Gate Is Open

Following the exegesis of certain passages in the *Analects* alongside historical sources and etymological analysis, I would like to propose that, as a result of Confucius's philosophy and didactic convictions, his front gate was *open* for students—providing they had a burning desire and commitment to learn.[8] This is again an important point that I find pronounced in many and varied dimensions, that is, that the gate might indeed be open for us (in this case, Confucius's disciples), but the hard work is left in our own hands; this 'burning desire to learn' constitutes the hinge that opens the gate. When the disciple is awarded the opportunity, it is up to him to follow his own path through commitment to self-cultivation; how nicely it resonates with the Chinese idiom, "Teachers open the door. You enter by yourself" 師傅領進門, 修行在個人.

This particular gate's exegesis of the master's front gate as an open invitation to embark on the path of education constitutes an exceptional case in the overall analysis of gate passages in the *Analects*. Indeed, as will be discussed in chapter 5, gates in Chinese humanistic philosophies tend to constitute a strict boundary of social conduct, rituality, and morality, that is—more closed than open.

Let us first examine three *men* composite characters that appear in the *Analects*, namely, *menren* 門人 (occurring eight times), *kongmen* 孔門, and *tongmen* 同門; *menren* has been traditionally thought to refer to the disciples of the master, whereas *kongmen* 孔門 is interpreted as the gate of Kongzi (literally, "people of the same gate"), that is, the community or fellowship of the master or the doctrine.[9]

What exactly does the "gate of Confucius" mean? Is it purely metaphorical or could it perhaps relate to his physical front gate? This might give us an interesting glimpse into the early stages of the evolvement of the community (and later on, the Confucian "family" or school of thought *rujia* 儒家). A clue might be found in one of the most famous lines in the *Analects*—and the first to open the whole text:

> The Master said, "To learn (something) and regularly practice (it), isn't it (a kind of) pleasure? Having disciples coming from afar, isn't it a happy occasion? To remain calm and unresentful (though) people don't know and acknowledge it, isn't it (a sign of) a superior person?"

> 子曰: 學而時習之, 不亦說乎? 有朋自遠方來, 不亦樂乎? 人不知而不慍, 不亦君子乎?

Different interpretations explain the placing of this passage right at the beginning of the whole compilation (as an opening *gate?*)—some suggesting that it stems from an emphasis on learning as the most important message of the text. Peimin Ni also maintains that in Confucian eyes it is not "bookish learning" sought after, but "practical learning that would result in the transformation of the person. Such a person will particularly appreciate the joy of having harmonious interactions with people, near or afar" (2017, 80).

In the overall hermeneutic of the passage, I find the character *peng* 朋 significant; traditionally rendered "friends," it is taken to express Confucius's delight in seeing his friends dropping by to pay a visit. However, the interpreter Bao Xian (6 BC–65 AD) referred to this very *peng* and postulated that it does not mean "friends," but in effect, "people who share the same gate" (study together under one master or, in other words, *disciples*) (Y. K. Lo 2014, 82). Is it indeed plausible that the reference is made to disciples coming from afar and *not* friends (or at least, not friends to begin with!)? It opens the possibility that Confucius's disciples had come from the far corners of the state and then stayed in close proximity to him—as part of their new "family." What indeed do we know about Confucius's disciples?

Primary and secondary materials point to some interesting characteristics of Confucius the teacher; it seems, for instance, from *Analects* 7.7, that it was sufficient to "pay" with a bundle of dried meat instead of paying the tuition fee (with currency). Also, it is documented that his disciples came from all over China; for instance, forty-three came from the state of Lu, six from the state of Wei, three from Qin, and two each from Chen and Qi, among other places (Y. K. Lo 2014). It thus stands to reason that there was great diversity in their socioeconomic background and education. In *Analects* 15.39, we learn that Confucius himself said, "(where) there is teaching, (there is no) class distinctions" (子曰: 有教無類), which means that a student's personal background was not relevant when he came to the master's gate seeking education.

In the chapter *Xunzi faxing* 法行, line 6, we have another clue as to this principle; here, Zigong (Confucius's disciple Duanmu Ci) emphasizes that genuine desire to learn is sufficient enough to be accepted at the master's gate—in exactly the same way that a physician admits all sick patients waiting at his gate (且夫良醫之門多病人). *Analects* 7.8 reads,

The Master said: "For (an undetermined mind), I will not open (the door), nor will I (offer to) develop (speaking skills), to someone who is unable to talk."

子曰: 不憤不啟, 不悱不發.

This passage emphasizes the act of opening, and in this case, an opening as *opportunity* on the journey of self-cultivation, education, and ethics. For a disciple to be awarded with the opportunity to learn with the master (to have the gate opening up to him), he must have a very determined mind as otherwise education would not be effective; as Slingerland says, "education is only effective when there is active, sincere, and appreciative engagement on the part of the learner" (2008, 245). Furthermore, beyond the metaphorical significance of this "open gate," we might ask whether the concrete front gate and house of the master served as the physical locus for the community; Yuet Keung Lo stresses that

> to get to know a student thoroughly, close contact and regular communication would definitely help. The physical proximity between the students' dormitories and their master's residence was crucial as it provided them ample opportunities to interact constantly with each other, and in a real sense, we can consider them to be living together in the same community. (2014, 86)

This postulation tells us something important about the type of teacher Confucius was. He kept his disciples nearby or in close proximity to his private home; he is not interested merely in the conveyance of knowledge into their heads . . . for him, teaching is a personal endeavor and a commitment, setting himself as a personal example, assisting and guiding his disciples on *dao* to self-realization. I believe this is the meaning of "sharing the same gate"—a space constituting the tangible (physical gate) and the intangible (ethics and values).

Although arriving from very different backgrounds, the disciples shared quite many personal traits, namely, an aspiration to change, transform, become a *junzi*, make an effort, dedicate themselves to study, and commit to self-cultivation. Through the application of knowledge in their everyday lives as a community, each and every member went through a transformation—from a disciple to a friend or even a family member. Thus, the passage above could be uttered (in retrospect) by Confucius as if saying, "Isn't it indeed a great joy to have *disciples* coming from afar?" We can assume that for the master, his own local community constituted a small-scale embodiment of his vision for the whole nation. I suggest that this close and intimate community, moreover, turned into a *family*—an ordered and constructed unit of particular hierarchy and etiquette in which every member fulfills his or her role with the father as head figure.

Was Confucius a father figure for his disciples? One clue might be found in the disciples' reaction to his death, a three-year mourning period—which is a rite reserved for fathers only. Furthermore, it is said that Zigong continued mourning him for an *additional* three years (Takigawa 1977). It is thus highly possible that Confucius had evolved to become a new "father" to his disciples—the significance of which would later transform him to be the father of the *Rujia* 儒家 school. In a reference to the *Daxue* 大學 (*Book of Great Learning*), philosopher Cheng Yi 程頤 (1032–1985) said that "the *Great Learning* is a book that was inherited from Confucius, it is the gateway to virtue for those who begin learning" (Ariel and Raz 2010, 400).

From this first step of "beginning to learn" (the gate opens) comes great harmony, one of the highest objectives of a Confucian society. Harmony *he* 和 can be thought of as a gestalt-like sum of the self-cultivation of each individual, and the relationship that develops between two individuals (the literal meaning of *ren* 仁). Thus, the master's front gate constitutes a *wai/nei* meeting point: from the *inside* of the master's home (and perspective) to the outside, and from the *outside* (the disciples' perspective) back inwardly—signifying the first step on the journey (*dao*) of self-cultivation.

However, let me stress a significant point: once these disciples entered the inner world of Confucian values, they approached other gates . . . gates that stand for established, value-specific rules, rites, and conduct of the Confucian doctrine. From the front gate that constituted an open invitation and opportunity for learning and transformation (symbolizing *no distinctions* between people), the disciples entered an inner world in which gates stand for strictly defined distinctions of propriety and morality.

The Mouth as Gate

We now move closer to personal space—to an individual's body-mind, and specifically, to the interesting conceptualization of the mouth as a gate. Sources analyzed here include poetry, hexagrams from the *Yijing*, the *Guiguzi*, and the *Spring and Autumn Annals*. Indeed, in the *Spring and Autumn Annals* the ears, eyes, nose, and mouth were conceived as the four officials who guard against excess pleasures that can enter the body and corrupt it. Through correlative thinking, these openings or gates of the body were conceptualized as state officials who need to be regulated. James D. Sellmann indeed says that "just as the organs (*guan*) of the body, have to be organized and managed to fulfill their function so do the state officials must be regulated to fulfill their proper roles" (2002, 69). The gates pertain to the delicate balance and decisions whether go forth, withdraw, or stand still.

Before I embark on textual analysis itself, an interesting etymological analysis sheds light on the gate metaphor in the act of speaking. In the *Shijing* (*Book of Poetry*), in the "Decade of Dang," the second line of Poem 6 reads, "do not hold my tongue; words don't die out" 莫捫朕舌、言不可逝矣. The whole poem, but particularly this line, emphasizes the need for a careful monitoring of words uttered—not only because it is the sole responsibility of the individual but also since words don't just fade away; they stay and have lingering impact on others. Hsiu-Fang Yang has analyzed the character *men* 捫 in this poem and claims that its original meaning is "to hold the door open/closed," in the same way that, for instance, the expression "to hold tears" (捫淚), can either mean "to stop the tears," but also "to let tears go, to wipe tears away." This means that the poem doesn't simply demand that no one can "shut me up" but by the same token, no one will tell me whether I can talk or not; no one is responsible for the words uttered from my mouth (or not) but myself. Again, it is the inherent potentiality of the gate that is stressed, meaning that out of two options (open or closed), it is up to man to choose![10]

As a manual for decision-making, the *Yijing* naturally advises on correct actions at certain times and circumstances, including the act of speaking. In the commentary of Wang Bi on Hexagram 13, for instance, a trigger and a hinge are mentioned in association with language and words—a key idea in association with the gate's mechanism and potential:

> Words and actions are the door hinge and crossbow trigger of the noble man (the door hinge and the crossbow trigger represent the master control that governs action). It is the opening of this door or the release of this trigger that controls the difference between honor and disgrace. Words and actions are the means by which the noble man moves Heaven and earth. So how could one ever fail to pay careful attention to them? (Lynn 1994, 58)

This very thin line between honor and disgrace is likened to a cross-bow arrow trigger—an extremely sensitive device that responds to the most minute movements and spatial changes, the result of which is the direction (and target) of the arrow.[11]

One particular text which is wholly devoted to rhetoric and the art persuasion is the Master of Spirit Valley, the *Guiguzi* 鬼谷子, which contains some intriguing postulations on psychology and rhetoric. Hui Wu, who studied the text, says that the *Guiguzi* "is recognized as China's earliest treatise devoted primarily to rhetoric. Compiled over many centuries, it comprises the teachings of Guiguzi (Master of the Ghost Valley), the first Chinese teacher specifically associated with the 'art of persuasion' during the pre–Qin Warring States period" (475–221 BCE) (2016, 503). The *Guiguzi* is rich with gate references with particular emphasis on two-leaved gates and their "opening-closing" mechanism. In fact, the name of its first chapter is "Open and Shut" *Bai He* 捭闔. However, the contextual theme of "closing and opening" in the *Guiguzi* is one's ability to control other people through speech (that is, rhetoric), and the act of "pushing into crevices," which carries the significance of "taking an opportunity." Most significantly, again, is the usage of "crevices" *xi* 巇 in the context of change and actualization.

To me, it directly relates to the concept of *shi* 勢 (inherent propensity) of "feeling the time, the place and circumstances" in order to choose the appropriate choice, but also correlatedly connects with the theme of openings, gaps, and cracks that signify a creation of a new state (actualization is the result of "taking an opportunity").

I find that the first chapter not only encapsulates the most basic mechanism of a gate's apparatus and its efficaciousness, but wholly manifests Chinese correlative thinking through several parallel spheres, for example, the mouth and a city's gates or checkpoints on the roads. Paragraph, 1.1 of the chapter "Open and Shut" says,

> Observing the "opening and the closing" of *yin* and *yang* is (the means through which) all things are named; it is knowing the gate of existing or perishing.

觀陰陽之開闔以名命物; 知存亡之門戶.

This evokes the gates of creation in the *Yijing* (chapter 2), but in a particular context, that is, from the cosmic down to the human sphere, and further down to man's most conspicuous trait—language and the mouth as its apparatus (in between the inside and the outside). As the saying goes, "words can kill"—what people say or how they say it can sometimes lead to heavy consequences all round. The passage continues:

> (Through) the observation of signs of change, (you can) guard and control (their) gate's doors.
>
> 見變化之朕焉, 而守司其門戶.

Yet again an important reference to the *Yijing* is made here, namely, that the observation of "signs of change" enables one to acquire practical wisdom—as a precondition for any conduct. In the *Yijing*, these deciphered signs were observed in heavens and earth, while here, I presume, it refers to any aspect of the human world. It does indeed make sense that if one's aim is to influence others, then one needs to observe people's behavior, weaknesses, and psychological traits as these might assist in his or her manipulations. In 1.2 it says,

> Shut down to open up others in order to understand what they seek. Open up to demonstrate what to do, or shut down to keep others quiet. When opening up for demonstration, respond to others' emotions; when shutting down to make others quiet, determine if they are sincere. Whether fitting or not, examine and understand their plans and strategies to clarify why they agree and disagree. Follow the will of others to hold your footing against different opinions. (Hui Wu 2016, 40)

Isn't that exactly a reference to the efficacious mechanism of the gate? Its inherent potency lies in its ability to either connect or separate through the control of the hinge or pivot. As said, the utterance of a word might carry heavy consequences, in the same way that a small hinge can open or close a huge gate; Qi Zhu refers to this hinge in the context of *shi* in warfare: "using a five-inch-long hinge mechanism to open and close a much larger and heavier door is equivalent to a general's use of the advantageous *shi* to overcome much larger opponents with smaller troops and minimal confrontations" (2008, 98).

The mouth as a device of speech constitutes a gate from which inner thoughts are rendered outside, with potentially great consequences, but it also refer to political activities. All these factors should indeed be thoroughly studied to reach deep fathoming (mo 摩) by an individual or a general: as the meaning of a strategy, that is, the planning and acting out according to the situation (shi). In chapter 8, we find an important and direct reference to the mouth as gate:

As for the mouth, it is the gate's door of the heart-mind.

口者, 心之門戶也.

To what heart-mind does the author refer? His own or another's? As the Guiguzi focuses on rhetoric, we can assume it is the second option: through the conscious manipulation of language, one can penetrate (go through the gate of) the heart-mind of others. Always noteworthy, in Chinese thought xin constitutes our thinking faculties as well as our feelings and emotions. If xin had been closer to its Western meaning (the seat of love, affections, etc.), we could have taken the above passage to refer to the relationship between man and woman (in which a man is trying to win a woman's heart through sweet words).[12]

However, the attempt at influencing others might relate to any dimension—from the very personal to the political. In chapter 16, we meet the cycle of yin and yang again, with the intriguing characteristic (which we have met previously) of the "tipping point":

(As) yang moves and circulates, yin stops and hides away;
(as) yang moves and goes out, yin conceals and goes inside;
(as) yang proceeds towards yin, yin reverses (to utmost) yang.

陽動而行, 陰止而藏; 陽動而出, 陰隱而入; 陽還終陰, 陰極反陽.

Then it reads,

Yinyang seek each other mutually, through (the act) of opening and closing. This is dao of yinyang in the whole universe; and the method of "man of rhetoric"; for previously to all things and events is (what is called) the gate to the round and square.

陰陽相求, 由捭闔也. 此天地陰陽之道, 而說人之法也。為萬事之
先, 是謂圓方之門戶.

The author makes a correlation between the cycle of yinyang and rheto-ric, between the square—as earth—and the round, for heavens. I suggest that the two lips of the mouth parallel heavens and earth, that is, the upper lip is heavens and the lower lip is earth, and in between is the emptiness through which words go out. This is precisely a double-leaved gate! But note the character *hu* 戶 that comes after the gate character *men* . . . Why is it there? Is it because when we talk, it is indeed only the lower lip (and jaw) that moves?

Another *men* is mentioned in chapter 52 of the *Daode jing*—especially interesting in the context of its closing mechanism:

> Halt your mouth; close your (body and mind) gates; and your life will not be over-exploited; open your mouth; add to your affairs; and your life will not be saved.

> 塞其兌閉其門, 終身不勤. 開其兌, 濟其事, 終身不救.

The character *sai* 塞 means "to stop" and is linked with *dui* 兌—a complex character of different meanings. For example, in the *Yijing* it stands for "joy" or "exchange" as a title of a hexagram, in some dictionaries it means "strategic point," and in Chinese medicine *dui* means "breath coming out of the mouth or speak" (exchange of breath or words); indeed, in chapter 9 of the "discussion of the trigrams," it is identified with the "mouth" (R. Wilhelm 1950, 279).[13] This rendering of the character *dui* as mouth corresponds better with the overall message of the chapter and the requirement to guard the senses at any given time.[14] To convey the meaning in everyday language, the line would go something like the following: "as long as one stops talking (mouth), and closes the gates of his senses and body, one will preserves his energy; when one opens his mouth, he just adds to his troubles and he will, eventually, bring ruin upon himself."

The advice to be constantly cautious and careful in what one says and what one lets inside is conspicuous, and it belongs to the overall attention given in numerous sources to the "gates of the body"; according to Wang Bi, gates are "the basis from which desires for action arise, and 'doors' are the basis on which desires for action are pursued" (Wagner 2003b, 297). Does the *Guiguzi* advocate manipulation and mere deceit through these schemes of influencing (and controlling) other people's minds? In large part, yes. However, the schemes emphasize an ability to carry negotiation through "direct responsiveness" *ying* 應 and "adapting to the situation" *yin* 因. In that sense, it resonates also with the *Art of War* by Sunzi (chapter 6).

Finally, in the *Ci Xi* ("The Great Treatise") 1.8 of the *Yijing*, it says,

> The Master said: "The noble-man stays in his room (but) his words travel outwards; if they are words of virtue, then even at a distance of a thousand *li*, they will be accepted with agreement. Let alone at closer circles! If (on the other hand), non-virtuous words come out of his room, then even at a distance of a thousand *li*, they will be accepted with objection. Let alone at closer circles! One's words influence the people, actions conducted in the close circle, are seen from a distance. The words and actions of the noble-man are like a pivotal hinge; (according to) this pivotal hinge, one's honor or disgrace are determined. By the means of words and actions, the nobleman can move heavens and earth, can he (afford to) be careless about them?!"

子曰: 君子居其室, 出其言, 善則千里之外應之, 況其邇者乎, 居其室, 出其言不善, 則千里之外違之, 況其邇者乎, 言出乎身, 加乎民, 行發乎邇, 見乎遠. 言行君子之樞機, 樞機之發, 榮辱之主也. 言行, 君子之所以動天地也, 可不慎乎.

Here we have a person staying inside his room, talking; his words flow out of the door and the outer gate—to the world outside. His words have great impact on people (even in circles far away), notwithstanding whether they are virtuous, wrong, or bad; furthermore, even words uttered and actions conducted within close circles are still seen at a great distance.

Then the author compares the nobleman to a pivot, a hinge of a gate: his words and actions move heavens and earth in the same way that an small axis can move a great gate; hence, the nobleman carries a great burden of responsibility—first, to himself as part of self-cultivation and his dedication to pursuing *dao*, but second, to those living close by, and further away to the multitudes out there. Even though he does not know them, his words and actions influence their course! The passage constitutes yet another instance of contextual circles that run from the mind to the cosmos, and back. Here, again, the *opening* is no less than an act of creation, change, and transformation (which can go both ways: to life or to destruction).

The correlate significance of the front gate, the mouth, and the mind seems to refer to everyday lives, and I will explain. The front gate is the point through which a person leaves his own home, goes out to meet society, or the threshold through which—he enters back inside. Going back inside means entering a familiar realm, the intimate, private, motherlike womb of the home. The mouth represents a different sort of communication—but it is an act that still occurs between two individuals or between an individual and society at large. They both signify the gradation in an individual's inside-outside strategy, that is, ranging between total openness (one's home is always open . . . or "I always say what I think") and withdrawal to the inside (both gates are closed). A most significant point is the lack of any absolute instruction as to both gates—decisions are always interlinked with time, situations, circumstances, location, and *shi*.

Chapter 5

Gates of Sociomoral Order
and Distinctions

Nowadays people no longer know how to read. When they read the
Analects, for instance, they are the same kind of people before they
read the book and after they read the book. This is no different
from not having read the book.

—Cheng Yi, Song dynasty Confucian[1]

The gates included in this chapter were found to symbolize moral values,
ritual propriety, and gender distinctions, which naturally positions them
in the sociopolitical dimension: individual, family, society, governance.
Importantly, the shared ideological framework of the gates compiled here
is the aspiration for personal, social, and political *order*, which means,
philosophically as well as practically, a formation of clear boundaries
and distinctions—as a strategy against the constant threat of chaos
and anarchy. Though we discussed the open front gate of Confucius in
chapter 4, further extracts from the *Lunyu* 論語, the *Mengzi* 孟子, and
the Classics are included here.

As mentioned before, in the context of social distinctions one particular gate plays an important role, namely, the *que* gate 闕. *Que* gates
emerged as an important symbol in the Zhou dynasty but by the Han
dynasty they referred not only to the sentinel of city gates but also to
the stone carvings that were erected in front of temples, courtyards, and
tombs. According to Qinghua Guo, each one of these *que* gates "had a

different function" (2005, 46). This "different function" is related to the peculiar structure of *que* gates: as opposed to the rudimentary structure of gates (as postulated in the introduction), *que* gates are named twin towers as they consist of two posts, each designed with an extended horizontal component but lacking in girders or inner doors that connect them together.

These gates consisted of a wooden-framed pavilion called *xie*, which was built on high walls or, in some cases, lacked walls altogether; in case they lacked walls, two smaller *que* were symbolically built next to the gate. Two fine examples of *que* gates are the Wu family cemetery at Jiaxiang in Shandong and the Gao Yi cemetery in Ya'an in Sichuan. Figure 5.1 shows the Gao Yi cemetery *que* gate—one of the best-preserved *que* gates in China.

Figure 5.1. A *que* gate erected at the entrance to Gao Yi graveyard. Public domain.

It is thus a unique type of gate that cannot be closed . . . in other words, and strangely enough, they are more open than a gate that can be opened. It is thus interesting to learn that the original definition of *que* was simply "a gap" (H. Wu 1995, 277), that is, emptiness! In addition, the *Shuowen jiezi* 說文解字 specifies that "*que* refers to *guan* gates," emphasizing the motif of "seeing" in both; it is interesting to note in this context that Daoist temples were also named *guan*—again, a possible hint at the significance of the sense of *seeing*. The study indeed found *que* gates in a number of different dimensions, playing different roles in each—on one hand, they mark social status, and on the other, they signify an open passage to the heavens: the former symbolized distinctions, the later symbolized open boundaries. A remarkable quote by Liu Xie (ca. 465–522) is given by E.Y. Wang in relation to *que* gates—which carries an added contextuality with the important   interplay between the formed and the formless:

> {in thinking on "how one encages heavens and earth in the realm of form," Liu Xie "saw the *que* gate as the anchor of this cognitive model," adding that, "my bodily form is by the rivers and seas and my mind is under the gateway of the palace of Wei. This is called thinking with the spirit"}. (2005, 295)

This is perhaps the underlying reason for *que* gates to oscillate between various "roles"—as they constitute by themselves a gradation between emptiness and concreteness. This may also be, by its own right, an instance of Chinese visual perspective and resolution—the shifting of ideological and metaphorical focus between the concrete shape of the gate and the vacuous passage that it offers. As this chapter focuses on the role of gates in social boundaries and distinctions—it is the concrete and formed perspective of *que* gates that will be discussed.

Que gates were valued by the nobility and aristocracy, as is recorded, for instance, in the *Chunqiu Gongyang Zhuan*: "the number of the *que* is two for a king, one for the nobility or grand officials" (Hung Wu 1995, 47). For the rulers of the Eastern Zhou, *que* gates fulfilled a further role as the bearers of legal documents and official announcements in front of a palace and in entrances to graveyards (Hung Wu 1995, 105). Remains of twenty-nine Eastern Han stone *que* gates were found throughout Henan, Shandong, Beijing, and Sichuan, while others are known from various texts; the *que* gate of Wang Ziya (the governor of Shu) from the second century BC, for instance, is documented in the *Li Daoyuan* records, which remarks that Wang's daughters used most of their savings in building it because "the gate alone could make their virtue renowned" (Hung Wu 1995, 277). Li-Kuei Chien mentions Ban Gu 班固 (32–92 AD), who believed that "one of the purposes of erecting *que* was to "distinguish the superior from the inferior" (2018, 78).

What about the role of other types of gates in the context of social conduct, behavior, and rituals? The Classics contain a rich array of gate rites that constitute detailed instructions as to appropriate ways of conduct when crossing a gate, standing in its midst, and so on. In the Announcement of King Kang in the "Book of Documents" *Shang Shu*, for instance, we find evidence of the gate's importance in political and diplomatic ritual behavior and conduct:

> The king went out, stood in the space in between the gate, when a high official led the princess from the Western regions inside—through the left (side of the) gate—while the duke of Bi led those of the Eastern regions through the right (side of the) gate.

> 王出, 在應門之內, 太保率西方諸侯入應門左, 畢公率東方諸侯入應門右, 皆布乘黃朱.

Indeed, this and numerous passages demonstrate the importance of the space within the gate itself (門之內) in formal meetings, containing highly specific instructions that carefully choreograph the situation—from the right positions that should correspond to one's rank and status (e.g., the right or left side of the gate) to detailed specifications regarding conduct, behavior, and speech.

Let us continue with *Analects* 6.17:

> Yong Ye: The Master said, "Can one go outside without using the door? How come no one follows *dao*?"

> 雍也:子曰: 誰能出不由戶? 何莫由斯道也?

Confucius actually states that no one can make a first step in the space "outside" without passing through the threshold first, that is, opening the door (*he*). The text can be interpreted in three different ways: taken literally, it points out that following *dao* is as simple as opening the door and stepping outside . . . so how come people don't do that? It might also mean that by "door" the author refers to the gate of the mind which needs opening to change and determination, as a precondition for (the onset of) the path (path outside the door = *dao*) of self-cultivation; as a third option, the text might refer to *how* a door is supposed to be opened . . . that is, a reference to ritualistic behavior, *li* 禮.

If indeed ritualistic behavior is the subject of this line, then it might constitute an expression of Confucius's frustration upon encountering impropriety in the most mundane behaviors—especially when it comes to people who wish to succeed on the path of self-cultivation. The whole line might be delivered in the opposite direction, that is, can one venture on the path of self-cultivation without *li*? The answer is easy . . . no, it is not possible, and those who readily understand this would find it easier to follow *dao*. *Li* means that each and every part of a behavior is carried out in the most accurate way possible, as the process of becoming a *junzi* involves the need to acquire extreme self-awareness: every detail counts. As Jones and Culliney state, "for Confucius nothing was more important than *li* because any participant in society should "not look unless it was in accordance with the rites" (1998, 398), as indeed the "Book of Rites" demonstrates with gate and door rites.

But the crucial point for the understanding of *li*, to my mind, is the course of *internalization* that is needed for its fulfillment—that is, by continuously being repeated, *li* eventually becomes second nature—it becomes an inseparable part of one's body-heart-mind (no conscious thought is actually involved!). It becomes *spontaneous* . . . as the way of the *dao*. I find the subject of Confucian ritual *li* to constitute an excellent point of difference between Confucian and Daoist thoughts—in relation to harmony *he* 和: whereas the Daoist approach is going back to the spontaneity and harmony of the natural world, Confucians also seek spontaneity of *dao*—but within the dimension of the human sphere, through ritual, as a system that confers, as Benjamin Schwartz says, "socio-political order" (1985, 67–68).

This *internalization* of the act of ritual into the body corresponds, according to Patricia B. Ebrey, to the concept of *shi* 勢, which "possesses equivalent authoritative regulating power and is an intrinsic aspect of the ritual itself" (1991, 16). Thus, the passage reflects the idea that as soon as one fully immerses himself in "ritual propriety" (which the opening of the door signifies), it is similarly easy to follow *dao* (or in other words, *dao* then constitutes a natural continuation). Slingerland refers to primary and mundane rites, and adds that the end destination to which they ultimately lead is the same, because "there has never been a person who has entered a room without using the door" (2006, 79).

One final exegetical note on this passage: the character used is not *men* 門 but *hu* 戶, a door of a house or a door inside a two-leaved gate. If it refers to the door of a house, the passage might carry an additional significance: the threshold between the private and the public, which perhaps hints at the departure point from which man goes out to become a *junzi*. Furthermore, isn't it one's very home, according to Confucius, that sets the example and source for any journey of self-fulfillment? (See chapter 4).

Indeed, the *Analects* contains specific rituals involving gates and doors, such as in 10.3–4:

> Enter the court gate and bow (so deeply), as if you squeeze your way through. Stand, but not in the middle of the gate; walk through, but without treading on the threshold.

> 入公門, 鞠躬如也, 如不容. 立不中門, 行不履閾.

The above constitutes only the beginning of a long passage of specific instructions, which describe the respectful way one should enter a palace gate. It intriguingly refers to the act of bowing inside the gate—an act that should be carried out as if there was no space between the posts, that is, in a similar way to entering a narrow tunnel. The bow is an act of honor: the lower the bow is, the more respect it conveys. The metaphorical minimization of the physical gap in the gate "forces" the person to express honor—the space itself constituting social *constraints*.

The passage continues with a description of the way one rises up back to an erect position, but dares not stand motionless in the middle of the gate! This is because, as we have discussed in the context of the private house, the threshold was reserved for people of the highest standing; it is a heavily invested line that encapsulates the complementary convergence of "inner and the outer." This symbolic threshold constitutes a "reminding device" for those entering the house, to stop, pay attention, be aware, slow down, contemplate; it means that no carelessness is allowed in this very singular midpoint.

It takes us back to the *wai-nei* question of ritual: the interrelations between inner intention and external performance, and the level of flexibility allowed, if at all; in other words, is *li* a sequence of external "robot-like" movements or an internal, authentic intention? Are they equal in importance? This is a controversial subject. Shu-hsien Liu, for instance, emphasizes that Confucius *was* actually flexible (about rituals), saying that he had "always been able to react spontaneously according to his time and situation in a proper way" (1974, 149). If we assume *li* to be altered with *shi* 勢 and *shi* 時, the gate becomes a locus of change and "in-betweenness" which allows for a certain spatial freedom while still functioning as "pillars of order" in the Confucian society.

From this perspective, any alteration in *li* customs might have a great impact on society, in the same way that a tiny hinge moves a huge gate: it has the potential to lead to far-reaching consequences—between order and disorder, morality and corruption. Jones and Culliney believe the same, saying that "there is no between . . . the only alternative to one, is the other" but that does not mean that the actual ritual cannot change with time (and then needs repeating correctly); the same authors claim that "*li* has an inherent potential for growth," and that "ritual for Confucius was an organic entity with potential for growth or diminution over time" (1998, 399). Thus *li* needs to respond to the changing needs of society as otherwise it would lose its stability (stability = continuity and order).

Some passages in the *Analects* include gatekeepers, a "job" that transforms any gate into a "barrier which might potentially open" for those walking the road. In the following passage from *Analects* 14.38, a guard stops Zi Lu at the gate:

> Zi Lu spent the night at Shimen; at dawn, the gatekeeper asked him, "Where have you come from?" Zi Lu said: "From the Kong family." The gatekeeper said: "It is he, isn't it, who keeps on going resolutely though he knows the task is impossible?"

> 子路宿於石門. 晨門曰: 奚自? 子路曰: 自孔氏. 曰: 是知其不可而為之者與? [2]

When the gatekeeper learns that Zi Lu has come from the household of Confucius, he asks whether Confucius is the one who "never gives up" even in the face of impossible aspirations. The gatekeeper as a "person in between" probably asks Zi Lu about the rumor he heard at the gate that such people as Confucius are strange and pitiable because they go on and on against all odds (it almost evokes the image of Don Quixote); they would make personal sacrifices for the education of the masses, even though the leaders themselves show nothing but corruption. Herrlee Glessner Creel writes, "The picture of this venerable gentleman, in some respect still unsophisticated, setting off in his fifties to save the world by persuading the hard-bitten rulers of his day that they should not oppress their subjects, is in some ways ridiculous. But it is a magnificent kind of ridiculousness, found only in the great" (1949, 52). Robert Eno (2016) comments that Zi Lu (formal name Zhong You) was one of Confucius's senior disciples who, according to early texts, had a strong personality and was deeply loyal to Confucius, but on the other hand was "somewhat (an) unrestrained man . . . whose disposition could be problematic." We can sense the loyalty of Zi Lu conveyed through the text (as otherwise he wouldn't have disclosed where he came from), and I would have loved to be "a fly on the wall" to hear the rest of the conversation: Did Zi Lu restrain himself in response to the gatekeeper's demeaning description of Confucius? The gatekeeper might have attempted to ridicule, but I argue that he actually pointed to a key characteristic of both the master and his doctrine: perseverance and determination.

Indeed, we can assume that one of Confucius's qualities was perseverance: never giving up, going on and on in spite of getting no sympathetic/attentive/intelligent ear on his way. From the doctrine's point of view, it reflects the idea that *dao* is a never-ending process, never a quick or straightforward linear progression. It is probably the way Confucius grasped his own life's endeavor as a teacher, but plausibly wished his own commitment to serve as a personal example to others. But the qualities of the gatekeepers are noteworthy: they *know* how to listen *wen* 聞 and ask questions *wen* 問 (both characters include the gate radical)—they are "in between" inside and outside so that they become a sort of a "seismograph of the times."

In reference to the various methods advised in the *Analects* as the means by which one familiarizes himself with the prevailing norms and practices of the world, Karyn L. Lai emphasizes "listening (e.g., 1.10; 2.18; 4.8; 7.28, etc.), asking questions (*wen*; 3.15; 5.15; 10.14, etc.), [and] having discussions" (2019, 199). It is noteworthy that these methods share a common denominator: the act always takes place in the space in between two active parties, and, come to think of it, isn't is exactly the space that a gatekeeper inhabits? The gatekeeper by definition occupies the space between the outside and inside and as the one with authority over passage, people confide in him, or perhaps indulge in gossip-like chitchat with him—probably because they wish to form some kind of *guanxi* with the gatekeeper.

Indeed, an investigation into the etymology of *guanxi* and its everyday expression of Chinese vernacular *mei guanxi* 沒關係, reveals some intriguing meanings: *guanxi* means influential relationships in society, the expectations for equal reciprocity, and mutual protection; *guan* 關 is a barrier, a watchtower, or a strategic pass, while *xi* means "to care for" (Weingardt 2016, 7), which hints at the expectations to be "cared for" by the gatekeeper, because, obviously, they control the coming and going, entering and exiting of each and every individual, which might very well mean their future and even fate.

It is thus reasonable that the gatekeeper was a figure worth befriending, influencing, or developing "special connections" (*guanxi*) with. With time he develops a high level of intuitive perception (recognizing people), knowledge (knowing people of all walks of life), reading and writing skills (going through documents), and a position which gives him power over people (allowing or denying passage). The gatekeeper in the passage embodies two themes: (1) the way ordinary people saw Confucius and (2) Confucius's own point of view (dedicating his life to helping his fellowmen and transforming ways of governance). Confucius struggles against ignorance, indifference, and corruption, and his frustration and exasperation is expressed in the above passage.

The Confucian gate constitutes the line that transforms a person from his "before" and his "after" through self-cultivation; it signifies the very onset of opening: an opening that constitutes an opportunity for transformation (by a teacher) and the development of inner determination. The hinge of the gate symbolizes practice and internalization of "ritual propriety," and the gate is also the meeting point between teacher and pupil / teaching and studying.

An additional passage that refers to *li* and includes a reference to listening *wen* 聞 and asking *wen* 問 is *Ba yi* 八佾 3–15:

When Confucius entered the Grand Temple, he asked about everything. Someone said, "Who said Confucius is a master of ritual? He enters the Grand Temple and asks about everything!" Confucius, hearing this, said, "This is the ritual."

子入大廟、每事問. 或曰. 孰謂鄹人之子知禮乎. 入大廟、每事問. 子聞之、曰, 是禮也.

This passage exposes an important meaning of *li* as well as elucidating Confucius's inner thoughts—it tells us that upon entering the temple, Confucius had started asking questions. As we are given no details on the nature of the questions, it might not be the relevant point in the passage—meaning that Confucius is being criticized for the very act of asking (and not for the questions' content) as being the *wrong li*. When Confucius hears that (criticism), he states that, in fact, it is *asking* that constitutes ritual.

Can it be inferred that the act of asking by Confucius constituted a criticism of people who blindly follow conventions? Charlene Tan stresses that the episode sheds light on Confucius's attitude to thinking and evaluating something *si* 思 (and consequently *xue*), saying that the need for *si* is "where an inquirer autonomously and actively participating in and making sense of something" (2014, 4).[3] This is beautifully articulated by Confucius in *Xian Jin* 先進 4, "Yanhui doesn't assist me at all; in response to my words, he actually says nothing" (子曰: 回也非助我者也, 於吾言無所不說). It thus seems that Confucius encouraged active participation and critical thinking, which also includes dialogues (questions and answers) on multiple aspects of the mundane.

But isn't that dangerous? Wouldn't people be raising doubts as to the very need for ritual propriety or its nature and form? *Li* is supposed to function as "social pillars" or "loci of steadiness," repeated again and again throughout the generations (as a tradition), and consequently—is it advisable to encourage doubt and criticism? I suggest that two Confucian ideas or concepts may explain and underlie the successful continuity of Confucian *li*, namely, shame *chi* 恥 and respect *jing* 敬. The following passage refers to *li* and *jing* but also to Zi Lu again and can thus serve us in discussing the interconnectivity of these concepts; in addition, it constitutes a remarkable instance of the use of *architecture* as a metaphor, in *Xue Er* 學而:

> The Master said: "What is the zither (*si*) of Zi Lu doing at my gate?" The other disciples began not to respect Zi Lu; the Master said, "Zi Lu has ascended to the (waiting) hall, but he has not yet passed into the inner chamber room."
>
> 子曰: 由之瑟奚為於丘之門? 門人不敬子路. 子曰: 由也升堂矣, 未入於室也.

Confucius does not approve of Zi Lu playing at his gate (or leaving the musical instrument in its midst); when other disciples had heard this, they immediately lost respect for Zi Lu. Realizing this, Confucius quickly amends the situation: he compliments Zi Lu on his "ascent to the hall," meaning first, that he managed to *enter* the gate (the doctrine and practice), and second, that he succeeded in learning and/or in making progress on the path of self-cultivation. However, he hasn't as yet reached the level required to enter the innermost room (as we have seen before); note how an architectural path constitutes a metaphor for the various stages on the Confucian path (*dao*): the tangible and visual forms of architecture and behavior are fused with intangible and hidden intention.

Outside → Gate → Hall → Inside (Inner Chamber)

It brings to mind the inner sanctum *ao* 奥 discussed in chapter 3 (in the *Taixuan jing*) as both passages exhibit the same parallelism between architecture and stages on the path of self-cultivation, but with an interesting and significant difference: in *Taixuan jing* the inner sanctum *ao* carries connotations of a deep and *mysterious* space which constitutes the world beyond—a state prior to any division or distinctions that can be reached (by the sage) by returning backward to formlessness; such descriptions of the beyond (sometimes in the context of the afterlife) are indeed mentioned in Daoist texts. I argue, however, that in the Confucian context, the inner chamber (as opposed to *ao*) actually stands for a deeper level of *distinction*, that is, deeper into the doctrine of correct propriety!

As an *inappropriate* act was carried out by Zi Lu inside the gate . . . it signifies the thin line between propriety and or impropriety, but also a physical "step backward" or a failure to proceed (as opposite to "returning to the mysterious" in the Daoist context). It might be that Zi Lu, as commented previously, possessed a somewhat unrestrained character, but was still appreciated by his master, so that he "promotes" him to the waiting hall (a physical step forward) as he doesn't want him to lose respect by his fellow disciples. I suggest he uses the situation as an example to others, saying something along the lines of "Zi Lu might have made a mistake here, but he is determined and hard-working and as a consequence he is already *inside* . . . if he continues with the same spirit, he might one day succeed to enter the inner rooms (of the doctrines, of *dao*), and I encourage you (instead of criticizing him) to do the same."

The respect *jing* mentioned in the passage deserves more attention; in the Confucian context, respect depends on the conduct of the recipient, which means that it is closely linked with *li* (as a way things are carried out). Pengbo Liu indeed says that "*jing* is closely associated with notions like *shen* 慎 (caution), *gong* 恭 (respectfulness), *ci rang* 辭讓 (deference), and is considered to be fundamental to *li* 禮 (ritual propriety)," that is, to the "way or manner in which one performs (it)" (2019, 52–53). It does seem that the disciples' loss of respect for Zilu did not stem from the "what" but from the "how": nothing about his music or the zither was wrong per se, but the timing and the location—at the gate.

Can we find another mention of these four components—that is, gate, master, disciple, music—that could perhaps shed more light or give some contextual reference? I believe the following passage from *Analects* 17:20 (*Yanghou* 陽貨) might just do that:

> Ru Bei wished to see Kongzi, (but) Kongzi declined due to illness; just when (the bearer of) the message went out of the front gate, Kongzi took the zither and sang . . . in order that (Ru Bei) might hear him.
>
> 孺悲欲見孔子, 孔子辭以疾. 將命者出戶, 取瑟而歌. 使之聞之.

Why did Confucius refuse to see Ru Bei (Zu Pei)? Was it because of Ru Bei's flawed character or inappropriate behavior? If Ru Bei was indeed arrogant and ill-mannered, as Jing-Bao Nie suggests (2011, 127), it might be that the master was not convinced of his sincerity or commitment and therefore "did not open his gate" (as said, Confucius stated that "for an undetermined mind, I will not open the door"). If the master was just aiming at brushing off someone who surprises him at the wrong time (something we are all familiar with), and lied because he did not want to come across as offensive and rude, he wouldn't have taken up the zither to play for Ru Bei's ears . . . in fact, isn't it more offensive to lie and then make certain that the addressee *knows* that he was lied to?[4]

What did the master then wish to achieve through the playing and singing at the gate? Slingerland remarks that "most commentors generally see the purpose of this insult to be to inspire Ru Bei to reflect deeply on his own behavior and reform himself" (2003, 209). But a conclusion must be inferred from this exegesis: that Confucius expected Ru Bei to *understand* the message, accrediting him with a character that "enables him to suffer and insult and consequently turn inward to discover its justice" (A. Olberding 2012, 124–25); indeed, assuming the master refused him audience because of his flawed character, it seems rather odd.

I argue that the exegesis of the passage depends on whether Confucius's lie was calculated or impulsive; as opposed to conventional views of the great master, some textual indications hint at the later possibility. Christoph Harbsmeier indeed suggests that the above passage (among others) points to some unfamiliar personality traits of Confucius, e.g., impulsiveness, cynicism, irony.[5] If so, both the lying and the zither playing demonstrate a total lack of respect for Ru Bei; as discussed above, lack of respect stems from the recipient's inappropriate demeanor, which means that Ru Bei must have done something seriously unethical, improper, or rude. If the act of lying was impulsive, the music might be a way of apologizing or softening the blow . . . as if Confucius is admitting that he is also a mere human being: impulsive, uncourteous, and faulty at times.

If, on the other hand, the two actions were calculated, I suggest an exegesis that is based on a *wai/nei* conceptual point of view (with the gate positioned in between): the three actions that coalesce at the gate are (1) request to enter the inside (outside-to-inside), (2) an act of lying and refusal to open the gate (the threshold or center is closed), and (3) playing the zither upon the exit of the bearer of the message (inside-to-outside). I argue that the first and third actions constitute a *type of ritual*, and I will explain. The scene took place at a specific time and circumstances, which were not right for either of the two protagonists: Ru Bei is not yet ripe at his current stage in life, and for some reason, it was not the right time for Confucius to accept him (or perhaps anyone) inside.

The master's lie constituted the appropriate *action* for this specific time. As opposed to Western thought and Abrahamic theology which (broadly speaking) are based on the principal of truth as *conceptually* tied with morality, meaning that a lie is always a lie, always frowned upon as wrong and forbidden regardless of situation, circumstances, or timing, the attitude to truth and deceit in Chinese thought seems untangled from consequential moral judgment; in other words, it is acceptable to lie (i.e., it is not immoral) if the situation calls for it (interestingly, the concept of *upaya* in classic Indian thought suggests the same). As Paul J. D'Ambrosio indeed states, "Confucian morality includes the use of falsity or deception . . . without appealing to any form of consequentialism. For Confucius and Mencius moral behavior is determined by the situation as a whole, not one or two elements of it. Accordingly, there is no need to apologize or make excuses for misrepresenting a situation or one's own psychological content when it is the appropriate behavior" (2015, 138).[6] After lying and refusing to open the gate for Ru Bei, Confucius utilized the ritualistic act of music that inherently (and without words) carry truth, harmony, and sincerity to the outside. The second act, thus, at the very center of the gate symbolizes *potentiality* for change for Ru Bei: the gate might open for you one day—it depends on you. Again, music is an important clue . . . as Yong-qiang Lei says in reference to Confucius, "he advocated music education and believed that music is an outside display of the human's inner emotion" (2016, 267).

Finally, an important clue as to what Confucius thought about the proper relations between inside (heart-mind) and outside (people, society) is found in part 12 of *yan yuan* 顏淵 of the *Analects*, which says, "the master replied: do not look at what is contrary to propriety; do not listen to what is contrary to propriety; do not speak (in a manner) contrary to propriety; do not behave (in a manner) contrary to propriety" (非禮勿視, 非禮勿聽, 非禮勿言, 非禮勿動).[7] It actually warns against *specific* content penetrating the mind, namely, anything improper or amoral. This requires strong internal discipline as our senses easily succumb to external stimuli . . . it demands self-control at the outset!

The gate as the line between chaos and order is particularly emphasized in the *Mengzi* 孟子 (ca. 371–289 BC), who stands only second to Confucius in the humanist tradition, "a fact officially recognized in China for over a thousand years" (Lau 1970, 1).[8] Mencius held that the human heart contains the "sprouts" of the "four principles" (*siduan* 四端), namely, *ren* 仁, *yi* 義, *li* 禮, and *zhi* 智; all four need to be nourished—just like seeds of plants in the soil.[9] To my mind, Mencius relates one's mind-heart *xin* 心, and the inner flow of *qi* in the body to man's self-cultivation and stages of the virtuous man—from the petty or "small" people *xiaoren* 小人 through *xianren* 贤人, *junzi* 君子, and *shengren* 圣人. An inseparable part of self-cultivation, as was found associated with gates, is a unique awareness to the three Mencian principles, namely, right timing (endowed by heavens *tianshi* 天時), advantages of the environment (earth *dili* 地利), and man's will and harmony (*renhe* 人和).

A passage from the *Gong Sun Chou* (公孫丑下) II, 10.1 says,

Mengzi said: "Heavenly timing" is not equal to advantages of "earthly position," "earthly position" is not equal to "(collective) human harmony."

孟子曰: 天時不如地利, 地利不如人和.

The emphasis here is the "advantages of position and topography" *dili* 地利 which is also important in the context of construction of houses (formulating concrete forms out of listening to the environment). Yet another reference is found in the *teng wen gong* 滕文公下 II, 6, which says, "building shelters on trees or piles where the land is low (marshy) and constructing caves where the land is high (loess and terrace)" (Guo 2001, 3). It thus "listens" to the environment by correlating the tall (trees) and the low (land) and the deep (cave) to the hilly (land).[10] As will be seen, the emphasis given in the *Mencius* on "listening to" the topography, terrain, and flow is closely related to the high significance of water and floods (chapter 1).

The first passage that refers to the flood is the *Teng Wen Gong* (滕文公上) I (the second is in the *Li Lou* [離婁下] II57):

In Yao's time, the world was not as yet stable, the vast flood waters overflowing everything (in the world). Vegetation was thriving, birds and beasts reproduced in great number. (Hence) the five grains could not be grown, and (because of the great number of birds and beasts), man was pressed for space. Roads marked by the footprints of birds and beasts crisscrossed throughout the Middle Kingdom. Only Yao felt anxiety (because of this). (Thus) he elevated Shun to high office, and Shun employed Yi as the one responsible for fire. Yi set fire throughout the mountains and the marshes (to cause) the birds and beasts to escape into hiding. Yu cleared the nine rivers and the courses of Ji and Ta, enabling them to flow to sea. He opened way for Ru and Han and cleared the course of Huai and Si, to flow into the Yangzi River. Order thus restored, the people of the Middle Kingdom could cultivate the land for food. During this time, Yu spent eight years away from home, and though he passed in front of (the gate of) his own home, he did not get in.

當堯之時, 天下猶未平, 洪水橫流, 氾濫於天下. 草木暢茂, 禽獸繁
殖, 五穀不登, 禽獸偪人. 獸蹄鳥跡之道, 交於中國. 堯獨憂之, 舉
舜而敷治焉. 舜使益掌火, 益烈山澤而焚之, 禽獸逃匿. 禹疏九河,
瀹濟漯, 而注諸海; 決汝漢, 排淮泗, 而注之江, 然後中國可得而
食也.當是時也, 禹八年於外, 三過其門而不入, 雖欲耕, 得乎? 后
稷教民稼穡. 樹藝五穀, 五穀熟而民人育.[11]

As discussed in chapter 1, Sinic society met harshly with the dual facets
of water and rivers, and it is thus no wonder that the flood became a core
metaphor in its culture. The account tells us of an ancient (Yao) time, in
which there was no order, floods prevailed, and people could not cultivate
their land nor live decent lives. Yao employed Yi and Shu (each with his
special authority and skills) to help the people cultivate their land. But
who are these ancient kings and sages? Julia Ching says that such figures
as Yao, Shun, Yü, T'ang, Wen, and others, gained the reputation "not
merely as political ruler(s), but an idealized human being" (1983, 6).[12]

The mythical figure of Yu symbolizes the order that is borne out of
chaos, and is thus a key figure in the exegesis of the passage; beyond the
immediate connotation with the flood, Anne Birrell found yet another
reoccurring figure associated with Yu, namely, *Kung-Kung*.[13] This is a
curious figure who seems to possess an inclination toward work or labor,
and who is described in one narrative as being in conflict with the god of
heavens who is responsible for keeping the heavens and the earth separate.
This association to boundaries is highly significant; keeping these entities
separate is a sign of "setting order" in the universe, as opposed to the
chaotic and formless state. Thus, if in conflict with the god who prevents
the universe from collapsing back to chaos, it seems that *Kung-Kung* is a
rebel or a subordinate who attempts to prevent order—he is predisposed
toward chaos. Anne Birrell comments, "*Kung-Kung*'s challenge, therefore,
may be viewed as an archetypal act of rebellion. Traditional commentators, and modern scholars, such as Bernhard Karlgren, have interpreted
Kung-Kung's act in the first passage above as usurpation" (1997, 231).
Within this conceptual framework of the struggle between order and chaos,
Kung-Kung is repeatedly accused of destroying the way and corrupting
paradise, and, intriguingly enough, his main weakness is promiscuity and
uncontrolled sexual libido. Uncontrolled sexual libido is thus positioned
analogously to chaos . . . now, if we go back to the Mencian passage with
this new information, a certain layer of significance is revealed. Mencius
argues that Yu's ability did not stem from mere technological knowledge,
but from his "innate knowledge and understanding of the principles of

nature" (Birrell 1997, 244). What exactly is this knowledge? Isn't it the knowledge of the "principles of heavens and earth," and of the "natural rhythm" of things—including a particular awareness to sexual activity?

How is all this related to the gates in the last line? Let us think of a certain man who, for many years, is far away from home . . . working without break, continuously and intensively, experiencing tiredness and hunger, and certainly, homesickness. Presumably, such men who spent years away from their home went through sexual abstinence. Indeed, Birrell states that "colourful though this vignette may be, neither it, nor the Mencian reference should be allowed to obscure its implicit motif of sexual restraint, which the euphemism of passing by one's gates or not visiting home almost disguises. This motif resonates with that of uncontrolled sexual libido attached to the mythical" (1997, 246). Can we therefore assume that the conscious decision "not to enter the gate" metaphorically stands for refraining from joining one's wife inside (that is, deciding to refrain from sexual activity). If so, Yu decided to refrain from sex three times—every time he passed in front of his gate. Why? I suggest that this decision stems from the exertion involved with the challenging and ambitious project of putting *order* in the world after the flood—in order to succeed in the task, he first *needs to put order* in himself (evoking the passage from the *Daxue* quoted in the introduction). This is an intriguing interplay between the ability to control the flood and the *control* of one's body and desires!

Yu, who is in control of the outside (controlling the flood and putting order in the world), but also of his inside (controlling himself), is put in opposition to *Kung-Kung*, who manages neither. As the gate embodies the in-betweenness amid order and chaos, it signifies the thin line between "having control" and "losing control." The minute the gate opens (even a tiny crack), all is lost (like the Dutch boy and his finger in the dam). It signifies, yet again, the efficacy inherent in each and every decision we make along the path and the far-reaching consequences that it may carry. In this context, there is yet another subtexted gate, namely, the "gate of femininity," the female vagina (characterized by *yin*, the dark, the gate that gives life, etc. in Daoist sources). It might be that the gate of Yu's private home signifies or is analogous to his wife's "femininity gate," which he consciously chooses not to penetrate. One of the sources to indicate this analogy is the *Laozi Xiang'er zhu* (*Commentary on the Laozi*), which says, "the female is earth. A woman resembles it. The vagina is the gate" (Stephan Eskildsen, 2015, *Laozi-Xiang*, 19–20).[14] This parallelism between sexual desire/behavior and order/chaos in the context of *Kung-Kung* and the floods is discussed by Paul Goldin:

> Thus, it seems that at the very beginning of time, "licentious-ness" 淫 and "dissolute pleasures" 湛樂 were already contrasted with the orderly government that preserves—and gains its strength from—the regular forces of nature. The fact that the names of both sins are based on aquatic images (overflow and dissipation) only strengthens their association with the flooding wares. *Kung-Kung* and *Kun* are beings who disrupt the flow of the rivers, so that "disaster and chaos" flourished together. (Goldin 2001b, 93)

Importantly, this sexual restraint is time dependent (as opposed to total celibacy) as the Mencian doctrine sees sexual desire as a natural need—similar to the need for food. Leon Antonio Rocha, investigating the etymology and development of the character *xing* 性 (human nature), refers to the famous correspondence between Gaozi and Mencius in relation to human nature, saying that "Gaozi states that the appetite for food and sex forms part of human nature, summed up in the famous phrase *shi se xing ye*. Here, sex is not represented by the character *xing*, but by *se*" (2010, 5).

However, notwithstanding the Mencian grasp of sexual act as a natural component of *xing*, it is clear that this urge should be restrained and controlled in a way that is parallel to the containment of *qi* and the heart-mind *xin*.[15] Mencius sees *qi* in a broader sense than the physical, as a substance that influences and even determines multiple facets of our emotional disposition *qing* 情, decision-making, knowledge, and wisdom *zhi* 智. Table 5.1 attempts to parallel *qi* of sexual desire and water according to the Mencius.

Table 5.1. A comparison of actual and metaphoric uses of water and *qi* in the *Mencius*.

Qi of sexual desire	Water
Mandatory for the continuation of life and is part of human nature.	Mandatory for the continuation of life and is part of the natural world.
When in surplus, in a state of over-flow, yi gets corrupted, licentiousness prevails, consequently, chaos.	When in surplus, in a state of over-flow (flood), all is ruined, conse-quently, chaos.

Source: Author provided.

The quality that can overcome overflowing states of *qi* is, according to the *Mencius*, man's will. In the *Gong Sun Chou* I (公孫丑上), it says,

The will is above *qi*, *qi* fills up the whole body. The will is first, *qi* comes second. Therefore, it is said: "Hold on to your will, (so there will be) no sudden loss of *qi*."

夫志, 氣之帥也; 氣, 體之充也.夫志至焉, 氣次焉. 故曰: 持其志, 無暴其氣.

Thus, a strong will and a determined mind can control *qi* but reaching such level of control requires practice, dedication, and also courage—all part of the journey of self-cultivation and fulfillment of potentiality. As said, an inseparable skill of that path is sensing timing and circumstances as a "doctrine of timeliness," which most simply holds, as Eno says, "that the correct action in any particular situation can only be assessed in context" (2016, 13).

Mencius's analogy that sees our incipient tendencies and sensual dispositions as vegetative sprouts (which, as mentioned, can both be cultivated), seems to be the target of criticism by Zhuangzi, as he uses the very Mencian terms "sprouts of benevolence and righteousness" in the *Qiwulun* 齊物論 ("Leveling-Out Opinions") 11 of the Inner Chapters, saying that from his own point of view, "the sprouts of benevolence and righteousness are all mixed up, and natural outlines chaotically intermingle, thus when it comes to evil (sprouts)—how can I possibly know to distinguish between them" (自我觀之, 仁義之端, 是非之塗, 樊然殽亂, 吾惡能知其辯). This means that Zhuangzi sees no categorial opposition between them, or, in other words, does not find objective ethicality possible.

To continue with gate passages in the *Mencius*, with emphasis on barriers and temporality, let us read the following passage from *Jin Xin* (盡心下) II:

Mencius said: "In ancient times, strategic gates were (put up and) used to defend against violence; nowadays, strategic gates are used to bring violence."

孟子曰: 古之為關也, 將以禦暴. 今之為關也, 將以為暴.

This passage constitutes a perfect example of "architecture as metaphor and correlation between concrete signifier (the gate) and abstract idea—as signified." As mentioned before, the character *guan* 關 is often rendered "to close," but I argue (to be discussed in chapter 6) that it refers to strategic gates which had been erected at narrow mountain passages as barriers against continuous threats, and later became an inseparable part of the borders between provinces and between the state and its neighbors.

Yuri Pines mentions an event surrounding Lord Ling of Qi 齊靈公 (r. 581–554 BC) which incorporates some of the main characteristics of warfare strategies in ancient China (such as the method of piling up horse carcasses to block the passage), but furthermore, demonstrates the importance of topography and the spatial singularity of narrow passages between mountains or between a mountain and a pond (as in this example). As times passes, these narrow passages develop into central (sometimes famous) "venous valves" of the Middle Kingdom; intriguingly, some of these checkpoints, as is mentioned in the quote, are still in use by the Chinese authorities today.

> The location of this event—the vicinity of Guang Hamlet—is precisely the location where the starting point of the Qi Long Wall was erected a century later. A narrow pass between the large pond adjacent to the ancient flow of the Ji River to the west and the Taishan Mountain massif to the east is an ideal topographic location to control the movement northward along the Ji River; even now it is still used as a checkpoint by the Public Security Bureau on the National Highway. Cumbersome chariots could be blocked in this pass and adjacent paths just by a single large chariot or by piling up horses' carcasses. Back then, there was no need to build a major wall: a small strategically located fortification (the "Gate of Defense") was enough to slow down the invaders. (Pines 2018, 756)

As Mencius lived during the Warring States period (that is, later than the period of the above quote), it is reasonable to assume that checkpoint gates or *guan* barriers were already well positioned at such central junctions and passages—heavily guarded against threats and invasions; however, Mencius's proclamation of a shift between ancient times ("strategic gates were [put up and] used to defend against violence") and his present time ("nowadays, strategic gates are used to bring violence"), might refer to his observation of a real change in the utility of these *guan* gates.

Starting out as mere defense barriers in which patrolling guards watched afar for threats and blocked the advances of enemies, these *guan* checkpoints had indeed constituted a strategy of "prevention of violence" and protection of the state, but it might be that with time they developed into loci from which violence was *initiated*—as points from which the state attacks. Did Mencius pass through these *guan* gates on his travels in the country? Did he conceive of these gates as representative of aggressive governing and population-control methods?

Let us now move to the challenging passage of *Jin Xin* (盡心下) II:

Gaozi said: "The sound of Yu's (musical instrument) surpassed the sound of King Wen's (musical instrument)."

Mencius said, "How come you say that?"

He said: "It (the musical instrument) is almost completely worn out."[16]

He said: "How is that sufficient (reason)? (See) the (carriages') ruts on the path through city gates—are they created by (the force of only) two horses?"[17]

高子曰: 禹之聲, 尚文王之聲.

孟子曰: 何以言之?

曰: 以追蠡.

曰: 是奚足哉?

城門之軌, 兩馬之力與?

The passage is open to quite a few interpretive directions, such as relating to the subject of music as ritual propriety, to aesthetic pleasures in general, or perhaps a discussion of "arriving at conclusions."[18] Disciple Gao argues that because the musical instrument has almost worn out completely, the sound produced in Yi times is better than in King Wen's times. The analogue made here between a "better sound" and "worn out" is surprising as we naturally assume that the more worn out an instrument or device is, the *worse* it would play or work (i.e., lacking in quality or efficacy).

Thus, what can this state of "worn out" mean? Perhaps it signifies "been through much use" ("have been practiced a lot") or just simply, an antique instrument. As Yu is mythologically older than King Wen, Ivanhoe explains it by saying that "Mencius is suggesting that Gaozi failed to recognize that Yu's bell was much older than King Wen's and hence subject to greater wear. (2002b, 160). Is Mencius referring to the quality of the music produced or to the joy it brings? The etymology of the character for music *yue* 樂 demonstrates a shared phonetic root with joy and happiness, and, by the early third century BC, as Erica Brindley stresses, "authors began to exaggerate this linguistic connection by asserting the equivalence of the two terms, music and joy" (2006, 2).

Taking all these points into consideration, the first half of the passage seems to say that due to the lengthy use of the instrument (hinting at practice, long-standing traditions, and time), the sound produced is better, and consequently, the musical ritual *liyue* 禮樂 is of higher quality. As we have discussed before, "ritual propriety" has internal and external facets, particularly when it comes to the relationship between the inner intention and psychological state, and the external sound produced. Peter Wong Yih-Jiun refers to this interplay of *wei/nei* in *liyue*, saying that in Confucian literature, "*liyue* is often given an inner-outer distinction according to function. Such a classical understanding is found in the following passage from the "Record of Music" *Yueji* 樂記: "Music (*yue*) acts within (*zhong* 中), ritual (*li*) works from without. Since music acts within, one's feelings are [rendered] genuine (*qing* 情); and since ritual works from without, one's appearance is [rendered] refined" (2012, 248).

The passage thus deals with music as representing ritual practice which requires continuous practice and learning. Willard J. Peterson notes that indeed "Mencius gave us no grounds for doubting that, used with care, perceptions, reasons, and traditions can be relied upon as a source of 'knowing'" (1979, 318). Mencius agrees with Gaozi that the music in Yu's time was better than in King Wen's time, but disagrees that it is the external appearance of the instrument (its degree of usage) and time/practice that constitute the only "factors of evaluation" for the quality of sound/music/ritual.

On the other hand, as music is closely linked with pleasure and joy, it might be a warning against overindulgence . . . indeed, was it Gaozi's mistake to criticize Confucians for being heavily indulgent in music (and pleasures in general)? As I have argued previously, in the same way that Mencius perceived a very thin line between order and chaos, between a barbaric behavior and a cultivated conduct, music can thus be accepted as an aesthetic and *correct* form of "ritual propriety," but it can become a source of overindulgence quite easily . . . simply by "crossing the thin threshold." If this happens, both music and ritual can transform from being "instruments" on the path to self-realization to a sought-after "end-target." Hongkyu Kim interprets the passage to represent "Gaozi's criticism of the Confucian inclination toward ritual and music" (especially by Daoists), and adds that, "of course, Mencius rebuked him for his criticism, and the dialogue between them comes to an end there, indicating that Mencius's logic prevailed" (2012, 68).

Indeed, the second part of the passage stresses that Mencius couldn't accept Gaozi's argument and logic, and this unwillingness is expressed through an ironic reference to the city gate's ruts. It is ironic because ruts at city gates cannot be created by two horses or a single chariot, but the lengthy accumulation of endless people treading, horses galloping, and the wheels of carriages. Even this analogy carries a few layers of significance. First, just as the ruts at the city gates' paths constitute the accumulated impact of the passage of multitudes, hence, in the same way, opinions, assumptions, and conclusions cannot be made based on *one* factor only (in this case, the state of the musical instrument).

Second, as will be discussed in chapter 6, the gate of the Chinese city constitutes the threshold between its inner sphere of culture, order, and long-standing traditions, and its external boundaries that are disorganized and disorderly. The ruts might represent a shift in rural-urban preference or attitude, as they hint at the city's size and population, commercial productivity, and so on. Thus, they might represent the successful progress of a city as a man-made achievement, that is, the city becoming a symbol of harmony, culture, and in-out trade. An interesting passage that relates to "how to do things in appropriate ways" is found in *Wan Zhang* (萬章下) II:

> If (a commoner) is summoned (the same way) as a sage, how dare he go? Let alone when a "man of virtue" is summoned in an inappropriate way! He who wishes to meet a "man of virtue" but conducts it in an inappropriate way, is (exactly) like wishing (and inviting) him to come in (but) closing the gate (in his face). "Internal propriety" is the path; "ritual propriety" is the gate. Only *junzi* are thus able to follow this path, going in and out of its gate.

以士之招招庶人, 庶人豈敢往哉。況乎以不賢人之招招賢人乎?
欲見賢人而不以其道, 猶欲其入而閉之門也. 夫義, 路也; 禮, 門
也.惟君子能由是路, 出入是門也.

This passage refers to ritual propriety, internal propriety *yi* 義, and the gate, and is made of the following logical sequence of reasonings:

1. Inviting a commoner in a way that is appropriate for a man of virtue will result in a refusal by the commoner. Why? Because even a commoner would realize that he was given undue honor.

2. Inviting a man of virtue in an inappropriate way constitutes a worst-case scenario . . . the man of virtue would not go.

3. The above (no. 2) parallels a situation in which a man of honor is invited and, when he is just about to enter the house/palace/court, the gate is being shut to his face. Even in our contemporary times (Chinese or Western), it would be considered highly disrespectful and/or shameful.

4. Then, we learn that this path (which can be appropriate or not), is in fact *yi*; and the said gate is in fact *li*.

5. Only *junzi* are able to follow this path, and only *junzi* are, thus, able to use the gate (to enter and exit).

Here again, it is useful to be reminded of the many and varied rites involving gates, in the Classics as well as the *Analects*; the gate's threshold constitutes a highly sensitive line as it stretches between the inner sphere of the "host" and the outer sphere of the "guest" . . . it is the threshold on which the most delicate and careful behavior is required, to prevent "losing face" and disrespect between the parties. I imagine it as a "choreographed dance" in which both parties coordinate and resonate simultaneously in order for the whole "singular moment in time and place" to be accomplished. The meeting of two parties (each from different backgrounds), reveals yet another layer of "ritual propriety"— one connected to the principle of complementary opposites; in order for such a meeting to succeed in harmony, both parties need to *give up* their respective "characteristic (personal or cultural) load," and converge in the middle ground of the threshold.

This is exactly why *li* is so important . . . it might be seen as an artificial and external behavior ("going through the motions"), but to the eyes, mind, and heart of the opposite party, it conveys humble respect, which, in return, causes them to reciprocate in the same manner. This is the very essence of diplomacy, ceremonies, and even mundane courteous manners, such as saying hello, shaking hands (West), or bowing (Japan). As for the third and fourth points above, if the way of inviting a man of virtue is wrong, it is like shutting the gate in his face; in extension, inviting a man of virtue through the wrong path which is *yi*, immediately makes *li* not useful! It means, I propose, that *li* is nothing without "internal propriety," genuine intention, and wisdom.

Furthermore, the passage defines ritual propriety as the gate, but the gate to what? I suggest that it is the gate that stands between the innermost world of the "virtuous man" (his internal, private realm) and the external environment and society (public domain). In other words, if the ritual is conducted correctly from within, the gate will open appropriately to the outside, and by "outside" it refers to society that observes it. Indeed, in order for traditions and knowledge to continue through the generations, the "virtuous man" must serve as an example to others. This is perhaps why Mencius brings former kings and sages as exemplars—as guidance for people and leaders of his time, because, according to Mencius, all people possess *yi* naturally but it constantly needs cultivation and guarding—or it might become corrupted.

Such a corrupted *yi*, I hold, is the meaning of the "gate which closes in his face" . . . because *li* would appear (even externally) ungenuine and inauthentic. This is intriguingly connected to previous passages that touched upon "ritual propriety" and its external-internal aspects. In the fifth section, it says that only *junzi* can follow the path (of internal propriety), and only *junzi* can indeed *use* the gate. In this context, I find it curious that the first "way" mentioned in the passage is *dao* 道 ("inviting a man of virtue in the wrong *dao*"), but the two "paths" mentioned later are actually *lu* 路, which can mean way, path, route, journey, and so on.

Delving into this point further, I have counted 25 *lu* and 150 *dao* in the *Mencius*, each of which is used for a different purpose and meaning. In the passage it is said, "not by the means or through *his dao*" (不以其 道), meaning that by "his/their" he refers to *xiaoren*, but *xiaoren*, though a virtuous stage, is still considered less advanced than *junzi* . . . thus, how can we explain that *dao* (arguably the most important term in Chinese philosophy) is used for *xiaoren* whereas *lu* is used for *junzi*? Jim Behuniak argues that Mencius grasped the proliferation of philosophies that advocate alternative courses as an obstacle to *dao*, and that in this context, *dao* can be understood as "teachings" and "courses advocated by these alternative schools" (2005, 23). If indeed *dao* in this specific passage refers to such "alternative courses," then perhaps the meaning of 不以其道 is "the way he is being summoned is not according to his teaching," and therefore it would be disrespectful to accept! On the other hand, the path *lu* mentioned in relation to the *junzi* constitutes the very journey of self-cultivation, emphasized to such a high degree in the *Mencius*.

This connects us back to the "seeds" of the four virtues, which, as Willard J. Peterson says, "have the same endowment, but differences in soil, weather, and cultivation affect the 'fruit' of essentially the same seeds" (1979, 313). These sprouts or seeds of the four virtues that are contained, according to Mencius, in one's *xin* and are represented as analogous to biological seeds of a plant—that need water, sunlight, and nourishment. Indeed, these "Mencian sprouts" need constant cultivation in the same way that man needs constant self-cultivation on the path to becoming a *junzi*. *Yi* is exactly that: nurturing *qi* through the accumulative practice of all that is correct and appropriate, and I believe that in this context, the *Mencius* refers to a wider circle of nature beyond man . . . the concept of *qi* together with the metaphor of seeds or sprouts, evokes a reference to the natural world and its continuous evolutionary process.

A tiny seed of a lofty tree contains all that it needs (as "genetic potentiality") but whether this potentiality would be fulfilled depends on its cultivation (soil, water, light, etc.) in the same way that man needs cultivation to bring his or her inner goodness and potential into fruition and fulfillment.[19]

The Longing to Break Gender Division: The Half-Open Gate

This is perhaps the most curious type of gate; it combines the context of social distinctions *and* the afterlife, and comes in the form of half-open gates depicted on tombs or as murals inside tomb chambers. These depicted scenes usually include a woman standing just behind a half-open or even slightly opened gate/doorway, peering out (figures 5.2 and 5.3). Intriguingly, the "women in the doorway" was a common motif in late Han dynasty exactly because in this era it was improper for women to cross the boundary of their "internal quarters" ("way of the women" *fu dao* 妇道) over to the front gate of the house or to the quarters of men.[20]

Figure 5.2. Woman at a half-open gate depicted on an Eastern Han period sarcophagus, Sichuan. After Paul R. Goldin (2001a). Illustration by the author.

Figure 5.3. A stone pillow depicting a woman at a half-open gate. Photo by the author.

In *Neize* (內則) 57 of the *Lijing*, we encounter the following gender-distinction instructions:

> Ritual propriety (*li*) commences at a cautious (set of relationship between) husband and wife, (because), as they build their home, they make outside and inside distinct. The men reside

in outside, the women inside. The deeper the mansion, the stronger its gates, guarded by gatekeepers. The men do not enter (the) inside, the women do not enter (the) outside.

禮, 始於謹夫婦, 為宮室, 辨外內. 男子居外, 女子居內, 深宮固門, 閽寺守之. 男不入, 女不出.

The line that says "they make outside and inside distinct" is of most significance. The gates between the inside and the outside mark the separation between the genders—a visual and cultural symbol of order and morality. The initial and basic state of these gates is that of guarded containment that, to my mind, carries a twofold significance: first, their mere existence is always a reminder of the *potential* danger of *breaking* the rules, which means the destruction of moral order and the potential deterioration to anarchy (the breaking down of conventional social constructs); the second significance constitutes the opposite . . . the gate in between the genders constitutes a *yinyang* type of fusion—of *both* male and the female characteristics—the sexual act that unites male and female.

Isn't it human nature to desire what you cannot have or what is banned? Intriguing it is, therefore, to find half-open gates depicted on tombs . . . expressing the desire (in the afterlife) for sexual freedom and the elimination of division between the genders, as shall be seen shortly.

Bret Hinsch studied this very subject and he writes,

> The distinction between inner and outer had a major impact on gender relations. Women came to be generally associated with inner spaces and men with the outer. Prescriptive rules separating the sexes employed these spatial metaphors, thereby taking segregation from abstract rhetoric to physical practice. These physical metaphors allowed the boundaries between women and men to become objectified in space. Separation of the sexes now went beyond work roles; the surrounding space of daily life was gendered, forcing men and women farther apart. (2003, 601)

When Sima Qian described the decadence leading to the fall of the Shang dynasty, he employed the dramatic image of men and women mixing freely among wasteful luxury. The implication is that the failure to segregate the sexes will bring on a dynasty's collapse—a theme that is repeated regularly in historical writing (e.g., the state of Jin was said to have sunk into chaos because the state's ruler failed to separate the sexes). According to this historical view, during the Han dynasty, rulers were "criticized for failing to keep men and women apart" (Hinsch 2003, 606).

Some of the scenes evoke an atmosphere suggestive of eroticism and sexual freedom—as representative of the "forbidden fruit," while others even go as far as depicting the "woman at the doorway" in explicit sexual scenes that convey an atmosphere of danger—a blunt and self-conscious representation of social taboos. The world behind the gates promises sexual delight, with the woman herself sometimes described as "wandering beyond the gates in search of satisfaction" (Goldin 2001a, 547). The gate challenges moral order, existing between the conventional and the forbidden, the separated and the united, between life and death; as Wu Hung says, this gateway "occupies a 'luminal position' and functions as an 'intermediary stage between life and death'" (quoted in Goldin 2001a, 539). The woman stands for a pathway between the mundane, tedious world in which a lady's erotic or sexual invitations constitute a fantasy and the fabulous world where such fantasies of sexual liberation actually become actualized (Goldin 2001a, 548).

The gate opens an "opportunity" for sexual and social freedom: women depicted as standing at half-open doors, peeping out or even involved in implicit sexual acts—socially considered taboo—evoke the excitement, fear, arousal, and imaginary dreams associated with the unknown world across the gate. In an intriguing way, even in this case—embodying the space in between real, concrete lives and ideal, imaginary worlds, the half-open gate constitutes a symbolic apparatus for the fulfillment of potentiality; here, potentiality refers to something that is universally human, that is, the fulfillment of desires, dreams, and wishful thinking that belong to the inner and private world of the individual— and its resonance-dissonance relationship with the external world. But yet again, it is tightly interconnected with culture: if we venture further out from the circle of the individual—to the wider sociopolitical circle, the half-open gate becomes a cultural symbol of freedom from social and moral constraints; from this point of view, it can be considered a representative of the long and winding path of philosophical debate that seems to characterize Chinese society from its early days, that is, whether to succumb and embrace the chaotic aspect of life (e.g., animalistic and natural instincts, the path of least resistance, Daoist spontaneity, etc.) or to fight against it in order to create and maintain order in the world (e.g., humanistic approach, Mencian self-control, etc.). I therefore argue that the half-open gate is not a mere curiosity or a private case of sexual fantasy but is in effect a semiotic landmark within Chinese symbolic culture.

Chapter 6

The Gate as Authority

The Construction of Order and Control

What is it that makes a man human?
It is his (ability to make) distinctions (decipher boundaries).

人之所以為人者何已也? 曰: 以其有辨也

—Xunzi 5

The gates explored in this chapter have been found to primarily function as barriers—a gate in a closed state. In this particular assembly of gates, the reason underlying their closed state is an ideology and aspiration for order and control as sought after by the authorities. By "authority" I refer to any figure or body in the sociopolitical dimension that decides on the behavior and movements of the individual and the populace, for example, governance, city municipalities, or warfare strategies. Within this sociopolitical framework that aspires for order, there are variances in how closed a gate is—from strict barriers between provinces to gates that close at certain times (e.g., gates of the city), and others. One of the most important types of gates in early China is the checkpoint gate—important both as a tool in the hands of state but also (and as a consequence) as an inseparable part of the daily life of anyone who ventured out of his village, city, and certainly beyond. The checkpoint gate constituted the openings along the boundary between states and provinces and manifested the state's aspiration for order and control of the populace. It is thus no wonder that it found its way into imaginary (philosophical and religious) journeys, as well as into Chinese folklore. With this type of checkpoint gate—*closed as default*—we begin this chapter.

Gates on the Roads: Journey as *dao*

As mentioned in chapter 1, city avenues were referred to as *dao*, and in the most general sense when it comes to Chinese thought, it is important (within the deeply philosophical significances attributed to the term) not to neglect or overlook this very concrete and "earthly" aspect of *dao*—a physical path or road along which one treads, and upon which gates are erected. It indeed corresponds best with "way-making," as suggested by Ames and Hall: "At its most fundamental level, *dao* seems to denote the active project of 'moving ahead in the world,' of 'forging a way forward,' of 'road building.' Hence, our neologism: 'way-making.' By extension, *dao* comes to connote a pathway that has been made, and hence can be traveled" (2003, 57). Thus "way-making" constitutes not only the active aspect of *dao* but its correlate manifestations in all dimensions and spheres, concrete and abstract. How indeed was *dao* referred to in the physical aspect—as a road? Do we have any textual reference to early China's roads and routes?[1] According to Needham, the Zhou administration classified different types of paths and roads according to width and length; this information, which was preserved in the *Zhouli* 周禮 (*Rites of Zhou*), distinguished between two types of roads, namely, *dao*—which refers to imperial highways that are wide enough for two chariots, and *jing* 徑, which refers to narrow paths that are passable only for one person or single-horse carriage (1971, 4). This classification is important as in some cases it sheds light on the conceptualization of *dao* (see discussion of *jing* in chapter 7). Roads fulfilled a crucial part in the efforts to control the movement of the populace in early China, particularly during the Qin and Han dynasties; this was carried out by the erection of checkpoint gates called *guan* 關 along roads and in between provinces; it was especially important at strategic points that constituted "the weakest links" and could potentially endanger the safety of the state.

At these checkpoint gates, gatekeepers questioned the people going in and out, examined their papers, and inspected their records (Sou 2018, 223). Anyone passing or leaving through these gates without authorization got punished, which ranged from tattooing to foot amputation. Travelers had to present "passports" and travel documents in order to pass the gates, while the names of officials who traveled as part of their duties were kept as a special list in the hands of "Gate Registers" *men ji* 門籍 (Sou 2018, 233).

One intriguing type of "passport" was the *fu* 符, a tally device that was usually made of two parts: one part was given to the official traveling while the other was kept with the gatekeeper; only when the two pieces matched each other completely was passage granted. How symbolic it is that only when two parts *conjoin* at the gate, it actually opens up, similarly to the complementary workings of the *yin* and *yang*. Such gate tallies were made of bronze, gold, and even jade and were made in the shape of various animals; an important animal for a tally was the tiger, named *hufu* 虎符 (figure 6.1), which was used by the emperor himself to command and/or dispatch the army. One of the earliest tiger tallies to be found (Warring States period) is exhibited in the Shaanxi History Museum's collection.

The text on this particular *hufu* states that the right half of the tally is held in the hands of the emperor, while the left half is issued to the governor of Duxian County. Only when these two parts conjoin to form the whole figure, a military message would be sent with an instruction to dispatch more than fifty soldiers.

Figure 6.1. A two-part Chinese *fu* 符 (gate tally) shaped as a tiger. Public domain.

When it comes to private road travel in early China, especially to unfamiliar territories (and certainly beyond China's borders), it must have evoked a mixed array of feelings and emotions in the traveler's heart-mind, such as curiosity but also fear and doubt. It probably also involved superstitions and prejudice as to remote places and its inhabitants ("the other"). Indeed, Daniel Sungbin Sou remarks that documents from the Qin and Han dynasties indicate that individual traveling was quite limited—precisely because of the fear to travel "across territory fraught with danger and uncertainty," and mentions the existence of *rishu* 日書 or "daybooks" that listed "inauspicious days to travel or places to avoid" (2018, 241).

Indeed, the fear of the unknown constitutes a shared theme in two types of correlating travels—the physical road and imagined journeys to the afterlife. Such checkpoint gates (and even their gatekeepers) constitute an inseparable part of real journeys and in parallel serve as models for imaginary journeys to worlds beyond. Guolong Lai explains that

> to understand what the otherworldly journey may have meant in early China, one must first consider the meaning of everyday journeys. The imaginary journey was likely modeled after real travels that people experienced during their lifetime. Death was conceptually regarded as 'a grand journey' (*daxing* 大行) and funerary rites were directly related to travel rituals. (2005, 167)

This is significant to the understanding of Chinese correlative thinking in general and to the meaning of journeys in the lives of the ancient Chinese. As "cosmology and the conception of the afterlife are inextricably connected" (G. Lai 2005, 11),[2] descriptions of otherworldly journeys demonstrate how their cosmological loci and the end destination varies according to the deceased's social status. Guolong Lai mentions, for instance, that war casualties or people who died of unnatural causes were buried in different loci, "located in the wilds of Mount Buzhou, the Gate to the Dark Capital in the northwest" (2005, 11). Mount Buzhou was considered "the nexus of the spirit world, the axis connecting the spirit and the human realm or the Gate of the Dark Capital (*youdu zhi men*) where the spirits reside" (G. Lai 2015, 163). Diagrams of the "Divination on the Placement of Doors" on bamboo strips were discovered in Qin tomb number 11 at Shuihudi, Yunmeng, Hubei Province.

In some tombs (e.g., the tomb of Li He in Shuangheng Village, Shaanxi), the front of the sarcophagus is incised with the image of a gate with a lock, flanked by two guards with a carved bird on top. In

Xi'an, tombs of high officials have been discovered with stone gates and stone outer coffins from the Tang dynasty. The gates are also carved with large pictures of beasts and the two stone blocks supporting the posts of the gate are sculpted to resemble squatting lions. Beyond archeological evidence, such cosmic encounters (e.g., with locked gates or gatekeepers) are richly described in numerous poems; Stanza 52, for instance, of the Chinese poem "Li Shao" by Qu Yuan (340–278 BC) refers to a curious encounter with the gatekeeper of heavens and earth: "I bade the gatekeeper of *tian-di* to open the gate-barrier, (but) he leaned on the Changhe gate and stared at me"(吾令帝閽開關兮, 倚閶闔而望予).

As mentioned before, the Changhe gate constitutes a barrier situated just before reaching the gate of heavens; its gatekeeper only stares at the protagonist and says nothing; the overall atmosphere is vague and mysterious and the scenario is enigmatic: What does this silence indicate? Is it a refusal to open the gate or an interval in time (*jian*) that represents (through emptiness) an opportunity for the protagonist to transform? Does he need to transform as a prerequisite for the gate to open?

Kirkova says the Changhe gate seems to be "a permanent landmark in the subsequent description of cosmic journeys, where it always tests the visionary travelers at the transitory point to heaven and indicates a passage between planes of being" (2016, 206). It was even suggested by the Neo-Confucian interpreter Li Guangdi that the *problem* (i.e., the delay at the gate) is not due to the protagonist at all . . . but actually signifies "the wise king not awakening" (Zikpi 2014, 410). Personally, the story evokes an immediate association with Kafka's parable "Before the Law" (1914)—one of the most iconic stories in Western literature that curiously involves a protagonist, a gatekeeper and a closed gate . . . it certainly begs for a comparative analysis.[3]

In tombs and mausoleums, gatekeepers are depicted at singular locations as semiotic reminders of their control—over the inner space but also over the soul's journey. As Tonia Eckfeld says, these surveillance guards "mark the beginning of the tomb tunnel and designate a change from the first zone outside the tomb's palace compound; to the second zone within the palace gates" (2005, 96). Similarly to checkpoints on real journeys, they had to monitor all movement in and out of the gates. At times we are witness to a visual representation of the gatekeepers' gaze (as in the above poem); Eckfeld notes that this gaze of the palace gatekeeper and his pointing index finger constitute an indication that the viewer required a tally that had to be matched with his own before he or she could proceed to the tombs' corridors and chambers (as discussed in chapter 5), adding that, "this gives the impression that those permitted beyond the wooden door are passing to a different and superior scheme" (2005, 98). I find these parallels between the world "under" (tombs), and the world "above" (the heavens), between life and the afterlife, between body-mind and the cosmos, and the necessity for gatekeepers and checkpoints in all these dimensions—nothing less than a fascinating instance of Chinese "correlative thinking." The checkpoint gate on the roads signifies a *potential* . . . a promise of discovery and/or transformation once one succeeds in crossing over—but on the other side, it might just prove itself to be a disillusion. E. Y. Wang aptly describes these gates on imaginary journeys as a "heartbreaking place," and adds that while the gateway

> promises a journey leading to the land ruled by the Queen Mother of the West and other frolicking immortals, one knows nothing of what lies beyond it. The Great Beyond is a country from whose bourne no traveler returns. Up to this point the living can accompany the spirit of the deceased on the journey; beyond this point, the deceased's spirit will have to fare for itself. This boundary is thus heavily invested psychologically, emotionally and symbolically . . . the pillar-tower gateway is therefore the setting for two separate, albeit related, actions: the journey toward the otherworld and the transformation of the deceased's presence into iconic figures—the double portraits—straddling the threshold between this world and the otherworld. (2005, 31–34)

The gate is thus loaded with the significance of a potential turning point in one's life and afterlife, a transformation or, possibly, rejection. Yet another instance of concrete-abstract homologies are gates that are depicted on tombs and symbolize the passage of the soul into the spiritual world, and include either a figure who greets the deceased at the entrance or an impressive procession of carriages that is welcomed by officials. Sofer and Rudolph remark that such processions were common in Han funerary carvings and, "have been interpreted by some scholars as representations of the journeys taken by the deceased when they were alive" (1987, 73).

E. Y. Wang describes the minute details included in such processional scenes, such as images of the Queen Mother of the West who resides in the immortal realm—as the ultimate destiny of the deceased—and emphasizes how "the overall composition accentuates the gateway's symbolic role" (2005, 31). In the *Baozishan* sarcophagus, we see an open gate through which a rider guides the soul of the deceased into the world beyond, which, as Angela Falco Howard writes, includes "images of entrainment, immortality and Confucian moral tales," implying a desire that the departing soul would enter through the *que* gate to an eternal realm of happiness (2003, 93) (Figure 6.2).

This illustrates the attempts made by the ancient Chinese to imagine and illustrate this thin yet immensely significant line between these spheres—where the gate of heavens is located. Historical documents indicate that though tomb architecture aimed at imitations of the living world, in some tombs actual *que* gates (which were supposed to be erected outside) were replaced with murals of *que* gates depicted *inside* the tomb (Sofer and Rudolph 1987, 49). Furthermore, Li-kuei Chien looks at archeological finds of *que* gates in the Shibeidi palatial complex built by China's first emperor, Qin Shi Huang, and connects it to the long folkloristic association of the area with myths and legends of immortals; though he emphasizes the difficulty in proving these theories, he speculates that it was this mythical aura surrounding the place that

Figure 6.2. *Que* gate depicted on an Eastern Han period stone sarcophagus. Photo: Courtesy of Dr. Hajni Pejsue Elias.

attracted the attention of the emperor in the first place, saying that, "the position of the twin towers relative to the Shibeidi and Heishantou palaces suggests that they may have been intended to connect the human and divine realms by serving as portals for immortals arriving from the celestial mountains in the sea" (2018, 72).

In Praise of Protecting Rulership

The aspiration for order seems to be exceptionally emphasized in a certain philosophical school known by several names, *fajia* 法家, *Huang Lao* 黄老, or (the arguably flawed name) "Legalism."[4] The main aspiration of this school of thought was the *creation of order* through strong governance—the meaning of which is ensuring the strength of the ruler while standardizing (creating uniformity in) everything around it, for example, rules, units of measurement, administration, etc. Such uniformed bureaucracy would be able to administrate rewards and punishments through an impersonal and efficient system. A conspicuous representative of this school is *Hanfeizi* (280–233 BC) and the text attributed to him—the *Hanfeizi* 韓非子. The text contains ninety-three occurrences of *men* 門—most of which have been found to stand literally and/or figuratively as a necessary device for the "protection of the current ruler from inimical elements." In many of these cases, as will be seen, the gates are consequently closed and even firmly bolted. But intriguingly there are a few gate passages that carry a different significance, which, perhaps not surprisingly, are contained within two chapters that are exceptional in their own right, namely, *the Jielao* 解老 ("Explanations on the *Laozi*") and *Yulao* 喻老 ("Analogies with the *Laozi*"). Indeed, in addition to questions surrounding the *Hanfeizi* in general, such as its authorship, these two chapters evoke further debates and controversies revolving around their close contextual association with *laoxian* thought (corresponding intertextually mainly with *the Laozi*, the *Huainanzi* and the *Guanzi*).[5] I thus suggest that investigating the meaning of these atypical gate passages might offer a novel point of view on these chapters, in particular, and the hermeneutics of the *Hanfeizi*, in general.

Out of the various correlations with the *Daode jing*, these two chapters exhibit a particular resonance with chapters 46 and 47, with emphasis on the need to suppress (close the gate on) one's desires, the importance of feeling content through the inner knowledge of sufficiency, and the intriguing idea (chapter 47) that the sage "penetrates into the knowledge of the universe without venturing out of his door, and sees into the way of the heavens without looking out through the window" (不出戶知天下; 不闚牖見天道). At the end of the chapter *Yulao* 17 in the *Hanfeizi*, the idea is expressed slightly differently: "The sage is able to know the universe without venturing out of his door, and is able to know the way of the heavens without peeping out of his window" (不出於戶, 可以知天下; 不闚於牖, 可以知天道). The main difference is in the characters *keyi* which stress an ability (something that needs cultivation and practice rather than an inherent gift one is born with).

As we have seen in chapter 4, Chinese correlative thinking might visualize architectural components (such as one's front gate) as openings on the boundary of the inner sphere of the body-mind—such as the senses (e.g., eyes, ears, etc.). In the above passage, thus, it would imply that sagely *knowledge* needs no external information to develop internally— meaning that as far as the sage is concerned, the gates of these openings can be closed. This is open to two interpretations, namely, that the sage can gain knowledge about the world from within (his knowledge is not dependent upon the state of the gates . . . open or closed is irrelevant), but, alternatively, that he actively needs to close them (as is pronounced in the *Daode jing*, the *Huainanzi* and other Daoist-inclined sources); the beginning of *Yulao* 17 indeed says,

> Hollow orifices are the doors and windows of the "superior brilliance"; ears and eyes are exhausted from all the sounds and colors, the "quintessential spirit" is exhausted by external appearances—and as a result there is no master inside.[6]

空竅者, 神明之戶牖也, 耳目竭於聲色, 精神竭於外貌, 故中無主.

Simply put, when the openings of the body are wide open (hollow, vacant holes), the internal spirit is exhausted, that is, damaged and spoiled and, consequently, there is no proper ground from which the unique ability of "superior brilliance" can develop or grow; furthermore, in such a state, Hanfeizi says, the body-mind is ruled by no-one: there is no master in the house.

I stress that when it comes to the *Hanfeizi*, its contextual backdrop of rulership, governance, and politics should always be taken into consideration—inclusive of the two Laozian chapters; thus, when referring to the *master* above, is Hanfeizi signaling to the wider circle of the kingdom or to governance in general? Should the king surround himself with high walls and bolted gates—not only for protection but also for the cultivation of a unique type of "political superior brilliance"?

Indeed, before we move forward to delve into gate passages associated with more direct political advice, I would like to remain in the Laozian chapter *jielao* to discuss a particular theme that makes three appearances in it (but is absent from the rest of the text), namely, foreknowledge *qianshi* 前識.

A gate and foreknowledge appear in the following passage (*Jielao* 7):

While Zhan He was in attendance with his disciples, the moo'ing sound of a cow was heard from outside of the gate; one of the disciples said: the cow is black (except for) its white forehead; Zhan He said: indeed, the cow is black but white is on its horns.

詹何坐, 弟子侍, 有牛鳴於門外, 弟子曰: 是黑牛也而白題. 詹何曰: 然, 是黑牛也, 而白在其角.

This is a curious passage. What is the purpose of such a guess and in what way is it important or significant? As the gate is presumably closed, they could not get a glimpse of the cow but only test their ability to "see" outwardly without the physical sense of sight—a miraculous demonstration of "knowing in advance" that Hanfeizi names foreknowledge *qianshi*; in the events that follow, Zhan He was proven correct—with the result of total admiration from his disciples and witnesses around. However, Hanfeizi is not impressed . . . he points out that instead of the whole exhausting procedure, any young ignorant man could simply go to the cow and see with his own eyes that her horns are covered by white cloth.

Indeed, the first and last lines of *Jielao* 7 further express Hanfeizi's aversion: it begins with "anticipating events and deciphering patterns prematurely is named foreknowledge; it is groundless and extremely meaningless" and the last line says, "one who plays with foreknowledge is like a flowery embellishment of *dao*—(it ranks) first in the line of foolishness and deception." Here Hanfeizi utilizes *Daode jing* 38 which says, "foreknowledge is (just) a flowery embellishment of *dao*, and is the beginning of stupidity" (前識者, 道之華, 而愚之始).[7] Importantly, Wang Bi also refers to foreknowledge as a negative aspiration and action—in his commentary on the *Laozi*, remarking that "generally speaking, [however,] ritual is [the result of the] wearing thin of truthfulness and credibility, and thus the beginning of [social] chaos. Foreknowledge is [the result] of the Way's becoming an [external] ornament, and [thus] the beginning of stupidity [violent and counter-productive government]" (Wagner 2003a, 241).

The two *Hanfeizi* passages above deal with perception and epistemological questions, that is, how do we know something about the world, what is the role, function, and reliability of the senses in the acquirement of knowledge, and particularly—whether sages possessed superior skills (that reach beyond the ordinary usage and abilities of the senses); these questions occupied the minds of Pre-Qin thinkers to a great extent, as is perhaps better known in the context of Daoist thought and sagely skills (see chapter 3). Miranda Brown and Uffe Bergeton indeed remark how "early Chinese thinkers also speculated about how sages 'saw.' They asked whether sages were endowed with extraordinary powers of sight and sound, they contemplated whether there were things that sages alone were able to detect, and they debated whether sages detected ruses" (2008, 641).

If indeed we analyze the two passage epistemologically and in relation to gates (openings) of bodily senses, we see that in the first, the gates should be closed in both directions in order to block external influence (to protect the "superior brilliance" *shenming*), but in the second instance, the gates don't need to open outwardly (for the sage to go out)—similarly to the *Laozi*. But why the warning and objection to foreknowledge? Isn't foreknowledge a superior skill of "internal premonition"—not unlike the ability of the sage to know the world without going outside? It seems the *Hanfeizi* follows the *Laozi* in negating foreknowledge due to some underlying characteristics it shares with *ritual*—because they are both grasped as external and shallow acts that are even potentially dangerous—as they can be utilized by crafty people in order to deceive others. It seems that in this instance, at least, Hanfeizi rejects deception and indirectness in both civil and military contexts—in a similar fashion to *Xunzi* 荀子 (but as opposed to the *Sunzi* 孫子).[8]

But there is a deeper, more "Daoist" reason to Hanfeizi's contempt to foreknowledge; Laozian knowledge is not subjective, structured, or defined; in the epistemological context, foreknowledge *qianshi* stands in opposition to *wuzhi* 無 (and to *wuwei*), that is, the efficacy of "not-knowing" or "no-knowledge" that leads to authentic life; in the Zhuangzian sense, knowing is perceived to function like a mirror: a full-present and singular "acknowledgement" of the phenomenal world. I believe this is the underlying reason for the words *dao zhi hua* 道之華 in the above lines: foreknowledge sees only the external and *specific* details of *dao* (the flower correlates with the whiteness on the cow's head), whereas *wuzhi* penetrates down to the roots of the plant (*dao*). Chapter 71 of the *Daode jing* indeed says, "to know (the value of) not-knowing is superior; not knowing (the danger of) knowledge is an ailment" (知不知上; 不知知病).

However, in the context of "having prior knowledge," the *Hanfeizi* does emphasize the importance of a different (but not unrelated) action that should be taken upon an inner feeling or premonition, that is, being *pro-active* instead of waiting for an event to unfold. Curiously, one such passage in *Yulao* 10 also makes reference to an illness (with intriguing insights from a medical point of view): it describes how a patient goes to the doctor and receives a prognosis and advice for immediate treatment; however, again and again the patient ignores the doctor's orders until, with the progression of the disease, it becomes too late . . . Hanfeizi urges that upon receiving or seeing the earliest (primordial) signs of something (in this case, a disease), he or she must act promptly; in another passage in *Shoulinxia* 說林下 ("Collected Sayings" I) 21, we learn of a person who senses or suspects that something is wrong with his neighbor, thus subsequently and immediately he moves out of his home . . . though everyone advises him to calm down and wait to see whether his suspicions are at all grounded . . . he listens to his inner voice, packs, and leaves.

But in fact, don't foreknowledge and pre-action share common ground? They both point to "sensing what is out there or what will happen soon" . . . and even in Daoist context there are references to knowledge that perceives the evolution of things from their very incipient roots—and yet the text clearly objects to the one and encourages the other. Andrej Fech likewise questions this contradiction and according to his interpretation, "this particular rejection of "foreknowledge" may also stem from the negative connotations of the preposition 'in front' (*qian* 前) as pointing away from the location of the Way. This explanation goes well with the depiction of 'foreknowledge' as 'flowery embellishment" of the Way and not its substance" (2017, 59). Finally, it is also plausible that the *Hanfeizi* contains some textual inconsistencies and/or different messages that vary according to the designated audience; Goldin indeed emphasizes that:

> The case of Han Fei and the Han Feizi is more complex because Han Fei was slippery. What Han Fei said varied with his expected audience, a point that most scholarship

on the Han Feizi—from the beginnings right down to the present day—has not taken seriously into account. Most of his chapters are addressed to kings; at least one, "The Difficulties of Persuasion" ("Shuinan"), is addressed to ministers; and for many chapters we can only guess at the intended audience. (2013, 1)

After all, it was Hanfeizi who formulated (for the first time) the idea of contrast and contradiction through the story of the all-piercing spear *mao* 矛 and the impenetrable shield *dun* 盾 that together constitute an inherent paradox—which also means an inconsistency between what one says and what one does.

Let us now move to other chapters in which gate passages deal with political advice to the king. The first appears in *Hanfeizi* 5, named *Zhudao* 主道 ("Way of the ruler"):

> When one is careless about closing his gate, and does not make sure it is strongly bolted, tigers will therefore (take advantage and) use it. If you are not cautious in your undertakings, if you do not hide their true aspect, then traitors will arise.
>
> 不謹其閉, 不固其門, 虎乃將存.

As the passage goes on it is clear that tigers represent traitors who aim at assassinating the sovereign and replacing him. The gate therefore stands for the need to "protect the ruler"—thus from the ruler's perspective, the very first step that he himself needs to take is to pay special attention to the gate and to the strength of the gate bolts! This is a wonderful demonstration of how an ideology or philosophy leads to entirely different methods and intellectual motivation, that is, as we discussed, in the case of *guan* watchtowers, the emphasis was put on the skills of patrolling and importantly, on seeing afar, whereas here the stress is on the physical bolting of the gate itself.

The text lists five different types of "blockage" that refer not only to the physical gates themselves (a palace or a city), but to ways that can be employed by (internal) officials or (external) traitors in order to seize power; it reads, for instance:

> Therefore, (as for) the ruler of men, there are five (types of) "blocking" (that could stop him from ruling): when the

state officials stop his ruling, it is one (type of blockage); when the state officials take advantage of his wealth, it is the second (type of) of blockage; when state officials issue orders without authority, it is the third (type of) blockage; when the state officials obtain righteous deeds (in their own name), it is called the fourth (type of) blockage; when they are able to set up their own close circle of men, it is the fifth (type of) blockage.

是故人主有五壅: 臣閉其主曰壅, 臣制財利曰壅, 臣擅行令曰壅, 臣得行義曰壅, 臣得樹人曰壅.

Instead of grasping the gate as a symbol of "right" or "wrong," "correct propriety" versus "wrong propriety," or a "value-oriented hinge" in the case of Confucius or Mencius (chapter 5), here we find that the gate and its threshold demarcate "current ruling authority" that stand in opposition and antagonism to any other ruling authority. This is a "one-sided gate" that separates and divides but also prevents the possibility of change! In advocating the means by which traitors can succeed in taking the ruler's power away, the ruler does everything in his *power* to further hold on to his *power*.

Yuri Pines offers an exegesis that reinforces this point of view, saying that according to Hanfeizi, "The ruler is first of all an institution, and as such he is beyond criticism: he is the apex of sociopolitical order, the counterpart of the Way, the embodiment of abstract principles that govern the cosmos and the society" (2013, 67).[9] Indeed, the gate constitutes an extreme case of airtight closure—it is shut impenetrable to anyone who does not belong to the close and immediate circle of the ruler. It symbolizes protection at all costs and stands against change, different opinions, or political tendencies. Is it because, according to Hanfeizi, the ruler is an institution that embodies cosmic order? Is "political earthquake" his deepest fear? An earthquake that would shake down the current and cosmic order of things—and bring about chaos?

In *Yangquan* 揚權, ("Raising authority") we read,

The gates of high ministers are big, just because many men are in fear of them.[10]

大臣之門, 唯恐多人.

The gates of officials might symbolize the concrete gates of their private residences . . . roaming high and thick, they symbolize the strength and wealth of their owners, and thus in the eyes of the common man, they signify this impenetrable threshold of social status that lies between them and the officials, but in addition, they evoke in them two types of feelings, namely, awe combined with fear (and perhaps detest), but also—envy and admiration.

In relation to concepts of rulership as expressed in the *Hanfeizi* and in relation to and comparison with the *Daode jing*, it seems that the dismissal of moral values as the basis of governance is mutual to both; instead, it is cosmic (not human) order that constitutes the root of good administration. David Shepherd Nivison sheds some light on the subject by referring to another gate extract in chapter 8 that defines the ruler as someone whose power is absolute because, though he is mysterious and silent, he manages, on the other side, to hold the ultimate weapons of control: " 'The ruler of men must prune his trees from time to time and not let them grow too thick, for if they do, they will block his gate.' The idea is explicit in *Laozi* 36, one of the sections that the *Han Feizi* comments on" (quoted in Loewe and Shaughnessy 1999, 804). From this perspective, the ruler's control over his people stems from the same root (literally speaking) as the cultivation of plants and trees; trees stand analogous to people who come to the gate (visitors are mentioned in the next line), and the "pruning of trees" parallels the "pruning of people" (their *cultivation*). Conceptualizing it as such, if the ruler manages to control the people through cultivation, his gate will be free of protests or uprising or, indeed, empty of fear. Under such circumstances the gate of the ruler can remain open! But "pruning" might carry an additional meaning—preventing the people from growing too spoiled or needy (just as trees grow too wild). Pruning them thus "keeps their heads down" to prevent them from "taking liberties," the aim of which is to keep the populace in reverence, awe, and most importantly, in order.

Gates as Warfare Strategy

As said in chapter 1, warfare fulfilled a crucial part in the development of thought and culture of early China; Roger Ames even argues that its intensity has been a defining factor "in the articulation of the distinctive correlative worldview of ancient China" (quoted in Olberding and

Ivanhoe 2011, 117–18). Gates naturally had a key role in the context of warfare—constituting the space that "can potentially be opened" along the wall or through the state, and thus their significance lay in the symbolic as well as in physical defense. A well-known text (which gained popularity in the West) that constitutes a treatise on military strategies is *the Sunzi bing fa* 孫子兵法 (*Master Sun's Military Methods*) written by Sun Wu during the Spring and Autumn period. The chapter *yongjian* 用間 ("Using Spies") reads,

> In defeating an army, attacking a city, or killing someone, what needs to be known in advance (are), the (names of) visiting attendants, (the names of) gatekeepers and all those in command; (our) spies must be required to ascertain all these.

> 凡軍之所欲擊, 城之所欲攻, 人之所欲殺; 必先知其守將, 左右, 謁者, 門者, 舍人之姓名, 令吾間必索知之.

We meet with the theme of gatekeepers again as the one controlling the hinge of the gate and holding the key to victory or defeat; deciding who is allowed to pass and who stays behind leads to the accumulation of power in the midst of this singular locale between governance (the rulers) and the ruled. In the case of spies, the importance of gatekeepers becomes even more pronounced (in comparison to gatekeepers on the roads) because, first, they have gathered familiarity with passers-by, probably knowing regular travelers by name, and second, they must have acquired a sort of "sixth sense" (almost like "sniffing") which "feels" that something is wrong and/or people trying to take on false identities (as spies probably did).

Thus, the key to a successful attack on a city is acquiring the names of those gatekeepers and people who go through the gates—this is preliminary knowledge that sets the background for a militant victory. The emphasis here is on preliminary "background checks" before any attempts to break down the gates by mere force. In the "Nine Terrains" (九地) paragraph 8, it is said,

> Therefore, the day you take up governance, break down all barrier-passes, destroy all gate (*guan*) tallies (*fu*), allow no passage for messengers, be strict over the imperial court,

punish their affairs. If the enemy's gate is open, certainly go in. First seize the (the enemy's) favorite place, and take over little by little, employ punishments as befit the enemy; this is how you determine your win in a battle. At the beginning, (be) like a maiden, so the enemy opens up the gates, then (act) as a running hare, the enemy will be too late to resist.

是故政舉之日, 夷關折符, 無通其使, 属于廊廟之上, 以誅其事, 敵人開闔, 必亟入之. 先其所愛, 微與之期, 賤墨隨敵, 以決戰爭. 是故始如處女, 敵人開戶, 後如脫兔, 敵不及拒.

The strategy presented here involves a set-up scheme in which blocking and opening of the gates play a key role; it is made of two parts: one points to the original kingdom of the new ruler (symbolic inside) and the other points to the new (conquered) kingdom (symbolic outside) of the enemy. The strategy involves trickery: pretending to be someone else (like a Trojan horse) and then quickly getting inside before the enemy realizes what is happening—behavioral tactics and timing.

A Scheduled Barrier: The Gates of the Chinese City

In his influential book *The Image of the City*, Kevin Lynch specifically referred to two main characteristics that underlie a city's uniqueness, namely, way-finding and imageability. He defined "imageability" as certain physical qualities (whether shape, arrangement, or color) in a city that facilitate "vividly identified, powerfully structured, highly useful mental images" that become the city's immediate recognized visuality (1960, 9). As for way-finding, it constitutes the experiential image etched in our memory and physical body through the immediate sensation of walking through a city—something that is deeply universal.

Looking at the Chinese city from this conceptual angle, and its unique imageability and certainly its characteristic *way-finding*, instantly surface. Indeed, as succinctly discussed in the introduction, the city constituted for the ancient Chinese the epitome of symbolism and *choreographed* living space; its planning, orientation, and construction followed cosmic concepts brought down to earth and accordingly designed. As early as the Shang dynasty, as Hellmut Wilhelm says, the city was called the "Heavenly City" and was the "site of gods and ancestors, an image and symbol of Heaven, as the creators of the Chinese culture had envisioned it" (1977, 93–94). By the Han era, the orientation of the Chinese city was formulated into a three-by-three grid of a "well-field system" called after its resemblance to the Chinese character for "well"—*jing* 井; this shape and system applied not only to the city *chengshi* 城市 but also to houses. John B. Henderson mentions an intriguing detail as to the "well-field system": "Fu Xi was believed to have first observed such a pattern on the shell of a turtle emerging from the Luo River. So even though the nine-palace formation, the graphic basis of the perennial Chinese cosmography, was credited to an ancient sage-king, its pattern was supposedly taken from the natural world. It was immanent in the structure of heavens and earth, or at least marked on the shell of a remarkable turtle" (1994, 204). It seems that the hands and mind of Fuxi were everywhere . . . to the extent of attributing to him the classic Chinese urban planning; furthermore, it stresses yet again the characteristics of *observing natural patterns* by the ancient Chinese (as discussed in chapter 1) and the consequential and correlative structuring of man's concrete world.

To go back to Kevin Lynch's urban theory, the term "way-finding" as the means by which one is "intuitively guided in a city" becomes even more literal when we think of the main south-north axis of the Chinese city (from ancient to late imperial times) as the concrete manifestation of the abstract idea of *dao*; along this axis are halls and gates that create a gradation in privacy and social status, which means that along it there is a scale of perviousness that controls who enters where . . . the closer one is to the immediate family, the deeper he is allowed in a private home, and the same goes for an imperial city, but this time the content that is being "managed" is not privacy but social status. Then we have walls (and gates in them) that are so significant for the Chinese city that the character *cheng* 城 actually means them both.

This spatial arrangement as an ideal pattern for urban settlement was first mentioned in the *Kaogongji* 考工记 (*Register of the Artificers*) that describes how carpenters demarcated the capital as a square with sides the length of nine *li*—each with three gateways (Jun 2013). Zhou, Zwahlen, and Wang comment that "in the excavation area . . . the well is surrounded with close-set semi-cylindrical piles; meanwhile, it is possible to see how another pictographic character *jing* 井 is derived from this image, even as an oracle bone inscription. The walls of the well were lined with close-set timber piles reinforced by a square wooden frame. The 28 piles in the outer part of the site may have been part of a shelter for the well" (2011, 1104; figure 6.3). As gates controlled the traffic flows in and out of the city, they became, as Sen-dou Chang notes, "the main factors determining the patterns of streets" (1970, 78). In the *jiangren yingguo* we find such standard design, which, according to Feng Jiren, produced a systemized theory of urban planning:

> When artisans designed a capital city, [they made the city] nine *li* long and three gates on each side [of the city walls]; in the city, nine roads from north to south and nine roads from west to east, and each road was as wide as nine wagons abreast; the ancestral shrine was in the left [of the city],

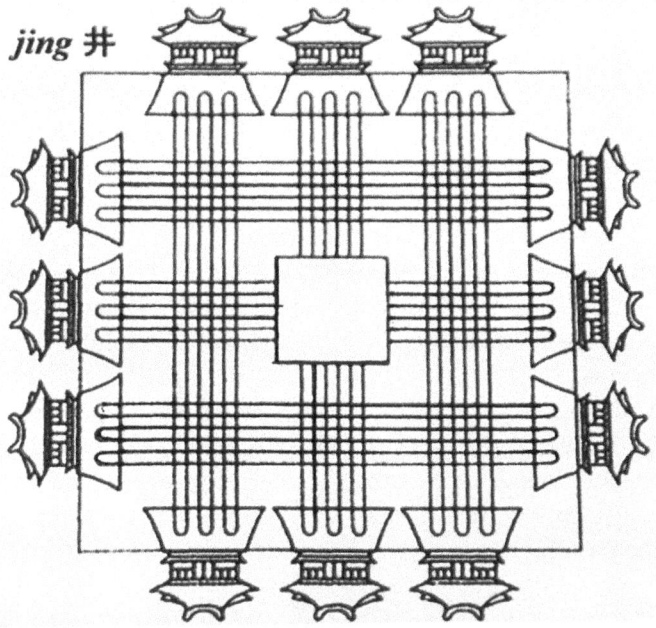

Figure 6.3. The three-by-three grid of a "well-field system" (a well, *jing* 井) of Han period Chinese cities. Public domain.

while the altars to the gods of soil and grain on the right; the audience chambers were in the front, while the market was behind [them]; the market and the audience chambers constituted an area of one hundred steps square. (2012, 31)[11]

The above paragraph is a testimony to the accuracy with which the city was designed and constructed—location, measurements, orientation—but it also demonstrates the existence of constant fear . . . an anxiety from those barbarian states that lurk behind the walls. The clear boundary the ancient Chinese wished to mark between their own civilization and "the barbaric other" says a lot about the way they grasped their own self-identity, culture, and state.

The significance of walls to Chinese cities (and its civilization in general) is evident in the fact that the name *cheng* 城 applies to both. Yinong Xu refers to the symbolic and psychological meaning of walls in Chinese culture and thought, saying that it "certainly derived from the characteristic way in which the Chinese of ancient times perceived and shaped the world. It points to the ultimate and Chinese desire to create and maintain order as much in the minds of the individuals as in society; which should be in accord with both the order of the world and the cosmos" (2000, 86). It is noteworthy that beside *cheng*, two other terms were used for cities, namely, *du* 都 and *yi* 邑, among which *yi* referred to a small-sized city or even town, while *du* referred to a capital city and a political center during the *Zhou* dynasty that constituted the place of residence of the ruler—from which he governs the state. A characteristic of *du* cities was the construction of ancestral temples in which memorial tables were enshrined—to protect and symbolize the clan system; from the Qin dynasty onward, *du* cities constituted the place of residence of the emperors.

Wall gates constitute a *possible break* in the continuous line of walls . . . grasped as the "weakest link" that must be protected at all costs; it is thus understandable that their control, supervision, and monitoring became first priority. In the Eight Observations of the *Guanzi* 管子, the following passage details their importance:

The main city wall must be well constructed, the suburban walls impenetrable, village boundaries secure from all sides, gates kept closed and residential walls and door locks kept in good repair. The reason is that if the main walls are not well constructed, rebels and brigands will plot to make trouble. If

suburban walls can be penetrated, evil fugitives and trespass-
ers will abound; if village boundaries can be crossed, thieves
and robbers will not stopped; if gates are not kept closed and
there are passages in and out, men and women will not be
kept separate. (Rickett 2001, 228)

The last line makes a curious reference to the separation of genders: if
gates are not kept closed and people just go in and out, then . . . men
and women will not be kept apart! It immediately evokes the theme
of half-open gates (discussed in chapter 5) that symbolizes the notion
that the segregation between men and women constitutes order, while
their union (sexual freedom) signifies its collapse into anarchy. Indeed,
it is not only in the context of gender segregation; the Chinese city
constitutes a sealed urban planning the reason for which, according to
Hong Xu was

> the authoritarian political system which was greatly strength-
> ened during the Eastern Zhou period, especially after the late
> Spring and Autumn period. The capital city planning from
> the time of the Cao-Wei period to the Sui and Tang dynas-
> ties not only retained the sealed type of planning from the
> past but also further divided the residential areas even more
> strictly based on social hierarchy. (2021, 9)

Within such a sealed city the walls and the gates constituted a membrane—only through its gates, can the city (as a living organism that
must function) communicate with the outside (trading with the outside
world, for instance) or serve as a social and political symbol; accordingly,
the walls varied in function, type and size, for instance, the *gongyu* 宮隅
(corner towers of the palace city), the *chengyu* 城隅 (corner towers of
the outer city), or *que* gates. Yinong Xu describes how city gates "were
in their own right undoubtedly the positions on which not only the
defense of the city itself but, by their social and conceptual implication, also the security of the whole prefectural area was concentrated"
(2000, 119).[12] The following is a passage from the *Guanzi* referring
to the walls and their guards: "Let there be a single road (leading to
each village) and let people leave or enter only one at a time. Let the
village gates be watched and careful attention paid to key and locks.
The keys shall be kept by the village commandant and a gatekeeper
shall be appointed to open and close the gates at the proper times"

(Rickett. 2001, 105). The control of the gates by the authorities turned them into an efficient tool of governance. The gates closed at regular intervals: the authorities closed them in the evening and opened them again at dawn. Naturally, they could also decide to shut the gates at any other schedule—whether it was necessary or as a type of punishment. Imperial capitals were divided into numerous quarters (*fang*) or blocks, and, as Sen-dou Chang says, "the blocks were protected by walls and were closed by gates at night" (1970, 63).

One of the most outstanding gates of Helu Dacheng ("the great city of Helu" Suzhou's former name during the beginning of the Eastern Zhou) was a Changhe Gate 閶闔門, which importantly, as mentioned, symbolized the gate of heavens (*Tianmen*).[13] Yinong Xu elaborates: "*changhe* is the name of the first gate leading to Heaven and also the name of the gate of the celestial Ziweigong, which is the center of the universe and is where the High God resides" (2000, 51). But importantly, it seems that Changhe gates were designed with the purpose of allowing the "winds of Changhe" to flow inside. What is Changhe wind? Yinong Xu says that this is one of the right winds of heaven which let the heavenly *qi* (cosmic breath) enter the city. This is yet again (as discussed in chapter 1) an instance of the attention given to the wind *feng* in early times and its conceptualization as rudimentary cosmic breath without which life cannot be sustained. But it is particularly interesting to find its role in architecture.

Naturally, at times of war the city gates turned into centers of commandment—both as high points from which soldiers could see afar (for any approaching attack) and as the loci from which the army protected the city; apparently, gates could also become the "living quarters" for soldiers, as Send-dou Chang says: "Usually the most striking features of the city's architecture and were intended to serve as living quarters for soldiers on duty at the gate, and as posts for archers in times of war" (1970, 64). But it was not only against human threats that the gates fulfilled a role; double-layered gates were constructed in "river-towns" as a special type of dike against floods—yet another instance of the close association between rivers, floods, and architecture in ancient Chinese culture. As the cities grew in size, the areas near the gates became the logical and comfortable location for markets (merchandise coming in and out of the gates). Sen-Dou Chang notes that in some cities, this resulted in the symmetrical development of markets near the four gates. The *Qingming shanghe tu* 清明上河圖 is one of the most famous scrolls ever to be painted in China, and its impressive gate (probably of the city of Kaifeng) (figure 6.4) is a wonderful portrayal of the busy hustle

Figure 6.4. A city gate depicted in the Song dynasty painting *Qingming shanghe tu*. Public domain.

and bustle, the comings and goings of camels, merchandise, and traders that pass through its two-leaved inner doors—only during daytime hours.

Attesting to their importance is the custom to bestow upon the gates various names and titles (related to an historic event, a war victory, or the name of a new ruler). This "naming of a gate" was carried out ceremonially and was a significant affair—for the rulership and the people. The significance of "naming" in the context of Chinese thought is well known—particularly in the humanistic philosophy and Confucius's principle of the "rectifying of names." Language was grasped as reflecting true order by itself, and thus, if a certain name or title is chosen inappropriately, order and harmony are at a risk of collapsing.

This is perhaps the reason for the fact that, as Yinong Xu says, "it was the names of city gates of Suzhou, rather than their form and style that were one of the major topics of description and argument in local gazetteers of all periods of history" (2000, 50). If we refer to the naming of gates from a Confucian point of view, gates can indeed be conceptualized as a *li* entity—a landmark upon which harmony and order prevail, and indeed numerous symbolic acts were performed at the gates or involved them, as is detailed in the Classics. Some examples: In the autumn of 669 BC, when the state of Lu suffered a severe flood, the authorities offered sacrifices at the city gate; also, when the leading forces of the Song conquered the Zheng in 698 BC, they conducted a highly symbolic act: they first burned down the Qu gate of the Zheng capital city, then they dismantled the ancestral temple, carried its rafters back home, and used them to build their own Lu gate (Xu. 2000, 53). This fantastic account attests to the synonymity of gate and identity and the symbolic act of using the building materials of the enemy for one's own temple and gate.

One of the main textual sources on city gates and defensive strategies is, in fact, the *Mozi* 墨子, which contains no fewer than 120 gate passages. For instance, in the context of city gates and their opening-closing schedule during day and night, *Mozi* 70.16 gives a detailed account of the strict gate policy of a Chinese city:

> The night drum should be within the main gate of the Defender. In the evening, the order is given for a cavalryman or messenger carrying an identification tally to close the city gate; in either case it must be a person of rank. At dusk, the drum is struck ten times and the gates and pavilions are all closed. Those walking about are put to death, [but first] they must be bound and questioned as to their reasons. Then the punishment is carried out. When daylight is seen, the great drum [is struck] and this allows people to move about. Each of the officers of the city gates enters and requests the key to open the gate. Immediately this is done, they return the key. (Johnston 2014)

The description sheds light on the level of specification and detail that revolved around the gates of the city: high-ranking personnel were handed the "job" of closing the gates, no walking about was allowed after closure, and severe punishments (to the extent of death) fall upon those who disobey these rules. When the sun comes up, people are allowed outside, and upon the sound of the drum, officers of the city gates request the key to the gate, and upon the fulfillment of their task (of opening the gates), they had to return it immediately.

Such a strict policy was designed to protect the city against unwanted elements, but also had a symbolic role as representing the long hand of governance. Chapter 52 of the *Mozi* is even named *bei cheng men* 備城門 ("Preparing city gates") and contains material and information on city walls and gates, as well as types of attacks, for example, "approaches" (*lin*), hooks (*gou*), battering rams (*chong*), ladders (*ti*), mounds (*yin*), water (*shui*), tunnels (*xue*), sudden attacks (*tu*), and more. Here, Mozi gives fourteen characteristics of walls and defense methods, and specific descriptions and measurements of "hanging gates"; in chapter 52.3, for instance, it says, "they should be 2 *zhang* high and 8 *chi* wide, and consist of two equal leaves. The two leaves of the gate should overlap by 3 *cun*, and there should be a covering of earth on each leaf not exceeding 2 *cun*" (Johnston 2014).

In chapter 52.20 it is instructed that "the main gate should always be closed. There should be two men to defend the gate and one man for each parapet. The road outside the city should be kept clear" (Johnston 2014).

Chapter 53, named *bei gao lin* 備高臨 ("Preparing against imminent attack") describes a plan of defense using kilns and fire: "when the enemy enters [the gate], drop the wheels and block it. Activate the bellows and create smoke" (Johnston 2014). However, in chapters 48.20 and 49.15, Mozi makes a metaphorical usage of gates in a very interesting way—making an analogy with disease: "There are many ways in which people can become sick. They can suffer from cold or heat. They can suffer from strain or fatigue. If there are a hundred gates and only one is shut, then how, all of a sudden, can a robber not enter?" (Johnston 2014); and from 49.15:

> You have much, but you have not used it to distribute to the poor. This is the second misfortune. Now you serve ghosts and spirits by sacrifice and that is all. And yet you say, "Where is my sickness coming from?" This is like having a hundred gates, closing one, and then saying, "How did the robber enter?" How is it possible to be like this and still seek good fortune from ghosts and spirits? (Johnston 2014)

In both passages Mozi enquires as to the nature of illness, specifically saying that a disease enters the body from many causes and reasons (in 48.20 it is specificized, e.g., cold or heat, strain or fatigue), but conceptualizing the disease as a moral problem: the rulers themselves and the state are wealthy, but the poor do not get their share.[14] The ruler does not follow *yi* 義 but expects that sacrifice to the ghosts and spirits will prevent misfortunes from happening . . . the disease is a misfortune and can thus enter from many openings (ninety-nine open gates, to be precise), out of which only one that is closed; it is obvious that with such a high degree of penetrability, it is impossible *not* to have a robber intruding.

In analogy, the sociopolitical state of corruption, injustice, and inequality parallels a city or a state with ninety-nine open gates . . . the act of sacrifice—probably considered by the ruler to be a "gate against misfortunes"—is absolutely useless. It is interesting that in comparison, as we have seen in the *Analects* (*Wan Zhang* II 萬章下)—*yi* was the path while *li* was the gate. How are we to understand Mozi's descriptions of severe and cruel punitive action and suppression of freedom (e.g., going outside during curfew hours is punishable by death)? Is he in favor of such means of control and defense or against them? Mozi preached *jian xiang ai* ("mutual universal love"), which calls for feeling love for all humankind equally—inclusive of those people who are outside of one's close circle. How is that reconcilable?

Does Mozi allow the usage of extreme defensive measures as long as one refrains from initiating aggressive attacks? Or is it perhaps his way of demonstrating the futile and tragic price of hatred and antagonism? John Gittings believes the latter, saying that "no one will attack anyone else if all regard themselves as part of the same big (international) family. If the rulers love the states of their others as if they were their own, no one will commit aggression" (2012, 5). As mentioned before, this is part of a continuous debate in early China on *wen* and *wu* (civil versus military life)—not simply as a choice between peace and war, but a deeper conversation on whether aggressiveness is justified in cases of self-defense, or at all.

From the point of view of chaos and order, war constitutes turmoil and collapse of current order—the breaking down of all known social and political constructs (forms), and peace can be thought of as social and political stabilization (or continuation of existing order and forms). In the midst of this tension between anarchy and order, gates symbolize the potentiality of both . . . when used in defense, they hold against anarchy (they keep away chaotic forces in the same way as a dam on a river); from the enemy's point of view, they constitute a potential opening for an obliteration of a nation's political continuity.

Finally, all above instances of gates as means of control in the hands of authorities share one denominator, namely, gatekeepers (and they fulfill a key role in other contexts, e.g., afterlife or the hagiography of Laozi (chapter 7). I maintain that these "keepers of the gate" and the temporospatial singularity they embody, carry significance beyond their mere "job description." As said, as they literally stand on the border—the threshold in between two spatial spheres (inside-outside)—they serve as representatives of law and authority. However, this in-between sphere is also a zone in which neither "side" (state) has more power over the other (similarly to "demilitarized buffer zones" and airports) . . . so that they carry an additional significance in the temporal dimension; that is, what gatekeepers do most of the time is wait . . . they wait at the border for passengers and the passengers wait at the border to approach them—an experience not altogether foreign in our contemporary world.[15]

Chapter 7

Destroy the Mind Barrier!

An Opportunity for Personal Transformation

To "divide," then, is to leave something undivided:

to "discriminate between alternatives"

is to leave something which is neither alternative.

"What?" you ask. The sage keeps it in his breast,

common men argue over alternatives to show it to each other.

Hence, I say: "to 'discriminate between alternatives' is to fail to see something."

—The *Zhuangzi*, Inner Chapters 2[1]

In this chapter, I introduce gates that were found to constitute a barrier *in the mind*, that is, a "formless form" that prevents the required transformation and breakthrough on the path (*dao*) of self-cultivation. It is my argument that three sources, namely, the *Zhuangzi*, the *Hagiography of Laozi*, and the Chan Buddhist text *The Gateless Barrier* aim at the destruction of this barrier as means of self-transformation, and, though they belong to different periods and genres, they do share an inclination toward Daoist philosophy and practice. The main address of these texts is a *cognitive* structure that is too rigid, blocked, or stuck in one-sided convictions or opinions or, as in the case of Laozi, stands for a *wuwei* "breakthrough" at the right moment and opportunity. The case of the various hagiographies of Laozi is especially interesting in this respect, as, according to my exegesis, though what the narrative presents us with is a classic gate-barrier in actualized form, it creates a synergy with the formless barrier in the inner-worlds of both protagonists, namely, Laozi and the gatekeeper.

In the case of Zhuangzi, we encounter an aspiration for the highest form of formlessness and nonattachment in the mind—a state in which one loses any strict sense of self and identity—in conjuncture (and in consequence to) vanishing into obscurity. Brook Ziporyn, exploring textual sources by the exegetist Guo Xiang 郭象 (252–312 AD), one of the most important interpreters of *Zhuangzi*, discusses "vanishing and disappearing" as an advocacy for change: "this is to vanishingly unify oneself with the ten thousand things and form one body with transformation" (quoted in X. Liu 2015, 412). In this state of mind one possesses no *ordinary* sight since it is a vision that sees no duality or distinctions: a "united field of light" on which even the gate itself disappears and dissolves.

Indeed, in the following Zhuangzian passages and narratives, the mental or cognitive structure that stands as an obstacle in the way of a "mergence with transformation" is preferential duality or the existence of a cognitive distinction—even in the form of a mere trace. A cognitive distinction is the outcome of preference or inclination, and, in the wide spectrum of mental and emotional preferences of the human mind, Zhuangzi emphasizes one of the most "deep-seated" inclinations, namely, the natural predisposition toward life—over death. Zhuangzian descriptions of life and death evoke some type of circular path that first goes back (or down) to the undifferentiated root (before demarcation into branches), and then ascends or elevates to a state that is beyond any opposites and preferences. This elevated state of mind constitutes a singular and unified space that not only transcends this or that pair of opposites, but necessarily needs to go beyond each of their *contextual fields* . . . life and death included. The story of Zhuangzi's wife as described in *zhile* 至樂 ("Utmost Happiness") 18 of the Outer Chapters, exemplifies this view in a beautiful way: "In the midst of the jumble of wonder and mystery, a change took place and she had a spirit. Another change and she had a body. Another change and she was born. Now there's been another change and she's dead. It's just like the progression of the four seasons, spring, summer, fall, winter" (Watson 2003, 113). We first learn that a spirit had been created out of change and then—a form, a body, which makes her an actual living thing; yet another change takes place and she dies. Through a sequence of changes, life as form appeared and disappeared—in the same way that the four seasons come and go, replacing each other in ordered sequence. In such a cycle, there is no distinction between life and death, or, to be more precise, they *are* two entities (as otherwise we wouldn't be able to refer to them separately), but they belong to the same continuous spectrum and, most significantly, neither side takes precedence or possesses an added value in relation to the other: they constitute transformations in constant flux and as such, no absolute value or definition can be attached to them. This is, I believe, the way body and mind are conceptualized in Chinese thought—as belonging to one continuum but possessing different characteristics. Indeed, the underlying root of life and death, body and mind, and all living things are the "myriad transformations" *wan hua* 萬化 which are the cycles of "being" and "non-being"; in between we find a place of indeterminacy: the gate itself as singularity or unity *yi* (一).

Steven Coutinho indeed says, "Zhuangzi turns our attention to the continuities, *yi* (一)—that constitute the natural world as an interlocking web of cyclical processes" (2004, 68). This is the place where one "lives forever" in a center that is constantly evolving and enduring forever and not in any physical sense. The meaning and cause of losing identity (that is, one's *false* self-identity) is that the mind becomes invisible; it also socially means that the person might become insignificant in the eyes of others.

Being insignificant in the eyes of others takes us naturally to the Zhuangzian narrative that relates to ego, pride, and one's social status, that is, the story of the "turtle in the mud" who is offered a job as the emperor's counsel, but replies something along the lines of "I prefer to drag my tail through the mud than accept this offer" in the *qiu shui* 秋水 ("Autumn Waters") of the Outer Chapters. This story demonstrates two themes, namely, the independent mind that is free from attachments, and the absurdity and futility of titles, chairs, or political positions. Harold Roth emphasizes that it is indeed no wonder that such ability of selflessness, impartiality, and spontaneous responsiveness became so desirable to those who held positions of governance as "it promised a sagely, almost divine clarity and the attendant wisdom not only to govern efficaciously but to also achieve total personal fulfillment" (quoted in Lopez 1996, 127).

In the Miscellaneous Chapters 14, there is a reference to the "pivot of the *dao*" *dao shu* 道樞 or "the dark and deep of the pivot" 冥

有樞. It is yet another locus of obscurity and invisibility—both on the cosmic scale and man's inner mind. The Inner Chapters *dao shu* refer to controversies, that is, debates on whether "this" side or "that" side is correct, again, pointing at a discriminating mind. The chapter *qiwulun* 齊物論 ("Leveling-Out Opinions") exemplifies it: "just now life, just now death, just now death, just now life" (方生方死, 方死方生), realizing that there is no distinction between life and death and "this" and "that"; it then continues, "the beginning of this pivot is in (standing at) the center of the ring" (樞始得其環中), in which one can respond continuously to any view or opinion—neither affirming nor denying.

The pivot of *dao* contains, at any given instance, all the vast ocean of possibilities. However, the difference is that the pivot acts similarly to the gate—an *act taken consciously by man*, because a pivot (like a hinge of a gate) is a device which needs conscious attention and consequential handling. These possibilities constitute the endless array of information, opinions, arguments, and moral evaluations of the human world, out of which, according to Zhuangzi, none suppresses the other. Furthermore, as Hans-Georg Moeller and Paul J. D'Ambrosio say, "Moral values—such as those created by Confucianism—intoxicate people's heart-minds and lead to moral fanaticism, which, as far as its destructive effects are concerned, is eventually indistinguishable from immoral fanaticism" (2017, 103). One of the most famous stories in the *Zhuangzi* directly addresses sociomoral conventions and concepts of justice, as well as cognitive inclinations, namely, Robber Zhi (盜跖) from the Miscellaneous Chapters. In the story, which constitutes an outright criticism of Confucian concepts of justice and ethical teachings, we are introduced (quite nonchalantly) to explicit and gruesome details that tell us something about Zhi's character, such as, for instance, that he eats people's livers (he is a cannibal), that he violently assails into cities and homes while abducting women, and, importantly from the Confucian point of view, he and his men pay no respect to the elders nor do they sacrifice to their ancestors. Confucius is said to visit Zhi with the hope of turning him away from sinful life, but when Zhi learns that it is Confucius who awaits him, he furiously utters, "Does it happen to be the imposter and hypocrite Kongzi from the state of Lu?" (此夫魯國之巧偽人孔丘非邪?).

Indeed, the tantalizing impact at the very beginning of this wonderful satire is the immediate contrast between the obviously *negative* description of Zhi and Zhi's attitude to Confucius as the hypocritical one; for the point to be made, Zhuangzi *needs* the characterizing of

Zhi to be "negative beyond doubt" . . . so that readers will be slightly shocked by Zhi, even perhaps abhor him—because one's own reaction to the characteristics, beliefs, values, and customs of another person or a different culture, for that matter, is indicative of his or her own set of values . . . thus, the narrative constitutes a mirror of the readers' own discriminating (*bian* 辨) mind between concepts of good and bad, moral and immoral; of course, for Zhuangzi, the *Ru* 儒 promotes this cognitive state of dichotomy further through the introduction of set values, for example, humanity *ren* 仁, propriety *yi* 義, ritual propriety *li* 禮, wisdom *zhi* 智, and more.

Thus the first point relates to Zhuangzian criticism of "this and that" way of thinking (discussed also in chapters 2 and 3), that is, the formulation of a set of virtues that is defined, articulated, and taught as a certain "this" (i.e., appropriate etiquette, sociopolitical roles, designated titles and names, etc.), consequently leaving everything else as "that"—the values that are not included in this structured system get thrown "outside of the gate" and conceptualized as wrong (*fei*). As long as the mind of the individual, as well as society at large, is preoccupied with *choosing sides*, both can find themselves stuck in a rut; indeed, according to Zhuangzi, the obstacle to transformation and change in the individual and social dimensions is the preferential and discriminating mind that inclines toward dichotomic thinking (see further analysis in the discussion). The aim of the Zhuangzian sage thus is to achieve a state of empty mind (empty as "not full" in its attachment with absolute values, opinions, virtues, beliefs) and settle into the axis of *daoshu* from which he observes the changes without being affected by them (it evokes the image of a mirror that reflects everything yet absolves nothing). This ability to be at the axis, the pivot, requires an elimination of everything . . . I see it as a kind of *distilling* out of which only the very essence remains, so that though the mind roams freely in emptiness, it is efficacious in the concrete world.

The second point in the narrative teaches us (then and now) a chapter in hypocrisy . . . indeed, the deliberate staging of Confucius and Zhi face to face—the great sage of high-brow morality with the personification of brutality, constitutes an intriguing summit of order and chaos. As he doesn't "play by the rules," Zhi is "out of order," that is, chaotic in nature—which constitutes part of his charm and charisma . . . whereas the Confucian idea of morality and order means people are assigned certain roles in society, such as "being a father," "being a son," "being a ruler," and so on. That was indeed what Confucius wanted from Zhi to begin with, that is, to offer him a civil position . . . to install this element of chaos inside the ordered system . . . perhaps as a manipulative way of eliminating or at least controlling this chaotic person who wouldn't "listen to reason" and social conventions. It might also be possible that Confucius, who flatters Zhi and even calls him a virtuous man, wishes to adopt Zhi's charisma and attractiveness for his own interests. This alone already exposes Confucius's double standards and at the same time demonstrates Zhi's lack of interest in rank, title, or money . . . well, he already achieved both status and money through other, less conventional, means.

It is then that Zhi makes a mockery out of everything that is held dear by Confucians: the holding of ancient texts and figures in high esteem, the rituals that do nothing in helping the people, the usage of things they don't make or work for themselves (e.g., food and clothes), advancing their own interests through empty gestures of brotherhood and ideals, and most importantly perhaps—walking among the people deeply convinced that they are morally superior (only they know what is right and what is wrong); in other words, being self-righteous . . . which constitutes an extreme instance of polarized, all-or-nothing way of thinking—indeed, far away from Zhuangzi's concept of "empty mind" and emptiness in general (see discussion for further implications).

The twofold significance of emptiness is expressed in another well-known narrative from the *Zhuangzi*, namely, Cook Ding (庖丁) in *Yang sheng zhu* 養生主 ("Mastery of maintaining life") in the Inner Chapters: we are told how Cook Ding works his knife through the empty gaps of a carcass but, astonishingly, the blade of his knife remains sharp. The knife itself "roams freely" in emptiness and it can be paralleled to the aimless wandering of the sage: *xiao yao you* 逍遙游 as they both constitute spontaneity and intuitive thinking.[2] Thus we have here, in effect, an intermingling of two states of emptiness: one characterizing the inner mind and the second the empty gaps in a concrete and external object. Cook Ding could not have *wandered* through the empty gaps with his knife without a mental pre-requirement of emptying out. Alan Fox says that "the attitude becomes what might be described as 'open-minded,' and action becomes non-contrived (*wuwei*), effortless, and unobtrusive" (1996, 64).

In chapters 2 and 3, we have already encountered gate passages in the *Zhuangzi*—some of which constituted a space in between the formed and formlessness, while others served as the place in which natural (in the biological sense) creation occurs. In the context of this chapter—the investigation of cognitive barriers—gate passages in the *Zhuangzi* continue to relate to the problematic consequences of Confucian values, to attachments of the mind and the concept of the heavens in the two-fold context of *wai/nei* (external versus internal). Let us begin with the Outer Chapters 5 named "Movement of the Heavens"), in which a "gate of the heavens" is mentioned. In the beginning, Zhuangzi describes how attached (and desirous of) people are to wealth, fame, and power, and the constant fear that is in their heart-mind of losing all these things; then Zhuangzi details a list of opposites, such as hatred and love, life and death, and taking and giving, as an illustration of Confucian "correctness" and the way name-rectifiers evaluate things on the basis of *shi-fei*. Those who are stuck in such dichotomous thinking cannot adapt to change and thence the "'gate of heavens' will not open in their heart-mind" (其心以為不然者, 天門弗開矣).[3]

When the "gate of heaven-like" (which signifies the natural way things act out of nothingness and nonexistence) is closed in the heart-mind, it forms a barrier which does not allow for any flow or interaction (complementarity) between the sides. This means that one is mentally "stuck." Also intriguing is the positioning of this "gate of heavens" in man's heart-mind . . . it is not only an example of correlative thinking, but a Zhuangzian view that heavens (*tian*) constitutes the sum of cosmic cycles which cannot be divided into absolute conventions and values. Indeed, Chong Kim-chong explains that *tian* in the *Zhuangzi* is related to its closeness to *zhen* (in *zhenren* 真人), because it is "largely a synonym for "nature," that is, the natural world and its regular phenomena. These are referred to in the 'Dazongshi' as what heaven does (天之所為者) without implication of any anthropomorphic entity who brings about these occurrences. Instead, this is meant as a contrast to what humans do (人之所為者)" (2011, 325). From this point of view, then, heavens constitutes the "self-so" cycle of things that constantly develops in absolute quietness; it is an existence completely immersed in the whole that carries no particulars of its own. The "gate of heavens" in one's heart-mind opens the sage to a state of formlessness. Chung-Yuan Chang argues that this state is not "absolute void," saying that, "when one reaches this state, one's inner being is in the state of ontological transparency" (1963, 250).

The following passage gives us yet another clue as to this "gate of heavens," which appears twice in the *Geng-sang Chu* 庚桑楚 in the Miscellaneous Chapters:

Existing (in) life; existing (in) death; he (now) exits, he (now) enters; entering and exiting—but his form cannot be seen, this is called "gate of heavens"; the "gate of heavens" is nonexistence, all myriad things stem from nonexistence.

有乎生, 有乎死, 有乎出, 有乎入, 入出而無見其形, 是謂天門. 天門者, 無有也, 萬物出乎無有.

At the end of this passage, there is a reference to *shengren*—the "utmost sage," as the place "where the *shengren* hides" (聖人藏乎是). As said before, life and death are but the same "spheres of existence" in the mind of the authentic man, or *shengren*. Importantly and probably a shocking concept to the majority of the people today, the notion of life does not evoke joy in his heart and the concept of death does not evoke sorrow in his heart. This exemplifies again the metaphoric role of the hinge or the axis at which no distinctions exists, and all is in a cyclic movement between *dao* and its manifestations.

How does it relate to the concept of "returning back" in the *Daode jing*? David Chai believes that "although the *Zhuangzi* did not explicitly use the word *return* here, it is nevertheless implied and forms one of his central philosophical constructs" (2012, 30). However, I argue that Zhuangzi takes the philosophy of Laozi one step further by grasping the gate itself to be a *trace* of dichotomy. The meaning implies is that the gate itself must be destroyed! According to David Chai, it is "only when the inner and outer realms of reality obscurely join does our dependency on the trace vanish and we can return to the time when things retained their original traceless nature" (2012, 68).[4] By becoming invisible altogether with the gate, the sage turns into the very axis of "efficacious emptiness" reaching the highest level of *wuweidao* 無為道, that is, though he is a visible agent he acts in the world as if he were invisible.

Laozi at the Gate

When it comes to hagiographies, it is noteworthy that they constitute by themselves an entity of "in-betweenness" as they stand between history, biography, and mythology. Their significance lies exactly in their *fictional* aspect—a literary narrative that developed through thousands of years to the point of becoming an established (distilled) story that conveys ideas and/or ideals to generations and generations to come. Mythologies and hagiographies are not taken to be accurate historical descriptions but, as they go down the generations, they distill further into a concentrated "national psyche" in which themes, narratives, and characters become their cultural DNA. When it comes to the hagiographies of Laozi 老子, the legendary author of the *Daode jing*, we enter a wide, complex, and controversial Sinological field. A. C. Graham explains that in the fourth century BC, the narratives grew out of the "need of a founder," with the character of Lao Tan being adopted to serve as an ideal Daoist (1986, 124).

The first mention of Laozi occurs in Sima Qian's "Records of the Grand Historian," which brings some biographical details about the legendary figure, namely, that he was born in the southern state of Chu during the Zhou dynasty, and that his personal name was Er (ear), his surname Li, and his style name Dan; we further learn from Qian's account that he worked in the Zhou archives, and (as is mentioned in other biographies) encounters Confucius—with whom he engages in conversations—a dialectical tool through which the author(s) wished to pronounce the superiority of Laozi's wisdom over Confucius (personally) and advantage of Laozian thought over Rujian doctrine, intellectually. It is even narrated how Confucius, upon his return to his disciples, admitted to having been overwhelmed by the "Dragon-like" presence of Laozi. Further accounts of Laozi (Lao Dan) are included in the *Zhuangzi* (chapters 11, 12, 13, 14, and 26), and the narrative is repeated with some variations in the *Liexuan zhuan* 列仙傳 (*Lives of the Immortals*), composed by Liu Xiang (79–8 BC). The character of Laozi continued to go through an incessant divinization process to become a deity of superior forces, for example, being able to metamorphose to become the very manifestation of *dao*.

Texts devoted to Laozi continued to be composed—each adding or altering this or that aspect of the legendary figure, such as the *Laozi ming* 老子銘 (*Inscription to Laozi*) written by Pian Shao in ca. 166 AD, or the *Laozi bianhua jing* 老子變化經 (*Classic on the Transformations of Laozi*) of the second century AD—in which a "quantum leap" in the conceptual-ization of Laozi is brought forth, namely, that Laozi had metamorphosed into his own mother and gave birth to himself—thus taking the line from chapter 1 of the *Daode jing* quite literally (有名萬物之母). The Daoist movement "Way of the Celestial Masters" of the second century AD further strengthened Laozi's mythologization by referring to him by the name of Lord Lao (Laojun 老君) or Most High Lord Lao (Taishang Laojun 太上老君).[5] His importance "crossed borders" and moved into other sematic fields when, in the Western Jin dynasty (265–317), the *laozi Huahu jing* 老子化胡經 (*Laozi converting the Barbarians*) was composed by Wang Fu 王浮, and related the arrival of Laozi to India in order to teach the barbarians and his eventual rebirth as the Buddha. The above (and very succinct) account of the remarkable evolvement of the figure and deity of Laozi clearly attests to the extent to which it became central to Daoist thought and (later) theological development and in Chinese intellectual history in general. Livia Kohn divides the narrative into the following stages: "(1) Laozi as *dao* creates the universe (creation); (2) Laozi descends as the teacher of dynasties (transformations); (3) Laozi is born on earth and serves as an archivist under the Zhou (birth); (4) Laozi emigrates and transmits the *Daode jing* to Yin Xi (transmission); (5) Laozi and Yin Xi go west and convert the Barbarians to Buddhism (conversion); (6) Laozi ascends to the heavens and comes back again to give revelations to Chinese seekers, founding Daoist schools (revelations)" (1998. 13). Each and every stage in the above legend is worth its own investigation, but in the context of the study of gates, the following discussion will be devoted to the very beginning of the scene—due to the central place a checkpoint gate (*guan* barrier) occupies in it. Indeed, we are told of a certain man named Laozi, who cultivated *daode*, who is on his way to leave, but, as he approaches the pass, he is stopped at the gate by the Guardian of the Pass, Yin Xi 尹喜; the guardian asks Laozi if he would be willing to put down his philosophy in writing—for his sake, which Laozi does by composing a text of 5,000 characters—the *Daode jing*.[6] The legend has geographically grown around the area of the upper Huang He (Yellow River), and specifically at a certain locus that is known in present-day China as *Hangu-guan* 函谷關, that is, Hangu Pass (checkpoint gate) in Lingbao County, Henan Province (see figure 7.1).

I decode three significant stages or contextualized components in this episode, namely, (a) the encounter between Laozi and Yin Xi, (b) the composing of the *Daode jing* and its transmission, and (c) the ensuing inner transformation of both Laozi and Yin Xi. The presence of a gate in this narrative is highly significant; as Steven Burik says, "Is it a coincidence that the legendary Laozi was stopped by the 'gatekeeper' and that this gatekeeper persuaded him to write down his teachings before he definitely moved to the other side?" (2010, 501).

Indeed, as discussed before, gatekeepers were an inseparable part of the lives of the Chinese people from very early times. It is therefore interesting and valuable to learn more on the second protagonist in the story, namely, biographical and personal details about Yin Xi. Let us begin with his very name: *yin* 尹 shows a hand holding a stick, symbolizing control or perhaps a brush used to write laws, which is apt for a gatekeeper; and the character *xi* 喜, a combination of mouth and drum, stands for joy and love.[7] I find it interesting that his name is made out of two opposite meanings, that is, on the one hand (literally), a stick, and on the other, a positive, heart-warming feeling. Does it hint at the quality of "in-betweenness" as inherent in the character of Yin Xi?

We might have further clues on Yin Xi from a text known by the title *Guanyinzi* 關尹子, believed to have been written by a man named Yin Xi (Zhou dynasty) who carried the courtesy name of Yin Gongdu 尹公度 or Yin Gongwen 尹公文. Unfortunately, the text itself has been lost.[8] However, we do find in the transmitted versions a mention of the character *guan* 關 (barrier) as the gate of Laozi's Yin Xi, and, moreover, that Yin Xi lived on Mount Zhongnan 終南山 in a straw hut, became the disciple of Laozi, and specialized in the art of reflecting the starry sky within his own body (Ulrich 2018).

Reflecting the starry sky within the body corresponds with and resonates with the image of a mirror that reflects everything yet stays unaffected; it is also yet another instance of the correlation between cosmos, heavens, body, and mind. In addition to being the epitome of in-between heavens and earth, Yin Xi's "job" itself constitutes in-betweenness on the social level, that is, on the one hand, he is no nobility, but he must, on the other hand, be quite literate . . . as gatekeepers had to approve travel documents. In addition, as said previously, through time and experience, gatekeepers develop some kind of sixth sense, special skills of observance and recognition; they ask *wen* 問 questions (as indeed he does with Laozi) and listens—listening can be literal or metaphorical, as in "feeling the moment." As gatekeepers supervise all comings and goings, the skill of observation is very much part of their work.

Indeed, Nathan Sivin refers to the way Joseph Needham interpreted the sage in the *Guanyinzi* text: "for every day the sage is responsive to the totality of phenomena *wu* 物, his mind is stilled, i.e., in a state of incipience" (1995, 42). In this context, let us not forget how Yin Xi noticed the special characteristics of Laozi: he *sees* his special aura (of purple color) and his wisdom—he recognizes his *dao*. Then, according to some texts, having read the *Daode jing*, Yin Xi goes through a transformation, and then, leaving his post behind, joins Laozi on his westward journey. The singular event contains temporality, spatiality, and circumstances, and it marks a once-in-a-life-time opportunity and the creation of the *Daode jing*. As Laozi decides to transform his philosophy from abstract thought to concrete text, a new connection begins between humanity and *dao*—through Yin Xi. This connection occurs at a specific locus—the gate—and its opening to transformation is enabled through a unique device, the *text* as hinge. As Burik says, "the gateway is the meeting place of humankind *Dao* precisely through language" (2010, 502).

The interrelationship between the inside and the outside occurs on multiple levels between Laozi's internal world and the outside world (which Yin Xi represents). I argue that the narrative is particularly Chinese, but universal at the same time. The struggle and constant dissonance between the innermost psyche of man and its connection and dialogue with the external world is something we all feel and share. This is especially so when it comes to the art (and act) of writing . . . a familiar emotion that is probably shared by people who write "for the drawer": a mixture of fear, hesitation, self-doubt, and so on; in fact, these feelings alone can constitute a mental barrier in the way of publishing, and consequently, in the way of self-realization and fulfillment of one's potentiality. It takes a quantum leap of courage and self-confidence to "take out to the light" the ideas that inhabit the deep and "dark" sphere of the inner mind.

Can we detect such fears or hesitation in Laozi himself? To begin, with, why did he decide to leave everything behind and disappear *without* trace (trace being his *dao* or philosophy put in writing)?[9] According to the narrative, Laozi decides to leave because the state (the kingdom) lost *dao* . . . but intriguingly, we gather that he was planning on leaving and taking his philosophy with him—the result of which could have been the disappearance of both philosopher and *written* philosophy (without textual trace, how can anyone know about it?).

It is only when Laozi is being approached by Yin Xi (symbolizing humanity as a whole), that Laozi agrees . . . because agreeing constituted the appropriate response to these specific *spatiotemporal* circumstances. It is noteworthy thus that Laozi did not *initiate* action . . . his action was, it seems to me, the ultimate manifestation of *wuwei* 無爲. The action did not involve any calculative or rational decision-making, but an intuitive and visceral deed of the moment (see discussion for further implications). It seems to me that, according to this narrative, the writing down of his *dao* actually constituted Laozi's own fulfillment of potentiality. Isn't it the meaning of the character "to steal" *dao* 盜 which carries the additional meaning of "to be secretive" (R. Wang 2012, 121)? It refers to the efficacy of emptiness that water, winds, and *qi* all share, that is, taking advantage of what is on the verge between the invisible and the visible, or, in other words, future unfolding of phenomenon that are (as yet) unseen to the ordinary man. Wang describes this skill as "aligning one's self with heaven's timing and terrain's placement" (2012, 121).

The gate in this narrative encompasses a wider circle: the structure itself and the mind of the person encountering it! Unless the mind is empty and spontaneous, the gate cannot open up to allow the person to stand at its center and disappear in the "great unity" (datong 大同). This spontaneity exists in anyone's mind-body—though it is deep, animalistic-like, and instinctive—but with time, as any skill, if it is "out of use" and is constantly being "covered" by educational forces and rationalizations, it becomes harder and harder to connect with it again. Going back to Laozi and the scripting of the Daode jing, the very text of the Daode jing (or any text, for that matter) can be grasped as de (concrete manifestation) of the de (human beings) of dao—a phenomenon that continues to change people's lives throughout the generations.

Yin Xi goes through transformation himself after having read the text, and I believe any reader of books experiences the transformative efficacy of a book—they can transform lives. Additionally, this hagiography is indicative of the importance and significance of the texts and books in the intellectual history of the Chinese. Isabelle Robinet notes that the Chinese compare the term jing with its homophone meaning "road" and, in this sense, it becomes a synonym for dao or way: "ching is the track or path that guides, shows, and unveils" (1993, 19), indeed, the same relationship as between dao and de. In addition, as said before, jing referred also to narrow, winding (indirect) paths for a single chariot or person (as opposed to dao) which might suggest that they are designated for the individual and not for the masses, meaning that each one of us must choose his or her own path and that we are alone in this endeavor. Indeed, the author(s) of the Daode use the first person point of view in expressing his feeling of aloneness, such as saying, "I alone" (wo do 我獨) in chapter 20.[10] One final point: Laozi's disappearance at the culmination of the narrative signifies that he became invisible—as a true sage. As chapter 57 of the Daode jing tells us, "Hence the sage says, I take no action and the people are transformed of themselves; I prefer stillness and the people are rectified of themselves; I am not meddlesome and the people prosper of themselves; I am free from desire and the people of themselves become simple like the uncarved block" (Lau 1964).

The gate in this hagiography has multiple relevant implications for twenty-first century lives and in the final discussion I ponder further into it. However, before we move on to *The Gateless Barrier*, I suggest one more insight associated with this hagiography, and specifically to Yin Xi. I imagine the gatekeeper's work is quite routine as people go in and out daily, and for lengthy periods of time there's nothing to do. Did Yin Xi contemplate a change in his life? Was he feeling the need for change before the dramatic meeting with Laozi? Was the seed of transformation already there but an external hand was needed to "push" him in the right direction (way, *dao*)?

It is not at all rare to encounter people in such a situation; think of people stuck in routine life, whether work-wise, in marriage, or in any other aspect, and upon reaching a certain age (whether as midlife crisis or sooner), an inner voice starts expressing doubts as to the current situation and in it are the sprouts of a desire for change. However, change doesn't come easy; it requires courage to take the risk (one might lose everything)—one needs self-confidence and inner conviction for a new beginning. Also, familiar notwithstanding, patterns are still needed as easily recognized road signs that point one's way. As for Yin Xi, it seems that it was the *Daode jing* that gave him the courage to go through such change and perhaps also listen to his inner voice (instead of routinely listening to others!); consequently, he transforms, "resigns" (gives up or lets go of the sociopolitical power that was invested in him as a gatekeeper), and starts taking steps on his own personal path—his *dao*.

Figure 7.1. Present-day Hangu Pass (the legendary gate in the hagiography of Laozi). Photo by the author.

The (Formless and Nonexistent) Barrier (in the Mind)

Regarding the ultimate barrier that has no form, I would like to offer my exegesis of *The Wumenguan* 無門關 (Jpn. *Mumonkan*), that is, *The Gateless Barrier*, a text that was compiled in 1228 AD—thus significantly deviating from the study's predefined historical framework. However, the title and opening lines of the text are too significant to be left out. The *Wumenguan* was compiled by Chan Buddhism (Jpn. Zen) monk Wumen Huikai (無門慧開), known also by his Japanese name, Mumon Ekai, who stayed in Ryushu temple studying methods to develop his disciples' potential.[11] The result is a collection of forty-eight cases or *koans*, headed by a title which, I argue, is the most significant of them all. The riddle in the title stems from different interpretations and consequential translations of the three characters it consists of.

I argue that rendering the title *The Gateless Gate* as it is better known in the West, misses on the fascinating wordplay and concealed meanings that it holds. First, let us look at the third character, which (I believe) holds the key to unlocking the whole compilation, namely, *guan* 關. As was discussed before, *guan* stands for a strategic gateway or a checkpoint on the road, so the most obvious choice is to render the title, "The Gateless Barrier"; however, note that the name of the author is in fact Wumen (full name, Wumen Huikai 無門慧開), which allows us the second translating option, namely, "The Barrier of Wumen" ("The *koans* of Wumen"). Yet there's a third option . . . the character *wu* 無 is traditionally translated here as negating the gate, that is, "no-gate" or "gateless," but could it be that the *wu* stands for emptiness? This would render the title "The Barrier of the Gate of Emptiness." Indeed, what is the correct one?[12]

I contend that the title constitutes a *koan* by itself and the riddle it presents to any reader at the very beginning (before one begins to read the text itself) is intentional; it serves as a mirror that reflects our desire to understand and rationally analyze a language . . . when in effect, the answer is staring us in the face: all three meanings are meaningless because they all point to the essence of the whole doctrine, namely, emptiness. This interpretation rests on three points. First, one of the main ideas of Chan/Zen Buddhism (and the *Zhuangzi* before them) is that one can practice "emptying out the mind" through *zazen* (sitting) meditation—but importantly, throughout all the activities of daily life, with special emphasis on the arts as *upaya* or "skillful means"; this daily practice leads to *kensho* (realizing one's true nature), and the attainment of effortless, natural flow and "ultimate liberation" (Low 2016); I thus believe the very act of composing the text was for Wumen an *upaya* practice and the product of "emptying out his mind." Second, a state of no-gate (as we have encountered in the *Zhuangzi*) constitutes the destruction of the gate itself as the last trace of duality; thus, the *gateless* means that nothing is left in this spatiotemporal sphere: just emptiness. Finally, the barrier *guan* is in itself a *koan* as an obstacle in the mind that prevents the disciple from realizing *kensho* and thus requires the adept to continue with daily practice until the destruction of the barrier—and the embrace of emptiness in the center of the mind.

Having laid out the three pointers to emptiness as the foundation of the title and the whole compilation, it might be beneficial to ponder further into *guan* as a barrier, that is, the *koans* themselves as barrier in the mind. T. G. Foulk suggests that *koans* are "devices that are meant to focus the mind in meditation, to confound the discursive intellect, freezing it into a single ball of doubt, and finally to trigger an awakening (J. *satori*) to an ineffable state beyond the reach of all 'dualistic' thinking" (2000, 15). These "devices" for enlightenment consist of various types of sayings, statement, riddles, questions, dialogues, and so on that contain some element of "startling-irrationality" or even gestures that leave the novice "speechless." The Japanese *Rinzai* tradition (临济宗, twelfth century) states that the aim of *koans* is "not to solve the paradox but to realize the hopelessness of any attempt to find solutions" (Heine 1990, 366)![13] This realization not only relates to the above suggested exegesis of the title, but furthermore conveys a dramatic message to human beings: as all phenomena are interconnected and nothing in the cosmos has its own fixed nature, the attempt by humankind to *isolate* things and phenomena in order to analyze them is not only futile but pulls them away from full realization of reality.

Furthermore, if all phenomena are in constant spontaneous flux, then there's a high level of chance and randomness in the cosmos—a scary prospect for man's attempts at control. However, according to Zen Buddhism, this does not mean that everything is meaningless . . . actually, the very realization and letting-go of the ego gives deep meaning to mundane life and the appreciation of the "here and now." In 1817, the poet John Keats coined the term "negative capability" as the state of "being in uncertainties and doubts," understanding that we cannot know it all, hence "letting go" the chase after "facts and reasons."

Realizing the "here and now" through the power of *koans* lies in their immediate efficacy in exemplifying that language and words, though necessary for everyday life, distance us from the immediate grasp of the "absolute." As discussed previously, words are "definers" that put limitations and boundaries on the things they point at: they encase things in man-made constructs! But in nature all phenomena are interconnected (this is modern ecology) and living in the moment means being one with this interdependency and connectiveness as an existence empty of attachment to anything steady.

One of the most important Doctrines to lay the foundations for this approach to human language and to emptiness is no doubt Nagarjuna's *Madhyamika* ("Teaching of Emptiness"), that, as Hsueh-li Cheng says, "laid the foundation of the anti-intellectual, irrational and unconventional teachings and practices in *Chan* (*Zen*) Buddhism" (1982, 10). Emptiness for Nagarjuna, "is emphatically not nonexistence, but, rather, interdependent existence" (Garfield 2002, 91). Interestingly, one of Nagarjuna's texts includes a gate in its title as well, namely, *The Twelve Gate Treatise*; referring to this, Hsueh-li Cheng says it "has been emphasized by Chinese Madhyamika Buddhists who were devoted to the doctrine of emptiness" (1982, 6). In this case, it is Nagarjuna himself who explains in his preface the reason for the use of gates in the title: "gate is the term for opening up, clearing the way and removing hindrances" (H. Cheng 1982, 51).

For Nagarjuna, a gate is thus a device that "opens out," connects, merges, and conquers obstacles, so it fits "the original purpose of the book, namely, that it is designed as the perfect way to get rid of extreme views and enter into the right view" (H. Cheng 1982, 108). It seems that the metaphor of the gate here resembles the potter's wheel *tianjun* 天鈞 or the whetstone *tianni* 天倪 in the *Zhuangzi*—through emptiness (*sunyata*, in Sanskrit), the two sides lose their identity and an empty state of "neither" or "this and that together" is created at the gate's dynamic liminality.

It is therefore the aim of the adept . . . to break the barriers in the mind through the barriers of *koans*, the means by which one is able to break free from rational, conventional thinking, judgments, emotional tendencies, attachments, opinions, and intellectual "baggage." *Koans* demand intuitive and spontaneous reaction, aiming at revealing the existential tension between the logical and the unconscious or intuitive (see the discussion for further implications). I visualize these "mind barriers" as "sunken sediments" which are very hard to destroy/remove or purge as time goes by; this is due to years upon years of accumulating cultural and educational content, psychological tendencies, and cultural conventions. This "shedding off" or "letting go" of all prior conceptions and illusions in the mind cannot occur through rationality and "thinking about," but only through a full, body-mind realization of emptiness. This is why Wumen, the author of *The Gateless Barrier*, writes in the preface to the text, "Buddhism makes mind its foundation and no-gate its gate. Now, how do you pass through this no-gate? It is said that things coming in through the gate can never be your own treasures. What is gained from external circumstances will perish in the end" (Sekida 2000, 26). When Wumen says that "Buddhism makes mind its foundation," he refers to the Buddhist doctrine as first and foremost a philosophy of the mental state, a psychological theory and practice. Having announced the framework, he now states that, no-gate is (the mind's) gate and that "things coming in through the gate can never be your own treasures." For Wumen (as for Zhuangzi), the mind's gate that stands between the external and the internal must be destroyed because as long as there is a distinction, the mind cannot break through and transform.

The way to "let go" of this confining reality is to make whole of internal and external, reality and illusion. Hence the reference to "external things," that "can never be your own treasures and will perish in the end," because, first, when the internal mind pulls external things in, it wishes to *make them its own* (enforcing its own identity on them), which is impossible in absolute reality, and second, because all things and phenomena are impermanent and transient. Such mental attachment to external things is the seed of an illusion, the consequence of which is suffering (duḥkha). It is not enough to open the gate! It needs to disappear altogether. This makes "The Gateless Barrier" close to gate extracts found in the *Zhuangzi*.[14]

I find an additional message in the text: the path to enlightenment begins with one's personal choice and continues with a determination and commitment to daily practice, as opposed to blindly following a scripture or a leader/teacher. Indeed, in the preface to the text, Wumen says, "as for those who try to understand through other people's words, they are striking at the moon with a stick; what concern have they with the truth?" (Sekida 2000, 26). When Wumen says that the *word* "moon" is not the *actual* moon, he refers to the same point I have made before, that is, that language and words constitute an illusionary tool to grasp phenomena; importantly, he is not negating language *per se*, but denying the possibility that language can be used as a tool *for enlightenment*. This resonates with Zhuangzi's famous lines from chapter 26 ("External Things"):

> Fish traps exist as the means of catching fish; once fish are obtained, though, the trap can be forgotten. Snares exist as the means of catching rabbits, once the rabbits are caught, though, snares can be forgotten. Words exist as the means of conveying thought and ideas; once thought and ideas are understood, words can be forgotten. Ha! How can I find a man who forgot the words, so I could have a word with him?

> 荃者所以在魚, 得魚而忘荃; 蹄者所以在兔, 得兔而忘蹄; 言者所以在意, 得意而忘言. 吾安得忘言之人而與之言哉?

That is to say, once tools fulfill their function, they are no longer necessary, and the same goes for words and language. The second part of the passage (starting with "Ha!") is extremely important because if it was absent, readers would probably take Zhuangzi to be a "highbrow philosopher" who belittles his fellow men for their pathetic need for language, but then, as a typical Zhuangzian "punch-line," Zhuangzi enlightens us by saying that he does indeed enjoy a chat . . . providing it is with a like-minded person who realizes that language is a mere tool and not the meaning itself.

Furthermore, one should not embark on this transformative process with the expectation of a "reward" awaiting at some imaginary other side: don't tread on the Dharma path in order to get somewhere (a target or destination); only when you go beyond words and distinctions you find that you have entered the gate or better still, you realize that it was open all along or never existed.

Proceeding with the text of *The Gateless Barrier*, we encounter the following gate *koan*: "The great Way is gateless, approached in a thousand ways, once past this checkpoint, you stride through the universe" (Sekida 2000, 172). The *koan* tells us that, potentially, there are many ways, skills, or experiences that can transfer us into (being one with) *dao*, and that once one breaks through the barrier in the mind, one is liberated and free. Also, *dao* has "no gate" because: (a) *dao* has no beginning or end; (b) once one thinks in terms of before and after (i.e., the gate), he is caught in limitations and distinctions; and (c) as said before, the gate itself disappears when one steps right into its "warp and weft" liminality, thence, enlightenment is reached.

An additional *koan* that has become well known tells us of a monk who asked Jōshū whether or not a dog has Buddha-nature and he replies *wu* 無!—that is, emptiness! (in Japanese, "*mu!*"). This is perhaps Wumen's way of saying that one should be aware of attaching himself to words and ideas, notwithstanding how beautiful or clever they are!—even the central idea of emptiness itself. Also, a desire to achieve emptiness as an act done *for the sake* of a certain target, loses the very *way* to enlightenment and realization. In addition, the answer *mu* reveals the ineffectuality of the question itself . . . because by demanding a "yes" or "no" answer, it again stresses dichotomic thinking.

Robert Aitken correctly identifies "barrier" as a checkpoint (*guan*) and says that "it thus refers not only to Mu as a theme but as a point of realization (1981, 88). Douglas R. Hofstadter (in his remarkable book The Mind's I), mentions *mu* in an imaginary dialogue between a crab and an anteater about Holism and Reductionism: "The answer of 'mu' here rejects the premises of the question, which are that one or the other must be chosen. By unmasking the question, it reveals a wider truth: that there is a larger context into both holistic and reductionistic explanations fit" (1981, 162). *The Gateless Barrier* is intentionally ambiguous as it plays on our misconceptions . . . how is it that the barrier (which is a closed gate) has no gate? Because the barrier is a barrier as long as there is a gate in it! Once you break the barrier, the gate is gone! I suggest this breakthrough and the realization that a barrier is actually not a real barrier happens to us in daily life; we encounter an obstacle (even a concrete one), and it seems unbreakable and knot-tight, but, as we approach it (spatially or temporally)—simply allowing for a certain interval of time (*jian, ma*) to mature—it suddenly dissolves and disappears, without logical explanation.

This is a familiar feeling in problem-solving: we aim at it incessantly, but no breakthrough occurs . . . so we let go, take a break (*jian*), forget about it, go to sleep . . . and suddenly the answer is there. Was it always there but we were *blocked* from seeing it? At times, these barriers come in the form of imaginary scenarios played in the mind, or as confabulation (inventing stories to fill in the gaps in memory), or even catastrophizing (thinking of the worst case scenario). The reason is that these barriers (born out of fear, doubt, anxiety) are in effect—nonexistent.[15] When we think of mind obstacles and the search for answers, the intellectual history of Chan/Zen Buddhism allows us a glimpse into the minds of its very masters and monks in their search for understanding the human mind.

One of the best known monks of the Chan tradition is Dogen (1200–1253), who was bothered by a question: If all humans are endowed with *hongaku* 本覚 or original enlightenment or Dharma-nature, why do we have to practice so much? Attempting at solving this paradox, he traveled to China on a boat, on which he (allegedly) met a Tenzo (head cook of a monastery). Seeing that he worked hard, the following dialogue ensued: "'Why, when you are so old, do you do the hard work of a Tenzo? Why do you not spend your time practicing *zazen* or working on the *koans* of former teachers? Is there something special to be gained from working particularly as a Tenzo?' The Tenzo burst out laughing and remarked, 'My good friend from abroad! You do not yet understand what practice is all about, nor do you know the meaning of characters'" (Uchiyama 1983, 11). This wonderful passage distills a Chan/Zen Buddhism lesson: the most profound is found in the most mundane of iterative skills (such as cooking)—as manifestation of *dao* into the concrete, that is, *de* 德.

The following image (figure 7.2) shows the gate of the White Horse Temple in Louyang, Henan; the temple is considered the oldest (Chan) Buddhist in China, founded in 68 AD.

Figure 7.2. The gate of White Horse Temple in Luoyang is regarded as the oldest Buddhist temple in China. Public domain.

Finally, I would like to draw attention to yet another Chan text that was composed by Yuanwu Keqin in 1125 during the Song dynasty (that is, roughly at the same period as *The Gateless Barrier*), namely, *Biyan lu* 碧巖錄 (Jpn: *Hekiganroku*) (*The Blue Cliff Record*); the text contains one hundred *koan* cases that had been formerly interpreted by Xuedou Chongxian (980–052)—one of the most prominent figures in Chan tradition and *koan* interpreters. Beyond the dozens of gate passages and references contained in the text, three *koan* titles revolve around a gate—certainly deserving a separate investigation in the future.

For now we have space to briefly discuss only one case (a single sentence really)—chosen for its uniqueness (and relevance to present-day Chinese vernacular): in case 87 titled "Medicine and Disease," Xuedou writes, "closing a gate and not building a cart, the road clears and opens by itself—to pass through" (閉門不造車, 通途自廖廓). Before modern times, the expression *bimenzaoche* meant that one does not need external knowledge in order to build or understand something (interestingly, in contemporary China the expression acquired the opposite meaning: that it is foolish and arrogant to try and build something without external knowledge such as expert advice, external investigation, etc.). Thus, although one is confined to the inside with gates closed (so he cannot look out or go outside), a cart can still be built based entirely on internal cognition and subjective knowledge; Steven Heine interprets the line in the context of Daoist thought, saying that "this image suggests the prevalence of subjective truth over objectivity" which means that one who is truly adept "navigates through free and easy wandering along an unobstructed path minus any need for assistance" (2016, 105).

The above *koan*, however, uses the expression in the negative: "closing a gate and *not* building a cart, the road clears and opens by itself—to pass through," for which I suggest four possible meanings (which are perhaps all interwoven together): (1) the cart symbolizes status, title, honor, etc.; "building a cart in order to go outside" parallels "building a name for myself in order to be someone important in the external world"; there is no need to build a cart when one is *inside*—meaning, insignificant, invisible! When one cannot be seen by the external world (the gate is closed for external eyes to see inside), one can roam freely through an open and wide road. The *Zhuangzi* contains a few passages in which a cart or carriage symbolizes status, for instance, in the *rangwang* 讓王 ("Allowed by Kings") in the Miscellaneous Chapters, Yuan Xian criticizes officials for their fake and inauthentic behavior, that they do learning as if for the people, but (in fact) only in order to promote themselves, their evil thoughts are concealed behind the façade of righteousness and benevolence, as well as their decorated horse-chariots

學以為人, 教以為己, 仁義之慝, 輿馬之飾.

Another story by Zhuangzi, funny every time, relates how the number of carriages one has actually indicates how lowly his level of flattery (to officials or kings) is (i.e., sorry but, literally referring, in today's vernacular, to arse-licking)—here it is from the *Lieyukou* 列御寇 in the Miscellaneous Chapters:

> Zhuangzi said, "When the Qin king had an illness, in order to get rid of boils and squeeze out acne wounds, a doctor was summoned—who arrived by carriage. He who licks piles obtains five carriages. Actually, as the treatment gets lower and lower, the number of carriages goes up. How did you, dear Sir, treat his boils? How did you obtain so many carriages? Walk away"!

> 莊子曰: 秦王有病召醫, 破癰潰痤者得車一乘, 舐痔者得車五乘, 所治愈下, 得車愈多. 子豈治其痔邪? 何得車之多也? 子行矣!

Besides the new understanding of the cart as symbolizing social status (with which one wants to go out and show off), and, as can be inferred from the last passage, is achieved through flattery and phony life, there are a few more possible interpretations for the cart: (2) it constitutes a metaphor for a tool that is consciously and deliberately built for a certain target outside; if the mind is constantly on the end reward (both the cart and external traveling)—spontaneity is lost, as is *dao*; (3) it stands for a teaching method, that is *upaya*—here Xuedou might be referring to himself as a teacher, saying something along the lines of "I am not building the cart behind closed gates—I am doing it openly for you to *see*—and if you (the disciple) are open enough to *see* (grasp, be enlightened), then the road will be wide and open for you to roam freely"; (4) still in the context of Zhuangzian thought, I suggest a hermeneutic closeness with the meaning of trace *ji*: as we have seen, as the gate symbolizes a trace of duality, it needs to be destroyed—in the present case, the "destruction" refers both to the gate (or, more specifically, to its open-closed state), and the act of building a cart. If we take the house as correlative to the body-mind (as we have seen in chapter 4)—by closing its gates as Laozi and Zhuangzi both advise, the inner sphere of the mind is *clear, spontaneous, and open* (unobstructed by outside influence)—therefore, one needs no tools in order to cross through (life); from this perspective, the cart might represent language, words, and texts, among other things (i.e., that are not needed for true enlightenment). This connects well with the previous Zhuangzian passage about tools that are no longer needed once they fulfill their designed purpose (which ends with Zhuangzi's invitation for a chat . . .).

Discussion and Further Reflections

A Chinese Gate's Resolution

A person of Jing lost a bow and was not willing to search for it, saying:

"A person of Jing lost it, a person of Jing will find it, so why search?"

Kongzi heard this and said, "If you leave out 'Jing,' then it is acceptable."

Lao Dan heard it and said, "If you leave out 'person,' then it is acceptable."

—*Lushi Chunqiu* 呂氏春秋
(*Master Lu Spring and Autumn Annals*), 239 BC[1]

In this discussion I will allow myself to wander further afield (beyond Chinese thought and culture) with the hope of demonstrating the wider relevance and applicability of the study—whether in contemporary times, comparative (East-West) thought, or cognitive-epistemological context. Let us begin with the gradation that has emerged out of the gate's investigation—ranging between the open and closed, and associated with the acts of opening and closing. Visually, this gradation may looks like this

kai 開 -----*men* 門 -----*guan* 關 / *he* 合 / *bi* 閉

The various degrees of openness constitute the levels of stretching or condensing of the space in between in each dimension on the Chinese psycho-cosmic continuum and ideality. In the context of creation (chapter 2) two-leaved gates are in continuous and iterative open-closed intermingling (e.g., the *Yijing*, *Huainanzi*). In the aspiration for the undifferentiated state—gates can either be open to begin with (*que* gate) or actually closed as a first step (e.g., the *Laozi*, *Zhuangzi*, etc.). When it comes the decisions and actions made by the individual, gates are open *or* closed (e.g., mouth, front gate, and mind); in the dimension of political thought, gates are *closed by default* by the authorities (aspiring for political order); and when it comes to the sociomoral dimension—we have encountered half-opened gates.

The visual graph of the early Chinese open-closed gradation that ensues, therefore, posits the highest degree of openness in the dimension of the mind (innermost sphere, tends to chaotic state) and the highest level of closedness in the political dimension (aspires for order). Intriguingly enough, this correspondence leads me to think of yet another possible trait of early Chinese "psyche": a graph in which the x-axis represents rising degrees of oppression by the authorities (abstract or concrete barriers erected to enforce political or moral order), and in which the y-axis corresponds with higher and higher degrees of mental freedom.

In the need to find a word or term that best conveys this open-closed gradation, I have found that "resolution" (as the title of this chapter) constitutes a most suitable "strange attractor" that encapsulates a few distinct meanings related to the thesis presented in this book: first, resolution (according to the Merriam-Webster dictionary) means the "adjustment of the degree of separation between things"—paralleling the gradation in the opening and closing of the Chinese gate; second, it denotes the "conversion of something abstract into another form," which corresponds with Chinese actualization (the concrete manifestations of ideas); and the third meaning—curiously enough—is its relation to *decision-making* (i.e., as in "I make a resolution to . . ." or "New Year's resolution, etc.).

Come to think of it, the above meanings also relate to circles of identity adopted by individuals or nations—hence the epigraph inserted above. How wittingly it expresses different concentric circles of identity and idealism *within* the framework of early Chinese thought: starting from the narrow "nationalist" circle (within the human sphere), widening further to one particular circle in the human sphere (Confucianism)—and then breaking out of the human sphere altogether to the natural world.[2] Beyond the point of view that it affords on Chinese thought, isn't it most relevant to the world, in general? It all pertains to choices we (individuals, cultures, nations, disciplines, etc.) make as to who or what we let in (inclusion, openness) or who or what stays outside (exclusion and closeness).

But in order for such a wide spectrum of possibilities (between open and close) to present itself for humans to choose from, a culture needs to be able to *discern* (*see*) the whole range of appearances of the phenomenal world—from forms that are there (visible) to the formless (invisible). This requires "lens" equipped with a very wide range of resolution that allows for a deep zoom in and a wide zoom out.[3] This is not a quality to be taken for granted (i.e., cultures differ in that respect), but in early Chinese thought the attention given to emptiness and to the sense of sight, such as passages we have encountered that deal with the ability to discern, see afar or and foresee beyond—indicate the utilization of such "lens" in early Chinese intellectual thought. This unique sense of sight is in constant interplay between the visible and invisible—whether in the inner sphere of the mind, or the play on light and dark, brightness and darkness, or a beam of light penetrating a gate (*jian*)—all these instances oscillate between the empty and the concrete—in correspondence to the *focus* of the sense of sight. Linda Rui Feng mentions certain Tang writings that demonstrate a premise "in which a subterranean, unseen topography coexists with a visible, above-ground counterpart" (quoted in G. Olberding 2022, 138)—an observation that sees both the visible and invisible world simultaneously. Furthermore, this adds another layer to the theme of openings, cracks, crevices, and passages that were discussed throughout the book—since openings, ruts, and cracks are passageways that connect the visible and invisible worlds together! As discussed in chapter 1, early Chinese observation resembled a scientific enquiry not only in the level of resolution, but by what is *not* left out. In reference to Zhuangzi's dialogue on *dao* in the *Zhibeiyou* 知北遊 ("Knowledge of the northern wander"), Needham remarks how in early China, "nothing lies outside the domain of scientific enquiry, no matter how repulsive, disagreeable or apparently trivial it may be" (Ronan 1978, 90). Mark Elvin indeed says that "China possessed in varying degrees all the styles of thought identified by Crombie as the eventual key components of science—the 'postulational' (like Euclidean geometry), the 'experimental,' 'hypothetical modelling,' 'taxonomy,' the 'probabilistic,' and the 'historical derivation'" (quoted in Robinson 2004, xxxviii).

Naturally, if we had space, this would lead us to the "Needham question" of "Why did modern science develop in Europe and not in China?" to which there are many answers (although asking why something didn't happen is based on the assumption that it should have . . . as if it is the only correct way for a culture to develop). However, one important characteristic of early Chinese investigation of external things (*gewu* 格物) might constitute part of the reason, namely, that it was always linked to practicality and actuality—not only aimed at solving immediate problems but also relational to the subject (the human enquirer)—as opposed to the Western aim of arriving at abstract, systemized theories and the separation between subject and object.

One aspect of Chinese material culture and aesthetics that requires a unique *seeing* and which also demonstrates the interplay between open and close is the art of landscape painting that "paints" a visual representation of the interplay between form and no form, visible and invisible. And importantly, the onset of each and every painting correlates or evokes cosmological ideas of "how it all began," that is, creation. It starts with a blank, empty, expecting paper: a cosmos that is "infinite with possibilities" but still framed within bounds; then comes the first stroke that acts as the very opening *kai* 開 of the scene—as the onset of creation. With the progression or, better still, *evolution* of this artistic act, forms slowly begin to appear, followed by an intermingling of "white and black," "being and nonbeing," "presence and absence."[4]

Furthermore, in Chinese painting, the principle of *kaihe* (open-join/close) connects the beginning and closure of a painting but also seals its higher and lower parts together. Importantly, the principle is thought to exist before the "first stroke" even takes place; indeed, Zheng and Dong say, "not only that *kai he* exists once (one) started painting, but *kai he* exist even without (one) has started to paint" (1992, 79). Upon completion of a Chinese landscape painting, one deciphers the forms that are present and visible *you xiang* 有像, (a mountain or a human figure), but simultaneously "sees without seeing" that "which is not there" and is without form *wu xing* 無形 or beyond form (such as the abyss in between mountains). If Shakespeare said that "the object of art is to give life a form," I would say that when it comes to early Chinese landscape painting, it is rather "to give invisible formlessness—(visual) life."

From the Chinese point of view, a painting constitutes a concrete manifestation of the emptiness—as the rudimentary "architecture" or warp-and-weft matrix of the cosmos that alternates between emptiness and actual things, between the invisible and the visible. Significantly, the preliminary state of emptiness "exists" simultaneously on the paper and in the mind of the artist (as a precondition). Through correlative thinking, this "act of creation" as the first "opening stroke" occupies place (and time) in multiple other dimensions, for example, an empty, open space awaiting architectural construction, the first step taken on one's *dao*, or the empty and dry terrain awaiting the first weak streams to fill its crevices, holes, depressions, and ruts.[5]

The importance of such empty passages in ancient Chinese culture and thought is related to various creation acts of opening or one splitting into two. Textual reflections on such processes are evident in several spheres, for example, the first division or separation of heavens and earth, the *yin* and *yang* out of *taiji*, opening lines in textual creation, the description of the evolvement of all living things, the first step on a journey or of a resolution, and the first line drawn to separate space and create architectural creation.

Indeed, the significance of *kai* as the act of opening is ubiquitous in many fields of Chinese culture and thought. In later Daoism, for instance, the scripture of "Opening the sky/heavens" *kaitian jing* 開天經 (sixth century AD) uses *kai* in the sense of creation, in which Lord Lao (as *dao*) rises from nothingness and instructs the world on how to evolve—in the evolutionary sense. *Kai* is important in Chinese medicine, as well: it constitutes a core idea and principle in association with internal gates and passages in the body. Consider the following line, for instance, from *Huang Di Nei Jing Ling Shu* ("The Ancient Classic on Needle Therapy"), chapter 52, titled "The Guard Qi": "Those who know the *qi* paths of the six short-term repositories, know how to untie knots, tie ends and ensure the security of the gateways" (知六府之氣街者, 能知解結契於門戶) (Unschuld 2016).

The meaning of "untying knots" is synonymous with the important character *tong* ("break through," encountered before), which, together with the character *qi* 契 points to the ability to "untie every knot and to open every door" that is considered a high achievement and actualization for health (but I presume it relates to other correlated fields as well). Here, the principle of open channels for the free and easy passage of *qi* requires open gates . . . interestingly, however, the character *he* in the line indicates that the gate mentioned is double-leaved—which means that these gates are not *always open*! Even here it depends on circumstances, situations, and temporality.

I find, however, that the full meaning of the act of "opening up" is revealed in one of the most ancient rituals of the Chinese civilization, namely, the oracle bones and the *yao* 爻 of the *Yijing*. The divinatory ritual of the oracle bones involved the drilling of hollows (凹穴 *ao xue*) in oxen bones or tortoises' plastrons, followed by a careful application of intense heat (fire) into them; this caused the bone to *open up* (i.e., make a crack on the other side)—to be interpreted as either auspicious *ji* 吉 or inauspicious *xiong* 凶—as a clue for future decisions and behavior (figure C.1). These crevices or veins that *opened up* in front of the diviner or the king himself took different forms *zhao* 兆, some of which developed into characters (the Chinese character for 'to divine' *bu* 卜, for instance, has probably developed from the shape of a crack).[6]

From the observation of signs from the natural world, such as bird tracks on the ground (*zhao* 爪), the Shang sought clues in marks on the bones—this time, signs that were created as the result of a human act: these crack-openings constituted the revelation or creation of a new world to ponder into—a glimpse into a new and unfamiliar world (evoking by association Tao Yuanming's story in chapter 1).

Figure C.1. A Shang dynasty oracle bone. Guimet Museum, France. Public domain.

As for the *Yijing*, before I discuss what I find significant about the shape/form of its *yao*, it is noteworthy that the character *kai* is used in describing the efficacious potential of the book: in *Cixi* I ("Great Treatise 1") 1, following a query as to the book itself, it is said, "the Changes opens up to the (knowledge) of the way all things reach fulfillment" (夫 易開物成務)—again, the act of opening equals revelation and knowledge, a penetration into the (yet) unknown.

Now, as for the *yao* themselves—these constitute a symbolic matrix that plays on continuity and breaks: the broken *yao* represents *yin* and the unbroken *yao* represents *yang*. In *Cixi* II.8, it describes the basic characteristics of the *yao* as the firm/strong and yielding/soft that continuously interchange (剛柔相易). The *visual choice* (in ancient China) to represent the *yin* by a broken line and the *yang* by a continuous one has always intrigued me (if indeed it was a conscious choice and not merely a consequence of using long and short yarrow stalks). I haven't been able to find sources (primary, Chinese or Western) that ask, "Why is that particularly so?" What is in a broken line that renders it to be *yin*, or the continuous line—*yang*? Perhaps the visual image of walls and gates can be used heuristically: the *yang yao* looks like a wall from above, that is, just straight uninterrupted line that has no gate or opening; the *yin yao* as looks like a wall with an opened gate—if we look at it from above.

The opening of the *yin* line—as a gate in a wall, invites change as it represents discontinuity, which means perhaps that change was more associated with the softer, yielding force of yin? Note also that they differ in their inherent tension, that is, the *yin yao* pulls inwardly as if wanting to connect back, while the two sides of the *yang yao* pull out—as if wanting to break. This tension represents a dynamic, physical tension in which opposite forces close in (*yin*) and open out (*yang*).

Moreover, the *visual structure* of the hexagrams plays a semiotic role in the constant flux of change in the universe as they go through phases of "waning and waxing"—paralleling the phases of the moon. Look, for instance, at the gradual *visual* change in the structure of the hexagrams as "waning" occurs (figure C.2), that is, the process in which *yin* (broken *yao*) grows in its number within the hexagram sequence, from bottom up: Hexagram 44 (*gou* 姤) to Hexagram 33 (*dun* 遯) to Hexagram 12 (*pi* 否) to Hexagram 20 (*guan* 觀) to Hexagram 23 (*bo* 剝) to Hexagram 2 (*kun* 坤)—the climax at which the cycle reaches a "tipping point," (full *yin*), and from which it will start its "waxing cycle," that is, becoming more and more *yang*. And visually, we see "gates" growing in their inner

Figure C.2. Waning pattern and *yin* cycle in the *Yijing* hexagrams. Image created by the author.

spaces (emptiness)—reaching a state of a "*que* gate" with no girder above.

When it comes to decision-making and strategies of behavior, the hexagrams of the *Yijing* "hide" a further "visual layer," namely, that as each *yang* line moves up (away from "ground zero"), any new state is likened to a dragon in different stages of action, for example, a "hidden dragon" (dormant, inactive, and invisible) to "emerging dragon" in line two (becoming visible but still inactive), to a "flying dragon" and then a dragon that "rises up to the sky"—until it reaches a "tipping point" and exceeds its own limits (feeling all-mighty, one behaves without regard to anything . . . a sign of *arrogance*).

Chinese characters are not unlike the hexagrams themselves, that is, they are both architectural constructs that are built from foundations (i.e., the radicals) up—with additional tiers of significance piling on top. If Daoists and certainly Chan Buddhists (starting from Nagarjuna) negated the possibility of language to describe *dao*, emptiness or the "here and now," humanists and other schools tended to take these formed constructs very seriously—as (literal) "pillars of continuity and social order."[7]

I have so far discussed *kai*, that is, the various manifestations and meanings of "opening up," but what about the various dimensions and situational contexts of the closed state of the gate? The dimension that demonstrated the lowest "degrees of freedom" (barriers) is sociopolitical, but as was shown, the advice to close the gates was also encountered in other dimensions—even in those in which the "highest degree of freedom" is aspired to, namely, the mind (particularly in Daoist-inclined schools). The conspicuousness of the advice to close the gates in these dimensions has been surprising.

I admit my own surprise with the conspicuous presence of closed gates in relation to the relative inseparateness of Chinese thought and medical concepts of the body (i.e., relative to Western tendency toward separateness; see below). Core Chinese ideas do create a holistic framework in which things interconnect and change constantly, such as *dao*, change, and the complementary nature of opposites, the character *xin* which denotes both the physical organ *and* the thinking and feeling faculties, the emphasis in Chinese medicine on unobstructed *qi* that flows through the meridians, the relative collectivist notion of individual and society, *correlative thinking* between domains of knowledge and disciplines, and more.

But the study found that within this relative matrix of interconnectedness and resonance, closed gates are also needed—in the same way that biological membranes constitute open channels between inside and outside but they must also need (according to constantly changing variables) to be able to block substances from penetrating the cell, the organ, or the whole body. Thus, I maintain that any attempt at defining the Chinese body as purely holistic or only weakly so, not only constitutes a binary trap by itself, but fails to grasp the essence of holism in general . . . interconnectedness does not mean that everything is always open and accepting (like some new age spiritualism) but that it is constantly in between connectiveness and separateness through a highly-tuned, relative, and case-dependent mechanism of change,

In the context of the relations between the inside and the outside, however, one clear conclusion of the study is the early attitude of the Chinese psyche to the inside: beginning with the innermost circle of the body-mind, to the home, the city, and the state, The predominant emotion that is conspicuous in many and varied texts is one of fear and anxiety of the *outside*! As said, it seems that the inside is not to be taken for granted and must be constantly protected. It is indicative of the extent to which the ancient Chinese either feared that order and harmony will collapse due to the intrusion and invasion of external forces, or believed that the interior is never strong or solid enough to stand on its own, and it thus needs constant care.

That the Chinese state had been continuously anxious about invasions (especially from northern barbaric tribes) and wished for order inside the state is indeed expressed through architectural gates that are closed by default, such as the watchtower *guan*. Yinong Xu also stresses the imminent threats that loomed over the Chinese, saying that "such [threats] had demonic implications to the people within since the potential ruin of the city, in a sense, was equivalent to *retrogression to chaos*" (2000, 47; my emphasis). This constant anxiety underlies the creation of the *Yijing* itself, in the sense that one has to be constantly worrisome (*youhuan* 憂患) as to every minute act, behavior, or decision taken along the way, as the wrong act might lead to failure, disaster, or just bad luck. Tze-ki Hon strengthens this view, saying in reference to the *Yijing* that "this proactive thinking may cause anxiety when people are constantly worrying about making mistakes" (2019b, 9). As it is said in *Xici* II 7, "The Changes came into use in the period of middle antiquity. Those who composed the Changes had in them fear and anxiety" (作 易者, 其有憂患乎). It is noteworthy, however, that even in the case of the political aspiration for order and control, the gate is not constantly and hermitically shut; recall the gatekeepers, for instance, that utilize "questioning and listening" combined with flexible attunement to time, location, and circumstances (see comparison with the Kafkian gate in chapter 6).

If I wish to relate this gate philosophy of "protecting the inside" to current times, it points to a mental ability to handle the potential harmful impact of the outside. Modern times only intensify the need for each and every one of us to "mind his or her gates" . . . in the technological revolution we are now experiencing, aren't we overflooded with information, news, data, social media, temptations, signals, and more? Indeed, how is one to control what goes in and what stays out through the bodily gates? This can be achieved through the cultivation of a balance between closeness (self-protection) and openness and flexibility. The gradation in the levels of gate perviousness is by itself a pronouncement of flexibility and a unique "listening" to circumstances—a far cry from strict separation and divisions, which is more typical to Western thought. Indeed, it was Heidegger who said that Western thought constitutes a search "for inappropriate brightness . . . it is pure brightness without proper sophistication" (Ma 2006, 155).

When intellectual attention is drawn to *one* of the two sides of a phenomenon as opposed to their interrelation (in-betweenness), the mind is being trained to think in an *either/or* default mode. This "either-or" thinking, also named "binary thinking," "tunnel vision," or "thinking in black and white," is sadly evident and conspicuous in our present era when people are either defenders or advocators of a certain ideological view or belief—so strongly, in fact, that they are unable to relate to the opinion of the other side, and, as we know too well, they would also be prepared to fight for their position/stand/faith with violence.[8] Reaffirming the attention given to the *inside* are Chinese ideas and practices of self-cultivation that relate to the mental sphere of *xin* that contextually can be thought of as a "psychology of the body." Erica Brindley says that "there are many interesting writings in early China that focus primarily on bodily operations that more or less correspond to what we would call the more psychological aspects of the body" (2006, 7). This Chinese framework of attention to what goes in and comes out as part of self-cultivation can be useful in our current times in no lesser degree (probably much more)—a conscious and mental (biological) membrane that would balance between chaos and order, rigidity and flexibility, openness and closeness.

When such a mental membrane is impenetrable to information from the outside, for instance, one could be stuck in repeated (mental) patterns of negative feedback—which diminishes the ability to change (and the inside becomes "full of oneself").[9] This is one of the layers of meanings in chapter 11 of the *Daode jing*: as long as the cup is full, it cannot accept fresh liquid, and in correlation, as long as the mind is full, it can accept new or fresh ideas, knowledge, or insights. Any container needs to first purge itself (empty out) so that change is allowed in. This is a natural fact: life has no "room" to grow if death did not clear some space first. This is the *yinyang* of Laozi and the *yinyang* of biological life. Such psychological patterns condition the person and prevent an authentic experience of reality, not to mention the ability to find joy in the here and now.

Interestingly, if psychologists once believed that serious mental problems are the result of a mental state that is *too open, borderless, and chaotic*, it is now believed to be the opposite! John Briggs mentions psychiatrist David Shainberg, who argued that "mental illness, which appears chaotic, is actually the reverse. Mental illness occurs when images of the self becomes rigid and closed, restricting an open creative response to the world" (quoted in Briggs 2000, 29). Thus, the mind needs repeated and continuous practice toward "knowing things without knowing," that is, acquiring knowledge but not through ordinary faculties.

This is how we return to the phenomenon that underlies it all: emptiness and in-betweenness. As said, Western attitudes to emptiness differed greatly from the Chinese, but in the twentieth century, new attention has started to be given to the subject of the liminal—a growing area of research in Western scholarship (such as the anthropologist Arnold Van Gennep who studied "rites of passage" as edgy or liminal events). However, it is Western science that reaches wider into the macrocosm and deeper into the microcosm to realize that emptiness is a fundamental essence of the universe.[10] Not only emptiness per se, but the role of mediatory spaces in physics or biology, such as, to name just a few, species that inhabit the mediatory niche between the sea and the beach, nerve synapses, and as emphasized, cell membranes. Even our bodies contain gates and valves at which threshold critical physiological process take place.[11] This constitutes the very meaning of the term "ecology," as "the study of the relationships between living organisms, including humans, and their physical environment" (with the gate as its organic component).

As said in chapter 1, quite many early texts hint of an understanding of the natural world in a way that resonates with modern biology. Raymond J. Barnett even claims that Daoist thought and modern science have "independently arrived at views which are similar in their essential features and that this similarity is not coincidental but rather quite understandable" (1986, 248).[12] Not only that early passages demonstrate a modern understanding of natural adaptation and evolution but they exhibit a "secular" understanding the world—one that does not require a personal, transcendent figure that orders and responds according to specific and individual conduct. The following passage from chapter 5 of the *Laozi*, for instance, reads, "the heavens and earth (don't act out of) humanlike benevolence, they treat the 'ten thousand things' as stray dogs" (天地不仁, 以萬物為芻狗); as Roel Sterckx says, "heaven was not transcendent or personified, but an overawing force that governed all" (2019, 12).

Indeed, the religious persuasions of a culture deeply influence individuals' behavior and inherent mindset; as an illustration of this idea, let us look at two passages in comparison—each from a different tradition: Chinese and Jewish. The Chinese passage is taken from the Lunheng 論衡 number 54 (composed by Wang Chong in the first century AD):

> The heavens, (by) granting *qi* right into all the ten thousands things, the grain recovers hunger, and silk and hemp protect from the cold. This is why man eats grain and wears silk and

hemp. This is not (however) that the heavens give birth to the five crops, silk and hemp purposely in order for man to eat and wear—and in the same way, the heavens cannot be blamed for the existence of natural catastrophes (as if they desired it to befall on man on purpose).

天者、普施氣萬物之中，穀愈飢而絲麻救寒，故人食穀、衣絲麻也. 夫天之不故生五穀絲麻以衣食人，由其有災變不欲以譴告人也.

Here humans are given a very important lesson . . . nothing in nature is made purposely for them and nothing in nature works personally and purposely against them. The second passage is taken from Genesis 1:29 of the Old Testament:

God said: I give you every seed-bearing plant that is upon all the earth, and every tree that has seed-bearing fruit; they shall be yours for food.

(וַיֹּאמֶר אֱלֹהִים הִנֵּה נָתַתִּי לָכֶם אֶת־כָּל־עֵשֶׂב ׀ זֹרֵעַ זֶרַע אֲשֶׁר עַל־פְּנֵי כָל־הָאָרֶץ וְאֶת־כָּל־הָעֵץ אֲשֶׁר־בּוֹ פְרִי־עֵץ זֹרֵעַ זָרַע לָכֶם יִהְיֶה לְאָכְלָה)

The discussion as to the implications of these two very different "set of tools" or "rules of the game" that are hereby given to humans is beyond the scope of this book (and could probably fill another).

Now, included in the early Chinese scientific-like observation of the world was a certain intuitive understanding of the intermingling of the forces of chaos and order—and the role of the thin line that stands in between them. I suggest the term *homeostasis* best describes this process: the membranous exchange with the outside (environment) of each cell and organism constitutes the very sphere in which it would either survive or perish—because each organism must preserve order in the same rate as its inevitable disintegration. Importantly, the term *homeostasis* is often misunderstood because of the Latin word *homeo*, which means "keeping the same state"—which might be interpreted as "allowing no change"! However, the "dynamic perspective" in modern biology realizes that actualized life depends on the constant response between the internal and external and on the ability to change. Without change there is no life.

This is an important realization: the survival of any organism is never promised nor guaranteed; it resembles a delicate seedling that needs proper care in order to grow . . . as the very character for life *sheng* 生 indicates. Robin Wang says that it "originally referred to a plant growing out of the soil. It can be a noun indicating life itself or a verb that conveys the generative living process" (2012, 12).[13] Thus the very delicate balance between chaos and order constitutes *life* itself and corresponds to the continuously changing balance between rigidity (closed gate) and flexibility (gradation of openness). Indeed, Richard J. Bird calls it "order within chaos," and says that "the traditional use of the word chaos signifies complete disorder, but modern science shows that there is a great deal of orderliness even in the patterns of chaotic systems (2003, 5).

This cosmic system is, on the one hand, individually exclusive, because any and every entity in it is unique (a form by itself), but on the other hand, it is collectively inclusive, because all and everything in the world is in it. It is an open system which presents all possibilities—through "open and closed" movements it can expand or decrease, stop or proceed. In 1978, James Grier Miller coined the term "living systems," defining them as "open self-organizing systems that have the special characteristics of life and interact with their environment." According to this model, all nature is a continuum, in which the endless complexity of life is organized into patterns which repeat themselves (1978, 1025). In the endless cycles of life, which necessitates an open system of interrelations, the decay of organisms is inevitable.[14]

As said, a system that is too rigid (stuck in its *form*) will not be adaptive enough to meet these life's challenges; complete isolation does not allow for life to thrive. This also applies to human lives: How is man to survive, evolve, and prevail, not to mention succeed and flourish?! It is here that we go back to self-cultivation—which actually begins with parenting and education as the starting point of a child and continues with the decisions and path-making (*dao*) of the adult.

This is the meaning of cultivation in general: the fulfillment of potentiality of any living thing constitutes the way through which their inherent power and natural tendencies emerge outward and are pronounced in the ontological world (as we have seen in the *Yijing*)— from *dao* to *de*. As a root idea of Chinese thought, *dao* remains in its deepest essence an entity that can be *way'ed*, that is, walked (or sailed along a river), and self-cultivation means a continuous lifetime process which is efficaciously manifested through practice and involves change and transformation, evident in Chinese arts (inclusive of martial arts).[15]

How are the above ideas of openness, closeness, and change relate to the model suggested for *dao* in chapter one? Rivers present two possible choices or strategies: flowing with its stream, which means flexibility, openness, and letting-go, and on the other hand, going against the stream, which utilizes conscious effort and involves the attempt to control the river (e.g., in the form of dams). If the reader recalls the narrative of the carp and the Dragon Gate, for instance, it constitutes an instance of self-cultivation that requires effort, planning, and a highly determined mind directed at a target. The other option of flowing down with the stream might sound *easier* (one of the meanings of *yi*) but requires courage and a deep letting go of one's ego and forceful mind (it takes courage *not* to be in control).

I maintain this is exactly the meaning of the following line in chapter 70 of the *Daode jing*:

My words are extremely easy to know, and very easy to practice; still, no one in this world is able to know them and no one is able to practice them.

吾言甚易知, 甚易行. 天下莫能知, 莫能行.

It is *easy* in a *wuwei* sense of behavioral strategy which runs along the path of least resistance: noninterference with the natural flow of things and events—an observation that watches the processional fruition of an event like a mirror.[16] Intriguingly, in the context of self-cultivation, if the reader recalls, the two strategies were found to correlate with architecture: three passages present the process and stages of self-cultivation with a sequence of architectural steps (the *xue er* in the *Analects*, a Zhou text that was posted on a gate, and the *Taixuan jing*, respectively), as follows:

Outside → Gate → Hall → Inner Chamber

Main Street → Alley → Gate → Courtyard → Outer Hall → Inner Chamber

Steps → Audience Hall → Gate → "inner sanctum" *ao* 奧.[17]

These acts of *dao'ing* start from an external gate and proceed to the innermost chamber *ao* (which signifies the highest accomplishment in the dimension of the mind). The significance of architecture here is twofold: (1) The repetitive nature of "using" architecture . . . we enter and exit a structure through a gate again and again—as an iterative process that constitutes the ordered pattern of life and of the human experience; just as architecture is repetitive in use, self-cultivation consists of a continuous course that arrives and departs at the same spatial point in a cyclic process—but each time a deeper realization and actualization is achieved. It evokes the passage from the *Daxue* (see introduction) that demonstrates the consecutive process of "implementing order"—from the cosmos down into the heart-mind and back again!; (2) Whereas the *dao'ing* itself is shared by both strategies, the direction is opposite! In the humanistic context, the direction is from the simple to the complex, a process of learning in which knowledge, conventions, and rules of differentiation are accumulated . . . whereas in Daoist thought (and Chan/Zen Buddhism), it goes back to the simple and empty—the "inner sanctum," which is deep and mysterious and accessible only to the enlightened whose mind lodges in emptiness *xu* 虛, in quintessential silence and clarity.

It is said in chapter 40 of the *Daode jing,*

> The movement of *dao* constitutes a return backward,
> Weakness is what *dao* employs;
> The "ten thousand things and phenomena" are created (and
>   given life) from Something,
> And Something is borne out of emptiness.[18]

I argue that the passage describes the natural phenomenon of entropy, which constitutes the process of deteriorating back to emptiness, the breaking down of all forms. Then, from emptiness things develop toward complexity (molecules, chains of molecules, cells, tissues, organs, a creature). It also refers to the inherent tendency of nature to "fall back" to chaos, instead of arranging itself in order.[19] But the passage carries an additional meaning: an aspiration for the mind to go back to the formless (lacking distinctions). At this locale, one is able to simultaneously see both order and chaos, and "this and that" as two manifestations of life.

Further testament to an early understanding of the natural propensity for entropy (and "tipping point") appears in the *Guanyinzi* 關

尹子 *Master Yin of the Pass:* "The construction of things is difficult; the destruction of things by the Tao is easy. Of all things under Heaven there is none that does not reach its completion with difficulty, and none that is not easily destroyed" (Needham 1956, 446). Difficult to construct but also prone to be destroyed, Chinese architecture itself is made out of the gradation between emptiness (*jian*) and the concrete. Perhaps resonating with chapter 11 of the *Laozi* (see chapter 2) and with *jian*, Japanese architect Yoshio Taniguchi once said, "architecture is basically a container of something. I hope they will enjoy not so much the teacup, but the tea." Here the philosophical tendency is toward the aesthetic experience of emptiness, and Zhuangzi took this orientation to the extreme: destroy all forms!

Remaining still in the field of architecture, the above instances of gradual steps connect us back to resolution and sense of sight. As one walks along the way (as part of cultivation), one acquires the ability to simultaneously look backward (into what has been before) and forward (the unfolding of *dao* in the temporal dimension). This is interconnected with the contextual direction chosen—as said, forward to the more complex (against the stream) or backward to the simpler (with the stream). Can we visualize this "looking backward" as a personal reflection on one's long life? A famous passage in the *Analects* constitutes such reflection on the stages Kongzi went through in his life's journey (*dao*):

> Confucius said: "At fifteen my aspiration was the product of learning, (then), at thirty, I stood for myself, (then), at forty, I was not confused anymore, (then) at fifty, I realized the mandate of the heavens, (then), at sixty, my ears (started to) obey (then), at seventy, though the heart-mind (still) desired, I didn't overstep the boundary"

子曰: 吾十有五而志于學, 三十而立, 四十而不惑, 五十而知天命, 六十而耳順, 七十而從心所欲, 不踰矩.

Confucius reflects back on his life, pondering on significant stages in his own personal evolvement through the *quantum stages or gates* on *dao*. As he grows older, an additional point of view of "looking back" is added: in correlation, I believe, to the way Confucius *historically* referred to those exemplary sages and kings of the past, he now reflects back on his own personal life and *dao*.

This conscious reflection of change and cultivation along one's life indicates the crucial role of continuous *practice* as a lifelong process of assimilation into the body-mind (until *li* becomes second nature!).[20] I find the last "leap" in Confucius's self-account (at 70) particularly interesting because of the character *ju* 矩 (mentioned only once in the *Analects*)—which I translated as "boundary"; but *ju* refers to a carpenter's ruler or square that is metaphorically used in various sources for the right, correct, and accurate way things and standards *should* be. Sometimes the very characteristic of the tool (and not its function) is used to designate the nature of things (i.e., the ruler is square and straight thus cannot be round—this is its nature and designated efficacy).[21] Confucius attests to having achieved the level of "following the heart's desire without overstepping the carpenter's ruler" . . . utilizing the metaphor of the ruler in two contexts. The first is as a tool that is square—representing earth—which stands in parallel to the "decree of heaven" at the age of fifty (thus, standing exactly in between heavens and earth, at the gate of in-betweenness). The second hints perhaps that though man's nature (*xing*) desires infinite expansion, it should, in actuality, stay within *bounds*—as in this sphere of in-betweenness true freedom and authenticity can be achieved.

As for *dao* in the humanist context, Confucius famously said that it is man who "broadens the way" (人能弘道), a strong statement that has invited many and varied interpretations. Is it the notion that man is able to grasp, manifest, and apply *dao* in his life and by this *expand* his capability—therefore achieving a "broadening of the (human) way"? Is it also because the self-actualization of the individual and of society cannot be separated? The second half of the line (*fei dao hong ren*) hints again (as we have seen previously) that *dao* does not do anything to assist or actively guide the people—it is man who needs to explore, cultivate, and entune himself with *dao*. It strongly emphasizes that man is solely responsible for his or her life.

In reference to the character *dao*, Robin Wang says that "it implies that one does not simply walk on the road mindlessly or aimlessly but with a direction and with mindfulness" (2012, 45). Not only minute awareness to where one goes and in which direction, but a constant carefulness as to every step along the way; as said, this carefulness stems also from an anxiety, a constant fear of "what is out there" in the political, social, and individual spheres. In the dimension of the body-mind, various methods and techniques (physical exercise, alchemy, etc.) developed for the purpose of achieving personal transcendence and eternal life, for example, breathing exercises which enabled the adept to return to womb respiration. As is said in the *Gaozi* 49:

中 義 守 不 忒 Guard the center of (your) internal propriety, and (you) will not err;
不 以 物 亂 官 Do not allow things to disorder your senses,
不 以 官 亂 心 Do not allow the senses to disorder your heart-mind.
是 謂 中 得 This is called obtaining the center.

This inclination means "skipping" the human circle and returning to the natural, instinctive, and spontaneous state, before the accumulation of "civilized deposits" in man's heart-mind (characterized by a low level of order). Though Zhuangzi does mention past sages who possessed perfect *de*, I argue that he refers to their ideal state of mind and not so much to the *historical* sense—as humanists did. It is a return to the basal state of mind in which the "higher self" (that analyzes and rationalizes), and the instinctive and animalistic self (which exists "here and now") are not separate!

I suggest that the various Chinese inclinations toward the chaotic or the ordered also correspond to a tendency toward continuity or discontinuity in the sociopolitical dimension; we see this phenomenon throughout Chinese intellectual history—as the tension between adherence to old notions and the search for new ways. In other words, the philosophical question that persistently occupied the minds of the Chinese (to date) is "What is the key to prevail, survive, and even succeed—on both the individual and the social levels, that is, the people and the state? Is it an adherence to the words and ideas of ancient sages—which means a *continuity* of old traditions and customs (inclusive of *li*), or should it be a search for change, reforms, innovations, or even a total transformation?" As Patricia Ebrey writes, "in each period Chinese have made use of what they inherited, but also have come up with new ideas and practices" (1996, 8).

The Chinese *pattern* of oscillating between form and emptiness, chaos and order, *yin* and *yang* that we repeatedly see is evident again in relation to holding on to tradition or aspiring for innovation and change, as textual evidence demonstrates both attitudes! For instance, Michael Puett discusses chapter 7 ("Jingshen") of the *Huainanzi*, saying that it starts with a narrative of how the inventions of the sages took non-sagely humans from a world in which they lived in caves, had no clothing, and barely had enough food to survive to one in which they all had all they needed to live and thrive. One of the keys to this celebration of innovation is that sages must be fully free from following the standards of the past so that they can be allowed to create anew whenever necessary! (quoted in A. Olberding 2011, 231)

It is truly an illuminating passage in the way it explicitly declares *innovation* and the *breaking free* of past standards to constitute the most important factors for survival and successful living (as relevant today as it was 2,200 years ago)! The text further emphasizes that all three (previous) dynasties fell because the rulers were overly beholden to precedent. On the other side we have the humanists, for instance, for whom ancient scripts, traditions, and rituals constituted the foundations to which all future generations must cling.[22]

The gate's chaos/order interplay relates to Chinese history in yet another way: it was during chaotic periods that philosophers suggested their innovative ideas (that is, new formulations of *dao*), the most familiar representative being Confucius. By "chaotic periods" I refer to mediatory or liminal eras that stretched between centrally ruled dynasties of relative sociopolitical rest and order. These Chinese "middle ages" constituted a breakdown of the central power followed by social unrest, rebellious uprisings, and general *chaos*.[23] Patricia Ebrey indeed writes that Chinese civilization, "progresses through a series of *yin-yang* life reversal of direction from excessive disorder to excessive order and back again. Thus periods of creative but frightfully deadly disorder are followed by the imposition of stringent political order, sometimes so heavy-handed as to be oppressive. But order eventually unravels into disorder once again, renewing the pattern" (1996, 333). Chinese political history, even in modern times, demonstrates a constant examination of the "degrees of freedom" allowed to the populace . . . it is interesting to note that this conscious balance as to borders and degrees of openness parallels an *internal* play between "making changes but keeping the current system" (the framework) versus a total revolution (the 1911 Chinese Revolution), and even in the present-day Chinese Communist Party.[24] This is because culture *is* the result of specific boundaries constantly evolving and changing—sometimes expanding or narrowing down, sometimes opening its gates and in other times, closing them down. No culture escapes these shifts as they are a constant feature of life itself—changing with the inevitable exchange between the inside and the outside through its membranous "gates."

In the context of culture and society, Chinese humanist philosophy aspires for the individual and society to "move as one," and in order to achieve that, "harmony" and "ritual propriety" are required on all levels—from the individual to the family to society and the nation at large.[25] According to the Confucian view, as we have seen, individuals are not isolated entities floating in a "sack" of society, exactly as the mind does not reside isolated in the "sack" of the body. The idea that the family is an exemplary unit of conduct and interrelationships is connected to the humanist emphasis on education, learning, and teaching. Indeed, how often do we hear the utterance, "education begins at home"? However, the potentiality of a child's future way (life) is infinite, that is, there are endless directions and possibilities for a child to evolve to . . . and whether or not children and adults can succeed in manifesting their inborn potential (called "element" in modern education), depends on the education and cultivation he or she receives in childhood and his or her own self-cultivation later on.

This chaos-order interplay is something we experience every day: the sun indeed rises every morning, but (on the other hand) weather and natural disasters are sudden and unpredictable. The same interplay takes place in our minds: in the midst of the mundane, unexpected things can suddenly befall upon us or strike us as enlightenment. It is noteworthy that in a similar way to the intermingling forces of yin and yang (each underlying the other), numerical calculations suggest that "some degree of order may persist beneath the chaos" (Maddox 1990, 421).[26]

I have suggested a few paragraphs back that the "gate-philosophy" is applicable and relevant today. The ancient Chinse awareness to the gates of the body-mind can become a new skill of self-cultivation in the twenty-first century—as a mental exercise, which I call "Mind Your Gates." The following instances illustrates the efficacy of the idea: (1) Mouth: if it is too open (there are no gatekeepers), one talks, chats, gossips, or argues simply for the sake of "making a point," or it might also be that one abuses language in an offensive manner and pollutes the "human environment," on so on; (2) Mind: if it opens up only to certain principles, ideas, or moral conventions, or when one is stuck in binary thinking, or if one is unable to "let go" and allow things to take their course (cannot act *wuwei*); (3) Nose: breathing in the wrong way (too fast or shallow). Within this suggested framework—which is directed more toward the self (i.e., as part of self-cultivation)—another theme that repeatedly surfaced is related to the *outside* that surrounds us, that is, the external environment, individuals, or society at large, namely, the immediate and potential consequences of our actions and uttered words. Importantly, the passages emphasized how a small hinge has the efficacy to control a huge and heavy gate, and, likewise, the smallest act or a single word possesses the efficacy of far-reaching consequences—evoking the scientific idea of the butterfly effect.

These are but a few examples as an attempt to demonstrate the practicality and applicability of ancient Chinese ideas. Further still, each of the above-mentioned openings works differently! For example, the ears are permanently "open gates" so that we cannot stop hearing (we can only close the gate by external blockage such as ear plugs or earphones); also, according to Chinese sources, we can develop the skill of *inner listening*, which is not dependent on the ears! The mouth is a double-leaved gate that opens and closes at our will so that we are able to control what, when, and how we say things; the eyes are also double-leaved gates but of a different sort, that is, we can close and open them at will, but not indefinitely: at a certain point they must close. In the same way as inner listening, as quite a few passages claim, one can develop the skill of inner seeing.

The skills of inner listening and seeing can be compared to "knowing things without knowing,"—that is, acquiring knowledge but not through ordinary faculties. Pregadio says that "Zhuangzi's analysis of the human mind is in fact an epistemology: since the Dao is ultimately unknowable through the ordinary mind, there is only one way to know it: through 'the knowledge that does not know'" or, through the formless.[27]

As seen, this knowledge—the combination of an abstract idea manifested in the concrete—gave rise to multiple methods, techniques, skills, and various strategies of behavior and decision-making that all relate to *dao* . . . which way should I take, where do I want to "go"? Where do I want to be in the spatiotemporal future which is unknown and invisible?

As the *Yijing* and additional texts demonstrate, the Chinese offered no determinism: the future is unknown and invisible and there are no absolute answers . . . only clues, traces, and sensory skills (*shi*) that together manifest an internal knowing as to the right choice as per time, location, and circumstances. Indeed, one key element in Chinese decision-making is timing; as Guolong Lai says, "timing is an important aspect of the early Chinese notion of a journey, which in one sense can be understood as the science of timing" (2015, 167). The *Mozi* contains a wonderful description of such decision-making that demands a spontaneous and quick response (timing) . . . as the slightest hesitation or doubt causes the gate to close. Minor Choices *xiao qiu* 小取 of chapter 11, passage 6 says,

> To be about to exit through the gate, is not to exit through the gate;
> to stop just before existing through the gate, *is* to stop exiting the gate.

且出門, 非出門也; 止且出門, 止出門也.

If one makes the decision to exit through the gate (that is, to venture outside, whether mentally or physically), but—just before actually doing it—retreats back and refrains from the act, either because of inability, a change of mind, or due to fears and doubts, then the intention and preparations and inner resolution don't mean a thing . . . what *does* matter however is the *applied* fulfillment of one's resolutions . . . this is at least what I believe Mozi is trying to say.

The second part of the line emphasizes that stopping before the gate *is* exactly what it is: an inability to carry out a decision in the external and formed world. This is yet again a relevant message: people can talk and talk about the change they want to make in their lives, but as long as it is not implemented in action, it is not worth much. We have discussed a particular narrative which points directly to an opportunity for change manifested by a gate (actually, a closed checkpoint), namely, the hagiography of Laozi.

In this case the gate opened up as an opportunity for transformation due to the techniques and methods *shu* of *wuwei* and *dao* 盜—"stealing" *dao* (enabling one to be one with *dao*) by feeling the moment, the locality, and all circumstances. What is required, though, in order to open the "gate of opportunity"? Only a quick, spontaneous, and courageous act will open the gate because it won't be open for long. I suggest that in this hagiography, the text of the *Daode jing* is the actualized manifestation (*de*) of *Laozi and Laozi* is the actualized manifestation of *dao* (a sequential series of *de*). In the same way that the text changed the life of the gatekeeper Yin Xi, the *Daode jing* has since continued to transform the lives of future readers (but this is not a given . . . the readers themselves need to be in a suitable state of mind and readiness for change).

We all go through change and transformation constantly—visually apparent in our outer appearance but people seem to take their "internal environment" as a constant (unchanging) "real and true self," which is bound in identity and in name. With the comprehension that change is inevitable comes a second realization: the necessity to develop skills of adaptation to life's ordered and chaotic facets (the meaning of *organic* life).

This philosophical stand that people are solely responsible for their lives, fully realizing the knowledge that life is devoid of some grand, teleological scheme demands people to walk along the liminal zone of *uncertainty*, somewhere between the ordered and the chaotic, between the open and the closed—on the threshold. To draw an image, it would be just like passing through an endless succession of gates, each monitored according to location, time, and circumstances. This might be a scary place to be when nothing is guaranteed or promised "beyond the gate": it is an opportunity with no certainties. But this is exactly where the skills of *shi* 勢 and *shi* 時 are required—as an inner knowledge that senses when, where, and how to act—or whether to act at all! To me, this constitutes some of the most general and yet most vital Chinese "advice" to people. This inner skill of timely behavior resembles the way one threads on the road (*dao*) when we take a hike, for instance: one carefully selects where to place each and every step, constantly evaluating one's actions and reactions at any given moment.[28] The idea of the importance of the where, when, and how one makes a first step is beautifully illustrated in chapter 63 of the *Daode jing*:

> A tree of huge girth is born from a tiny tip,
> A platform of nine tiers starts from a hip of earth.
> A thousand *li* journey begins with the first step (on the ground).

合抱之木, 生於毫末. 九層之臺, 起於累土. 千里之行, 始於足下.

A first step signifies the decision to embark on the journey; second, the *way* this first step is conducted will determine all consequential progress and development—whether in nature, architecture, or man's life. It also points to the wisdom of *waiting* for the right moment. At times, the ego wishes to act out or impatiently say something *now* . . . but taking an interval *jian* 間 of time might allow for the natural dynamic of things to take place—realizing that one cannot force a fruit to ripen . . . as all things have their own unique cycle, dynamics, and rhythm.

The *Yuandao* expresses this need to be adaptive, courageous, and "reflexive" in one's decisions as the result of an intuitive mind (as opposed to the rational, calculative mind). Achieving this kind of responsiveness is the result of cultivating a *wuwei* mind—a spontaneous, *ego-less* "self-so" behavior. In the *Daode jing*, it constitutes a philosophy directed at the individual and leaders, advising for a "feminine" principle, of softness and flexibility, as opposed to other ways of dealing with conflicts and obstacles (e.g., aggressiveness). It also recommends that, like water, human beings should be able to go down to lowly places, of which they are (conventionally) afraid (looking into an abyss can be a scary experience) or for which they carry contempt.[29]

Indeed, the ego desires the lofty places that sit high above others . . . like a king sitting on the throne; but Laozi wonders whether people can excel at *bending* instead of fighting, being flexible instead of hard, being able to *bend* at times (like a bamboo) and yield. Visceral knowing is more an instinctive knowing that "acts" like water, streaming along "the path of least resistance" or *wuwei*. This behavioral and mental philosophy can pose a real challenge for a lot of people: first because the idea that the weak and soft can prevail (better than the strong and hard) is counterintuitive in many cultures (especially Western), and second, letting go and *wuwei'ing* is not easy for people who need to be "in control" . . . What does being in control mean? It is the constant calculating and thinking faculties that consciously observe and manage from above—distancing the mind from its physical and instinctive (even animalistic) roots.

This is presented in the *Zhuangzi* through an interesting variety of craftsmen who possess the highest *shi* 勢 of materials, which means knowing how to work and flow along with the natural propensity of materials. I see it as the *melding together* of the emptiness in the mind and emptiness outside. In the *Zhuangzi*, some devices serve as metaphors to this efficaciousness: the hinge *daoshu* 道樞, the potter's wheel *tianjun* 天鈞, and the whetstone of heavens *tianni* 天倪. They all stand for the "unity of two," a center in which the diffusion and harmonizing of being and nonbeing occurs. This harmony is the way *dao* functions through emptiness and annuls all dichotomies, thus returning to the order of natural balance, and continuous, spontaneous responsiveness—as said, "when the hinge is fitted into the socket, it can respond endlessly" (Watson 2003, 35).

Indeed, in order for the hinge to be efficacious it needs to be well fitted in its socket—to have the freedom of space, of emptiness so that out of this void it can then respond endlessly to the changing circumstances. This wandering, which constitutes the complete letting-go of social conventions, opinions, preferences, or, in fact, any distinctions in the mind, enables one to observe all phenomena without attachment, judgment, or inclination—it is a state of no distinctions at all, in which even the gate itself disappears.

This empty state of mind cannot be expressed through language; as one "forgets oneself" and loses all sense of time, one enters a "state of flow" that does not need be to defined or confirmed by words. The Western psychologist who probably got nearest to describing and even naming this state of mind, in which a person becomes fully immersed in an activity was Hungarian-born Mihály Csíkszentmihályi, who called it "flow"—ego falls away, time flies by, all is in the present time, and one feels pure joy. This aesthetic performance or aesthetics of living (meditation in motion) is the root of any artistic expression and its creative source. This point is beautifully described in Lu Ji's *Theory of Reading and Writing of Medieval China*, in which the author investigates the sources of creativity and the fear of losing one's inspirational muse. Wendy Swartz writes about the wheelwright Bian from the *Zhuangzi*:

> It is like a dancer flinging her sleeves to the rhythm of the beat,
> Or the singer delivering his sounds in response to the strings.
> This is undoubtedly what Wheelwright Bian could not speak
>   about,
> Hence nor is the most flowery discourse able to capture its
>   essence. (2020, 150)

I find the image of the dancer most apt because, first, the character for dancing *wu* 舞 (found on oracle bones) contains the character for emptiness (*wu* 無) and, second, it depicts a woman shaman dancing while holding feathers or plumes in her hands (Ronan 1978, 107). Several ideas combine together in this analogy, that is, emptiness, a connection with higher force (as shamanistic ritual), femininity, and creativity.

Dance offers further insights: the ability to be one with the music and its rhythm, be immersed in the "here and now," letting the body flow spontaneously—all this demands a freedom in the mind! (This is the opposite of the familiar acute sense of "self-consciousness" in a dance party.) It takes me back to the character *heng* 恆—as the ability to stay calm and centered and uninfluenced by external eyes and criticism; this points to an open gate through which external signals *can* indeed penetrate, but they bear no impact on the mind—exactly like a calm boat in stormy waters. Wendy Swartz continues in saying that

> according to Lu Ji, the workings of creativity, natural as a dancer flinging her sleeves to musical beats and undeliberate as a singer sounding his response to musical notes, can no more be revealed in language than Wheelwright Bian's craft. The unmanageability, even unpredictability, of the creative force is already foreshadowed in the preface of the "Rhapsody," where Lu Ji writes: "As for grasping an axe to hew an axe-handle, even though the model is not far, yet the permutations that follow the movements of hand are truly difficult to convey in language." (quoted in Kroll and Silk 2020, 151)

As I have argued before, these are not mystical experiences, nor is meditation: it is a state of body-mind in which one "sits" in quietness, and the mind is brought to zero, to "in-betweenness," to emptiness.

Meditation allows for a heightened inward awareness, a high resolution with which to observe internal and external events, and its training leads to a concrete body-mind assimilation of change, emptiness, and impermanence; slowly through practice it might lead to the destruction of the walls that surround us. I have mentioned Chinese painting, martial arts, and dancing . . . but perhaps music constitutes a more familiar example of training and repetition; think, for instance, of a pianist who plays the same piece over and over again. As said in regard to the three architectural paths (as cultivation), each time his performance—as the fulfillment of *potency* (*de*)—elevates and deepens. With practice, the pianist lets go of the reading of the notes and of thinking about what comes next, or in one way or another being self-conscious, and is fully engaged in the present moment. This level of music playing (as in many other skills and arts) is *beyond* verbal teaching or description (*it cannot be taught*, only practiced) as it constitutes a moment of clarity and exhilaration (the pianist forgets his or her self). As said, it is a cyclic path that repeatedly goes through the same points of entrances and departures, beginnings and ends (*ao*).[30] Studies offer an understanding of this type of acquiring knowledge through practice—the first looks at the internalization of the practice through memory and is called "procedural memory," in addition to models that break down the process to stages, namely, the Fitts Model (1954) and the Dreyfuss Model (1980) of skill acquisition.

In Daoist sources the emptied state of the mind is illustrated through visual images, such as, the "horse gallop" (that is seen through the gate in a flash) and wandering *you* 遊. To many people (especially those characterized by logic and preplanning) and perhaps in comparison to the rational West, aimless wandering seems too random to understand and accept (albeit follow). However, Zhuangzian wandering is not without consciousness or awareness, but a unique skill of utilizing the senses, without the interference of the ego or the "thinking and planning faculty." According to Zhuangzi, this is the "authentic man" who wholly feels the situation, time, space, and *shi* combined.

But in early China there were many voices . . . different from the Daoist inclination toward the "empty mind" or Zhuangzian wandering; actually, as we have seen, humanist philosophies tended toward the "full mind" of substantial knowledge—which puts distinctions into human society (whether of status, morality, gender, etc.). Thus, these two types of thinking can be thought of as the analyzing faculty that plans and is conscious to every move, and the intuitive and spontaneous one that corresponds to "here and now."

We also oscillate between the "I" or self that thinks, analyzes, and controls and the unconscious, spontaneous, and instinctive self that is bonded with the body and is closer to *ziran*.[31] Can modern theories of cognitive psychology as well as current studies of the human brain set a background to these two types of thought? The two hemispheres that make up the human brain function interconnectedly, and while the left specializes in analytical thought and language, the right specializes in intuitive and creative thought. This constitutes a "working framework" of two complementary systems in which the rational "higher self" makes certain that the instinctive and fast (our animalistic roots) is under control, so it does not make impulsive and rush decisions.

In parallel, Daniel Kahneman formulated a model of two systems: system 1 operates automatically with little or no effort, whereas system 2 allocates attention to the effortful mental activities that are often associated with the subjective experience of agency, choice, and concentration (2011, 20–21). System 2 constitutes our identity—the self that is aware of its existence and consciously makes decisions and thinks. This system tends to "overtake" system 1 by letting us believe that our bodies and mind are under our control; however, acting and working almost unnoticed, system 1 can generate ideas by itself. This spontaneous and instinctive system is more chaotic, less predictable, and quicker than the logical system that is inclined to ordered and rational calculation.[32]

Can't we perhaps combine these chaotic and orderly sides of our personalities through awareness to both? This might lead to the very starting point with which we have begun—the "gate of creation" in the *Yijing* and the gate at the end of chapter 1 of the Laozi. Isn't it the ability to be entwined with both our chaotic and orderly sides that allows for creativity (something new being born—a creation)? It means continuously re-creating ourselves through endless "transforming gates."[33] A painting by the Song dynasty artist Chen Rong (figure C.3) named *Nine Dragons*, portrays this chaotic *flow* so well: the dragons are soaring amidst the clouds, the mists, the whirlpools, and fire—their inner vigor is combined and entwined with the chaotic and dynamic forces of nature.

These soaring dragons visually evoke shapes and patterns of cloud formation (figure C.4)—so just as to give a comparative expression of this Chinese sense of chaos-in-order in nature, I add an image of a natural cloud formation.

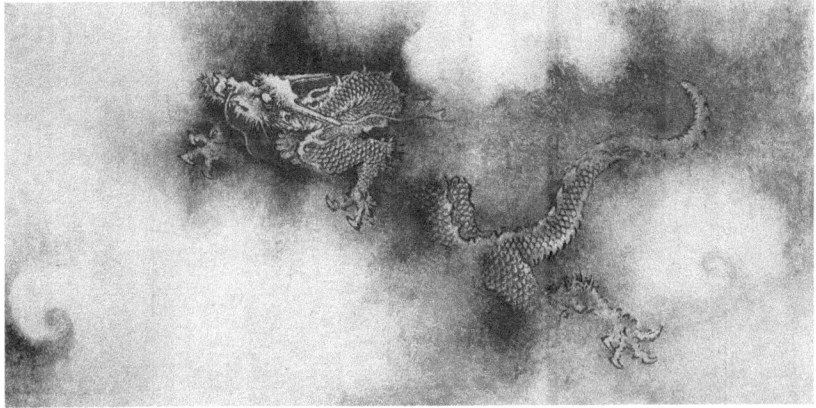

Figure C.3. Chen Rong, *Nine Dragons*, 1244. Ink and color on paper. Courtesy of the Francis Gardner Curtis Fund. Wikimedia Commons.

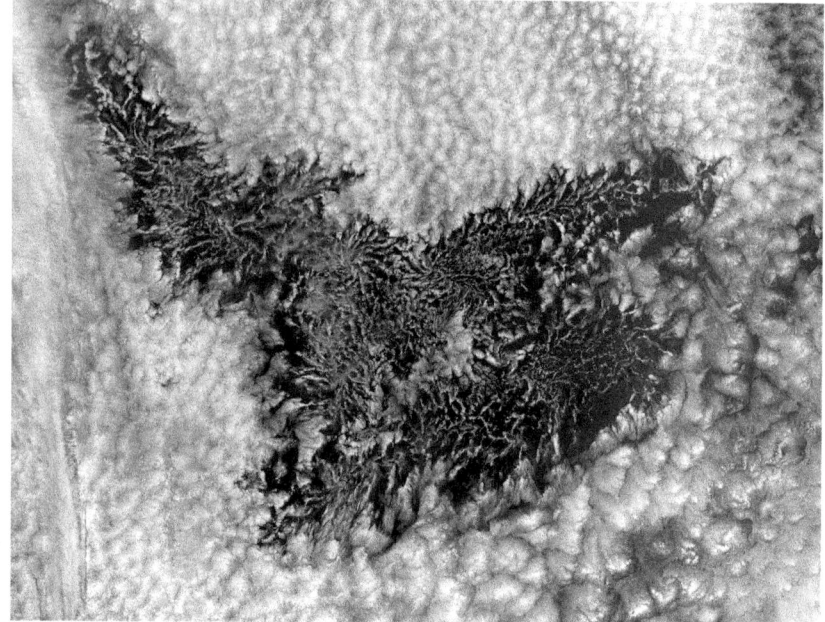

Figure C.4. A NASA (Visible Earth) image of clouds. Public domain.

To end, I choose the words of Wang Bi on the *Laozi*: "As a book, the *Laozi* can almost be covered completely with a simple phrase: **AH!** It does nothing more than encourage growth at the branch tips by enhancing the roots!" (Lynn 1999, 37).

Referring specifically to the *Laozi*, notwithstanding, I find in this concise passage some essential aspects of Chinese thought: an organic interplay between what can be expressed in words or only through image, a chaos-order interplay, human creativity and evolutionary creation, the transformational potential of the "space in between"—the gate. It appears the humble Chinese gate teaches us the importance of minute choices—visioned as a mindful and careful yet spontaneous treading through this life of ours . . . when we realize how short, quick, and fragile life is, every act of opening or closing—determines which path (among all others) was chosen—taking us full circle back right back to Borges's Garden of Forking Paths. To me, it always evokes Zhuangzian thought and Chan (Zen) Buddhism . . . first, that enlightenment is found in the most mundane of tasks and in iterative skills; second—being able to pass through this short life with lots of good humor . . . of course it would be Zhuangzi (Outer Chapters, "Streams of Autumn" 6) who would be able to contain it all in thirty characters:

The life of all things seems so sudden and quick—like the galloping of a horse; no movement lacks stillness, no (unit of) time lacks change; what to do? What not to do? Indeed! [I]t is all about self-transformation.

物之生也若驟若馳, 無動而不變, 無時而不移,何為乎? 何不為乎? 夫固將自化.

Or perhaps we can end with the British way of humorously coping with human existentialism . . . as is expressed by Basil in *Faulty Towers*:

Basil: "Zhoom! What was that?

That was your life, Mate!

Oh, that was quick.

Do I get another?

Sorry, Mate. That's your lot." (1979, Season 2, Episode 7)

Notes

Introduction

1. This opinion stems from two reasons: (1) Due to the huge cultural and historical gap, Chinese concepts should be kept as they are, e.g., *dao* and not "way." (2) Each Chinese concept constitutes such a vast world of meanings, associations, and connotations that no single foreign word can possibly convey it wholly.

2. See Fox (2017).

3. The idea of translating *tian* as "sky" or even "skies" may sound strange and inapt because it reduces the complex and multifaceted term "heavens" (in the context of human belief) to the "astronomical" sky; however, in Hebrew and Judaism the word *skies* (*shamaim*) שמיים is actually synonymous to God.

4. In an interview with Emma Brockers in the *Guardian*, 2011.

5. Boucher (1948).

6. As Borges was highly interested and attracted to Chinese philosophy, I wonder whether the gate's textual location at the very end of the last line resonates with the gate at the end of *Daode jing* 1; see Lidan Lin, 2017, "The Novel or the Garden? Borges' Postmodern Dialogue with China," *Journal of East-West Thought* 7, no. 4.

7. Descartes saw animals as possessing a merely machinelike body, without a soul or a mind—as a soul is a unique gift awarded by God only to human beings; this view was strongly backed by Christian belief of the superiority and right for domination of humans over animals (it was Voltaire who dared voicing criticism over the morally justified medical vivisections on animals conducted by his eighteenth-century contemporaries). In this context, a small note to Edward S. Slingerland, who, in his book on mind and body in early China (2019), indeed agrees that the Cartesian view that sees animals as mere automatons that cannot feel pain or distress is "bizarre, implausible, and morally repellent," but then adds that this view "is almost entirely unknown to any but professional historians of philosophy" (275); but this "almost entirely unknown" view was very much known

247

to a lot of animals at the time—many were horrifically tortured for no reason whatsoever. This illustrates the extent to which philosophy *does* matter (it has the potential to impact lives significantly whether in a positive or negative way). To return to the subject at hand, as the reader knows, the nineteenth century experienced a radical change with the appearance on the stage of Darwin—who shook the European world by presenting continuity between animals and human beings, something the Christian world had a hard time accepting (as do some extremely religious Jewish and Christian communities *today*).

8. For further reading, see Kanming Zeng, 1999, *Dragon Gate* (A & C Black and White).

9. Ge Hong (283–343 AD). "The book of the master who embraced simplicity" *Baopuzi* 抱朴子 (Henderson 1994, 226).

10. In 2022, the Jixia Academy ruins were discovered in Zibo City, Shandong Province—the result of five years of excavation.

11. Many questions and scholarly controversies surround the Xia dynasty: Is it a legendary dynasty or a historical one? Sarah Allan, for instance, treats the period as mythological, saying that "the genealogy of the Xia rulers can be divided into three eras: the earliest, a clearly mythological period, is from the Yellow Lord, Huang Di, to Yu the flood hero's son Qi" (1991, 64). Other scholars disagree; for a discussion, see Li Liu and Hong Xu, 2007, "Rethinking Erlitou: Legend, History and Chinese Archaeology," *Antiquity* 81, no. 314: 886–901.

12. Due to its fundamental relation to journeys and borders, the gate theme is conspicuous in many and varied literary works, typically challenging the protagonist on his journey of self-discovery (e.g., *The Neverending Story* by Michael Ende includes three different gates encountered on the path, such as the "Great Riddle Gate," or as a singular liminality, e.g., *Kafka on the Shore* by Haruki Murakami, in which the gate constitutes "a place where it might be possible to bridge or bypass certain distinction" (Mehigan 2008, 166).

13. For instance, Mount Osore in Japan is believed to be an entrance to the underworld (called *jigokudani*, meaning, "hell's valley or mouth"); in ancient Greece and Rome, stories of entering the otherworld through caves are abundant (such as Aeneas and Hercules, who both entered it through a cave at the edge of Lake Avernus in Naples); even Pluto's Gate in modern-day Turkey is said to be the entry gate to the underworld.

14. Gates and doors are common metaphors in multiple cultures; think, for instance, of the idioms "when one gate closes, a new one opens" and "a foot at the door," among others.

15. The term "deep elements of a culture" is part of Edward T. Hall's Cultural Iceberg Model (Granatta 2016, 68), which sees the external and conscious part (the surface) as what we can see (customs, rituals, costumes, etc.) and the deep traits as hidden below (core tendencies, values, beliefs, and patterns of thought) and which underlie (external) behavior.

16. In his 1979 book on Homeric gods, Walter F. Otto says that "it is Hermes' nature not to belong to any locality and not to possess any permanent abode; always he is on the road between here and there" (*The Homeric Gods: The Spiritual Significance of Greek Religion* [New York: Pantheon], 117).

17. In fact, the above correspondence (i.e., Slingerland-Behuniak) constitutes part of a heated debate among Sinologists on this very subject—pertaining as to whether or not Chinese thought and medical practices contains "strong holism" or "weak holism" (as Slingerland defines it)—in comparison to the strong or radical dualism of Western thought (with Cartesian philosophy as its most extreme view). This will be discussed in relevant chapters and the final concluding chapter.

18. Umberto Eco states that stairs constitute an example of a conceptual metaphor: "even if no one is going up that stair at present and . . . even if stairs are never used again by anyone,' it still denotes 'the possibility of going up'" (C. F. Munro 1987, 120).

19. It is only in radical body-mind dichotomy that ideas such as Descartes's *cogito, ergo sum*—can indeed grow: the idea elevates the human thinking faculty to an independent, separate and all-ruling position (in fact, almost godly) to the extent that it validates our living existence!

20. Certain philosophers such as Heidegger embraced emptiness while existentialists such as Sartre conceived it as something that cannot be escaped (essentially different from East Asian philosophies and Buddhism). As opposed to the way in which Chinese art manifested emptiness in the concrete, it is only recently in the West that a new form of art "plays" with this theme, e.g., Yves Klein (*The Void*); musician John Cage, who famously sat for hours playing "nothing"; and later on, the birth of ephemeral art (e.g., Christo, Julian Voss-Andreae), which (it seems to me) brings it closer to the singular creation of Buddhist mandalas—the epitome of *upaya* or "skillful means" that manifest (through form) the transitory and empty nature of the world and assists the devotee in the practice of nonattachment.

21. Furthermore, Michael Farrell examines Derrida's work *Of Grammatology* (published in 1967), and says that Derrida "examines the Western philosophical tradition of a perceived tendency for 'ethnocentrism' (analyses suggesting the superiority of 'Western man' over other groups), 'phonocentrism' (a prioritizing of speech over writing broadly defined), and 'logocentrism' (the notion of irreducible 'ideal' or 'transcendental' meanings). Derrida refers to logocentrism as 'the metaphysics of phonetic writing'" (2014, 91).

22. It seems, however, that this dichotomic concept is starting to lose ground even in Western culture and thought.

23. See also Wang Shuren and Zhang Lin, 2009, "The Roots of Chinese Philosophy and Culture—An Introduction to 'Xiang' and 'Xiang Thinking,'" *Frontiers of Philosophy in China* 4 (1): 1–12.

24. Antonio Cua refers to this passage, saying, "the Great Learning suggests four steps: cultivating one's life, regulating one's family, ordering one's state and clearly manifesting one's character to the world. The four steps are like concentric circles that extend outward, enlarging one's social space—from self to family to state to universe" (2013, 45).

25. The character *he* 和 is quite polysemous, according to meanings awarded to it by different schools of thought; however, in the context of parallels between different domains of knowledge, Chenyang Li points to the preparation of food as an analogous image! He mentions Shi Bo, a scholar-minister (of Western Zhou), who "praised early sage-kings that they harmonized (he) five flavors to befit the taste" and that "the ancient scholar minister Yan Zi, "formulated the notion of harmony on the model of making soup and producing music" (2008, 424). An additional instance of culinary parallelism is chaos *hundun* that is correlated with wonton soup.

26. In the third-century *Sanwu liji* (by Xu Zheng), we read an account of this separation act between the heavens and the earth (the creation of the *first* boundary): "Heaven and Earth were mixed together in chaos, like a chicken embryo, and Pangu was born within them. Over the course of eighteen thousand years, Heaven and Earth parted ways: clear *yang* became Heaven, and turbid Pangu lay within them; each day he underwent nine transformations, so that he became more divine than Heaven and sager than Earth. Heaven rose higher by a yard each day; Earth became thicker by a yard each day; Pangu grew by a yard each day. Continuing like this for eighteen thousand years, Heaven reached its ultimate height, Earth reached its ultimate depth, and Pangu reached its ultimate size" (Goldin 2008, 8).

27. The ideological and practical meanings of self-cultivation differ among the various Chinese schools, e.g., *zhishen* 治身 and also *xiushen* 修身 refer to the attainment of personal discipline through the cultivation of morality and social conduct and learning (etymologically, *xiu* 修 also means "study"). Benjamin Coles says that "for early Confucianism, such self-cultivation typically focused on 'external' aspects such as acquiring the familiarity with classic literature such as the Poetry (*shi* 詩) that was the mark of a cultured person and becoming proficient in the traditional rites (*li* 禮) that governed personal and social conduct" (2019, 388). But there were other types of self-cultivation, such as "inner training" (*neiye* 內業) and "techniques of the mind" (*xinshu* 心術), etc.

28. *Men* has received scholarly attention as part of hermeneutic analyses of ancient Chinese texts; Doeringer (1982) took the gate as forming a passage between absolute and relative realities; Ames and Hall (2003) saw the swinging door as a device that enables *dao* to open out to creativity; Ariel and Raz (2010) identified the gate with the very text of the *Daode jing*; Burik (2010) suggests that the act of shutting the gate means "to open up to the world without artificial inhibitions."

29. I am referring, for instance, to texts of later Daoism such as the *Neidan* 內丹 or the *Cantong qi* 參同契 (The Seal of the Unity of the Three) and Daoist alchemy, in general; the subject of Grotto-heavens *dongtian* 洞天, or an in-depth study of Buddhist sutras and scripts. As for specific themes that were found associated with gates but surpassed the available space of this volume, e.g., Mount Kunlun and Xiwangmu 西王母 (Queen Mother of the West), and its associated text *ruoshui* 弱水 (Weak River or Weak Water)—a mythical geographical locale that constitutes a central theme in a vast literal corpus formulated between the Warring States and early Han dynasty. The narrative surrounding this river relates to gates not only in the context of water and rivers (see chapter 1) but also because it was thought of as a *barrier* against unworthy people.

Chapter 1

1. Wagner (2003b, 149).

2. Is there a relation between pattern *li* and *ming* 命? Xiaosui Xiao argues that an earlier cognate of *ming* was "ling," which means "command," hinting that the Shang people asked their gods for specific "commands"; thence, from *ling* as "command," *ming* became associated with the heavens—as an all-pervading cosmic power (2006, 3).

3. For an intriguing elaboration on the concept of *li* 理, see Ziporyn (2014).

4. It is interesting to note that, as opposed to the West, it seems the ancient Chinese cartographers did not pay attention to the shape or characteristics of the world/earth as a whole, as they did for *tianxia* ("all under heavens") which is China itself; Henderson believes that "the geographical isolation of Chinese civilization may have contributed to Chinese cosmographers' lack of interest in outlining, either realistically or schematically, the form of the world as a whole" (1994, 203).

5. It is important to point out that, perhaps counterintuitively, the *fengshui* doctrine did not always enjoy a unanimous opinion and popularity; in effect, it seems that it received quite an ambiguous attitude from the various sectors of ancient Chinese society, and some even dismissed it. Xu Yinong mentions this interesting point, saying, "this ambiguity was brought about not only by the ambivalent stance of the majority of individual intellectuals towards *fengshui* but also by their different backgrounds of education and self-cultivation" (2000, 223).

6. Chaos has been rendered differently by various scholars, each positioning it either at the very chaotic side or on the verge in between (defined by form but still merged as one)—Victor Mair (1994) calls it "Lickety," "Split," and even "Wonton" (the soup as constituting the biological "primordial soup"), while Norman Girardot defines chaos as "any 'turbid, murky, confused, undifferentiated, or disorderly' condition" (1978, 299).

7. As far as I can tell, only one study conducted by Girardot in 1978 thoroughly examined the meanings and relationship between chaos *hundun* and disorder *luan*. Girardot analyzed the occurrences of both characters in a variety of early texts and says that, in relation to "Daoist" sources, for instance, they mean the following: "(1) In the Chuang Tzu (and it would seem for the other early Taoist texts), the terms *hun-(tun)* and *luan* are frequently paired in a contrasting way within the context of the paradise lost theme. *Hun-(tun)* . . . for the Taoists it seems to represent the true 'order' of the Tao that was present during the paradise time. This ideal prompts various political and mystical proscriptions for 're-turning to the beginning' before the 'great confusion' [*ta-luan*] caused by the coming of the culture" (1978, 313). I found this immensely helpful in deciphering the meaning of *hundun* in the *Zhuangzi* (chapter 6).

8. Mengzi emphasizes the use of tangible tools by society (technology) so that man is able to materialize the *shi* 勢 out of any substance, to enable the efficaciousness of man's actions. Willard J. Peterson remarks that "even sages, whose capacities might be presumed to exceed those of an ordinary man, still need to use inexhaustible cultural artifacts—woodworking models, musical models, governmental models—which contribute to a better world" (1979, 316). Chung-ying Cheng mentions that in the *Xici* of the *Yizhuan*, it says, "a list of inventions based on the reflection of the trigrammatic symbols is given. The hexagram *li* (離) gives rise to fishnet, the hexagram *yi* (益) gives rise to plough and the hexagram *shihe* (噬嗑) gives rise to market. Invention thus includes *concrete utensils and abstract institutions*" (2011, 348).

9. Louise Barrett says that "the idea that human cognitive systems (or, if you prefer, minds) are not limited to brains alone but incorporate various environmental resources and tools—that is, the notion of 'cognitive integration' or the 'extended mind' (Clark 2008)—seems crucial to the generation of a satisfactory evolutionary account of human behavior, not least because there is abundant evidence to suggest that the invention of certain artifacts and practices has transformed our understanding of ourselves and the world around us" (Barrett 2018, 204).

10. Yang Lihui researched the history of the myth in texts as well as in current Chinese rituals. For more information, see Lihui Yang and Deming An, with Jessica Anderson Turner, 2005, *A Handbook of Chinese Mythology* (Oxford University Press).

11. Original Chinese, 千里之行, 始於足下.

12. Some interesting theories make an attempt at deducting its origins in the shape of Chinese characters, that is, that the square ideographs underlie the orderly arrangement of Chinese architecture.

13. The significance of *jian* 間 (*ma* in Japanese) in Japanese culture, national psyche, art, and aesthetics cannot be overstressed, but that's for another volume.

14. The *huang* in the term "August Emperor" is curious as it is usually rendered yellow (hence, *huangdi*,' the Yellow Emperor). However, Fabrizio Pregadio (2010, 505) explains that it is "often used in ancient literature as equivalent to *huang* 皇 (august, venerable, superior). But Huangdi 皇帝 or "August Emperor" is the name of the heavenly god Shangdi 上帝. Thus, the Yellow Emperor was placed on the same level as the highest heavenly god, with four emperors (who personify the four compass points) as his subordinates.

15. Cai Yong, of the Han dynasty, is our most important source for information on the Bright Hall. He wrote the *Treatise on the Bright Hall and Monthly Ordinances* (*Mingtang yueling lun*).

16. Robin Wang says that "a key part of ancestor warship rituals of reverence was to build a proper tomb for the body and the *po* 魄 soul. Given its association with *po*, the earth and darkness, the tomb was called 'the house of *yin*'" (2012, 110). It might be worth mentioning that there is an ongoing debate as to the number of spirits (two, three, or indeed ten); Stevan Harrell emphasized that "almost every number from one to a dozen has at one time or another been proposed as the correct one" (1979, 521).

17. *Mingqi* 明器, literally "spirit articles" or perhaps "mandate articles," are tomb furnishings, consisting of objects and figurines, which were specifically designed and produced for the dead; the architectural models have always been an invaluable source of knowledge on ancient Chinese construction design and technology. Another intriguing aspect of the custom is that it is still alive today. Especially noteworthy in Taiwan, it nowadays involves all the latest gadgets and technological items the dead can wish for; thus, the deceased's family can buy at special stores any creative cardboard models they desire for their departing beloved, such as mobile phones, cars, etc.

18. Joseph. R. Allen says that the Chinese language is "a meta-language (i.e., a language whose referent is language itself) of the most real kind: not theory, but rather the basic material of linguistic competence" (1992, 189).

19. It says in the *Mengzi*, for instance, "it is difficult to impress with words someone who has wandered in the gate of a sage" (trans. D. C. Lau); as will be discussed, in the *Lunyu* the word for Confucius's disciples are named "people of the same gate."

Chapter 2

1. John Major et al. (2010).

2. The oracle bones and the *Yijing* can be considered "the parents" of early Chinese attempts at seeing afar and penetrating deeply into the hidden order of the cosmos, but texts from later dynasties (e.g., *Han Shu* 漢書), reveal that

it persisted in the form of a complex system of portentology—as a "specialized field of knowledge that aims at fathoming the concealed mechanisms at work beneath the spectacles of history and the world at large" (Espesset 2016, 5).

3. A translation note: I find that the best way to render the multifaceted character *tong* 通, is "breakthrough for unification," which corresponds to its basic meaning of "going out through an empty passageway and hence uniting everything." Lynn (1994) translates *tong* 通 as "free flow," which, I argue, misses a certain strength and direction involved—the result of which is unification.

4. Kirkland asserts that in the most general way and throughout history, Daoists have generally been "people who agreed that they should refine and transform themselves in order to attain a full integration with life's deepest realities" (2004, 75).

5. Chapter 42 has received multiple interpretations, partly due to the question of whether or not it refers to a "real" cosmogenic timeline (a consequential process of "before" and "after" in the origin and evolvement of the universe) or a mere metaphoric and schematic description. James Behuniak Jr. compares the chapter with the Warring States' text *Taiyishengshui* 太一生水 (*Great One Produces the Waters*) with the aim of understanding the meaning of each stage; for more details, see Behuniak (2009).

6. Robinet adds that "while the Taoists state that *taiji* is metaphysically preceded by *wuji*, which is the Dao, the Neo-Confucians say that the *taiji* is the Dao" (quoted in Pregadio 2010, 1058). This attests to the intricacy of the *taiji* concept and the various meanings attributed to it by the different schools of thought as well as through history.

7. A. C. Graham indeed said (in reference to this chapter) that "each is a combination of something and nothing; the hole in the wheel which takes the axle, the empty space inside the vessel, doors and windows in the house, are nothing yet belong to the things which could not be used without them" (1990, 346). It connects the "usefulness" of the things discussed (vehicle, pottery vessel and room) to its usefulness only, and *you* 有 is taken to be connected to the existence of thing itself (that is, *you qi zhi yong* just means that "there exists a useful device").

8. The character *yi* is conventionally translated *change* and sometimes rendered "easy" (which, to me, always evokes the concept of "the path of least resistance"), but there is an additional explanation which I find intriguing. In his book *The Mandate of Heaven* (2002), S. J. Marshall notes that on the oracle bones the character refers to "sacrifice to the sun" (it consist of "giving hand" and sun). Marshall says that "the context suggesting a ritual intended to change overcast conditions and rainy weather, and bring the sun out again" (15). This means that the "change" aimed for is "bringing the sun"—that is, a change from dark to light; Marshall further suggests that the title *Zhouyi* ("the change of Zhou") refers to the actual image of a dynasty emerging like sun rays from behind the clouds of an oppressive regime!

9. See www.hanziyuan.net.

10. Reins and horsemanship as symbolizing ways of governance constitute a familiar Chinese metaphor, which transforms according to philosophical tendencies. At times, the skillful usage of reins symbolizes the key for correct horsemanship and governing the people (through strict control), whereas other political attitudes dismiss its importance. The chapter "Xing shi jie" 形勢解 in the *Guanzi* 管子, for instance, praises a charioteer by the name of Zaofu, who cared and "listened" to the horses' state and capabilities—as a metaphor for wise and enlightened governance. Zaofu was good at looking after his horses, watering, and feeding them, estimating their strength . . . so that they never got tired (even on long journeys); thus, "charioting is the mere holding of reins" (馭者操轡也)—not Zhaofu's method (造父之術非馭也)—which elevates his governance to a wiser and more superior level.

11. Schwartz marks one of Zhuangzi's passages in the Outer Chapters ("Perfect Enjoyment") as attesting to these transformations in Nature itself, saying that, "Chuang-tzu presents us with images of the "incipient germs" (*chi*) of animal and plant life which produce entirely different creatures depending on the natural habitat in which they find themselves. In the water they become break-vines . . . on the edge of the water, they become frog's robes . . . so all creatures come out of these incipient germs and return to thereto. Watson aptly describes this whole passage as "a romp through ancient Chinese nature lore." What is celebrated here is the delightfully inexhaustible and protean transformation of nature" (1985, 220).

12. As an analogue idea, a new theory of evolution has emerged in the last few decades by some scholars (Carl Woese and Barbara McClintock, among others) as new findings demonstrate *quantum leaps* in evolution—a theory called "saltationism" or "punctuated equilibrium"; it finds that alongside gradual evolutionary adaptations (through genetic mutations), dramatic ("quantum") transformations also take place. See, for instance, Arild S. Foss, 2013, "Evolution: Giant Leaps or Half Measures?" *ScienceNordic* (https://sciencenordic.com/animal-kingdom-evolution-forskningno/evolution-giant-leaps-or-half-measures/1384326).

13. Nagarjuna (150–250 AD) is one of the most influential Indian philosophers and the main founder of the Madhyamaka school ("Middle Way"). Nagarjuna claimed that there are two levels of truth in Buddhist teaching: Ultimate Truth (*paramārthasatya*) and a Relative one (*saṃvṛtisatya*). A comparative investigation of the gate and emptiness in Chinese sources and Nagarjuna's concepts cannot be attempted here.

14. The first chapter has consequently received countless translations; in fact, there is even a website wholly dedicated to it (see http://www.bopsecrets.org/gateway/passages/tao-te-ching.htm).

15. Though it is agreed that the text constitutes an edited outcome of multiple authors, perhaps in different periods, the legendary figure and author Laozi became synonymous with the text.

16. As the word "omnipresence" is associated with Western monotheist religious connotations, I find the synonyms word *ubiquitous* to constitute the best rendering of *dao* in the opening lines; also, as opposed to the religious and transcendental feel of "omnipresent," ubiquitous is rendered as more commonly "present, appearing, or found everywhere."

17. For a most enlightening discussion of the exegesis of these opening lines, also in regard to matters of linguistics, see the following articles: Bo Mou, 2000, "Ultimate Concern and Language Engagement: A Re-examination of the Opening Message of the *Daode jing*," *Journal of Chinese Philosophy*, 27, no. 4: 429–39; or Cao (2013); or Sagmu Oh, 2017, "A Re-examination of the Paradox of Dao," *Dao*, 16: 483–501.

18. Hansen stresses that the first *dao* should be read as plural, meaning that, "any prescriptive system put into words gives inconstant guidance" (1992, 216), adding that this might be addressing those who claim to have the one constant *dao*. Moss Roberts maintains that since *dao* is transcendent and also immanent, it resembles time or nature, but it still "does not obey the same rules as the rules governing humans" (2001, 28).

19. In quite a number of pre-Han sources *chang* is given the meaning of "constant" and "enduring," e.g., in the *Zhuangzi*, "miscellaneous chapters" (in the "delight in the sword-fight"), *dai yi chang shan* 帶以常山 is translated (by Legge) as "enduring hills."

20. Kurtis Hagen and Steve Coutinho assert that this popular understanding might have been derived from later commentaries, either Buddhist or influenced by Buddhist thought (2018, 31). As for the various meanings of *chang*, see *The Historical and Comparative Encyclopedia of Chinese Conceptual Schemes*, online at http://tls.uni-hd.de/procSearch/procSearchLex.lasso.

21. I am as surprised as Qingjie Wang who wonders how come "the philosophical meaning of *heng* has rarely been discussed by Laozi scholars either in the East or in the West" (2000, 1). The character appears in the *Daode jing* more than thirty times, similarly to *chang*.

22. *Heng* is significant in other textual sources, such as the *Yijing* (易經) and its commentaries—both as a hexagram and an important philosophical category. D. C. Lau might be the first Western scholar to discuss *heng* in the new introduction of his translation of the *Laozi*. But his discussion focuses more on its philological aspect rather than the philosophical meaning.

23. As we have seen, the metaphor of water is not particular to Daoist sources but omnipresent almost in all Chinese philosophical texts. However, as with *dao*, the metaphor has received different interpretations according to philosophical inclinations and/or historical periods.

24. The character that, alongside *chang dao*, manifests this transformation between the formless and the formed is *de*; it constitutes the way the potency inherent in the ten thousand things and phenomena is efficaciously expressed and materialized—as the very omnipresence of *dao* in the world.

25. This exegesis suits the notion held by some scholars that Laozi was *forced* (not asked) to write the text and hence these paradoxical lines. My exegesis is different (see chapter 7).

26. Indeed, Galia Patt-Shamir explores the theme of the mother in the *Daode jing*, suggesting an analogy between mother and way, because they are both "fully responsible for *being* (*you* 有)" (2016, 251). For an additional discussion of the image of the mother in the *Daode jing*, see Constance Cook (2015).

27. This definition as to "being in an undifferentiated state" appears in the important Qing dynasty text on Chinese painting, "Twenty four modes/moods/categories of painting" *er shi si hua pin* 二十四畫品, written by art critic Huang Yue 黄钺; Loreta Poskaite refers to *miao* as "marvel," saying that "this unity or something marvelous is behind the world of human proportions and images ('marvel beyond the painting'—*miao zai hua wai* 妙在畫外)" (2020, 150).

28. In the *Xisheng jing* 西昇經 (Scripture of Western ascension), it says, "Emptiness and nonbeing, the vague and obscure, are the root of all being" (Kohn 1991, 25). The void, therefore, has a double function, in two analogous spheres: it is the root of all being (i.e., something indefinable from which the manifested living world is created), but an inseparable part of any being, and, importantly, a prerequisite for mental, inner transformation

29. Some examples include *kensho* 見性 (Jpn. lit. "seeing one's (true) nature"), *qishi* 啓示 (Chin. lit. "open to the manifestation"), and *ehara* (Heb. lit. "enlightenment").

30. For more information on this intriguing type of gates, see Chen Tao et al., 2010, "Preliminary Study on Memorial Archways in Ancient Huizhou of China," *Advanced Materials Research*, vols. 133–134: 1179–84.

31. The reference to the natural world and its relations to humans constitutes an important issue which (again) refers to the subject of boundaries. In his book *The Concept of Man in Early China*, J. D. Munro writes that "the Taoist sage would never distinguish himself from other animals, but would easily consider himself now as a horse, now as an ox, and so forth. The special qualities that human have are temporal, and are this insignificant. The whole intent is to end the thought about man's uniqueness, and to drive man from the center of the stage" (1969, 130).

32. The *Taixuan jing* 太玄經 (*Canon of Great Mystery*) was composed by the (mid-Han) scholar Yang Xiong 揚雄, who took the *Yijing* as its basic construct.

33. In this time and age, "leaving no trace behind" could be adopted as an apt "slogan" by any group or organization wishing to save the planet and promote sustainable tourism.

Chapter 3

1. Michael Nylan adds that the "Mystery" is "one of the first systematic responses to the Book of Changes (*Yi ching*)" which "can also help us reconstruct

the original imagery, structure, and meaning of that sacred canon in relation to other classics, such as the Book of Documents and the Book of Odes" (1994, 1).

2. See Raoul Birnbaum, 1989, "Secret Halls of the Mountain Lords: The Caves of Wu-t'ai shan," *Cahiers d'Extrême-Asie* 5: 115–40.

3. *Ying* 營 is a challenging character; it occurs in various Chinese medical texts in the sense of *nutrition* (such as in the *lingshu jing* 灵枢经, chapter 8), but also as "unity of spirit"; in reference to the phrase *zai ying po* 載營魄, Michael Stanley-Baker says that "by the time the term appeared in the Han dynasty *Daode jing*, the phrase *zai ying po* came to refer not to out-of-body travel, but to inward-looking, embodied cultivation of spiritual unity" (2019, 7).

4. In relation to the "breath" in chapter 10, some scholars see it as an important clue to or proof of the existence of a systemized method of breathing exercises and meditation in the time the *Daode jing* was compiled; Michael LaFargue, for instance, regards chapter 10 as "the most detailed instruction for meditation in the *Daodejing*" (1992, 61).

5. Beyond the impressive variety of subjects included in the twenty-one chapters of the *Huainanzi* ("from astronomy and calendric to government and the art of warfare" [Lau and Ames 1998, 3]), its historical background is intriguing: in the Book of Han (*Han Shu* 漢書) and in Sima Qian's "Records of the Grand Historian," it is narrated how Liu An 劉安—the king of Huainan (淮南)—paid his nephew, emperor Wu, a visit in 139 BC and presented him with a copy of the *Huainanzi*. The records make it clear that "the work was the product of many hands, which includes a group of men called 'masters of esoteric techniques' (*fangshushi*)" (Major et al. 2010, 17). Vankeerberghen claims that "scholars disagree as to whether Liu An revolted, plotted revolt, or merely reacted to pressures from the central court" (2001, 67). For a review of translators and interpreters of the *Huainanzi*, see Michael Loewe, 1994, "Review: 'Huang Lao Thought and the 'Huainanzi,'" *Journal of the Royal Asiatic Society*, 3rd series, 4, no. 3: 377–95.

6. The *Yuan Dao* constitutes a poetic rhapsody dedicated to *dao* and its inherent potency *de* 德, which naturally evokes the *Laozi*; according to Major et al., the *Laozi* serves as its "principal source" (2010, 45), but they emphasize that its richness might be symbolizing the diverse voices of the times (second century BC). The name that was given by writers of the Warring States and early Han periods to these diverse voices was *baijia*, the "Hundred Traditions" (which actually appears three times in the *Huainanzi*), which, Major et al. add, implies, "great variety, fluidity, and diversity of thought" (2010, 30).

7. As said in the introduction, Mount Kunlun has repeatedly surfaced in association with the gate along two other themes, namely, Xiwangmu and the Hollow Mulberry Tree; I theorize that the gate constitutes the common motif shared by these three entities in the context of Chinese mythology and

cosmology. The myth of Xinwangmu and Mount Kunlun have been referred to as the "axis mundi" of the universe, a central cosmological entity which might function in the same way as gates. Robinet says that "Kunlun and *hundun* are the same closed center of the world" (quoted in Pregadio 2010, 525). For some background on Xiwangmu in the Han dynasty, including an intriguing passage that links her with doors in Chinese folklore, see Jean M. James, 1995, "An Iconographic Study of Xiwangmu during the Han Dynasty," *Artibus Asiae* 55, no. 1/2: 17–41.

8. The *Changhe* gate is mentioned in various pre-Han sources, such as the *Han shi waizhuan* 韩诗外传 ("The Outer Commentary to the Book of Songs by Master Han"), the "Records of the Grand Historian" *Tàishǐgōng shū* 太史公書 (Sima Qian 司馬遷) and multiple times in the *Huainanzi*.

9. The passage could also be a description of the soul on its journey to the afterlife; in that case, then, the "above" and "below" might correspond to the soul's two parts, namely, *hun* 魂, which goes up to the heavens, and *po* 魄, which goes down to earth (for which tombs were built).

10. The Chinese Spirit *shen* is a complex and multifaceted term; however, according to Wing-Tsit Chan, *shen* or *guishen* carries four different meanings: "In ancient times *shen* usually refers to heavenly beings while *kuei* refers to spirits of deceased human beings. In later-day sacrifices, *kuei-shen* together refers to ancestors. In popular religions *shen* means gods (who are good) and demons (who are not always good). In Neo-Confucianism *kuai-shen* may refer to all these three categories but more often than not the term refers to the activity of the material force (ch'i)" (1963, 790).

11. Out of social constraints, moral conventions, and religions worldwide, some behavioral strategies have been formulated with the aim of dealing with external stimuli; these can be categorized into two main methods, namely, active coping and avoidance. Think, for instance, of sexually abstinent men from different religions—one actively cultivates his body-mind to cope with sexual desire, the other *avoids* coping with the stimuli by attempting to eliminate the "source of the stimuli," in this case, the feminine body (e.g., the *abaya* robe or the elimination of women from public space).

12. Hans-Georg Moeller translates chapter 52 in the following way: "Fill the openings, close the entries, be unencumbered by the termination of the body. Open the openings, be busy with affairs, and you will not be saved from the termination of the body" (2004, 35). He then relates it to the killing of *hundun* in the *Zhuangzi*, the act of which actually happens through 'making openings in his body,' and says, "in that way, an opening becomes synonymous to danger, decay and death." See my discussion of *hundun* in the *Zhuangzi* chapter.

13. In the *Zhuangzi*, *nang* 囊 appears in the famous passage from the Outer Chapters, named "cutting up satchel," where it refers to thieves that steal the

whole sack instead of trying to open it; I wonder, after studying its metaphorical meaning in the *Yijing*, whether *Zhuangzi* really refers to an actual sack or to the mind of people. This needs further investigation.

14. Interestingly, *nang* constitutes part of *qing nang* 青囊, which is an old term for *fengshui*; the first time it is mentioned is in the "Book of Jin" *Jin shu* in which it relates the story of Guo Population, who was handed nine volumes of burial books from a person by the same name who took them out of his *blue cloth bag*. More research is needed to establish whether or not that is the only legendary reason for its usage in the name; it could simply be that it meant "the study of the blue (surface of the) universe" (the blue refers to sky and water).

15. In addition to this interpretation, Victor Mair suggests a fundamental connection between the early form of the character *hundun* 渾沌 and the famous Chinese *wonton* soup, pronounced and written in early times, *huntun* 餛飩: "The undifferentiated soup of primordial chaos. As it begins to differentiate, dumpling-blobs of matter coalesce. . . . With the evolution of human consciousness and reflectiveness, the soup was adopted as a suitable metaphor for chaos" (1994, 386). However, some dispute this theory because *wonton* soup does not appear in pre-Han texts, at all. Nonetheless, I believe that *wonton* soup, as an image, could indeed render this stage in the evolution of life, when forms begin to appear and each living thing is defined by an "enveloping line" that defines the relationship with its environment.

16. The *Zhuangzi* became a canonical scripture or *jing*, as "reflected in the honorific title *Nanhua zhenjing* 南華真經 (Classical scripture of southern florescence) conferred upon it by Emperor Xuanzong of Tang in 742" (Moeller and D'Ambrosio 2017, 11). The *Zhuangzi*—in text and content—raises many questions regarding authorship, textual coherence, and contextual relations with the *Laozi*. See A. C. Graham, 1986, "How Much of the Chuang Tzu Did Chuang Tzu Write?," in *Studies in Chinese Philosophy and Philosophical Literature*, ed. Graham (Singapore: National University of Singapore), 283–321.

17. Published at http://www.frankwstevenson.com/articles/question-of-the-wind-in-zhuangzi.html.

18. The question of whether or not early "philosophical" Daoism (*Laozi* and *Zhuangzi*, mainly) included practical meditative and breathing techniques is quite controversial; Harold Roth believes such techniques existed quite early, as hinted by a jade knob (dated to 380 BC) that carries a sorites argument about breathing techniques and their relation to life and death (1997, 298).

19. Moeller and D'Ambrosio interpret the story as a parody and relate exactly to this lack of "happy ending," saying that, the "big bang" that one may have eagerly hoped for is eventually an implosion into emptiness" (2017, 78). The authors believe that Zhuangzi is ridiculing the possibility of a "grand narrative" that explains everything, and we indeed encountered the association

of "questions and answers" to gates. Wu Kuang-ming sees Mr. Hundun as the manifestation of "absolute kindness, unconditional acceptance" (2007, 278).

20. *Jing* is a well-known term in Chinese medicine and self-cultivation techniques in religious Daoism and various longevity skills. It refers also to the refined essence, the perfected; an extract; spirit, sperm, seed, etc.

21. There is an interesting parallelism here with chapters 50 and 55 of the *Daode jing*, particularly the following extracts: "I have heard it said that one who excels in safeguarding his own life does not meet with rhinoceros or tiger when travelling on land nor is he touched by weapons when charging into an army. There is nowhere for the rhinoceros to pitch its horn; There is nowhere for the tiger to place its claws; There is nowhere for the weapon to lodge its blade. Why is this so? Because for him there is no realm of death" (chapter 50); and "one who possesses virtue in abundance is comparable to a new born babe: poisonous insects will not sting it; ferocious animals will not pounce on it; predatory birds will not swoop down on it" (chapter 55) (trans. D. C. Lau).

Chapter 4

1. Owen (2016, 4:33–36).

2. Other descriptions relate status to the entrance, for instance, that ministers enter from the right side of the door only, and only the ruler can occupy the center. Slingerland points out that "some commentators argue that only the ruler was permitted to tread upon thresholds, and therefore a minister doing so would represent an act of insubordination" (2006, 99). The middle axial path which was reserved to the highest figurehead is evident in later dynasties (such as the Ming and Qing), and several monuments indeed reflect that (e.g., the Forbidden City, the Temple of Heaven).

3. A beautiful poem by modern-day author Lin Yutang (died 1976) takes the reader along a circular path deeper and deeper into his home-mind . . . his mental happiness so tightly bound with his home: "In the dwelling there is a garden, in the garden there is a house, in the house there is a courtyard, in the courtyard there is a tree, on the tree there is the sky, in the sky there is the moon, what a fortunate life!" (extracted from an online article on Li Yutang at web.archive.org/web/20130809193313/http://www.umass.edu/wsp/sinology/persons/lin.html).

4. Altman indeed sees privacy as a dialectic boundary process whereby a person is differentially accessible or inaccessible to others; see Altman, 1976, "Privacy: A Conceptual Analysis," *Environment and Behavior* 8, no. 1. For more on the cultural analysis of the home as indicative of degrees of openness and closeness, see Mary Gauvain, 1981, "A Cross-Cultural and Dialectic Analysis

of Homes," in *Spatial Representation & Behavior across the Life Span Theory and Application*, ed. L. Liben., A. Patterson, & N. Newcombe (New York: Academic Press), 283–319.

5. One interesting character that emphasizes the analogy between architectural gates and mental or emotional gates is *men* 悶 which is made out of 門 (concealed) + 心 heart/emotions → gloomy, depressed feelings concealed in the heart → anguish/agony (caused by melancholy). This is important as it hints at the gates of our body and *xin* 心 (heart/mind).

6. Mozi explains in chapter 15: "nowadays, individual people only know to love their own household and usurping another's household. Nowadays, individual people only know to love their own persons and not to love the person of others; they have no qualms about promoting their own persons and injuring he persons of other" (Johnston 2013, 76).

7. In the *Zhong yong* 中庸 ("Doctrine of the Mean"), it says, for instance, "Confucius said: the noble man realizes the mean; the petty man opposes it. The noble man realizes the mean because he is completely attuned with it" (仲尼曰: 君子中庸. 小人反中庸. 君子之中庸也、君子而時中). And, in the same source, it is said: "As for the center *zhong*, it is the great root for all (creatures) under the heavens; as for harmony *he*, it constitutes the very attainment of *dao*" (中也者, 天下之大本也; 和也者, 天下之達道也).

8. The *Analects* was probably written by Confucius's own disciples but also by "second-generation disciples some seventy years after his death. The surviving text was probably formalized at around the Western Han period" (K. Lai 2008, 20). In chapter 5, I discuss additional "Confucian gates."

9. The term occurs in other humanist sources, such as the *Mencius*: in *Gaozi* 告子下 II, it says, "I desire to stay here and receive instruction (professional teaching) from (at) your gate," (願留而受業於門), which means, "let me be your disciple."

10. Chinese poetry constitutes yet another facet of "correlative thinking," such as the poetic form called *xing* 興 ("Evocation") which consists of two parallel couplets: one from the natural world and the other from the world of man. The *Shijing* (*Classic of Poetry*), uses two principles or "literally tools" named *fu* 賦 and *bi* 比 that have influenced all genres of Chinese literature to date, including philosophical texts (!) in the form of dialectics and even the usage of complementary opposites. For an in-depth discussion of *xing*, see Karl S. Y. Kao, 2003, "Comparative Literature and the Ideology of Metaphor East and West," in *Comparative Literature and Comparative Cultural Studies*, ed. Steven Totosy de Zepetnek (West Lafayette, IN: Purdue University Press), 356.

11. The crossbow and its trigger are ancient Chinese inventions that had immense impact on Chinese military history, and some argue that its influence goes even further into Chinese thought in general; it was invented during the

Zhou dynasty and was first used to protect buildings from attackers. Its importance lies in the fact that it helped in the development of the idea to make long-range weapons, in fact, just like the gun in the Western world. It consisted of horizontally mounted bow, with a stock and trigger mechanism that allowed for the firing of multiple arrows and the ability to operate it using one hand; the trigger was made of metal, usually bronze.

12. Xin is rendered heart-mind to avoid the (Western) separation between body and mind; however, Slingerland claims against the "holistic view" of the Chinese (lacking dualism), and says that while xin is "certainly identified in some way as an organ in the body, the xin in Warring States discourse is clearly singled out as a very special type of organ, with qualitatively unique powers: it is the locus of intentions, rational thought, language use, categorization, and voluntary willing. Because of these qualitatively unique powers, it is often contrasted with the other bodily organs, and is in fact the only organ to be singled out and contrasted with the body as a whole" (2013, 15).

13. Indeed, James Legge translated the passage as follows: "Let him keep his mouth closed, and shut up the portals (of his nostrils), and all his life he will be exempt from laborious exertion. Let him keep his mouth open, and (spend his breath) in the promotion of his affairs, and all his life there will be no safety for him" (Chinese Text Project at ctext.org).

14. Keeping the meaning of dui as "exchange" could still work—as the utterance of words that goes out of the mouth is indeed an exchange between one's thoughts and an external recipient.

Chapter 5

1. S. Tan (2016, 134).

2. Slingerland adds that a similar opinion to that of the gatekeeper is pronounced by two additional figures in Analects 14.2 and 14.3: "confronted wherever he goes by indifferent or actively immoral rulers, Confucius should simply give up" (2006, 170).

3. Si is not merely thinking; it is a loaded term which includes contemplating, understanding, making analogies and judgment, drawing inferences, etc.

4. In the Za Ji II of The Classic of Rites, Ru Bei is mentioned in the context of mourning rites: he is sent to Confucius by Duke Ai in order to learn the proper mourning rites for Xu You, and these rites were apparently documented (恤由之喪，哀公使孺悲之孔子學士喪禮，士喪禮於是乎書). As the zither si is mentioned in the Analects and the Classic of Rites in the particular context of funerary rites, I wonder whether the two passages are intertextually linked, i.e., that by denying Ru Bei audience and playing the zither, Confucius

actually means to say, "There is nothing I can teach you through words; the most important element in mourning rites is musical harmony and playing the zither." This needs further study.

5. See Christoph Harbsmeier, 1990, "*Confucius Ridens*: Humor in the *Analects*," *Harvard Journal of Asiatic Studies* 50, no. 1: 131–61.

6. It is beyond the scope of this book to seriously discuss the subject of truth and deceit in Chinese thought and culture, especially in comparison to Western notions; Jing-Bao Nie discusses the cultural Western-Chinese cultural gap in regard to these concepts, presenting various nineteenth-century interpretations of this very passage (which disturbingly attribute its meaning to the general disregard of the Chinese people for truth). See Nie (2011, 127).

7. An interesting comparison would probably be the Japanese "'three wise monkeys,'" Mizaru, Kikazaru, and Iwazaru, whose advice refers to the active blockage of *content*, that is, "'see no evil,'" "'hear no evil'" and "'speak no evil,'" respectively.

8. Mencius employed unique linguistic means in order to deliver his arguments, being direct and sometimes argumentative, and on multiple occasions using analogies to "make a point." The principle of human nature *xing* 性 is central to Mencius's teaching, especially his emphasis on the original and universal "inner goodness" of man, which directs us to know right from wrong (the child on the verge of the well is one of the most famous examples given). This internal goodness is inherent similarly to any physical need or characteristic of the body.

9. Yi 義 is commonly translated as "righteousness" or "rightness," but I find that such rendering takes it into the lexical context of Western notions. Mencian *yi*, to my understanding, is the whole, comprehensive set of ethical codes that constitutes a man's inner integrity and commitment; it is a combination of (1) an internal obligation towards social norms and conventions, which also constitutes a disposition that weighs any behavior on the scales of "honorable or shameful" and refrains from and negates the latter; (2) an internal moral compass that guides man's actions; and (3) a conscious decision (as part of self-cultivation) to internally guard oneself from external temptations and distractions. I thus prefer to translate *yi* as "internal propriety" and *li* as "ritual propriety" as its external manifestation. Deborah Cao attempted at "breaking down" the meaning and exegesis of *yi* and reached the conclusion that "it is about the right or appropriate thinking and acting from one's own viewpoint, with rational action, self-restraint to resist temptation and the fortitude to do one's duty in one's social relations and interactions, and preserving one's integrity" (2019, 22).

10. Qinghua Guo refers to this paragraph, detailing two building types that indeed correspond to topography, the first, a nest type called *chao* (lit. "bird nest") of the Youchao Shi (lit. "the tribe who has nest") who lived at the

Yangzi River basin (present-day Chaoxian, Anhui Province); and the second, a cave type called *xue* (lit. "cave") represented by dwellings on the loess upland where the Yellow River runs through. Remains of both types were excavated in prehistoric sites of Hemudu culture (in the south) and Yangshao culture (in the north) (Guo 2001, 3).

11. The *Shizi* 尸子, composed by Shi Jiao 尸佼 (390–330 BCE), contains a similar passage that describes in detail the physical deterioration of Yu during his labors: "for ten years he did not visit his home, and no nails grew on his hands, no hair grew on his shanks" (Birrell 1997, 246).

12. Yu is mentioned in multiple sources as the idealized mythical figure that creates order out of chaos; to name but a few, the *Classic of Mountains and Seas*, the *Huainanzi*, *Songs of Zhou*, the *Guanzi*, the *Discourses of Zhou*, the *Mencius*, and the *Tribute of Yu*. Anne Birrell notes that "of all the mythical figures associated with a world deluge, Yu is the earliest in the textual tradition. As early as the 'Classic of Poetry' we have six references to Yu . . . Yu is more exactly described in this text as the god who demarcated all the earth's land, the god of tilling, and the god who regulated water courses and so ended the world deluge" (1997, 241).

13. William G. Boltz offers an interpretation of the name *Kung-Kung*, saying that it actually corresponds to his function, that is, a "personification of the flood itself" (quoted in Birrell 1999, 97).

14. Bokenkamp points to this as evidence that the author of *Laozi-Xiang'er* likely knew of and approved of the sexual rite known as the "Merging of *Qi*" (*heqi* 合氣), as part of later "religious Daoism."

15. For further discussion of the relationship between *qi* and heart-mind *xin*, see Alan K. L. Chan, 2017, *A Matter of Taste: Qi and the Tending of the Heart in Mencius* (Honolulu: University of Hawaii Press), 42–71.

16. Most translators take the character *zhui* 追 to refer to a bell—probably the bronze *bianzhong* 編鐘 used in court rituals during the Zhou period. If the passage refers specifically to *bianzhong*, it seems to hint at ritual propriety; also, as for the "worn out" reference, it can either be the bell itself or its shaft (on which it is hanged). But as the first line refers to the sound itself, I believe it points to the bell and not the shaft. Keith Wilson, curator of the tomb of Marquis Yi (dated to 433 BCE), which includes a huge set of bronze bells, says that "we're hearing an almost exact sound from 2,500 years ago; bells are fixed pitch instruments, a bell is a bell is a bell unless you start chipping away at the metal" (https://www.smithsonianmag.com/smithsonian-institution/bronze-age-chinese-bells-tells-story-ancient-innovation-180964459/). Thus, it is surprising that the "better sound" is analogous to the state of "worn out" and not the opposite.

17. Some translators rendered the literal "two horses" in the text as "carriage" or a single vehicle of transportation; in the most general way, though, a few archaeological sites (such the site of the Terracotta Warriors of the first

emperor Qin Shi Huang and the Anyang site), as well as textual and linguistic evidence suggest that during the Shang period, the norm was to use two horses per a single vehicle (see Gernet 1996, 51), while later on, in the Eastern and Western Zhou periods and into the Qin dynasty, chariots went through many changes, including the addition of two horses to one row. This is why I prefer rendering it as "two horses"—to draw on the possibility that Mencius emphasizes the smallest transport unit possible. For an in-depth study of Chinese wheeled vehicles—mainly in the Chinese Bronze Age, see Anthony J. Barbieri-Low, 2000, *Wheeled Vehicles in the Chinese Bronze Age (c. 2000–741 B.C.)*, Sino-Platonic Papers, No. 99.

18. In reference to the complex analogies and arguments made by Mencius, D. C. Lau said that "it is not unusual for a reader of the Mencius to be left with the impression that in argument with his opponents Mencius was a sophist with little respect for logic. Not the least contributory factor to this impression is the type of argument which centers round an analogy. Yet it is difficult to believe that a thinker of Mencius' caliber and reputation could have indulged consistently in what appears to be pointless argument or that his opponents were always effectively silenced by non sequiturs. The fault, we suspect, must lie with us" (1970, 235).

19. The image of seeds coming to fruition, or roots growing into branches constitute a reoccurring image and metaphor in Chinese thought; Chinese medicine similarly grasps a healthy human body as a "healthy garden" if it goes through the natural (positive) cycle of the five phases, *wuxing* 五 : earth (soil), metal, water, wood (tree), fire.

20. Archeology teaches us that this segregation continued well into later dynasties. In 2011, for instance, a Song dynasty tomb was excavated in Dengfeng, the chamber of which was covered in colored murals depicting everyday scenes; one of them shows a woman peeping through a half-open gate. See details and photo at http://en.people.cn/90001/90783/91324/7311514.html.

Chapter 6

1. Of course, China's most famous route is the Silk Road *Sichouzhilu* 絲綢之路, in which the character *lu* 路 is used for "road"; but although the name is derived from the Chinese silk that was traded along its routes, it was used as a general name for the trade and communication routes between Eurasian civilizations; the term itself was mentioned for the first time in a series about China that was published in 1877 by German geographer Baron Ferdinand von Richthofen: the "Silk Road" is a direct translation of the German term *Seidenstraße*.

2. The study of gates in the context of imagined journeys to the afterlife stresses the complexity of the general subject of death in Chinese thought and

beliefs. Indeed, as Philip J. Ivanhoe says, "what we do find in traditional Chinese attitudes towards and responses to death is difficult to represent in any summary fashion: this difficulty reflects not only the diverse media and forms of expression evident in Chinese culture but also the great variety of beliefs, attitudes and practices found throughout the Chinese tradition" (Olberding and Ivanhoe 2011, 1). Journeys were dependent upon status, geographical orientation, and more. This means that within the limited space available, it would be impossible to investigate all its various aspects.

3. In the last scene of Kafka's narrative, the gatekeeper roars in the protagonist's ear, "no one else could ever be admitted here, since this gate was made only for you. I am now going to shut it" (Glatzer 1971, 23). Was Kafka referring to the futility of finding meaning in life or to blind indifference and power of judicial systems, governments, or bureaucracy? Though Kafka himself was an atheist (by his own account), we cannot separate the story from Western and monotheist religious context (the Old Testament's God of the law)—even on some unconscious level (in fact, it seems to me that Kafka makes use of the "inaccessibility" of God as a proof of his existence). The significance of the gate metaphor here lies in the unfathomed distance between man and God— inherently different to the relationship and relatedness between man and the gods (and spirits) in Chinese tradition and faith. In tempospatial terms, the border and the gate in the parable signify "infinite distance" and also "infinite time" (waiting at the border) as well as "inaccessibility" that is associated with a monotheist God. Existentialist philosophers (such as Derrida, Heidegger, and Sartre) took the story as the embodiment of life's absurdity, the contingency of existence and society as "the other."

4. The term "Legalism" is problematic; it puts the emphasis on the use of punishments in the hands of an absolute power, but the Chinese term *fajia* 法家 is much more complex, as the character *fa* 法 is multifaceted and carrying meanings beyond the mere "law" or "legality"; in his article "Persistent Misconceptions about Chinese 'Legalism,'" P. R. Goldin says that "though *fa* can surely include 'law,' it covers a much larger semantic range, and it is precisely in this larger range that the word usually has to be located. The two basic meanings of *fa* are 'method' and 'standard'" (2011, 7). Goldin adds that "even in imperial China, *fa* tended to mean something more like 'government program' or 'institution' than 'law'" (2011, 7). For further discussion and reference to the text of Shang Yang (d. 338 BC), commonly thought of as a *fajia* thinker, see Pines (2012). Besides Hanfeizi, other notable pre-Qin "Legalists" are Shen Dao 慎到 (275–350 BC), Shang Yang 商鞅 (390–338 BC), and Shen Buhai (400–337 BC).

5. For an excellent investigation of the commentarial strategies employed by the two chapters and the central place the *Laozi* occupies in Chinese commentarial tradition, see Hendrischke, 2022, "The Commentarial Strategies of 'Jie Lao' (Explaining the Laozi)," *Monumenta Serica Journal of Oriental Studies* 70, no. 1.

6. *Shenming* 神明 is a multifaceted and important term in pre-Qin thought that is heavy with and open to various translations and meanings—intriguingly ranging from external deity-like cosmogenic forces encompassing the complementary efficacy of *yin* and *yang*, the heavens and earth, the moon and the sun, etc., to inner sagely prowess and wisdom. I follow Sharon Small, who concludes in her article on the exegesis of *shenming* that "*shenming* is ability, not spirit. It is ability either of our mind or either of the cosmos, just as Dao can be heavenly Dao (*tiandao* 天道) or humanistic Dao (*rendao* 人道), *shenming* can belong to heaven or the human, depending on context" (2018, 17). In the present *Hanfeizi* passage, I postulate *shenming* as an inner ability that penetrates directly into the very roots of the phenological world—just like a meditative gaze into a bright and illuminating flame. In an attempt to convey this meaning, I have translated it as "superior brilliance"—in the same way that we might refer to a very intelligent person as "brilliant" or as someone who possesses a brilliant mind, but with the added layer of deity-like abilities, hence, superior.

7. Further study is required into the subject of foreknowledge and its relatedness to *ritual*—its authenticity in the context of externality and internality.

8. Importantly, some scholars question the presence of *qianshi* altogether; by quoting an almost exact line from the *Zhibeiyou* 知北遊 (in the Outer Chapters) of the *Zhuangzi*, Robert Moss, for instance, wonders whether *qianshi* belongs to the original text at all: "Ritual is the bedecking of the Way and the source of social disorder. Thus it was said, 'Pursue the Way by unlearning day by day.' This interesting *Zhuangzi* passage suggests that the puzzling words *qianshi* may not belong in the text at all; it also shows that two *Laozi* references—to this stanza and to stanza 48—were cited as authority and related to one another by the author of the 'Zhibeiyou'" (2001, 209).

9. But Yuri Pines goes on to say, "yet the ruler is also an individual—and as we have seen, quite often a mediocre one. Han Fei's major concern is to prevent the ruler's flawed individuality from harming the political fabric; and the only way to do so is to dissuade the sovereign from actively intervening into political life. Thus, amid repeated warnings to the ruler not to delegate his power of authority (i.e., personnel promotions and demotions), he also demands that the ruler exercise this power only in accordance with impartial laws and regulations, limiting his personal input in policy-making to the degree of complete invisibility" (2013, 67). For further discussions on Hanfeizi, see Paul R. Goldin, ed., 2013, *Dao Companion to the Philosophy of Han Fei* (New York: Springer).

10. This line can be interpreted and translated in many ways; the traditional translation posits the "many men" at the gates of high ministers, as Burton Watson indeed translated in 1964: "Take warning when there are many men gathering at the gates of the high ministers." Beyond the fact that I cannot find the "take warning" anywhere, I believe that the 之 in "大臣之門" refers only to *chen* 臣 and the adjective "big" defines the gates, the whole part of which

stands before the reason given: I take *wei* 唯 as "only because" as a reference to "feared by many men" (恐多人).

11. Original Chinese: 匠人營國、 方九里、 旁三門、 國中九經九緯、 經涂 九軌. 左祖右社、 面朝後市、 市朝一夫.

12. Yinong Xu continues by describing the evolvement of gates-towers through to the second half of the Ming and the Qing periods, saying that they "assumed the function of public time-reckoning, alarm-raising and command signaling. There were thus loci from whence the maintenance of social order and security was transmitted . . . the city gates by their practical attributes represented the openings through which the function of government was carried out" (2000, 119).

13. The term *tianmen*, gate of the heavens, will appear in almost any chapter of this study, philosophical texts included. It is noteworthy that in the Han dynasty an expression developed: *tianmen, dihu* 天門, 地戶, meaning "gate of the heavens, door of earth"; Mura Kunio tells us that "a comparatively early example of both expressions used in conjunction is in the *Wu Yue Chunqiu* 吳越春秋 (*Spring and Autumn Annals of the States of Wu and Yue*), a work probably dating from the Han period but containing later additions" (quoted in Lagerwey, 1993b). When the King of Wu, Helü (r. 514–496 BC) was building the city walls of Suzhou (Jiangsu) according to the plans of Wu Zixu 伍子胥, he made a gate in the northwest to represent the gate of the heavens, and a gate in the southeast to represent the door of earth. The placement of the gate of the heavens in the northwest and the door of earth in the southeast is explained by the principle of Chinese cosmography and topography "that there is an 'insufficiency' or a 'gap' (*buzu* 不足) of Heaven in the northwest and of Earth in the southeast" (quoted in Pregadio 2010, 978).

14. The usage of medical metaphors reminds me of the Buddhist "Four Noble Truths," which begins with identifying the root problem of suffering in the same way that a doctor makes a diagnosis.

15. It brings to mind the way immigrants *wait at the borders for times infinite*—just to have the chance to have a new home—or foreign workers who are employed in neighboring rich states and go through the demeaning experience of crossing the border twice a day.

Chapter 7

1. Graham (1981).

2. In the discussion, I dedicate some space for a comparative dialogue with modern theories of human cognition, in which I detect in Zhuangzian thought (spontaneous and instinctive) the fast and automatic thinking studied by Daniel Kahneman.

3. There could be an alternative interpretation: that the list of opposites (e.g., hatred and kindness, death and life), can actually be used as "instruments for change" for a "correction" of one's self, so that the translation could be something along the lines of "alas, those who are indeed able to 'use' these instrument are precisely those who do not hold these values high! And the reason man does not realize this is because the 'gate of heavens' (in their heart-mind) hasn't been opened!"

4. For an elaboration on the interesting character *ji* 跡 see David Chai (2019).

5. There are quite a few controversies surrounding the hagiographies of Laozi, particularly in regard to the issue of "philosophical" and "religious" Daoism, i.e., whether they constitute one intellectual continuum or not. For a detailed account, see Liu Xiaogan et al., 2015, "Daoism from Philosophy to Religion," in *Dao Companion to Daoist Philosophy*, vol. 6, ed. Liu Xiaogan (New York: Springer).

6. Original Chinese of the said narrative: 老子修道德, 其學以自隱無名為務. 居周久之, 見周之衰, 乃遂去. 至關, 關令尹喜曰: 子將隱矣, 彊為我著書. 於是老子乃著書上下篇, 言道德之意五千餘言而去, 莫知其所終.

7. It seems that the character *yin* pointed also to a local authority responsible for important places and monuments, which perhaps included gates. Source: https://hanziyuan.net.

8. It is also known by the name *Wushang miaodao wenshi zhenjing* 無上妙道文始真經 (*Perfect classic of the beginning of the scripture of the supreme wonderful Way*); it presumably contained nine chapters, but was sadly lost soon after the Han period. The text reappeared during the Southern Song period 南宋 (1127–1279), but, unfortunately, there is no telling whether it resembles the original.

9. See additional discussion in Dor (2013).

10. The character *Jing* 徑 appears only once in the *Daode jing* (chapter 53) and in conjugation with (and in relation to) *dao*: "If I was sent as a formal messenger, I would acquire some knowledge and (therefor) walk along the great ways (*dao*); (but) the great ways have been destroyed, so the people like the narrow paths (*jing*)" (使我介然有知, 行於大道, 唯施是畏大道甚夷, 而民好徑). My translation is unconventional: most translators seem to conceptualize *jing* negatively—as a lower choice or a detour made by the ordinary people; I believe that the small, hidden, and indirect paths actually better suit Daoist context, and that the first words (formal messenger *jie* 介, and "having wisdom" *you zhi* 有知) point to what Laozi actually dislikes . . . stately positions and acquiring wisdom (wisdom in the Confucian sense).

11. Though they shared fifty-three years of their lives, Wumen (1183–1260) in Longxiang monastery, China, and Dogen (1200–1253), known as Kōso Jōyō Daishi 高祖承陽大師, in Kyoto and Eihei-ji temple, it is questionable whether they ever met; Dogen returned (to Japan) from his travels in China in 1227—a year before the compilation of Wumen's text. Though known to oppose *koans*,

Dogen in fact used, commented on, and developed a unique approach to their usage. Steven Heine says that, "the use of *koans* by Dogen after his return to Japan can be analyzed in terms of several stages leading up to the development of a uniquely innovative approach to *koan* interpretation" (2004, 2).

12. I have also come across a different rendering for the title, namely, *The great path, the gate of nothingness, has no gate*, as translated by the Numata Center for Buddhist Translation and Research, an edition published in 1999.

13. In his book titled *The Koan: Texts and Contexts in Zen Buddhism*, T. G. Foulk says that there is a "tendency among Western students of Zen to call anything that becomes the sustained focus of an existential problem of life crisis a 'koan'" (2000, 26), with which I agree . . .not any difficulty in life is a *koan* . . .as Foulk continues, "the idea that 'anything can serve a koan' is a modern development" (26). *Koans* developed in the specific context of mind transformation as they allow for a conscious awareness of the "fixed templates or molds" people think, feel, and react; *koans* work through language to demonstrate its (i.e., language's) limitations and fixation characteristics. It is also a Chan/Zen guided process and a multiple-stage way; thus, this tendency, I believe, to treat any life crisis as a *koan* is an oversimplification of this ancient (but still in use) tool for mind awakening. More will be said in relation to this subject in the concluding chapter.

14. This is not surprising: Chan Buddhism *chan zong* 禪宗 is the "child" of the intermingling of Mahayana Buddhism and Daoist philosophy (in the beginning of sixth century AD). In both there is an emphasis on the human language and its constraints on the mind. For a thorough examination of the *liminology* of language in both the *Zhuangzi* and Chan Buddhism, see Youru Wang, 2014, *Linguistic Strategies in Daoist Zhuangzi and Chan Buddhism* (Routledge).

15. *Wumenguan* is not the only text in later Daoism and Chan/Zen Buddhism to use a gate in its title; for instance, the *Script for Penetrating through the Barriers* written by Liu Yi Ming in the Qing dynasty (1644–1911), continues to be revised and published by Daoist masters and practitioners. One such master is Xing De, of Wudang Kongfu Center, who wrote the book *The 49 Barriers of Cultivating the* Dao; it demonstrates how gates continue to serve as learning and practicing tools by Daoist practitioners in present-day China.

Discussion and Further Reflections

1. Qiyou Chen (1984, 45).

2. The epigraph hints that humanistic philosophies always remained within the human sphere; however, certain humanistic philosophers pointed to and discussed the natural world, the heavens, or the cosmic dimension. One of these philosophers is Mencius, for instance, who (as was discussed), touches upon the cosmic in concept of *qi*, for instance, as the energy or life force that exists

everywhere and "fills one's body" (and is "directed by the will"). As Kaibara translates in relation to the *Mencius*, "one has to nourish it with integrity and place no obstacle in its path and it will fill the space between Heaven and Earth" (2007, 13). In addition, Mencius refers to man's innate "goodness" (*xìng shàn* 性善) as rooted in our nature, which means it is pre-existing and an inseparable part of the universe; it is also named as "sprout"—thus, it can be viewed as a cosmic or heavenly principle, or, indeed, the natural world.

3. With the aim of demonstrating the sheer scale of emptiness in the universe and the visual correspondence between the micro and macro worlds, one can watch scientific videos that zoom out of earth to space and then zoom back in—to the inside of cells, covering almost the whole phenomenal worlds of forms and emptiness ("almost" because they don't go further inside to the atomic and subatomic level); see, for example, https://www.youtube.com/watch?v=X-3Oq_82XNA.

4. A (remarkable) comparative analysis of Chinese and Western painting is Francois Jullien's *The Great Image Has No Form, or On the Nonobject through Painting*, published in English in 2009 by the University of Chicago Press.

5. When discussing Chinese painting, in general, and the significance of the first and single stroke, in particular, it naturally takes us to the famous seventeenth-century painter Shitao, who wrote about the significance of this "one stroke" *yihua* 一画 (or, the "primordial line"), saying that it is the root of the "ten thousand *xiang*" (W. Wong 1991, 119).

6. This relates to the intriguing subject of the relationship between written signs (their visual shape/form) and reality, and between *xiang xing* 象形 and *hui yi* 會意, and also to the question of *wen* 文 and the *zi* 字. See, for instance, Francoise Bottéro, 2002, "Revisiting the wén 文 and the zì 字: The Great Chinese Characters Hoax," *Bulletin of the Museum of Far Eastern Antiquities* 74: 14–33.

7. J. R. Allen indeed refers to Chinese written graphs, saying that they "[perform] the dual role of signifier and signified" and adds that Chinese is therefore 'a meta-language'—a language whose referent is language itself' (1992, 189).

8. For example: left wing/right wing in politics, religious/secular in monotheism, and others . . . Obviously, this does not mean, as we know from modern Chinese history itself, that such mode of "binary thinking" cannot occur outside Western culture on the political or individual level.

9. For further discussion of rigid dichotomous thinking, see Atsushi Oshio, 2012, "An All-Or-Nothing Thinking Turns into Darkness: Relations between Dichotomous Thinking and Personality Disorders," *Japanese Psychological Research* 54, no. 4: 424–29.

10. To compare it to the "real" cosmos out there, it is estimated today that there are around two hundred billion galaxies in the observable universe, and their arrangement resembles a honeycomb-like structure, with cavities (bodiless

empty space) that constitute its largest structures—some reaching the length of one billion light years.

11. The "Gate Control Theory of Pain" for instance, which involves a threshold, a "tipping point," and a hinge that responds to the smallest of changes (Melzack 1996, 132).

12. Physics and in particular quantum mechanics has been "corresponding" with Chinese philosophy for the past few decades. The *yinyang* complementarity was compared to the "wave-particle duality," as well as the "Heisenberg uncertainty principle." Famously, Niles Bohr, the Nobel laureate, had designed his own coat of arms (in 1949), emblazoning it with the *yinyang* symbol along the Latin words *contraria sunt complementa* ("opposites are complementary"). Two (best-selling) books were written on the subject (including Buddhist philosophical and psychological ideas): *The Tao of Physics* (Fritjof Capra 1975) and *Dancing Wu Li Masters* (Gary Zukav, 1979). The books received praise but also criticism by physicists who claimed they oversimplified.

13. Japanese culture seems to embrace and express this idea in the aesthetic and artistic, e.g., *haiku* poetry, dry Zen gardens, *wabi-sabi* aesthetics, etc.

14. In fact, the actual development of organisms, from embryology to adult life, constitutes a simulation process of life and death! An organism takes on the particular shape because certain cells or tissues grow while others die; thus, a development always consists of two processes: one is cell division (adding to life), and the other, cell death (apoptosis).

15. Importantly, in comparison to Western thought, it is never a linear journey of target and result (which might lead to "forgetting the way in the middle"); Bruce Lee was one of the first teachers of martial arts to bring this idea to Western audiences. He is known for his emphasis on emptiness and meditation as a precondition to any *kungfu* practice.

16. The dynamic and behavior in nature of "the path of least resistance" is connected to the "branching tree pattern" (also called "dendritic pattern")—a common spreading behavior in many and varied systems and dimensions (e.g., the branching-out of plants, in the flow of rivers, in the pulmonary system of the lungs, blood arteries, nerves, etc.). It also resembles the phylogenetic tree which presents the evolution of species.

17. One further note on *ao*: it is highly significant in Japanese culture, thought, and aesthetics; one conspicuous instance is the text titled *Oku no Hosomichi* 奥の 細道 composed by the seventeenth-century Japanese poet Matsuo Basho; the title literally means "the narrow way to the north," in which *oku* 奥 was a remote place in north of Japan, but in parallel, "deep inside"; in other words, Basho's journey (*michi = dao*) constitutes both an external and internal exploration.

18. Original Chinese: 反者道之動; 弱者道之用。天下萬物生於有, 有生於無

19. We are in fact most familiar with the phenomenon: the house will inevitably become more disorderly with time, and famously, a drinking glass will

break into pieces, but the event of these pieces gathering themselves back into the shape of a glass has never been seen . . . it is our everyday experience that continuous effort is required to (at the very least) keep the current order, let alone bring it to a higher level of order (low entropy).

20. The idea is even pronounced in texts of embryology. Anna Andreeva and Dominic Steavu notice that "in fact, the association between the genesis of individual life and the genesis of the cosmos had been established since the earliest surviving descriptions of embryology" (2016, 114).

21. A good instance is *Huainanzi* 1.19, which refers to the carpenter's square in the context of established ways of both the natural and the human worlds: "thus, scholars have the established format of essays; women have unchanging standards of conduct. The compass cannot become square, and the carpenter's square cannot become round, nor can the marking cord become crooked and the angle rule become straight. The constancies of Heaven and Earth are such that climbing up a hill does not make you taller and sitting on the ground does not make you shorter" (Major et al. 2010).

22. The Legalist gate has demonstrated a negation and even a destruction of the past (in the case of the Qin Xin Huangdi, and thousands of years later, Mao Zedong) and formulated a future of extreme order manageable through *fa* "laws and punishments"; their vision did not point backward, but to the present and the future. In this case, we have met with barriers, the closed gate that either protects the governance and/or controls the behavior of the populace.

23. As becomes more and more clear in relation to the Western Middle Ages, some important social shifts, technological advancements, and "quantum leaps" in new ideas have taken place in this period. If it was once thought to be of little significance (and even downright "negative," to the extent that a part of it is known as the "Dark Ages"), new studies shed new light on its importance; see, for instance, Chris Wickham, 2007, *Framing the Early Middle Ages: Europe and the Mediterranean, 400 to 800* (Oxford: Oxford University Press).

24. Indeed, the same "dialectical play" can be seen in the Chinese Communist Party, consisting of conservatives and reformists, the latter attempting reforms but believing in keeping the same political ideology. Raviprasad Narayanan says that "Chinese reformers, led by Deng Xiaoping, attempted to gradually transform orthodox doctrine into a more elastic pro-capital and investment attractive ideology while retaining essential socialist values" (2006, 331). In this context, the economic reforms led by Deng Xiaoping manifests this extraordinary Chinese ability to make far-reaching changes (reforms) while keeping the conceptual framework (communism).

25. This point is related to the tension and relationship that exist between an individual and its group, or the collective (society), which brings us to the much debated subject of individualism versus collectivism. The prevailing theory

points to agriculture as the root for these social evolvements—rice paddy culti-vation leading to strong mutual dependency and cooperation versus individually owned and managed agriculture in the West. See, for instance, T. Talhelm et al., 2014. "Large-Scale Psychological Differences within China Explained by Rice Versus Wheat Agriculture," *Science* 344, no. 6184: 603–608.

26. Hayles states that there are "two main "branches" of chaos theory: one concerned with "the order hidden within chaotic systems" and the other with the "order that arises out of chaotic systems" (1991, 8–9).

27. https://plato.stanford.edu/entries/daoism-religion/#Zhua

28. It is of course close to the concept of mindfulness, which has become very popular lately (*too* popular in the sense that it is used superficially or without practice—to the extent that it becomes belittled). This refers to the mind as being *present* and embodied in everyday experience; mindfulness techniques are designed to lead the mind *back* from its preoccupation with self, thoughts, and "distancing one off the center" to the immediate experience of the environment and situation at hand.

29. I would like to stress two points in relation to the Daoist advice to bend at times or go to lowly places like water and to the "path of least resis-tance"; each constitutes an excellent instance of cultural gaps between Chinese and Western thought. I have noticed how (especially in America) the principle is found to be contemptible! In America it is taken to be the path of the lazy person who puts no effort or work into getting his or her ambitions fulfilled. I have come across opinions expressing the idea that "*following the path of least resistance guarantees failure in life*." Indeed, it is similar to the way Chinese *wuwei* had been interpreted (in the nineteenth century) by Western scholars and nonscholars alike as literally "doing nothing."

30. Francois Jullien, writing on the Chinese art of painting, refers to music, introducing a remark made by Wang Bi: "As soon as 'sound' is produced, it is divided up or separated into the notes of the musical scale. If it is not one note that is emitted, it is necessarily one of the others. The 'capacity to govern the whole' (Wang Bi) that prevailed before sounds could be distinguished from one another is thereby lost" (2009, 47).

31. Gong Hua'nan notes in regard to the etymology of *ziran*, that according to the *Guang ya* dictionary, the second character *ran* literally means "achieve-ment and completion" which turns the whole expression to mean "fulfilment of potentiality" and "self-actualization" of the living world (2008, 393).

32. Space does not allow for an in-depth discussion of this interesting subject, but, in the context of decision-making and the Western debate of free will versus determinism, new studies of the digestions system and its gut biome suggest that the body (that operates on its own and not under system 2), plays a significant role even in decisions we take in life.

33. Yet again, reflecting on cultural gaps, when Descartes said *cogito ergo sum* ("I think, therefore I am"), he referred to the "thinking faculty" of system 2, thus *further separating* it from the physical or "bodily" *immersed feeling* of system 1.

Bibliography

Primary Sources

Bian Shao 邊韶. *Laozi ming* 老子銘 [Inscription for Laozi].

Birrell, Anne M. 1997. "The Four Flood Myth Traditions of Classical China." *T'oung Pao Second Series* 83, no. 4/5: 213–59.

CHANT (Chinese Ancient Texts) Database. http://www.chant.org.

Chen Cengbi. 1992. "*Lu Ban jing* 魯班經." *Zhongguo da baike quanshu*. Beijing/ Shanghai.

Chen Daming. 1993. *Yingzao Fashi Damuzuo Yanjiu / A Study on the Structural Carpentry System according to Ying Zao Fa Shi*. Beijing: Wenwu Publishing.

Chen Qiyou 陳奇猷. 1984. *Lüshi Chunqiu Xinshi* 呂氏春秋新釋. Shanghai: Shang-hai Guji Chubanshe.

Cheng Hsueh-li. 1982. *Nāgārjuna's Twelve Gate Treatise: Translated with Introduc-tory Essays, Comments, and Notes*. Studies of Classical India 5. Springer.

Chinese Etymology 字源. https://hanziyuan.net.

Gao Heng 高亨. 1998. *Zhouyi dachuan jinzhu* 周易大傳今注. Jinan: Qilu Shushe.

Goudian Laozi 郭店 老子. https://ctext.org/excavated-texts.

Graham, A. C. 1990a. *The Book of Lieh-Tzu. [Liezi* 列子]. New York: Columbia University Press.

Guanyinzi 關尹子. [*Master Yin of the Pass*]. http://chinaknowledge.de/index.html.

Guiguzi 鬼谷子. https://ctext.org/gui-gu-zi.

Hanfeizi 韓非子. https://ctext.org/hanfeizi.

Huang Kan 皇侃. 1991. *Lunyu jijie yishu* 論語集解義疏. Vol. 2. Taipei: Guangwen.

Jing dian wen xian 經典文獻. https://ctext.org/ancient-classics.

Johnston, Ian. 2014. *Mozi: The Book of Master Mo*. Penguin Classics.

Kim Hongkyung. 2012. *The Old Master: A Syncretic Reading of the Laozi from the Mawangdui Text A Onward*. Albany: State University of New York Press.

Knoblock, John, and Jeffrey Riegel. 2000. *The Annals of Lü Buwei: A Complete Translation and Study*. Stanford University Press.

Laozi bianhua jing 老子變化經. [*Scripture of the transformations of Laozi*].

Lau, D. C., trans. 1970. *The Mencius*. [*Mengzi* 孟子]. Penguin Books.

Liu Xiang 劉向. *Liexian zhuan* 列仙傳 [Immortals' biography].

Liu Zhao. 2003. *Guodian Chujian Jiaoshi* 郭店楚簡校釋. Fuzhou: Fujian Renmin Chubanshe.

Lu Ban jing 魯班經 [known also by the name of "Mirror of woodwork craftsmen"].

Lunyu 論語. https://ctext.org/analects.

Lynn, Richard J. 1994. *The Classic of Changes: A New Translation of the I Ching as Interpreted by Wang Bi*. New York: Columbia University Press.

———. 1999. *The Classic of the Way and Virtue: A New Translation of the Tao-te Ching of Laozi as Interpreted by Wang Bi*. New York: Columbia University Press.

Major, John S., Sarah A. Queen, Seth Andrew Meyer, Michael Puett, and Judson Murray. 2010. *The Huainanzi: A Guide to the Theory and Practice of Government in Early Han China*. New York: Columbia University Press.

Mawangdui Laozi 馬王堆老子. https://ctext.org/mawangdui.

Nylan, Michael. 1994. *The Elemental Changes: The Ancient Chinese Companion to the I Ching: The Tai Shuan Ching of Master Yang Hsiung*. SUNY Series in Chinese Philosophy and Culture. Albany: State University of New York Press.

Profound Words of the Blue Bag. 1985. *Qing nang ao yu, Yang Yunsong, Qin ding si ku quan shu*. Taibei: Yi wen yin shu guan.

Rickett, A. W. 2001. *The Guanzi: Political, Economic and Philosophical Essays from Early China. A Study and Translation*. Princeton University Press.

Sekida Katsuki. 2000. *Two Zen Classics: Mumonkan And Hekiganroku*. John Weatherhill.

Shisanjing Zhushu (十三經注疏). 1990. In *Zhouli Zhushu*. Shanghai: *Shangwu Yinshuguan*.

Shizhao Pu, ed. 1938. *Hui Tu Lu Ban Jing* 绘 图鲁班经. Shanghai: Hong Wen Publishing House.

Slingerland, Edward. 2006. *The Essential Analects: Selected Passages with Traditional Commentary*. Hackett Press.

Sunzi bing fa 孫子兵法 [The art of war or Master Sun's military methods].

Taixuan jing 太玄經 [The great mystery]. https://ctext.org/taixuanjing.

Takigawa kametaro. 1977. *Shiki kaichu kosho*. Taibei: Hongye Shuju.

Wagner, Rudolf G. 2000. *The Craft of a Chinese Commentator: Wang Bi on the Laozi*. Vol. 1. Albany: State University of New York Press.

———. 2003a. *A Chinese Reading of the Daodejing: Wang Bi's Commentary on the Laozi with Critical Text and Translation*. Albany: State University of New York Press.

Waley, Arthur, trans. 1937. *Excerpts from the Shih Ching (The Book of Songs)*. Boston: Houghton Mifflin.

Wang Bi commentaries: *Zhouyi lüeli* 周易略例 / *Zhouyi zhu* 周易注 / *Laozi zhilüe* 老子指略 / *Laozi zhu* 老子注.

Wilhelm, Richard, trans. 1950. *The I Ching or the Book of Changes*. Translated into English by Cary F. Baynes. Bollingen Series. Pantheon Books.

Wu Hui. 2016. *Guiguzi: China's First Treatise on Rhetoric. A Critical Translation and Commentary*. Southern Illinois University Press.

Xisheng jing 西昇經 [Scripture of western ascension].

Yingzao Fashi 營造法式.

Zhang Lianggao. 2002. *Jiang xue qi shuo* 匠学七说. Beijing: Zhongguo jian zhu gong ye chu ban she.

Zhang Xue. 1992. "Shuowen jiezi 說文解字." In Zhou Gucheng 周谷城, ed. *Zhongguo xueshu mingzhu tiyao* 中國學術名著提要. Shanghai: Fudan *daxue chubanshe*.

Zhuangzi 莊子. https://ctext.org/zhuangzi.

Secondary Sources

Adamson, Peter, ed. 2019. *Health: A History*. Oxford Philosophical Concepts Series. Oxford: Oxford University Press.

Aitken, Robert. 1981. " 'The Cloud of Unknowing' and the 'Mumonkan': Christian and Buddhist Meditation Methods." *Buddhist-Christian Studies*. 87–91.

Allan, Sarah. 1991. *The Shape of the Turtle: Myth, Art, and Cosmos in Early China*. Albany: State University of New York Press.

———. 1997. *The Way of Water and Sprouts of Virtue*. Albany: State University of New York Press.

Allen, Joseph R. 1992. "I Will Speak, Therefore, of a Graph: A Chinese Metalanguage." *Language in Society* 21: 189–206.

Allinson, Robert A., ed. 1989. *Understanding the Chinese Mind: The Philosophical Roots*. Oxford University Press.

Ames, Roger T. 1998. *Wandering at Ease in the Zhuangzi*. Albany: State University of New York Press.

———. 2011. *Confucian Role Ethics: A Vocabulary*. Albany: State University of New York Press.

———. 2015. "The Great Commentary (*Dazhuan* 大傳) and Chinese Natural Cosmology." *International Communication of Chinese Culture* 2, no. 1: 1–18.

Ames, Roger T., and David Hall. 2003. *Dao De Jing: Making this life significant: A Philosophical Translation*. Ballantine Books.

Andreeva, Anna, and Dominic Steavu. 2016. *Transforming the Void: Embryological Discourse and Reproduction Imagery in East Asian Religions*. Brill.

Ariel, Yoav, and Gil Raz. 2010. "Anaphors or Cataphors? A Discussion of the Two *Qi* 其 Graphs in the First Chapter of the *Daodejing*." *Philosophy East and West* 60, no. 3: 391–421.

Bachelard, Gaston.1964. *The Poetics of Space*. Orion Press.

Barnett, Raymond J. 1986. "Taoism and Biological Thought." *Journal of Religion and Science* 21, no. 3 (September): 297–317.

Barnwell, S. A. 2013. "The Evolution of the Concept of *De* 德 in Early China." *Sino-Platonic Papers*, no. 235 (March).

Barrett, Louise. 2018. In *The Routledge Handbook of Evolution and Philosophy*, edited by Richard Joyce. Routledge.

Basso, Keith H., and Henry A. Selby. 1976. *Meaning in Anthropology*. University of New Mexico Press.

Behuniak, James, Jr. 2005. *Mencius on Becoming Human*. Albany: State University of New York Press.

———. 2009. "'Embracing the One' in the *Daodejing*." *Philosophy East and West* 59, no. 3: 364–81.

———. 2019. Review of *Mind and Body in Early China: Beyond Orientalism and the Myth of Holism*, by Edward Slingerland. *Dao: A Journal of Comparative Philosophy* 18, no. 2: 305–12.

Bird, Richard J. 2003. *Chaos and Life: Complexity and Order in Evolution and Thought*. Columbia University Press.

Birrell, Anne M. 1999. *Chinese Mythology: An Introduction*. John Hopkins University Press.

Boucher, Anthony, trans. 1948. "Jorge Luis Borges." *Ellery Queen's Mystery Magazine* 12, no. 57: 101–110.

Briggs, John P., and David F. Peat. 2000. *Seven Life Lessons of Chaos: Spiritual Wisdom from the Science of Change*. HarperCollins.

Brindley, Erica Fox. 2006. "Music, Cosmos, and the Development of Psychology in Early China." *T'oung Pao*, 2nd ser., 92, no. 1: 1–49.

———. 2012. *Music, Cosmology and the Politics of Harmony in Early China*. Albany: State University of New York Press.

Brown, Miranda, and Uffe Bergeton. 2008. "'Seeing' Like a Sage: Three Takes on Identity and Perception in Early China." *Journal of Chinese Philosophy* 35, no. 4: 641–62.

Burik, Steven. 2010. "Thinking on the Edge: Heidegger, Derrida and the Daoist Gateway." *Philosophy East and West* 60, no. 4: 499–516.

Cao, Deborah. 2019. "Desperately Seeking 'Justice' in Classical Chinese: On the Meanings of Yi." *International Journal for the Semiotics of Law—Revue international de Sémiotique juridique* 32, no. 1: 13–28.

Cao Feng. 2013. "A Review of the Issues Related to 'Names' in Lao Zi's First Stanza." *Contemporary Chinese Thought* 44, no. 4: 72–91.

Cassirer, Ernst. 1955. *The Philosophy of Symbolic Forms*. Yale University Press.

Chai, David. 2010. "Meontology in Early *Xuanxue* Thought." *Journal of Chinese Philosophy* 37, no. 1: 90–101.

———. 2012. "Nothingness, Being, and Dao: Ontology and Cosmology in the Zhuangzi." Ph.D. diss., University of Toronto.

———. 2019. *Zhuangzi and the Becoming of Nothingness*. Series in Chinese Philosophy and Culture. Albany: State University of New York Press.

Chan Wing-tsit. 1963. *A Source Book in Chinese Philosophy*. Princeton University Press.

———. 1964. "The Evolution of the Neo-Confucian Concept of *Li* as Principle." *Tsing-Hua Journal of Chinese Studies*. 123–48.

Chang Chung-yuan. 1963. *Creativity and Taoism: A Study of Chinese Philosophy, Art & Poetry*. Julian Press.

Chang Sen-dou. 1970. "Some Observations on the Morphology of Chinese Walled Cities." *Annals of the Association of American Geographers banner* 60, no. 1: 63–91.

Chen Guo-Ming. 2008. "*Bian* (Change): A Perpetual Discourse of *I Ching*." *Intercultural Communication Studies* 17, no. 4: 7–16.

Chen Guying. 2016. *The Philosophy of Life: A New Reading of the Zhuangzi*. Translated by Dominique Hertzer. Brill.

Cheng Chung-ying. 1977. "Nature and Function of Skepticism in Chinese Philosophy." *Philosophy East and West* 27, no. 2: 137–54.

———. 1991. *New Dimensions of Confucian and Neo-Confucian Philosophy*. Albany: State University of New York Press.

———. 2011. "Interpreting Paradigm of Change in Chinese Philosophy." *Journal of Chinese Philosophy* 38, no. 3: 339–67.

Cheng Linsun and Yuan Haiwang. 2009. *Berkshire Encyclopedia of China*. Berkshire.

Chien Li-kuei. 2018. "Gateways to Power and Paradise: Twin Towers in Early Chinese Architecture." *Archives of Asian Art* 68, no. 1: 67–86.

Ching, Julia. 1983. "The Ancient Sages (*Sheng*): Their Identity and Their Place in Chinese Intellectual History." *Orient Extremus* 30: 1–18.

Chong Kim-chong. 2011. "The Concept of *Zhen* 真 in the *Zhuangzi*." *Philosophy East and West* 61, no. 2: 324–46.

Coles, Benjamin. 2019. "Guo Xiang and the Problem of Self-Cultivation in Daoist Naturalism." *Religions* 10, no. 6: 388–405.

Colin, Ronan A. 1978. *The Shorter Science & Civilization in China*. Vol. 1. Cambridge University Press.

Cook, Constance (2015). "'Mother' (*Mu* 母) and the Embodiment of the *Dao*." *Journal of Chinese Philosophy* 42: 1–2.

Coutinho, Steve. 2004. *Zhuangzi and Early Chinese Philosophy Vagueness, Transformation and Paradox*. Routledge.

Creel, H. G. 1949. *Confucius and the Chinese Way*. New York: Harper & Row.

Cua, Antonio. 2013. *Encyclopedia of Chinese Philosophy*. Routledge.

D'Ambrosio, Paul J. 2015. "The Value of Falsity in the *Mencius*: Early Confucianism Is Not Consequentialism." *International Communication of Chinese Culture*. Vol. 2.

Derrida, Jacques. 1978. *Structure, Sign and Play in the Discourse of the Human Sciences*. Routledge.

De Waal, Frans. 2001. *The Ape and the Sushi Master: Cultural Reflections of a Primatologist*. New York: Basic Books.

Doeringer, Franklin M. 1982. "The Gate in the Circle: A Paradigmatic Symbol in Early Chinese Cosmology." vol. 32. no. 3. *Philosophy East and West*.

Dong, Xinbin, and Zheng Qi. 1990. "The Discussion by Category on Antithetical Concepts in Chinese Painting" (*Zhongguo Huihua Dui'ou Fanchou Lun*). Nanjing: *Jiangsu Meishu Chubanshe*.

Dor, Galia. 2013. "The Chinese Gate: A Unique Void for Inner Transformation." *Journal of Daoist Studies* 6: 1–28.

Ebrey, Patricia B. 1991. *Confucianism and Family Rituals in Imperial China: A Social History of Writing about Rites*. Princeton University Press.

———. 1996. *The Cambridge Illustrated History of China*. Cambridge University Press.

Eckfeld, Tonia. 2005. *Imperial Tombs in Tang China, 618–907*. Routledge Curzon.

Elman, Benjamin A. 1989. "Imperial Politics and Confucian Societies in Late Imperial China: The Hanlin and Donglin Academies." *Modern China* 15, no. 4: 379–418.

Eno, Robert. 2016. *Tan Gong: "Liji," Chapters 3–4. Translation, Notes and Commentary*. https://scholarworks.iu.edu/dspace/handle/2022/23425.

Eskildsen, Stephen. 2015. *Daoism, Mediation and the Wonders of Serenity*. Albany: State University of New York Press.

Espesset, Grégoire. 2016. "Sketching Out Portents Classification and Logics in the Monographs of Han Official Historiography." *Bochum Yearbook of East Asian Studies* 39: 5–38.

Farrell, Michael. 2014. *Investigating the Language of Special Education*. Springer.

Fech, Andrej. 2017. "'Place' in the Philosophy and Biography of Laozi." *International Communication of Chinese Culture* 4: 53–64.

Feng Jiren. 2012. *Chinese Architecture and Metaphor: Song Culture in the Yingzao Fashi Building Manual*. University of Hawaii Press.

Foulk, T. G. 2000. "The Form and Function of Koan Literature. A Historical Overview." In *The Koan: Texts and Contexts in Zen Buddhism*, edited by Steven Heine and Dale S. Wright, 15–45. Oxford University Press.

Fox, Alan. 1996. "Reflex and Reflectivity: *Wuwei* in the *Zhuangzi*." *Asian Philosophy* 6, no. 1: 59–72.

———. 2017. "A Process Interpretation of Daoist Thought." *Frontiers of Philosophy in China"* 12, no. 1: 26–37.

Francois, Jullien. 2009. *The Great Image Has No Form, or on the Nonobject through Painting.* University of Chicago Press.

Fraser, Chris. 2016. "The Mozi and Just War Theory in Pre-Han Thought." *Journal of Chinese Military History.*

Fung Yiu-ming. 2010. "On the Very Idea of Correlative Thinking." *Philosophy Compass* 5, no. 4: 296–306.

Garfield, Jay L. 2002. *Empty Words: Buddhist Philosophy and Cross-Cultural Interpretation.* Oxford University Press.

Ge Zhaoguang. 2014. *An Intellectual History of China: Knowledge, Thought, and Belief before the Seventh Century CE.* Vol. 1. Brill's Humanities in China Library.

Geaney Jane. 2012. "Self as Container? Metaphors We Lose by in Understanding Early China." *Antiquorum Philosophia* 5: 11–30.

Geiger, Heinrich. 2013. "Sign, Image and Language in 'The Book of Changes' (Yijing 易经)." *Frontiers of Philosophy in China* 8, no. 4 (December): 607–23.

Gernet Jacques. 1996. *A History of Chinese Civilization.* Cambridge University Press.

Girardot, Norman J. 1978. "Returning to the Beginning and the Arts or Mr. Huntun in the Chuang-tzu." *Journal of Chinese Philosophy,* no. 5: 21–69.

———. 1983. *Myth and Meaning in Early Taoism: The Theme of Chaos (Hun-Tun).* University of California Press.

Gittings, John. 2012. "The Conflict between War and Peace in Early Chinese Thought." *The Asia-Pacific Journal* 10, issue 12, no. 5.

Glatzer, Nahum Norbet. 1971. *Kafka Franz, 1883–1924: The Complete Stories.* Schocken Books.

Goldin, Paul R. 2001a. "The Motif of the Woman in the Doorway and Related Imagery in Traditional Chinese Funerary Art." *Journal of the American Oriental Society* 121, no. 4: 539–48.

———. 2001b. *The Culture of Sex in Ancient China.* University of Hawaii Press.

———. 2008. "The Myth That China Has No Creation Myth." *Monumenta Serica* 56: 1–22.

———. 2011. "Persistent Misconceptions about Chinese 'Legalism.'" *Journal of Chinese Philosophy.*

———, ed. 2013. "Dao Companion to the Philosophy of Han Fei." *Dao Companions to Chinese Philosophy.* New York: Springer.

Gong Hua'nan. 2008. "How Is the Arrival of Things Possible?" *Frontiers of Philosophy in China* 3, no. 3.

Goodman, Howard I., trans. and ed. 2010. Li Yuqun 李裕群: "Review of Discoveries in Wei-Jin Nanbeichao Archeology since 2000." *Asia Major* 23, no. 1.

Graham, A. C. 1969/70. "Chuang-tzu's Essay on Seeing Things as Equal." *History of Religions* 9, no. 2: 137–59.

———. 1981. *Chuang-Tzu: The Inner Chapters.* Hackett.

———. 1983. "Taoist Spontaneity and the Dichotomy of 'Is' and 'Ought.' " In *Experimental Essays in Chuang Tzu,* edited by Victor Mair, 3–23. University of Hawaii Press.

———. 1986. *Yin-Yang and the Nature of Correlative Thinking.* Quirin Press.

———. 1989. *Disputers of the Dao.* LaSalle, IL: Open Court Press.

———. 1990a. *Studies in Chinese Philosophy.* Albany: State University of New York Press.

Granatta, Paolo. 2016. "Culture as Mediatization: Edward T. Hall's Ecological Approach." *Immediaciones de la Comunicacion* 11: 57–70.

Granet, Marcel. 1934. *La Pensée chinoise.* Paris: La Renaissance du Livre.

Grundmann, Joern Peter, ed. and trans. 2022. *Space, Time, Myth, and Morals: A Selection of Jao Tsung-i's Studies on Cosmological Thought in Early China and Beyond.* Vol. 3. Brill.

Guo Qinghua. 2001. "The Formation and Early Development of Architecture in Northern China." *Construction History* 17.

———. 2005. *Chinese Architecture and Planning Ideas, Methods, Techniques.* Axel Menges.

Hagen, Kurtis, and Steve Coutinho. 2018. *Philosophers of the Warring States: A Sourcebook in Chinese Philosophy.* Broadview Press.

Hansen, Chad. 1992. *A Daoist Theory of Chinese Thought: A Philosophical Interpretation.* Oxford University Press.

Harley, J. B., and David Woodward. 1987. "Cartography in the Traditional East and Southeast Asian Societies." In *Cartography in the Traditional East and South East Asian Societies,* edited by Harley and Woodward. Vol. 2, bk. 2 of *The History of Cartography.* University of Chicago Press.

Harrell, Stevan. 1979. "The Concept of Soul in Chinese Folk Religion." *Journal of Asian Studies* 38, no. 3: 519–28.

Hay, John. 1994. *Boundaries in China.* Reaktion Books.

Hayles, Katherine N., ed. 1991. *Chaos and Order: Complex Dynamic in Literature and Science.* University of Chicago Press.

Heidegger, Martin. 1971. *On the Way to Language.* Translated by P. D. Hertz. New York: Harper and Row.

Heine, Steven. 1990. "Does the Koan Have Buddha-Nature? The Zen Koan as Religious Symbol." *Journal of the American Academy of Religion* 58, no. 3.

———. 2004. "Koans in the Dogen Tradition: How and Why Dogen Does What He Does with Koans." *Philosophy East & West* 54, no. 1.

———. 2016. *Chan Rhetoric of Uncertainty in the Blue Cliff Record: Sharpening a Sword of the Dragon Gate.* Oxford University Press.

Henderson, John. 1994. "Chinese Cosmographical Thought: The High Intellectual Tradition." In *Cartography in the Traditional East and South East Asian*

Societies, edited by J. B. Harley and David Woodward, 203–27. Vol. 2, bk. 2 of *The History of Cartography*. University of Chicago Press.

Hinsch, Bret. 2003. "The Origins of Separation of the Sexes in China." *Journal of the American Oriental Society* 123, no. 3: 595–616.

Hofstadter, R. Douglas. 1981. *The Mind's I.* Basic Books.

Hon, Tze-Ki. 2019a. "Chinese Philosophy of Change (*Yijing*)." In *Stanford Encyclopedia of Philosophy*, edited by Edward N. Zalta.

———. 2019b. "Coping with Contingency and Uncertainty: The Yijing Hexagrams on Decay and Discordance." *Sungkyun Journal of East Asian Studies* 19.

Howard, Angela Falco. 2003. *Chinese Sculpture*. Yale University Press.

Huber, Jörg, and Zhao Chuan. 2011. *A New Thoughtfulness in Contemporary China: Critical Voices in Art and Aesthetics*. Transaction.

Hwang Ming-chorng. 1996. "Ming-Tang: Cosmology, Political Order and Monuments in Early China." Ph.D. diss., Harvard University.

Iljic, Robert. 2001. "The Problem of the Suffix -*Men* in Chinese Grammar." *Journal of Chinese Linguistics* 29, no. 1: 11–68.

Ivanhoe, Philip J., trans. 2002a. *The Daodejing of Laozi*. Hackett Classics.

———. 2002b. *Ethics in the Confucian Tradition: The Thought of Mengzi and Wang Yangming*. Hackett.

Jing Liu. 2017. "Be-ing (*you* 有) and non-be-ing (*wu* 無) in the *Daode jing*." An *International Journal of the Philosophical Traditions of the East*.

Johnston, Ian. 2014. *The Book of Master Mo*. Penguin.

Jones, David, and John Culliney. 1998. "Confucian Order at the Edge of Chaos: The Science of Complexity and Ancient Wisdom." *Zygon* 33, no. 3.

Jun Wenren. 2013. *Ancient Chinese Encyclopedia of Technology: Translation and Annotation of "Kaogong ji" (the Artificers' Record)*. Routledge.

Kahneman, Daniel. 2011. *Thinking Fast and Slow*. Penguin Books.

Kaibara Ekiken. 2007. *The Philosophy of Qi*. Colombia University Press.

Kierman, Frank A., ed. 1974. *Chinese Ways in Warfare*. Harvard East Asian Series.

Kirkland, Russell. 2004. *Taoism: The Enduring Tradition*. Routledge.

Kirkova, Zornica. 2016. *Roaming into the Beyond: Representations of Xian Immortality in Early Medieval Chinese Verse*. Brill.

Knapp, Ronald G. 1999. *China's Living Houses: Folk Beliefs, Symbols, and Household Ornamentation*. University of Hawaii Press.

Knapp, Ronald G., and Lo Kai-yin, eds. 2005. *House Home Family: Living and Being Chinese*. University of Hawaii Press.

Kohn, Livia. 1991. *Taoist Mystical Philosophy: The Scripture of Western Ascension*. Albany: State University of New York Press.

———. 2015. *New Visions of the Zhuangzi*. Three Pines Press.

Kroll, Paul W., and Johnathan A. Silk, eds. 2020. *At the Shores of the Sky: Asian Studies for Albert Hoffstädt*. Boston: Brill.

LaFargue, Michael. 1992. *The Tao of the Tao Te Ching*. Suny Series in Chinese Philosophy & Culture. Albany: State University of New York Press.

Lai Guolong. 2005. "Death and the Otherworldly Journey in Early China as Seen through Tomb Texts, Travel Paraphernalia, and Road Rituals." *Asia Major* 18, no. 1.

———. 2015. *Excavating the Afterlife: The Archaeology of Early Chinese Religion.* University of Washington Press.

Lai, Karyn L. 2007. "Understanding Change: The Interdependent Self and Its Environment." *Journal of Chinese Philosophy* 34, no. 1.

———. 2008. *An Introduction to Chinese Philosophy.* Cambridge University Press.

Lai, Karyn L., Rick Benitez, and Hyun Jin Kim, eds. 2019. *Cultivating a Good Life in Early Chinese and Ancient Greek Philosophy.* Bloomsbury Academics.

Laing, Ellen Johnston. 2017. "Carp and Goldfish as Auspicious Symbols and Their Representation in Chinese Popular Prints." *Arts Asiatiques* 72: 97–109.

Lakoff, G., and M. Johnson. 1980. *Metaphors We Live By.* University of Chicago Press.

Lamont, Michele, and Virag Molnar. 2002. "The Study of Boundaries in the Social Sciences." *Annual Review of Sociology* 28: 167–95.

Lau, D. C. 1964. *The Tao Te Ching.* London: Penguin Classics.

———. 1970. *Mencius.* London: Penguin Classics.

Lau. D. C., and Roger T. Ames. 1998. *Yuan Dao: Tracing Dao to Its Source.* New York: Ballantine Books.

Lee Sang Hae. 1986. "Feng-Shui: Its Context and Meaning." Ph.D. diss., Cornell University.

Legge, James. 1885. *The Li Ki.* Generic Press.

Lei Yong-qiang. 2016. "On the Functional Significance of Confucian Music Education." In *Proceedings of the 2016 International Conference on Humanities and Social Science,* 267–72.

Leslie, Donald. 1956. "Contribution to a New Translation of the *Lun heng*" *T'oung Pao* 44: 100–149.

Lewis, M. E. 2005. *The Construction of Space in Early China.* Albany: State University of New York Press.

———. 2006. *The Flood Myths of Early China.* Albany, NY: State University of New York Press.

Li Chenyang. 2008. "The Philosophy of Harmony in Classical Confucianism." *Philosophy Compass* 3, no. 3: 423–35.

Li Feng. 2013. *Early China: A Social and Cultural History.* Cambridge University Press.

Li Hongmei. 2014. "Analysis of the Application of Traditional 'Feng Shui' Theory in Modern Home Space." *CSCanada Studies in Sociology of Science* 5, no. 3: 105–109.

Li Min. 2008. *Social Memory and State Formation in Early China.* Cambridge University Press.

Li Xiaodong. 2002. "The Aesthetic of the Absent: The Chinese Conception of Space." *Journal of Architecture* 7, no. 1: 87–101.

Li Xiaodong and Yeo Kang Shua. 2002. "The Propensity of Chinese Space: Architecture in the Novel Dream of the Red Chamber." *Traditional Dwellings and Settlements Review* 13, no. 2 (Spring): 49–62.

Liu Jeeloo and Douglas Berger, eds. 2014. *Nothingness in Asian Philosophy.* Routledge.

Liu Pengbo. 2019. "Respect, *Jing*, and Person." *Comparative Philosophy* 10, no. 2.

Liu Shu-hsien. 1974. "Time and Temporality: The Chinese Perspective." *Philosophy East and West* 24, no. 2: 145–53.

Liu Xiaogan, ed. 2015. *Dao Companion to Daoist Philosophy.* Springer.

Liu Zhenhua. 2014. "Analysis of Flood Disasters from 206 BC to 1949 in China." *Computer Modeling & New Technologies* 18, no. 11: 750–57.

Lo, Vivienne. 2000. "Crossing the *Neiguan* 'Inner Pass': A *Nei/wai* 'Inner/Outer' Distinction in Early Chinese Medicine." *EASTM* 17: 15–65.

Lo Yuet Keung. 2014. "Confucius and His Community." In *Dao Companion to the Analects*, edited by Amy Olberding, 55–79. Springer Academic.

Loewe, Michael, and Edward L. Shaughnessy, eds. 1999. *The Cambridge History of Ancient China: From the Origins of Civilization to 221 BC.* Cambridge University Press.

Lopez, D. S. (ed.). 1996. *Religions of China in Practice.* Princeton Readings in Religions. Princeton University Press.

Low, Albert. 2006. *Hakuin on Kensho: The Four Ways of Knowing.* Boston: Shambhala.

Loy, David. 1985. "Chapter One of the Dao Tê Ching: A 'New' Interpretation." *Religious Studies* 21.

Lynch, Kevin. 1960. *The Image of the City.* Cambridge, MA: MIT Press.

Ma Li. 2006. "Deciphering Heidegger's Connection with the *Daodejing*." *Asian Philosophy* 16, no. 3: 149–71.

Maddox, J. 1990. "Order in the Midst of Chaos." *Nature* 347.

Mair, Victor H. 1994. "Wandering on the Way: Early Daoist Tales and Parables of *Chuang Tzu*." New York: Bantam Books.

Marshall, S. J. 2002. *The Mandate of Heaven.* Columbia University Press.

Mehigan, Tim. 2008. *Frameworks, Artworks, Place: The Space of Perception in the Modern World.* Rodopi.

Melzack, Ronald. 1996. "On the Evolution of Pain Concepts." *Pain Forum* 5, no. 1: 128–38.

Merrill, Ronald T., and Michael W. McElhinny. 1983. *Geomagnetism: The Earth's Magnetic Field: Its History, Origin and Planetary Perspective.* Orlando, FL: Academic Press.

Miller, James Grier. 1978. *Living Systems.* McGraw-Hill.

Moeller, Hans-Georg. 2004. *Daoism Explained: From the Dream of the Butterfly to the Fishnet Allegory.* Open Court.

———. 2017. "Hundun's Mistake: Satire and Sanity in the Zhuangzi." *Philosophy East and West* 67, no. 3: 783–800.

Moeller, Hans-Georg, and Paul J. D'Ambrosio. 2017. *Genuine Pretending: On the Philosophy of the Zhuangzi*. Columbia University Press.

Mortice, Zach. 2008. "Sun, Soil, Spirit: The Architecture of Mario Botta." *AIArchitecture* 15. https://info.aia.org/aiarchitect/thisweek08/0509/0509d_botta.htm#:~:text=The%20first%20gesture%20of%20an,this%20idea%20of%20limiting%20space.

Munro, C. F. 1987. "Semiotics, Aesthetics and Architecture." *British Journal of Aesthetics* 27, no. 2.

Munro, J. D. 1969. *The Concept of Man in Early China*. Stanford University Press.

Narayanan, Raviprasad. 2006. "The Politics of Reform in China: Deng, Jiang and Hu." *Strategic Analysis* 30, no. 2.

Needham, Joseph. 1956. *History of Scientific Thought*. Vol. 2 of *Science and Civilization in China*. Cambridge University Press.

———. 1971. *The Social Background*. Vol. 7 of *Science and Civilization in China*. Cambridge University Press.

Newell, William. H. 2010. "Undergraduate General Education." In *The Oxford Handbook of Interdisciplinarity*, edited by R. Frodeman, J. T. Klein, and C. Mitcham, 360–71. Oxford University Press.

Ni Peimin. 2017. *Understanding the "Analects" of Confucius*. Albany: State University of New York Press.

Nie Jing-Bao. 2011. *Medical Ethics in China: A Transcultural Interpretation*. Routledge.

Nielsen, Brent. 2013. *A Companion to Yi Jing Numerology and Cosmology*. Routledge.

Olberding, Amy. 2012. *Moral Exemplars in the "Analects": The Good Person Is That*. Routledge.

Olberding, Amy, and Philip. J. Ivanhoe, eds. 2011. *Mortality in Ancient Chinese Thought*. Albany: State University of New York Press.

Olberding, Garret Pagenstecher. 2022. *The Exercise of the Spatial Imagination in Pre-Modern China: Shaping the Expanse*. De Gruyter Press.

Owen, Stephen. 2016. *The Poetry of Du Fu*. Vol. 1. De Gruyter.

Patt-Shamir, Galia. 2016. "To Beget and to Forget: On the Transformative Power of the Two Feminine Images of the *Dao* in the *Laozi*." In *The Bloomsbury Research Handbook of Chinese Philosophy and Gender*, edited by Ann A. Pang-White, 249–66. Bloomsbury.

Peterson, Willard J. 1979. "The Grounds of Mencius' Argument." *Philosophy East and West* 29, no. 3.

Pilgrim, Richard B. 1986. "Intervals ('Ma') in Space and Time: Foundations for a Religio-Aesthetic Paradigm in Japan." *History of Religions* 25, no. 3: 258–59

Pines, Yuri. 2012. "Alienating Rhetoric in the Book of Lord Shang and its Moderation." *Extrême-Orient, Extrême-Occident*.

———. 2013. "Submerged by Absolute Power: The Ruler's Predicament in the *Han Feizi*." In *Dao Companion to the Philosophy of Han Fei*, edited by Paul R. Goldin, 67–86. Springer.

———. 2018. "The Earliest 'Great Wall'? The Long Wall of Qi Revisited." *Journal of the American Oriental Society* 138, no. 4: 743–62.

Poskaite, Loreta. 2020. "Authenticity/Genuineness/Truth (*Zhen* 真) in Chinese Traditional Art Theories and Aesthetics." *Art History & Criticism* 16, no. 1.

Pregadio, Fabrizio. 2005. *Great Clarity: Daoism and Alchemy in Early Medieval China.* Stanford University Press.

———, ed. 2010. *Encyclopedia of Taoism.* 2 vols. Routledge.

Qi Zhu. 2008. "Shi in Architecture: the Efficacy of Traditional Chinese Doors." Ph.D. diss., Hong Kong Polytechnic University.

Queen, Sarah, and Michael Puett, eds. 2014. *The Huainanzi and Textual Production in Early China.* Boston: Brill.

Rawson, Jessica. 1999. "The Eternal Palaces of the Western Han: A New View of the Universe." *Artbus Asiae* 59, no. 1/2.

Roberts, Moss, trans. and comment. 2001. *Dao De Jing: The Book of the Way.* University of California Press.

Robinet, Isabelle. 1977. *Les Commentaires du Tao To King jusqu'au.* VIIe siècle, Paris: Universitaires de France.

———. 1993. *Taoist Meditation: The Mao-shan Tradition of Great Purity.* Albany: State University of New York Press.

Robinson, Kenneth G., ed. 2004. *Joseph Needham: Science and Civilisation in China.* Vol. 7, pt. 2, *The Social Background.* Cambridge University Press.

Rocha, Leon Antonio. 2010. "*Xing*: The Discourse of Sex in Modern China." *Gender & History* 22, no. 3: 1–5.

Rochat de la Vallée, Elisabeth. 2012. "*Shen* (Spirit, Soul) in Chinese Religion and Medicine." *Charles Strong Trust Lecture Publication.*

Roth, Harold. 1991. "Psychology and Self-Cultivation in Early Taoistic Thought." *Harvard Journal of Asiatic Studies* 51, no. 2.

———. 1997. "Evidence for Stages of Meditation in Early Taoism." *Bulletin of the School of Oriental and African Studies* 60, no. 2: 295–314.

Schwartz, Benjamin I. 1985. *The World of Thought in Ancient China.* Harvard University Press.

Sellmann, James D. 2002. *Timing and Rulership in Master Lü's Spring and Autumn Annals (Lüshi chunqiu).* Albany: State University of New York Press.

Shih, Vincent Yu-chung, trans. 1959. *Liu Hsie: The Literary Mind and the Carvings of Dragons: A Study of Thought and Pattern in Chinese Literature.* New York: Colombia University Press.

Shulman, David, and Guy G. Stroumsa (ed.). 1999. *Dream Cultures: Explorations in the Comparative History of Dreaming.* Oxford University Press.

Sivin Nathan. 1995. *Medicine, Philosophy and Religion in Ancient China.* Variorum.

Slingerland Edward. 2003. *Analects: With Selections from Traditional Commentaries.*

———. 2008. "The Problem with Moral Spontaneity in the Guodian Corpus." *Dao.*

———. 2011. "Metaphor and Meaning in Early China." *Dao* 10, no. 1.

———. 2013. "Body and Mind in Early China: An Integrated Humanities–Science Approach." *Journal of the American Academy of Religion* 81, no. 1: 6–55.

Small, Sharon Y. 2018. "A Daoist Exploration of *Shenming*." *Journal of Daoist Studies* 11: 1–20.

Smith, Richard J. 2009. "Mirror of the Mind: The Evolution of the Zhouyi in China and Beyond." Paper for the Fourth International Conference of Analytical Psychology and Chinese Culture, Fudan University, Shanghai.

Sofer, A. C., and R. C. Rudolph. 1987. *Stories from China's Past: Han Dynasty Pictorial Tomb Reliefs and Archeological Objects from Sichuan Province, China.* The Chinese Culture Foundation of San Francisco.

Sou, Daniel Sungbin. 2018. "Crossing Borders: Control of Geographical Mobility in Early China." *T'oung Pao* 104: 217–50.

Stanley-Baker, Michael. 2019. "Health and Philosophy in Pre- and Early Imperial China." In *Health: A History*, edited by Peter Adamson. Oxford University Press.

Sterckx, Roel. 2019. *Ways of Heaven: An Introduction to Chinese Thought*. Basic Books.

Stevenson, Frank. "The Question of the Wind in Zhuangzi." http://www.frank-wstevenson.com/articles/question-of-the-wind-in-zhuangzi.html.

Sun, F., C. Fang, Z. Wang, and T. Yan. 2014. "Philosophical Foundation of Chinese *Feng Shui* Geography and Man-Land Relationship." *Tropical Geography* 34, no. 5: 581–90.

Swartz, Wendy. 2020. *Reading Philosophy, Writing Poetry: Intertextual Modes of Making Meaning in Early Medieval China*. Harvard-Yenching Institute.

Tan, Charlene. 2014. "Beyond Rote-Memorization: Confucius' Concept of Thinking." *Educational Philosophy and Theory* 47, no. 5: 1–12.

Tan Sor-hoon, ed. 2016. *The Bloomsbury Research Handbook of Chinese Philosophy Methodologies*. Bloomsbury.

Tang Man-to. 2018. "The Distinction between the 'Abstract West' and the 'Concrete East' from a Linguistic Perspective. *Kritika* 12, no. 1: 201–14.

Tseng, Lillian Lan-ying. 2011. *Picturing Heaven in Early China*. Harvard University Press.

Tu Wei-ming. 1985. *Confucian Thought: Selfhood as Creative Transformation*. Albany: State University of New York Press.

Uchiyama Kosho. 1983. *From the Zen Kitchen to Enlightenment: Refining Your Life*. Weatherhill.

Unschuld, Paul U. 2016. *Huang Di Nei Jing Ling Shu: The Ancient Classic of Needle Therapy. The Complete Chinese Text with an Annotated English Translation*. University of California Press.

Van Ess, Hans. 2005/6. "Argument and Persuasion in the First Chapter of 'Huainanzi' and its Use of Particles." *Oriens Extremus* 45: 255–70.

Vankeerberghen, Griet. 2001. *The "Huainanzi" and Liu An's Claim to Moral Authority*. Albany: State University of New York Press.

Viollet, Pierre-Louis. 2007. *Water Engineering in Ancient Civilizations: 5,000 Years of History*. CRC Press.

Wagner, Rudolf G. 2003b. *Language, Ontology, and Political Philosophy in China: Wang Bi's Scholarly Exploration of the Dark (Xuanxue)*. Albany: State University of New York Press.

Wang, E. Y. 2005. *Shaping the Lotus Sutra: Buddhist Visual Culture in Medieval China*. Seattle: University of Washington Press.

Wang Qingjie. 2000. "*Heng Dao* and Appropriation of Nature: A Hermeneutical Interpretation of Laozi." *Journal of Asian Philosophy* 10, no. 2.

Wang, Robin. 2012. *Yinyang: The Way of Heaven and Earth in Chinese Thought and Culture*. Cambridge University Press.

Watson, Burton. 1961. *Records of the Grand Historian of China*. Vol. 2. New York: Columbia University Press.

———. 2003. *Zhuangzi: Basic Writings*. Columbia University Press.

Weingardt, Heidi M. 2016. "Friends with Benefits: The Evolution of Chinese *Guanxi* in Conjunction with the One Child Policy and Improvements in Communicative Technologies." Undergraduate honors theses, University of Colorado Boulder.

Wheatley, Paul. 1971. *The Pivot of the Four Quarters: A Preliminary Enquiry into the Origins and Character of the Ancient Chinese City*. Chicago: Aldine.

Wilhelm, Hellmut. 1977. *Heaven, Earth and Man in the Book of Changes*. University of Washington Press.

Wills, John E. 2007. "Journeys Mostly to the West: Chinese Perspectives on Travel." *Huntington Library Quarterly* 70, no. 1.

Wong, Peter Yih Jiun. 2012. "The Music of Ritual Practice: A Reinterpretation." *Sophia* 51, no. 2.

Wong, Wucius. 1991. *The Tao of Chinese Landscape Painting: Principles & Methods*. New York: Design Press.

Wu Hung. 1995. *Monumentality in Early Chinese Art and Architecture*. Stanford University Press.

Wu Kuang-ming. 2007. "'Emperor Hundun 渾沌': A Cultural Hermeneutic." *Dao* 6, no. 3: 263–79.

Wu Nelson. 1963. *Chinese and Indian Architecture*. George Braziller.

Wu, Tinghai, Bin Xu, and Xuerong Wang. 2016. "How Ancient Chinese Constellations Are Applied in the City Planning? An Example on the Planning Principles Employed in Xianyang, the Capital City of Qin Dynasty." *Scientific Bulletin*. 61 (October): 1634–36.

Xiao Xiaosui. 2006. "Yijing: A Self-Circulating and Self-Justified Chinese Cultural Discourse." *Intercultural Communication Studies* 15, no. 1.

Xie Wenyin. 2000. "Approaching the *Dao*: From *Laozi* to *Zhuangzi*." *Journal of Chinese Philosophy* 27, no. 4: 469–88.

Xu Hong. 2021. *Dynamic Interpretation of Early Cities in Ancient China*. Berlin: Springer.

Xu Ping. 1998. "Feng-Shui Models Structured Traditional Beijing Courtyard." *Journal of Architectural and Planning Research* 15, no. 4.

Xu Yinong. 1996. "The City in Space and Time: Development of the Urban Form and Space of Suzhou until 1911." Ph.D. diss., University of Edinburgh.

———. 2000. *The Chinese City in Space and Time: Development of the Urban Form and Space of Suzhou*. Honolulu: University of Hawaii Press.

Yang Hsiu-Fang. 2013. "On Shijing's 'Do Not Hold My Tongue' (莫捫朕舌): An Etymological Explanation." *Bulletin of Chinese Linguistics*.

Yang Xiaoshan. 2003. *Metamorphosis of the Private Sphere: Gardens and Objects in Tang–Song Poetry*. Harvard East Asian Monographs 225.

Yu Zhou, François Zwahlen, and Yanxin Wang. 2011. "The Ancient Chinese Notes on Hydrogeology." *Hydrogeology Journal* 19: 1103–14.

Zhang Dainian and Edmund Ryden. 2002. *Key Concepts in Chinese Philosophy*. Yale University Press.

Zhao Dunhua. 2007. *Dialogue of Philosophies, Religions and Civilizations in the Era of Globalization*. Washington, DC: CRV Publications.

Zhao Guoping. 2012. "The Self and Human Freedom in Foucault and Zhuangzi." *Journal of Chinese Philosophy*.

Zhu Jianfei. 2004. *Chinese Spatial Strategies: Imperial Beijing, 1420–1911*. London: Routledge Curzon.

Zikpi, Monica Eileen McClellan. 2014. "Translating the Afterlives of Qu Yuan." Ph.D. diss., University of Oregon.

Ziporyn, Brook. 2014. *Beyond Oneness and Difference: Li and Coherence in Chinese Buddhist Thought and Its Antecedents*. Albany: State University of New York Press.

Index

Afterlife, Chinese concepts
of, 12–13, 25, 143, 259n9;
architecture of, 12–13, 47–49, 166,
168; *daxian* 大限, 10; half-open
gates, in the context of, 158–162.
See also spirit; soul
Analects, The, 6, 51, 121–25, 136,
138–40, 144, 146, 156, 188,
229, 231–32. *See also* Kongzi;
Confucianism, *rujia*
Anyang, archeological site of, 262.
See also oracle bones
Ao 奥, 43, 72, 81–82, 86, 119–20,
140, 229–30, 241; Japanese culture,
importance in, 273n17
Architecture, 1, 3, 5, 24; as sacred
act, 3; Chinese, 16–17, 39–50, 56,
77, 106, 111, 119, 121, 142–43,
152, 169, 184, 218, 229, 230–31
August Lords, 35
Auspiciousness, Chinese preoccupation
with, 25, 111–12; as luck, 224
Authentic living/man, in the
Zhuangzi, 96, 102–103, 139, 173,
198, 220, 242
Axis, 21, 39, 54, 166, 196, 216; *axis
mundi*, 99; of *dao*, 105; in Chinese
architecture, 19, 40–43, 46, 108,
131, 188, 195; mount Kunlun, in
context of, 258n7

Bagua, 40
Baopuzi (*The book of the master who
embraced simplicity*), 1
Being and non-being, 8–9, 70, 193,
195, 218, 239, 257n26–27
Bell, Chinese, 107, 154, 265n16
Benmo 本末 (Roots and Branches),
concept of, 13, 14, 72, 73, 74, 84,
244
Biology, modern science of, 16, 70,
226–27, 63; Chinese philosophy,
in context of, 7, 9, 23, 54, 62,
70, 73, 75, 77, 94, 100, 158, 197,
223, 225; emergent behavior,
13, 18, 23; evolution, 2, 9, 15,
28, 54, 62, 174, 226, 255n12;
entropy, theory of, 83, 230, 274;
homeostasis, concept of, 14; path
of least resistance, 30, 38, 83, 161,
229, 239, 254n8; primordial soup,
251n6; saltationism, 63n12; tipping
point, 61, 129, 221–22, 271n11,
230. *See also* chaos; membrane,
biological
Blue Cliff Records, The, 212
Body-mind, concepts of, 6–7, 9–11,
14, 43, 75, 76, 79, 80, 88, 100,
104, 125–26, 168, 171–73, 187,
214, 223, 232, 235, 241, 249n19,
259n11. *See also* Descartes